KNOWING, NOT-KNOWING
AND SORT-OF-KNOWING

KNOWING, NOT-KNOWING AND SORT-OF-KNOWING

Psychoanalysis and the Experience of Uncertainty

Editor

Jean Petrucelli, Ph.D.

For the American Psychological Association
Division of Psychoanalysis (39)

KARNAC

First published in 2010 by
Karnac Books Ltd
118 Finchley Road
London NW3 5HT

British Library Cataloguing in Publication Data

A C.I.P. for this book is available from the British Library

ISBN-13: 978-1-85575-657-1

Typeset by Vikatan Publishing Solutions (P) Ltd., Chennai, India

Printed in Great Britain

www.karnacbooks.com

In loving memory of my grandmothers,
Theresa and Mary
and to
Melinda
With affection and appreciation over the years...
for all the broken records

CONTENTS

vii

ACKNOWLEDGEMENTS

It occurs to me that my immersion in the analytic world has served a purpose far beyond my clinical work. It feels like a comfortable home that invites constant renovation in thinking that has broadened my sensibility and perspective on life. My engagement in analytic wisdom, beginning with my work in eating disorders and addictions, moving to meditations on longing and desire, and then toying with the metaphysics of knowing, is a continuation of playing with ideas that influence and inspire my pursuit of novel approaches to the problems I confront in my work and life. The analytic world, in particular, my analytic home at The William Alanson White Institute, has also afforded me the opportunity to meet fascinating and thoughtful colleagues who continue to inspire me, as have my patients who on a daily basis impart wisdoms I carry with me forever.

I would like to acknowledge the people, without whom this book would never have come into existence, beginning with the American Psychological Association Division of Psychoanalysis (39) board members, in particular Jaine Darwin, Nancy McWilliams and Henry Seiden. I am extremely grateful for their faith and trust that afforded me the unprecedented opportunity to publish some of the exciting papers that were presented at the APA Division of Psychoanalysis

39 conference that took place April 2008 in NY. This compelling conference, produced by Natalie Shear and her associates, came to fruition because of the hard work of many.

For more than two years, my co-chair extraordinaire, longstanding friend and colleague, Melinda Gellman, and I met with invaluable steering committee members. Each member, with their unique blend of expertise, contributed to this vast undertaking: Seth M. Aronson, Philip Blumberg, Andrew Eig, Robert Grossmark, Jill Howard, Sheldon Itzkowitz, Jill Salberg and Janet Tintner. Together as a team, they brought their remarkable skills and unstinting devotion, to the task of crafting and shaping, the themes, panels and activities for this five day conference which yielded many brilliant papers and panels, of which regrettably, only a few could be included here. I am especially grateful to my esteemed chapter authors for their well-regarded contributions to contemporary psychoanalytic thinking on this topic, the experience of uncertainty, which has made my role as editor straightforward and gratifying.

The theme of this project and the weaving of these papers into a book was facilitated by a number of individuals who each deserve mention and thanks: Philip Bromberg for his much appreciated and out-standing (in the spaces or not) contributions to the analytic field which provide us with memorable ways to know, not-know and sort-of-know … many things; Paul Stepansky for his generosity of advice; Elizabeth Howell, for writing *The Dissociative Mind*; and Donnel Stern, a mentor, muse and leader of our reading group, that provides me with the opportunity to absorb and learn from our collective experience and ideas.

I cherish and value the help of a few colleagues and friends that have read various parts of this book and offered detailed critiques and commentaries; Donnel Stern, Ruth Livingston, Janet Tintner, Jill Howard, Nick Samstag and members of my writing group, led by Sue Kolod, whose comments and feedback were enormously helpful. I am indebted to Joseph Canarelli for his expertise and skillfulness in assisting me to edit parts of this book. I would also like to especially thank Oliver Rathbone at Karnac for his continued belief in me, support and backing of a project of this magnitude.

Finally, I would like to express my love and appreciation to my parents; my mom, who was a spelling maven way before spell check;

my dad, may he rest in peace as he continues to watch over all of us; and my family—Steve, Jules, Jade and Nina for their unending patience of my unavailability and for their support, laughter, love, dancing, snorting and 'gerbiling' … without them nothing would feel as good as it does and life would be terribly uninteresting.

ABOUT THE EDITOR

Jean Petrucelli, Ph.D. is Director and Co-Founder of the Eating Disorders, Compulsions and Addictions Service since 1995 at the William Alanson White Psychoanalytic Institute in New York City; where she is also a Fellow, Supervising Analyst; member of the teaching Faculty and Founding Director of the Eating Disorders, Compulsions & Addictions one year educational certificate program which began in 2006. She is Editor and chapter author of the book *Longing: Psychoanalytic Musings on Desire* (Karnac Books, 2006); Co-editor and chapter author of the book *Hungers and Compulsions: The Psychodynamic Treatment of Eating Disorders and Addictions* (Jason Aronson Inc. 2001), and contributing author in the following books: *Body to Body: Beyond the Talking Cure* (Analytic Press, 2006); *What Do Mothers Want?* (Analytic Press, 2005); *Handbook of Addictive Disorders: A Practical Guide to Diagnosis and Treatment* (Wiley Press, 2004); and *Hope and Mortality: Psychodynamic Approaches to AIDS and HIV* (Analytic Press, 1996). She is an Associate Editor for the journal *Contemporary Psychoanalysis*; and was the 2008 Co-Chair of the American Psychological Association's Division 39 conference in New York that led to the creation of this anthology.

Dr. Petrucelli, specializes in the interpersonal treatment of eating disorders and addictions and has lectured extensively at universities, private and public high schools, middle schools and treatment facilities. She is a psychoanalyst, in private practice on the upper Westside in New York City.

CONTRIBUTORS

Mark J. Blechner, Ph.D. is a Fellow, Training and Supervising Analyst at the William Alanson White Institute. He is Editor-in-Chief of the journal *Contemporary Psychoanalysis*. He is the author of *The Dream Frontier* (The Analytic Press, 2001) and *Sex Changes: Transformations in Society and Psychoanalysis* (Routledge, 2009).

Jill Bresler, Ph.D. is a psychologist in private practice In New York City. She serves as an adjunct clinical supervisor for the Center for Psychological Services of Pace University. She is a graduate of the New York University Postdoctoral Program in Psychotherapy and Psychoanalysis.

Philip M. Bromberg, Ph.D. is a Training and Supervising Analyst of the William Alanson White Psychoanalytic Institute, and Clinical Professor of Psychology at the New York University Postdoctoral Program in Psychotherapy and Psychoanalysis. He is an Editorial Board member of *Contemporary Psychoanalysis, Psychoanalytic Dialogues, Journal of the American Academy of Psychoanalysis*, and is a Consulting Editor of *Psychoanalytic Inquiry*. In addition to his numerous journal articles, Dr. Bromberg is perhaps most widely recognized as author of *Standing in the Spaces: Essays on Clinical Process, Trauma,* *and Dissociation* (1998), and *Awakening the Dreamer: Clinical Journeys* (2006), both volumes published by The Analytic Press.

Wilma S. Bucci, Ph.D. is a Professor at the Derner Institute, Adelphi University; Chair of the Research Associates of the American Psychoanalytic Association (RAAPA); Member of Faculty of the Research Training Program of the International Psychoanalytical Association; Visiting Professor in Psychoanalytic Research, at University College, London; Honorary Member of the American Psychoanalytic Association, and the Institute for Psychoanalytic Training and Research (IPTAR); and Honorary Member and Co-Director of Research at the New York Psychoanalytic Society and Institute.

Sandra Buechler, Ph.D. is a Training and Supervising analyst at the William Alanson White Institute; Supervisor for the Psychiatric Institute internship and postdoctoral programs; and Supervisor at the Institute for Contemporary Psychotherapy. Dr. Buechler has written extensively on emotions in psychoanalysis, including papers on hope, joy, loneliness, and mourning in the analyst and patient and has authored the books, *Clinical Values: Emotions that Guide Psychoanalytic Treatment*, published by Analytic Press, July, 2004, and most recently, *Making a Difference in Patients' Lives: Emotional Experience in the Therapeutic Setting* (Routledge, 2008).

Joseph Canarelli, L.I.C.S.W. is in private practice in Seattle. He is on the Board of Directors of the Northwest Center for Psychoanalysis/ Seattle, where he also has served as the coordinator of the Community Education Program. He is a consultant for the Northwest Alliance for Psychoanalytic Study.

Richard A. Chefetz, M.D. is a psychiatrist in private practice in Washington, D.C. He was President of the International Society for the Study of Trauma and Dissociation (2002–2003), former Chair of their Dissociative Disorders Psychotherapy Training Program (2000–2008), and is a Distinguished Visiting Lecturer at the William Alanson White Institute of Psychiatry, Psychoanalysis, and Psychology. He is a faculty member at the Washington School of Psychiatry, the Institute of Contemporary Psychotherapy & Psychoanalysis, and the Washington Center for Psychoanalysis, in Washington, D.C.

Barry Cohen, Ph.D. is a psychologist in private practice in New York City and Teaneck, New Jersey. He serves as an adjunct clinical supervisor for both the Center for Psychological Services of Pace University, and the Doctoral Program in Clinical Psychology at the Ferkauf Institute of Yeshiva University. He is a graduate of the New York University Postdoctoral Program in Psychotherapy and Psychoanalysis.

James L. Fosshage, Ph.D. is Past President of the International Association for Psychoanalytic Self Psychology (IAPSP); Past and Current President of the Association for Autonomous Psychoanalytic Institutes (AAPI); Board of Directors, National Institute for the Psychotherapies (NYC); Founding Faculty, Institute for the Psychoanalytic Study of Subjectivity (NYC); and Clinical Professor of Psychology, New York University Postdoctoral Program in Psychotherapy and Psychoanalysis.

Katie Gentile, Ph.D. is Associate Professor of Counseling and Gender Studies and the Director of the Women's Center at John Jay College of Criminal Justice in New York City. She is the author of a number of journal articles and book chapters on eating disorders, dating violence, the impact of violence and the creation of resistance, and the psychological development of time and space. Her book, *Creating Bodies: Eating Disorders as Self-Destructive Survival*, was published in 2007 by The Analytic Press/Routledge. She serves as contributing editor for the journals *Studies in Gender and Sexuality and Psychotherapy* and *Politics International*, and is the Co-Chair of the biannual on-line colloquium series for the International Association of Relational Psychoanalysis and Psychotherapy. She is a licensed psychologist and trained psychoanalyst who practices in New York City.

Caryn Gorden Psy.D. is a Clinical Psychologist and Psychoanalyst, practicing in NYC. She is a faculty member at The Stephen Mitchell Center, and serves as an adjunct clinical supervisor for the Doctoral Program in Clinical Psychology at the Ferkauf Graduate School of Yeshiva University. She is a graduate of the New York University Postdoctoral Program in Psychotherapy and Psychoanalysis.

Elizabeth Hegeman, Ph.D. is a Training and Supervising Analyst at the William Alanson White Institute, Supervising Analyst at the Institute of Contemporary Psychotherapy, and Professor of Anthropology at John Jay College of Criminal Justice, CUNY. Dr. Hegeman is on the editorial board of *Contemporary Psychoanalysis*.

Sandra G. Hershberg, M.D. is the Director of Psychoanalytic Training and Training and Supervising Analyst at the Institute of Contemporary Psychotherapy and Psychoanalysis and is on the Faculty of the Washington Center for Psychoanalysis. She is an Associate Editor of the *International Journal of Psychoanalytic Self Psychology* and on the Editorial Board of *Psychoanalytic Inquiry*.

Elizabeth F. Howell, Ph.D. is a psychoanalyst, traumatologist and specialist in the treatment of dissociative disorders in private practice in NYC. She is author of the book, *The Dissociative Mind*, as well as numerous articles on dissociation and on gender. Dr. Howell is on the trauma faculty of the National Institute of the Psychotherapies, and the Dissociative Disorders Psychotherapy Training Program, sponsored by the International Society for the Study of Trauma and Dissociation. She is the Book Review Editor for the *Journal of Trauma and Dissociation*; and an Adj. Associate. Prof, at NYU Master's Program. She is the recipient of the 2006 Cornelia Wilber Award, for outstanding clinical contributions in the field of dissociative disorders for the Int. Society for the Study of Trauma and Dissociation.

Sheldon Itzkowitz, Ph.D. is a supervisor of psychoanalysis at the New York University Postdoctoral Program in Psychotherapy and Psychoanalysis, the National Institute for the Psychotherapies, and the Department of Psychiatry at The St. Luke's Roosevelt Hospital Center. Dr. Itzkowitz is Co-Chair of the Interpersonal Track of the New York University Postdoctoral Program in Psychotherapy and Psychoanalysis; President of the Division of Psychoanalysis of The New York State Psychological Association; Associate Editor of *Psychoanalytic Perspectives*, and is in full-time private practice in Manhattan.

Susan Klebanoff, Ph.D. is a clinical psychologist and psychoanalyst in private practice in New York City and a graduate of the New York University Postdoctoral Program in Psychotherapy and Psychoanalysis. She is the co-author of *Ups and Downs: How to Beat the Blues and Teen Depression* (Price Stern Sloan 1999).

Peter Lessem, Ph.D. is on the faculties of Institute for the Psychoanalytic Study of Subjectivity of the National Institute of the Psychotherapies and the Professsional Psychoanalytic Study Center. He is in private practice in New York City working with individual adults and adolescents as well as couples.

Edgar A. Levenson, M.D. is a Fellow Emeritus; Training & Supervisory Analyst and Faculty Member of The William Alanson White Institute, in NY. He is an Adjunct Clinical Professor of Psychology at the New York University Graduate Studies Division; Honorary Fellow at the Postgraduate Center for Mental Health; Honorary member of the American Psychoanalytic Association; Life Fellow in the American Academy of Psychoanalysis; and Distinguished Life Fellow in the American Psychiatric Association. In 2006, he received the distinguished Mary S. Sigourney Award. Dr. Levenson is author of: *The Fallacy of Understanding; The Ambiguity of Change; and The Purloined Self* as well as over one hundred other publications.

Arnold Modell, M.D. is a practicing psychoanalyst, Clinical Professor of Psychiatry at Harvard Medical School, and Training Analyst at the Boston Psychoanalytic Institute. His contributions to the psychoanalytic literature span fifty years and include his two most recent books *The Private Self* (Harvard University Press) and *Imagination and the Meaningful Brain* (MIT Press).

Rachel Newcombe, L.I.C.S.W. has a private practice of psychoanalytic psychotherapy in Eastsound, Washington. She serves on the Board of the International Forum for Psychoanalytic Education and is Co-chair of the History and Psychoanalysis Committee and is part of a study group in Orcas Island.

Adam Phillips is a psychoanalyst and writer. The author of several books—most recently *Side Effects* and *On Kindness* (written with Barbara Taylor)—he is a member of the Association of Child Psychotherapists and the Guild of Psychotherapists, and works in private practice in London.

Allan N. Schore, Ph.D. is on the clinical faculty of the Department of Psychiatry and Biobehavioral Sciences, UCLA David Geffen School of Medicine. He is Editor of the *Norton Series on Interpersonal Neurobiology*, and a reviewer on the editorial staff of 32 journals. He is a member of the Society of Neuroscience, and the American Psychological Association Division of Psychoanalysis, from which he recently received the 2008 Scientific Award. He will present an Invited Plenary Address to the 2009 APA Convention of the American Psychological Association in Montreal. Dr. Schore's activities as a clinician-scientist span from his theoretical work on the enduring impact of early trauma on brain development, to neuroimaging research on the neurobiology of attachment and studies of borderline personality disorder, to his biological studies of relational trauma in wild elephants, and to his practice of psychotherapy over the last four decades.

Abby Stein, Ph.D. is the author of numerous articles on interdisciplinary research, criminal psychopathology, female sexual predation, child maltreatment, and states of consciousness during violent crimes. She completed a two-year post-doctoral fellowship at the prestigious William Alanson White Institute of Psychiatry, Psychoanalysis, and Psychology in 2008. Dr. Stein teaches in the Interdisciplinary Studies Program at John Jay College of Criminal Justice, and is the Director of the college's Vera Institute of Justice Fellowship Program.

Janet Tintner, Psy.D. is a Supervisor of Psychotherapy; Steering Committee member of the Eating Disorders, Compulsions & Addictions Service; and Faculty Member at the William Alanson White Institute. She also supervises at Teachers College at Columbia and Rutgers University.

Karen Weisbard, Psy.D. is a graduate of the Northwest Center for Psychoanalysis—Seattle. She served as the co-director from 2003–2006. She currently serves as a Board member of the institute. She has a private practice in Seattle, Washington.

Jessica Zucker, Ph.D. is a psychotherapist in Los Angeles. Her dissertation on women in pornography garnered the American Psychological Association, Division 39, Section III Dissertation Award, a Robert J. Stoller Foundation Grant, and the Josephine Bernstein Award for Qualitative and Quantitative Research.

INTRODUCTION

This project of knowing, not-knowing and sort-of-knowing began in the Men's Department of Bloomingdales, which is where I was standing when I received the phone call from Jaine Darwin, Chair of the APA's Division of Psychoanalysis (39) Program Committee, inviting me to chair the Division's 2008 Spring Conference in New York City. I knew at that moment what I didn't want to know that I knew—that something was going to be asked of me to which I "should" say no but would, in fact, say yes. Jaine Darwin's mission was to choose the unsuspecting sacrificial lamb and convince her or him that the task was not daunting, while leaving out the actual sacrifices of life and time that one would have to make. Well … mission accomplished … because those of you who know and respect Jaine, as I do, also know that Jaine does her job well. I was in, and thus began this adventure.

The first step was to pick a co-chair: I turned to one of my oldest and dearest friends of thirty some years, Melinda Gellman. Together Melinda Gellman and I chaired the five day conference, the annual meeting of Division 39 (Psychoanalysis) of the American Psychological Association. The meeting was called "Knowing, Not-Knowing and Sort-of-Knowing: Psychoanalysis and the Experience of Uncertainty".

How did we come to this topic? Several influences—Bromberg, Stern, Hegeman, Davies, Lyons-Ruth, Mitchell and others—seen through Elizabeth's Howell's book, *The Dissociative Mind*, studied in a reading group led by Donnel Stern that inspired our thinking. Elizabeth Howell (2005), in her masterful overview of the dissociative mind, underlines how dissociation pervades psychic life. Even though dissociation theory has existed side by side with the concept of repression in the history of psychoanalytic thinking, for many years it was less examined, treated as if it belonged only to trauma theory. Today, though, because the relational model, in which the concepts of dissociation and the multiple self have become central, is widely appreciated in psychoanalysis, dissociation is receiving much more attention within psychoanalysis than it has before. Co-chair Melinda Gellman and I decided that it was time to feature dissociation, to give it the prominent place it now deserves on the map of Division 39.

The second step was to gather a conference committee. We chose the members: Seth M. Aronson, Philip Blumberg, Andrew Eig, Robert Grossmark, Jill Howard, Sheldon Itzkowitz, Jill Salberg, and Janet Tintner. This talented and innovative group met with us on the Upper West Side of New York City for two years, brainstorming and designing this enormous event. In our pursuit of what we knew, didn't know and sort-of-knew, we addressed conference themes, panels and fun events that spanned the principles of uncertainty from postmodern analytic thinking to rock and roll. We allowed ourselves to think and play outside the analytic box, venturing into the terrain of not-knowing and sort-of knowing, hoping to create a memorable lived-through event that would engender ongoing curiosity and liveliness in our work as psychoanalysts.

Our collaboration resulted in a rich blend of more than 80 panels, presentations and meetings. The conference was held at the Waldorf Astoria Hotel in New York City and we had over 1100 attendees.

The success of surviving the conference gave me the courage to undertake another massive project—the compilation of this book, which unfortunately represents only a fraction of the many wonderful papers that were presented at the conference. This anthology is comprised of 27 chapters written by various clinicians and scholars, diverse in their thinking, type of training and backgrounds.

* * *

So much of our work is steeped in uncertainty, a fact that Freud recognized in 1893 when he described "the blindness of the seeing eye" as an experience in which one knows and does not know a thing at the same time. His insight, startling at the time, and still provocative today, has generated many competing theories regarding the way the mind is structured, leading to questions about the art of psychoanalysis such as:

Are we uncovering layers of repressed material and/or encountering a multiplicity of selves?

What psychic processes keep certain experiences out of the awareness of patient and analyst?

What is the place of dissociation and trauma in psychoanalysis?

What does the body communicate and how does this material express itself?

How does the body express or collude with not-knowing?

How do we learn from and use uncertainty in our clinical work and within ourselves?

And, of course, the overriding question for psychoanalysts:

How do we come to know the things we know and tolerate the ambiguity inherent in not-knowing or, more confusing still, sort-of knowing?

This anthology grew from clinicians grappling with these and related issues. The chapters invite exploration of the way the mind is structured around knowing and not-knowing. Analyst and patient confront things they know they know and things they know they don't know, but they also confront things they sort-of-know or sense they know. The contributing authors of this book, from multiple points of view and theoretical positions, consider, in their own ways, what makes an experience knowable, unknowable, or sort-of-knowable.

It seems fitting to begin this anthology with a chapter by Edgar A. Levenson, because his work reveals an unmistakable respect, even reverence, for the ultimate unknowableness of human experience. Part One of this book, "Stalking the Elusive Mutative Experience", includes only his paper, "The Enigma of the Transference". Throughout his 60 years of contributing to psychoanalytic discourse, Levenson has maintained an interest in the process of therapeutic action. Levenson challenges us as psychoanalysts to consider the phenomenology of what we do when we … do what we know how to do. He introduces the unique kind of confusion or uncertainty or not-knowing that invariably precedes new understandings and new beginnings.

Levenson reminds us that metapsychologies are essentially ontologies; that is, they are worldviews, and as such are ineluctably immersed in their time and place. He takes the position that they are neither right nor wrong, but rather relevant or irrelevant.

Part Two, Chapters two and three, consist of the two memorable keynote addresses delivered at the conference by Philip M. Bromberg and Arnold H. Modell. Their papers have been preserved as oral presentations.

In Chapter two, "The Nearness of You: Navigating Selfhood, Otherness and Uncertainty", Philip M. Bromberg addresses what he considers "the next phase" of psychoanalysis—how we, as clinicians, can contribute to not only effective psychotherapy but more centrally to our evolution in thinking about the "individual mind" and the "relational mind". He offers the view that the affect-based, right-brain to right-brain dialogue between self and other, if it lacks a cognitive context for too long a time, leads to what we are calling "sort-of-knowing", as well as to the quality of uncertainty that is basic to the experience. Bromberg suggests that "sort-of-knowing" is always at least somewhat dissociative; that is, we are aware of it more implicitly than explicitly. This chapter deals with "sort-of-knowing", both as a normal mind/brain process that helps us get through each day with minimal stress, and "sort-of-knowing" as a means of protecting ourselves from what may be too much for the mind to bear. Bromberg draws upon a work of fiction to illustrate how certain people, those for whom the early development of intersubjectivity has failed to take place or has been severely compromised, are in times of emotional crisis, especially vulnerable not just to "uncertainty" but to the annihilation of the boundary between selfhood and otherness. They can become unable to navigate this boundary. Bromberg's chapter illustrates how the ability to strengthen one's readiness to process trauma depends on a relationship with an important other who relates to one's subjective states as important to him or her—and to whose mental states one can reciprocally relate.

Arnold H. Modell in his keynote address, Chapter three, "The Unconscious as a Knowledge Processing Center", writes about the unconscious as a process, uniquely constituted in each individual's history, an "area of the psyche in which knowledge is processed". He reflects that the psyche "retains in memory a lifetime of emotionally significant experiences and emotionally salient fantasies", while the unconscious waking state works continuously and synthetically, functioning analogously to the unconscious at work in dreams. Modell draws our attention to the recontextualization of memory "in accordance with later experience", as "fully consistent with contemporary neuroscience's understanding of memory". Highlighting the function of memory in organizing and maintaining an unconscious self, Modell also considers loss of self feeling, the "inner feeling of vitality and aliveness of the self ... noticed only in its absence", as a dangerous state: "When this occurs the consequences can be disastrous, for the individual has lost touch with all that they value ... when the self lacks a sense of its own vitality, a sense of its own aliveness, it is also unable to simulate or imagine the future consequences of one's action".

Part Three (Chapters four to eight), entitled, "Dissociation— Clinical, Diagnostic and Conceptual Perspectives", elucidates dissociation by focusing on three of its most extreme manifestations: psychopathy, dissociative identity disorder (DID), and masochism. Chapter four, Abby Stein's paper, "Shooting in the Spaces: Violent Crimes as Dissociated Enactment", explores the links between early maltreatment and adult aggression, through the lens of contemporary psychoanalytic theories of dissociation and enactment. Using case material, Stein disputes prevailing beliefs about criminal character and motivation—for example—that criminals operate "without conscience", that sex murderers are driven by deviant fantasy, or that psychopathy is "inborn". What emerges is a more nuanced picture of the ways that childhood trauma shapes criminal violence.

Chapters five to seven take on the clinical, diagnostic and cultural challenges presented by Dissociative Identity Disorder. Sheldon Itzkowitz, Chapter five, discusses his remarkable DVD video clip of a therapy session with "Yolanda", a woman diagnosed with dissociative identity disorder. Itzkowitz's video clip clearly and poignantly illustrates his patient in the throes of her identity shifts and the dramatic changes of posture, speech and cognition that accompanied these changes in her self-states or, in DID language, "alter" personalities. Itzkowitz's case of Yolanda is then discussed in Chapters six and seven by Elizabeth Howell and Elizabeth Hegeman, respectively.

Howell, in Chapter six, "Dissociation and Dissociative Disorders: Commentary and Context", interweaves a discussion of Itzkowitz's case with an exploration into the history of DID and a discussion of the dissociatively based contradictions in public knowledge of this condition. In her discussion of Itzkowitz's case, Howell explores the relationships, interrelationships, and functions of various alter personalities in DID cases. She defines the concept of "procedural" identification with the aggressor, which clarifies the underlying dynamic behind self abuse in DID and the lack of its awareness, and likewise reflects on the astonishingly high prevalence of child sexual abuse in DID patients, exceeded only by the frequency of its denial. In discussing the history of DID she takes us from Freud and Janet through the present day to locate various reasons why this diagnosis had all but disappeared and why it has come back into focus. Howell also considers how the dissociative organization of individuals may mirror the dissociation of our society.

In Chapter seven, "Multiple Personality Disorder and Spirit Possession: Alike, Yet Not Alike", Hegeman brings her experiences as an anthropologist and a psychoanalyst to bear on a discussion focusing on the similarities and differences between spirit possession and DID. Occurring in non-Western cultures where multiple self-states are culturally acceptable, the possessed is embedded in some cultural contexts that contain and accept the experience of possession. Hegeman compares these cultures to our Western culture where the self is conceptualized as singular and bounded, and the person suffering from DID is more likely to be pathologized, ostracized, and shamed. This comparison of spirit possession and DID highlights the effects of our cultural rejection of altered states, showing that it overlaps with rejection of the traumatized self to create the "not known", rejected, dissociated self.

In the final chapter in Part Three, Chapter eight, "Masochism and the Wish to Rescue the Loved One: A View from Multiple Self Theory", Peter Lessem examines masochistic relatedness from a multiple self state perspective that posits the centrality of dissociation in psychic life. For some masochistic patients, Lessem writes, disavowed vulnerable self states are identified in the exploitative loved one. He posits that rescuing the loved one from their perceived plight feels crucial to the patient's own well-being and therefore structures in large part, his or her experience of the relationship.

Moving into the realm of experience, Part Four, "When Experience Has a Mind of Its Own", includes a series of papers by Jean Petrucelli, Mark J. Blechner, and Adam Phillips. These papers focus on the phenomena of how sometimes experience can lead the mind, be it through dissociation, panic or the experience avoided by the act of getting away with it. Petrucelli, in Chapter nine, "Things That Go Bump in the Night: Secrets after Dark", explores the role of secrets in two clinical cases, a student/dominatrix and a physical trainer/night binger, with "secrets" being the dissociation between the different parts of the self. The effects of these secrets revealed on the patient and their family are explored. According to Petrucelli, although dissociation may help one to cope in some situations, it ultimately complicates life at other moments and contributes to the silence of secrets. Secrets, she says, can be one way that the mind deals with experience, creating double lives that seem to have lives of their own, and can only be revealed when they are truly ready to be known.

Chapter ten, "Psychoanalytic Treatment of Panic Attacks", Mark J. Blechner, reports his clinical data on three patients. He describes an effective treatment that offers a different perspective on panic disorder from the approach that suggests that with panic disorder—no real danger exists and that the patient's anxiety is inappropriate. While each of the three patients had different backgrounds, each had a life circumstance that should have caused him or her to be very afraid and each dissociated from the seriousness of the fear-causing situation. Blechner suggested to his patients that they might begin to tackle their anxiety disorder by addressing the fear-causing situation directly, something that actually enhanced their anxiety. However, in every case the panic attacks stopped. Blechner suggests that for some patients dissociation may play a major role in panic attacks.

Adam Phillips muses in Chapter eleven, "On Getting Away with It", on the difference between not doing something because you believe it is wrong, and not doing something because you think you might be punished for it. What does the prevalent childhood wish to get away with things entail? Since the super-ego requirement of guilt is integral to Freud's model of the mind, Phillips wonders what the structure and function of this fundamental, apparently unrealistically evasive wish to get away with things might be. He considers the possibility that the fantasy of avoiding being caught facilitates developmentally essential forms of transgression.

Part Five, "How Do We Know and How Does It Change: The Role of Implicit and Explicit Mind/Brain/Body Processes", includes Chapters twelve through sixteen. These chapters explore the ways in which knowledge and research about the implicit and explicit domains, in the context of relational experience, reconfigures concepts of memory, learning and a sense of self in the developing brain and, furthermore, contributes to a theory of mind. The findings of Allan Schore, Wilma S. Bucci, James L. Fosshage, Richard Cheftez, and a discussion by Sandra Herschberg, emphasize the primacy of relational experience and how this experience informs our notion of how psychoanalysis leads to change, particularly in the areas of attachment, infant observation, and neuroscience.

Allan Schore, in Chapter twelve, "The Right Brain Implicit Self: A Central Mechanism of the Psychotherapy Change Process", utilizes a neuropsychoanalytic perspective to describe how right brain implicit functions operate at the core of psychotherapy change processes. Schore discusses the critical roles of not only implicit cognition, but implicit affect, communication, and regulation in the psychotherapeutic context, especially in patients with early forming severe self pathologies associated with attachment trauma. A major focus of his work is on right brain unconscious processes in both patient and therapist that are expressed in stressful affect-laden clinical enactments, an essential relational context of the change process. As he has written for the last two decades, Schore argues here that the right brain represents the psychobiological substrate of the human unconscious.

Wilma S. Bucci, in Chapter thirteen, "The Uncertainty Principle in the Psychoanalytic Process", explores how, from the perspective of multiple code theory, the analytic interaction is seen as inherently unpredictable, emerging for each person and each dyad, determined by activation of subsymbolic bodily experience and connection to the symbolic domain, in memory and in the present, in the constantly changing matrix of the relationship.

James L. Fosshage, Chapter fourteen, "Implicit and Explicit Pathways to Psychoanalytic Change", discusses how the interconnections of the implicit/non-declarative and explicit/declarative systems are pivotal for understanding the pathways to therapeutic change. Based on how these systems encode information for processing and the various factors that enable conscious accessibility of the implicit, Fosshage proposes two fundamental, interrelated pathways of change, one involving explicit reflective exploration and the other focusing on implicit learning that occurs in the psychoanalytic encounter.

Richard Chefetz, Chapter fifteen, "Life as Performance Art: Right and Left Brain Function, Implicit Knowing, and Felt Coherence", explores how the "wish to die" may be a fantasy escape-hatch from an unbearable world, and how, if the wish progresses to an action, tragedy is the outcome. He examines the example of a woman who had an unusual childhood habit that formed the basis of an adult communication that involved her fantasy of suicide, a fantasy that had become action and was proceeding toward conclusion. Chefetz highlights the importance of attention to dissociative processes and implicit ways of knowing as enactive communication and its transformation to explicit knowledge. He maintains that the achievement of a sense of "felt coherence" is an implicit goal of mindedness that is an extension of attachment goals of "felt security". In Chefetz's chapter, a neurobiologic heuristic is proposed that adds to our understanding of dissociative process. The importance of the left brain in emotional understanding expands the model of right-brain to right-brain emotional communication.

Sandra G. Hershberg, in Chapter sixteen, "Bridging Neurobiology, Cognitive Science and Psychoanalysis: Recent Contributions to Theories of Therapeutic Action" discusses the chapters by Schore, Bucci, Fosshage and Chefetz and comments on the ways in which implicit and explicit domains are conceptualized cognitively, neurobiologically and psychoanalytically, informing the ways in which we think about psychoanalytic change and therapeutic action.

The first chapters of this book addressed the role of experience in knowing, not-knowing, and sort-of-knowing. Then the focus moved to a consideration of the role of the brain. Part Six, "How Bodies are Theorized, Exhibited and Struggled With and Against: Gender, Embodiment, and the Analyst's Physical Self", shifts the focus to the body. In the first installment of Part Six, Chapter seventeen, "Lights, Camera, Attachment: Female Embodiment as seen through the lens of Pornography", Jessica Zucker remarks on how women's bodies have always been a site of desire, pleasure, and objectification, and how 1970's and 80's feminist thought grappled with the ways in which our culture viewed female sexual desire and longing as something to be sequestered and tamed inside the domestic and relational sphere. Zucker presents another perspective on female sexuality, one that was also developing during this period. This second perspective moved the debate out of a binary stalemate into the complications and paradoxes that continue to define issues of female sexuality and embodiment to this day. In her research, Zucker interviewed twenty women who work as actors in pornography and tried to understand the enormous complexities of these women's self-states. Zucker asked them to reflect on how they made meaning of their lives vis-à-vis the choice to merge sex with work. What emerged were poignant narratives reflecting pivotal developmental moments in mother-daughter relationships which, in turn, shaped their own sexual embodiment.

Katie Gentile, in "Purging as Embodiment", Chapter eighteen, focuses on a treatment with a 24 year old woman who, in the first month of therapy, got pregnant with a boyfriend she was not sure she wanted to continue seeing, and with a child she did not want, and married within two weeks only at her mother's insistence. This woman purged multiple times per day, but did not binge. Gentile explores how much of this woman's story was told with her body and how the author/analyst responded in kind, as a primary avenue of relating in the treatment. Gentile views this case through feminist and multicultural theory.

In Chapter nineteen, "The Incredible Shrinking Shrink", Janet Tintner, discusses the impact of her own weight struggles on her patients. Tintner focuses on her patients' difficulty verbalizing conflicting feelings about her weight loss, utilizing case material to trace the stages of her process. Tintner illustrates the disturbing feelings underlying her hesitation and the hesitation of her patients to speak. Tintner reflects on the obstacles to authentic dialogue, especially when it comes to the body.

Moving now from the body to the interrelationship of technology and knowing, Part Seven, "I Know Something about You: Working with Extra-Analytic Knowledge in the Analytic Dyad in the Twenty-First Century", is introduced by Jill Bresler in Chapter twenty.

The theme of this section is that current technology creates an environment in which it is increasingly easy to "know" each other via means we cannot control, thereby making it likely for analyst and patient to obtain knowledge of each other through means external to the analytic situation. Bresler studies the complexities of what patients and analysts know about each and how they know it.

Although the psychoanalytic inquiry is predominantly intended as an exploration of the patient's psyche, personal history, intrapsychic and interpersonal dynamics, the analyst, as a participant observer in the process, inevitably presents him– or herself to the scrutiny of the patient. What patients allow themselves to observe and to know about their analysts provides the analyst with an in vivo experience of their patient's ability to perceive, tolerate, and selectively inattend aspects of the other in the interpersonal situation. Barry Cohen, Chapter twenty one, in "Double Exposure ... Sightings of the Analyst outside the Consultation Room" reflects on clinical dynamics that arose in the treatment of a long term patient whose rigid reluctance to experience the individuality of the analyst became confounded when the patient serendipitously saw a television program featuring the analyst and his family.

Caryn Gorden, Chapter twenty two, "Who's Afraid of Google?" focuses on a clinical vignette that focuses on the way in which extra-analytic disclosure (through an internet search) influenced an analytic treatment. Specifically, Gorden explores how an analyst's privacy was compromised and how that event impacted the dyad and hence the analysand's treatment. She explores the co-constructed, enacted aspects of the analysand's intrusion into the analyst's personal life, the multi-dimensional transference-countertransference configurations that arose, and how the patient's "knowing" both interfered with and enhanced his treatment.

In Chapter twenty three, "Six Degrees of Separation ... When Real Worlds Collide in Treatment", Susan Klebanoff explores a therapeutic dilemma involving self disclosure after she learns that her long term patient is a close friend of her cousin's. Klebanoff discusses transference and countertransference implications of disclosure in light of both the patient's and the therapist's personal histories.

The final section, Part Eight—Chapters twenty four to twenty seven, "Omissions of Joy", explores the inherent anxiety still faced by the analyst who decides to self-disclose. In particular, these chapters address the disclosure of the analyst's joyful feelings. With few exceptions, the capacity for and experience of joy has received little attention within psychoanalysis. Analysts tend to think about it implicitly: that is, we hope analysis will enable our patients to lead richer lives marked by an array of joys. But what of joyful moments between and within each member of the clinical dyad during the analytic process itself?

When events of the analyst's life are revealed, their content often involves tragically sad or devastating situations that may be disruptive to the treatment. But what if an analyst's experience is joyous? Joy, our authors reflect, can be just as unhinging as tragedy and equally transformative. In three of these chapters, psychoanalysts Joseph Canarelli, Rachel Newcombe, and Karen Weisbard write about private experiences of love and joy that turned their worlds upside down, paradoxically inducing secrecy and shame in themselves. Responding to these papers, Sandra Buechler highlights the papers' themes of loneliness, intimacy, and moments of joy. All four papers explore a desire for and ambivalence about being professionally known and not known when it comes to the experience of joy.

In Chapter twenty four, "Silence, Secrecy and an Analyst in Love", Canarelli considers some typical instances of joy within his analytic practice. Finding himself newly in love and consequently preparing to relocate his practice out of state, he considers the challenge posed by his own joy—namely, what to tell his patients about why he is moving.

In Chapter twenty five, "The Underbelly of Joy", Newcombe tells us that although she never thought she would leave New York City, she did. Newcombe had imagined belonging to the decade club, analysts who have practiced in New York City for three, four, or even five decades. But instead she found herself faced with loss, and love, and more loss, and the heartbreaking process of terminating with patients. In the midst of all this turmoil around leaving and endings, she shared the details of her life with only a few colleagues, convinced that a "real analyst" lives a chaos free life. Her newfound joy was overshadowed by shame, then loneliness. Newcombe's chapter is a story about the desire to be known personally and professionally and how silence turned into speaking.

In Chapter twenty six, "The Intersubjectivity of Joy", Weisbard grappling with the tension between a one-person and the two-person psychology takes a more theoretical approach that relational psychoanalysis seeks to elaborate. She describes experiences of joy as intersubjective dilemmas that express both the need to be independent, separate, and unique, and the desire to be dependent, connected, and found worthy and lovable by others. To illustrate her ideas, Weisbard describes a personal experience that interacted with a clinical case, and that showed her how joyful experiences in the outside world can potentiate and deepen intersubjectivity and how this deepening may shift experiences of joy.

Sandra Buechler, in the final chapter (twenty seven) of this anthology, contextualizes these three papers, exploring the fundamental nature of joy as a human emotion. Buechler asks if we can make generalizations about what evokes joy in people or if, instead, each experience of joy remains unique and personal for each individual and beyond generalizations.

* * *

In gathering these wonderful papers together I realized that any such "tying up" really goes against the grain of this project and its theme. We know, do not know and sort-of know things in many different ways and for a vast array of reasons. From unconscious to conscious, from dissociation to affective aliveness, our experiences are multifaceted, pervasive, encompassing. Inside our minds and outside, in our relations with others, in our personal and our professional lives, the way we know, not–know and sort-of-know shapes and is shaped by the very complicated dynamics of social, cultural, political, physical, economic and familial relations.

And so, as much I would like to tag on a summary "happy ending" to this anthology (and maybe even tried to do so by concluding with the section on joy)—I would argue that psychoanalysis is not about simple narratives—those stories with a beginning, middle, and neatly packaged happy end. Rather, we keep learning that psychoanalysis is really about a myriad of possibilities, about all we continue to know, not know and sort-of-know. Indeed, it is an extraordinarily exciting time of new ideas opening up all over the place, of constant shifts, emerging questions, and expanding horizons that reach beyond our wildest dreams.

This collection of papers, written by today's analysts writing from their own personal experience, spans individual minds. In immersing myself in their stories I have come to question and think differently about a number of things I thought I knew. Our authors draw experience and knowledge from anthropology, they examine the link between neurobiology and psychoanalytic thinking, they grapple with today's burgeoning technology, they address once taboo subjects, and they examine their own frailties. Moving from the pervasive to the particular, from the unseen to the seen, from psyche to soma, from the extreme to the normative, from murder and brutality, and finally, to joy, this collection represents the best of many dedicated clinicians and theoreticians who accept psychoanalysis as a mysterious art and who are devoted to working with, and through, knowing, not knowing and sort-of-knowing with themselves and their patients.

Each section of this book and each individual paper in this anthology stands on its own. My hope is that you will read and savor these papers much as you would a collection of short stories: with a curious mind, an open heart, and an understanding that there is so much more to know ... not know and even sort-of-know.

I am certain—yes, I know—that you will come away with much to ponder.

Jean Petrucelli, Ph.D.
Editor

PART I

STALKING THE ELUSIVE MUTATIVE EXPERIENCE

CHAPTER ONE

The enigma of the transference

Edgar A. Levenson, M.D.

Psychoanalysis from its inception has been biased towards theory, metapsychology, presumably the font of the mutative therapeutic action. Far less emphasis has been put on the phe-nomenology of therapeutic action; that is, on *how* people change. This valorization of metapsychology is increasingly coming under scrutiny, however, as the erstwhile sharp-edged doctrinaire distinc-tions between positions blur and attention shifts to an emergent neu-ropsychological paradigm; at this stage of knowledge really more a metaphor than a genuine model (Pulver 2003). In other words, now that it is less clear that we are right and that you are wrong, we are all beginning to wonder what it is we are doing when we do what we all know how to do.

Metapsychology, for all its claim to ontological truth, always reflects the current culture, the social context in which we are all imbedded, but of which we are largely unaware. As Gregory Bateson said, the point of the probe is always in the heart of the explorer (Bateson 1979: 87). The current emphasis on the vicissitudes of early mothering, especially as described in attachment theory, reflects a cultural change, from the patriarchal, Oedipal-oriented (conflict and envy) world in which I both grew up and became an analyst, to a

3

matriarchal, nurturing one in which mothering (early) and empathy is privileged. One also notes, not inconsequentially, that the demographics of psychoanalysis have shifted from largely male and medical to female and psychological along with a radical shift in the economics. Believe it or not, when I entered the field in the early fifties, psychoanalysis was the second highest paid medical specialty and we had waiting lists! Clearly this made for a therapeutic milieu that tolerated more frustration and tempted therapist less to over-aggressive interventions.

But does anyone entirely believe that if secure attachment takes place, all subsequent troubles are weathered: Oedipal, family, sibling, peer group, societal, mid-life and old age? Whatever happened to the father? It would appear that although we are ostensibly ecumenically intended, agreeing to disagree amicably, psychoanalysis is still split into what Cooper called a "growing plurality of orthodoxies", adamant, entrenched, and highly politicized (Cooper 2008: 235). Yet, surely everyone from Freudian to relationist is on to something, has grasped some aspect of our proverbial elephant, the nature of mind.

Once the "Ghost in the Machine", mind, and its correlate, consciousness, has become of cardinal interest (Levenson 2001). We are now in the Age of the Mind. The nature of consciousness is hotly debated in a virtually medievalist sectarianism amongst the mentalists, the functionalists, the materialists, and the mysterians (Damasio 1994). Suffice it to say that the debate centres on whether consciousness is merely an epiphenomenon of the brain—an inevitable outcome of organic complexity—or, whether it is of another essence altogether.[1] Consciousness, as Damasio says, is "the last great mystery and may lead us to change our view of the universe we inhabit" (Damasio 1994: 21).

I would suggest that our current focus should be, not so much on competing metapsychologies and their interpretive sets, as on how mind *works*; how experience is processed and integrated. As Jonathan Miller put it, "we are the unwitting beneficiaries of a mind that is, in a sense, only partially our own" (Miller 1995: 64). We must

---

[1] See Chalmers (1996) and Searle (1997) for a discussion of a belief in a fundamentally irreducible consciousness.

understand the phenomenology of change, how people comprehend their being in the world, and how the analyst's presence and interactions foster flexibility and growth.

Regardless of theoretical doctrines, all analysts are struck by two oddly autonomous parameters of observation: first, the flow of consciousness as it is evidenced in the patient's narrative—the unconscious associations, the "red line" of coherence that runs through the ramblings of a session—and second, the transference enactment, the way analyst and patient behave with each other in the course of the inquiry. Clearly, both the interpersonal and the intra-psychic co-exist: the relationship between the intersubjective world and the still mysterious internal processes of change must be synthesized. Integrating these two strikingly incompatible aspects of the analytic process has been, for me, consistently the most puzzlingly and yet rewarding aspect of the therapeutic endeavor.

The patient's flow of consciousness, the intra-psychic, is the classic *sine qua non* of the analytic process—not necessarily limited to free-association, since the same order is equally evident in a detailed inquiry. As Bollas put it:

> [there is an] *understandable and inevitable tension between the goal of free association and the wishes of the analyst to understand the material: as free association unbinds meaning—in what Laplanche terms and celebrates as the "anti-hermeneutics" of psychoanalysis—while interpretation creates and binds meaning. No sooner are such understandings established than the workings of the unconscious, evident through free association, break the interpretation into particles of meaning, which constitute a "use of the Object", hopefully celebrated by the analyst's unconscious working along similar lines even as such use disperses his interpretive creations. (Bollas 1999: 70)*

The second striking manifestation is, of course, the relationship between the patient and the therapist, the uncanny way the two play or enact, or re-enact, the very patterns that are under inquiry This is of course the storied transference, these days considerably loosened from Freud's original constraints, but still clearly central to the process.

I want to proceed to two clinical excerpts. The first illustrates the coherence of the patient's unconscious flow of associations, which seem, at least at first view, to be independent of the therapist's participation. It very much reflects Masud Khan's aphorism that we are the servants of the patient's process. The second example, also a dream, illustrates less the flow of unconscious associations than the intricate interweaving of content and transference enactments.

This first patient, a thirty-year-old man, has a dream about three weeks into therapy. He is "with another guy". Perhaps they are reviewing his portfolio. That's all. That's the dream. Who is the guy? He doesn't know. He is thinking of working for a friend of his mother's brother—his famous uncle Max, the family patriarch, who is wealthy and powerful and helps them all with their problems, financial or personal. Oh yes, there are snakes floating around overhead. Also something like hieroglyphics, bits of information. Any other associations? Other ideas? None. Suddenly he remembers that the dream takes place in his parent's garage, at their country house. What about the house? His parents own an isolated country house. He often visits there without them. He must enter the house through the garage, which is always left unlocked. He must first reach over a shelf in the dark to find the light switch. Then he must reach over deeper into the dusty, cobwebbed space to find the house key. Then he must take the key around to the front of the house and open the main door. Otherwise, he could enter through the garage, go down the stairs from the garage to the cellar—a very spooky place that he has always avoided—and then he can go up the back stairs into the house. He never *ever* goes into the cellar. The garage is scary enough since it is never locked. Every time he opens the door, he expects to be attacked by "a bum or bear or something".

Why doesn't he just have another key to the front door? Why not leave another key hidden near the front door? It's not clear; he never thought about it. Does his father go through all this when he uses his house? Where were the bits of hieroglyphics? The associations begin to proliferate: to the movie, *Indiana Jones and the Temple of Doom*. It seems that entering the garage is like the movie—always hidden rooms, monsters, having to reach through icky bugs and snakes—Indiana Jones' Achilles heel, his phobia. What about snakes? Constrictors … not vipers … constriction … squeezed. He doesn't have a snake phobia, but he hates spiders!

Hieroglyphics come back into play. He was always interested in archaeology, thought it would be a wonderful thing to do. It is his grandfather and father's interest. Grandfather would spend weeks meticulously repairing antique vases, from his homeland. His father also loved antiquities. When my patient was a child, his grandfather would play with him, breaking a vase, burying the pieces and having him find them, dig them up and reconstitute the item.

This profuse flow of associations to a very brief dream, some totally spontaneous, other a consequence of my detailed inquiry, seem to come from some entirely autonomous source. They are, to put it technically, metonymic not metaphoric; that is, they are private associations.[2] Only the patient knows their relevance, as compared to metaphor, which is in the common domain, a story. Certainly the therapist has no idea where it was headed, although he did ask detailed questions that focused the odd omissions.

One certainly could infer a transferential subtext. The patriarchal Uncle Max who helps everyone, the fascinating game of inquiry and reconstitution (Freud, after all, considered psychoanalysis an archaeological process), the coded messages; all point to a view of transference and of the therapy. Is it a game to make the patriarch happy? Does it really engage him? The questions proliferate, but for the moment I want simply to show how this dream has a blatant associative aspect and a much more implied and less self-evident transferential dimension.

The second dream is far more elaborate, richly metaphoric, and chock full of blatantly obvious transferential implications. Indications of an associative flow are sparse. For this fifty-year-old woman, it is her first dream in vivid colour and occurs one year into therapy. She is at a conference where she meets Osama Bin Laden. He is her height, hazel eyes; something seems to be wrong with his right shoulder. He asks whether she hates him. She explains that she is Jewish and pro-Israel. She's telling him "straight". He's listening, looking her straight in the eye. Then Bin Laden wants to kiss her. He chews food and then passes it to her lips; like a mother bird or wild dog (note the polarities of nurturance—a bird or a carnivore). This, he explains, is "an old Indian custom". He has a virus, she is thinking of getting him medicine (she doesn't seem concerned about catching some disease from being fed by him).

---

[2] See *The Purloined Self* (Levenson, E. [1991]) for elaboration of this theme.

In contrast to the first dream, her associations are minimal: namely that her mother visited India twice (without her father). I point out to her the stunningly obvious—that I am her height, have hazel eyes and when she started in therapy with me a year earlier I'd just had shoulder surgery; my right arm (same side as in the dream) was in a sling for many weeks (the right side in both cases). This dream is a veritable palimpsest of unconscious process: first, the content, her apparent unawareness of perfectly obvious themes; her present- ing me with the themes so that I can pre-chew them and force-feed them back to her—which, of course, I proceed to do by explaining the dream to her. Does she need to be told that her feelings about Osama are ambivalent? That he represents the therapist? All he lacks is a name tag!

She has wonderful dreams—at least at that stage of the therapy— that make me feel very clever and insightful and I usually fall for "interpreting" them to her. If they are so obvious why doesn't she see them? How can someone so smart be so dumb? It is a prime example of R.D. Laing's dictum about mystification: the patient learns not to know what the patient knows she knows but is not supposed to know (Laing 1967). In this dream, although there are many rich threads of inquiry into her history, the interactive replay of those themes with the therapist is most instantly obvious.

These two dreams illustrate the polarities in the dialectic between the intra-psychic process of unconscious flow and the interpersonal process of transference enactment. How do competing psycho- analytic groups deal with these two apparently dissonant aspects of the process? Why don't analysts simply use both parameters of therapy flexibly, moving freely between them? As the clinical cases suggest, each seems so striking that one is tempted to think, "Ah. So that's how it works!' And, as I shall elaborate, psychoanalytic groups do seem to privilege one or the other as a means of institu- tional definition.

It all used to be much simpler. In the Good Old Days, you either were or were not an analyst: this, of course, was decided by the pow- ers that be. The White Institute was not. Simple as that. It was a prag- matic application of Popper's (1959) principle of falsifiability—you can't say what a thing is if you can't say what it isn't. Psychoanalysts defined themselves by declaring who wasn't. The struggle for status, prestige, patients and candidates invokes a polarization: them/us.

The minute you are convinced you are right and that your system is the only Truth—you've established a religion. Current ecumenism allows for multiple versions of psychoanalysis, some of which admittedly may strain the definition of the process. But at least we now talk to each other.

In 1983, Greenberg and Mitchell published their seminal *Object Relations in Psychoanalytic Theory* (Greenberg and Mitchell 1983). By subsuming virtually every psychoanalytic position under the rubric of "relational" (including the Kleinians, Kohutians, Interpersonalists, Winnicottians, and so on), they politically outflanked and isolated the Freudians; essentially pressuring them to participate in an ecumenical movement that may have had as much to do with pragmatics as any genuine substantive synthesis. Ironically, the Interpersonal position—the original apostates—may currently be closer to contemporary Freudians than to our other presumably "relational" cohorts.

At about the same time, Merton Gill presciently identified the problem in a paper read at the William Alanson White Institute (Gill 1983). Gill, who has been perhaps the most conciliatory of the Freudian analysts on the committee that in 1942 expelled the early group of Interpersonalists from the American Psychoanalytic Association (for among other shortcomings not conforming to the five-day/couch rule), had been drifting towards an interpersonalism of his own. He and I corresponded over my book, *The Fallacy of Understanding* and he came to White and attended some of our Clinic meetings (Levenson 1972). In 1982, he gave a remarkable talk at White, in defying the then current draconian bans, an act of no small moral courage. He had reviewed the entire corpus of Interpersonal writings, and with his fresh and original intelligence, he saw that there were, as he said, two dichotomies in psychoanalysis:

> *I refer to the distinction between two major cleavages in psychoanalytic thought. One cleavage is between the interpersonal paradigm and the drive-discharge paradigm. The other cleavage is between those who believe the analyst inevitably participates in a major way in the analytic situation and those who do not. I came to realize that I had assumed that these two cleavages ran parallel to each other, or at least that those who adhered to the interpersonal paradigm would also ascribe to the analyst a major participation in the analytic situation.*
> *(Gill 1983: 201)*

You will note that he accepts the relational/drive dichotomy as valid. He goes on to say that variations in the use of the second parameter cut across Institutional and metapsychological loyalties and affiliations. He is, in essence, saying that within any psychoanalytic group, there will be marked variations in this second cleavage—variations which one might consider as a continuum of activity, running from analysts who see themselves as the curative event in the patient's life (charismatic or restitutive), to those who see the cure as the analyst curing herself (analysis of countertransference), to those who believe in the analysis of resistance and transference as getting out of the way of the patient's self-curative potential, some self-regulating (intra-psychic) activity on the patient's part. The spectrum runs from the mutative effects of the analyst's engagement to emphasis on the unimpeded flow of consciousness.

These are, obviously, different stations on the currently loosely defined and delineated continuum of "transference". Nevertheless, when psychoanalysts work, they—every one—monitor the interpersonal field closely, whether to influence it or in order to get it out of the way. This sometimes inadvertent attention to the transference may be far more relevant to the cure than metapsychological considerations.

Freud's (1905) case study of Dora is considered the emblematic origin of his thinking on transference. This three-month treatment ended with an abrupt and unanticipated termination. Dora had told Freud at the beginning of the session that she would not continue. Freud continued his inquiry, ignoring her statement. At the end of the session, she said goodbye pleasantly and came no more! Freud's first reaction was hurt—why did she treat me so shabbily? But Freud being Freud, he morphed his disappointment into the concept of resistance and transference.

Erik Erikson subsequently made much of Freud's complicity in the female repression of the day—that is to say, that Dora had good reason to be angry (Erikson 1968). I would like to take it all one step further and suggest that *her response was inevitable no matter what Freud did!* Psychoanalysis begins when even the best-intentioned efforts fail. It is the analysis—not the avoidance—of the failure that defines transference and countertransference and constitutes the major leverage of the process.

In 1914, in *On the History of the Psycho-analytic Movement*, Freud defined the centrality of transference:

> Any line of investigation, no matter what its direction, which recognizes these two facts (transference and resistance. ed) and takes them as the starting point of its work may call itself psychoanalysis, though it arrives at results other than my own. (Freud 1914a: 298)

And about the same time in *On Narcissism*:

> [T]he whole structure of psychoanalysis stands apart from metapsychological considerations, which can be replaced and discarded without damaging the structure. (Freud 1914b: 147)

People resist change, for whatever reason, and that resistance takes the form of an interaction with the therapist *that recapitulates, in action, the very issue under discussion.* Freudians saw this enactment as a resistance to a confrontation with unconscious fantasy, and consequently interpreted *away* from the transference in order to get back to the fantasies. Currently, most of us interpret *into* the transference since we see it as a fruitful area of inquiry. We all agree that what happens between the patient and therapist is integral to the cure. We differ on what it is: the elucidation of fantasies projected onto the therapist, or the field of interaction itself.

It is my contention that transference is far more enigmatic, indeed uncanny, than one might suspect, not simply a form of resistance to change as the Freudians would have it, but rather some *mysterious, inherent, correlate of the inquiry*—inherent, inasmuch as it may be a natural aspect of cognitive process, not an artifact of anxiety or defense.

So then, the two striking phenomenological aspects of the analytic praxis are the patient's flow of consciousness and the uncanny tendency of their simultaneous relationship to play out or *mirror* what is being said. If the patient tells you how hurt he was by his father's criticism when he was a child and then gets hurt that you are ending the session five minutes early, it may matter less whether you interpret it as a distortion carried over from his childhood, or as a real enactment between the two of you that he is over-valuing, or even if you wonder why on reflection you ended the session earlier, the real value may lie in the recognition that *something is being replayed.* Why this should be so, requires the elaboration of a number of axioms.

First, all experience (perception) is an interpretation. This is not an issue of philosophic realism. How one experiences a bear, or for that matter a potential lover, depends, not just on the immediate circumstances (the bear is blocking your passage on the trail or sunning itself in a zoo enclosure), but on socio-cultural experience: that is to say, memory. Perception *is* ninety per cent memory—the "mind's best guess" (Gregory 1966: 2).

Second, all interpretation is selectively biased. Perception is always distorted or constricted; however caused, it is the *sine qua non* of neurosis. But how? There is a spectrum of possibilities: simply the necessity to select from multiple perspectives; by the force of unconscious drive; by interpersonal anxiety (out of awareness); or by being misled by other people, deliberately or unconsciously (mystification). Our therapeutic endeavours with the patient are all about omissions, what is left out of awareness—be it by repression, inattention, dissociation, or mystification.

From my point of view, all experience is interpersonally determined. Cognition itself is interpersonal. The interpersonal modus is contagious anxiety. Sullivan's concept posited that it was the anxiety of the significant other, the necessary caretaker, that frightened the child, causing a wave of contagious anxiety that then was responsible for the subsequent mechanisms of neurotic denial (Sullivan 1953). This disruptive anxiety creates a cognitive dissonance which is then obscured by the other, largely through the medium of language. The child is *mystified*; that is, he or she learns through the pressure of anxiety to not see what is there to be seen. They must learn to "close the eyes". This was, one notes, the theme of Freud's dream about his father's death, and not incidentally the Greek meaning of *mystes*—to close the eyes, to not see.

This is not to suggest that there is not distortion at play in patients' current lives. I am not implying that all the patient need do is see what is there to be seen. Mystification and its concurrent anxiety operate most strongly in early life events, but current events reiterate the earlier patterning. It is not that the patient is wrong about the present, but rather that the affect and, more importantly, the sense of semiotic confusion and impotence, resonate powerfully to earlier experience. The patient is not wrong in perceptions, but the affect and sense of helplessness surely are. As Fonagy, the eminent attachment theoretician put it:

> *We move away from the model where an early relationship is princi-*
> *pally seen as the generator of a template for later relationships. Instead,*
> *we argue that early experience no doubt via its impact upon develop-*
> *ment at both psychological and neuropsychological levels determines*
> *the "depth" to which the social environment may be processed. Sub-*
> *optimal early experiences of care affect later development by under-*
> *mining the individual's capacity to process or interpret information*
> *concerning mental states that is* essential for effective function-
> ing in a stressful social world. *(Fonagy, Gergely et al. 2002: 7; my*
> *emphasis)*

Axiomatic to my view of therapy is that one cannot *not* interact: one cannot *not* influence. The major instrument of mystification is language; language being not merely speech, but the sum of all its semiotic cues: non-verbal—that is, tonal, prosodic—and nuances of irony, sarcasm, and humour. The child learns, as Laing put it, to not know what it knows it knows; that is, the child is essentially talked out of her perceptions. But language, unfortunately, is less about communication of information than about deception and control—power. This "anxiety of influence", as every therapist is aware, may keep the patient from accepting insights from the therapist who may well be right but experienced as intrusive (Bloom 1973). So, again from the interpersonal view, resolving neurotic conflict means getting a better grasp of what's going on around you and *to* you; that is, mastering the semiotic world of experience.

Mystification, then, is the gap between what is said and what is shown: between *langue* and *parole*, speech and language (Levenson 1983). Mystifications severely limit the possible range of responses, so that neurosis becomes a type of cliché. According to the old psychoanalytic aphorism: the patient knows only one way of doing something and that doesn't work; or, alternatively, it works *too* well to allow change! It follows that the major instrument of demystification is the matching of what is said against what is done. The therapist and patient talk, and that talking is an interaction because it is not possible to talk without taking a selective position regarding the content; and that selective position is a bit of behaviour with the patient. Speech *is* behaviour: to repeat the earlier postulation, one cannot *not* interact. The Interpersonal field of patient/therapist is an enactment of what is simultaneously talked about. This may well be not some consequence of psychoanalytic inquiry, or stress of the field, *but an intrinsic part of semiotic communication.*

This experience of transferential enactment is often eerie. For example: analysts may find themselves imitating, or mirroring, the behaviour of patients. Years ago, I worked with a depressed and self-devaluing young woman. I caught myself, on leaving the office in the evening, imitating her strange gait. In another more extensive example, I had a vivid experience of this mimetic response. A sixty-year-old man was telling me about his childhood, how he felt tortured by his father's teasing, which was always ostensibly playful. He was the younger of two brothers, with an eight-year age gap, and he was always ragged about things he really could not be expected to have grasped at his age. As he tells me about the teasing, he begins to laugh and laugh and—when I said to him that he sounded on the edge of tears—he broke into sobs, saying how much he loved his father. Two weeks later, on his first session after his return from a ski trip, he turns on me in a rage as he is leaving at the end of the session, and says: "Why were you laughing at me when I first came in?"—staggering me.

After he left, I realized that I had started laughing when I had gone out into the waiting room to greet him. I thought I was glad to see him—but why laughter? And, in truth, as I tried to review it, I had been feeling, very faintly, something akin to ridicule. He was on to something and I told him so during the next session. I still don't entirely understand my reaction.

We tend to think of empathy as affective, as containing the patient's fear of emotional flooding; that is, empathy is the ability of the therapist to grasp the patient's affective experience and to contain it. But what of imitation? I suspect that imitation is a powerful therapeutic response, trying to capture the patient's experience by essentially embodying it. It is quite possible that patients may be, not so much relieved by the experience of the therapist's empathic holding, permitting a restitution of a developmental deficit, as much as being given an opportunity to learn, by imitation—from the therapist—a theory of mind, or empathy for others; that is, change may be less a matter of containment and restitution and more that of new learning.

Here we get into fascinating aspects of current neuropsychological research. The dichotomies between left and right brain are now long familiar and hardly require repetition (Schore 1994). However, I would like to spell out some remarkable new findings on what have been called "mirror neurons". There are fascinating developments in the phenomenology of learning, and—fueled by new techniques of brain monitoring—in the study of consciousness and mind. There are corresponding studies in child development and mother–child interaction. Children, we are told, learn first mimetically, imitatively. Acts such as tilting one's head or sticking out one's tongue call out an imitative response from very young infants. As the children mature, they imitate, experience the imitation, and then categorize the experience in language.

In a 1998 article, *Awareness, insight and learning* I tried to elaborate on the body/mind linkage and this possibility—that learning may be first bodily, first imitative, mimetic, and *then* cerebral (Levenson 1998). This suggests the interesting possibility that psychoanalytic insight may be first experienced and *then* formulated; that the direction of learning may be, not from the head to the body, but quite the opposite—a matter of what is said about what is experienced.

> *The rigid divide between perceptive, motor, and cognitive processes is to a great extent artificial: not only does perception appear to be embedded in the dynamics of action, becoming much more composite than used to be thought in the past,* but the acting brain is also and above all a brain that understands. *(Rizzolatti and Sinigaglia 2008: xi; my emphasis)*

It is a common clinical experience that Interpretations of both meaning and awareness (Gill 1983) work better *after* enactment. If interpretations precede enactment it doesn't work. At best, one gets intellectual agreement, compliance, from the patient.

Mirror neurons were first reported in 1995 by Iaccomo Rizzolati at the University of Parma (Rizzolatti and Sinigaglia 2008; Iacoboni and Mazziotta 2007). Mirror neurons are neurons that fire both when an animal performs and acts, and when it observes another animal performing the same act. This mirroring or imitation is felt by some researchers to be the next big thing in neurological discovery, the "great leap forward" in human evolution, the next cognitive revolution, after the Copernican, the Darwinian, the Freudian, the discovery of DNA and the genetic code. Now the claim, admittedly florid, is made that empathy, language, and theory of mind may all depend on this mirroring capacity. Also claimed, but open to a good deal of question, is that autistic children may lack mirror neurons, and that that lack may account for their inability to empathize. However hyperbolic this may be, it is clear that mirror neurons may open the door to a new understanding of how people learn through interaction, through behaviour as well as language (Ramachandran 2000).

All this certainly opens the door to a conception of psychoanalytic learning qua change as the matching of interpretation to transference. How does this speech/action parallel process translate into therapeutic praxis? I have written before of the algorithm of therapy (Levenson 1983). It consists of three components: frame, inquiry, and enactment. The frame is a set of constraints defined outside and before the psychoanalytic interaction. It provides the patient, and more importantly, the therapist, with a sense of safety and containment. It protects both participants from becoming over-anxious and limits the risk of mutual out-of-awareness interactions.

The therapist and patient engage in a verbal inquiry that may be free-associative or may be of a more detailed nature. Inevitably this leads, not to greater clarity, but to a deconstructed inquiry: coherence is lost, tangential associative threads emerge. Dreams and leaps of association occur. In the process of pursuing the inquiry, the enactment I have been explicating takes place.

Menninger called this direction of flow the "therapeutic cycle"; that is, when the process was proceeding correctly, the material cycled from the present, *through the transference*, and then to the history and back to the present. Note that the useful recall of the past only occurs after the resolution (enactment with therapist) of the transference (Menninger and Holzman 1973: 15). A therapy that links present difficulties to past experiences is educational but not quite psychoanalytic in scope, without the transition through the patient/therapist enactments.

Summary

I am proposing that the therapeutic power of psychoanalysis does not depend on the primacy of metapsychology, or on the presumably mutative interpretations thereof. Metapsychology is ontology; and the claim to knowing—to having a coherent theory of causality and treatment—undermines our appreciation of how little we understand about how people experience change, and its underlying neuropsychological processes. Sullivan is purported to have said, God keep me from a clever psychoanalyst! Humility truly is the beginning of wisdom.[3]

Observation of the praxis of therapy—what it is that we actually do, the act of therapy—illuminates two cardinal aspects of the process: the patient's flow of consciousness, and the analyst's vocal and behavioural participation. In that process, Freud saw very early that patient/therapist interactions got in the way of change. What he saw as resistance to insight with all its ramifications, we now see as enactment. Enactment, as I see it, differs from "acting-out", that anathema of psychoanalysis. Acting-out is a breaking of the frame, when some out-of-awareness material emerges as a disruptive piece of behaviour in or out of the therapy room. How we assess enactment varies. I view it as an inherent part of the interaction, necessary to the process and the cure, not as a by-product of pathological defence.

One might well see this dialectic between speech and action in terms of the long-established neuropsychological paradigm of a right brain/left brain dichotomy. However, more recently, the discovery of so-called mirror neurons has suggested that mirroring may be a vital part of relating to another, as vital an *embodied* aspect of empathy and theory of mind as affective empathy; that is, I know you because I feel your feelings. The original distinction between sympathy and empathy is considerably obfuscated in current psychoanalytic discourse. Much of what therapists call empathic response is simply sympathy and solicitude, since the therapist often cannot have a real grasp of the patient's experience. For true empathy, we must experience to some degree what the patient experiences; mirroring or imitation may serve that purpose, albeit in an adumbrated form. Bodily learning, "embodied cognition", may be an essential part of the therapeutic process. To quote Saporrta:

---

[3] See Richards (2003) for an eloquent plea for a measure of humility.

Cognitive scientists and linguists are coming to a new appreciation of Freud's body ego in their recent emphasis on embodied cognition. This is an appreciation that the experience of the body in motion and the body's encounter with the world structure the way we think and the metaphors and language through which we conceive of ourselves and the world. There is evidence that the influence of the body and physical context is not limited to early development but has an ongoing influence on the structure of thinking. *(Saporrta 2008; my emphasis)*

The inquiry (flow of consciousness, detailed inquiry, and drift of topics) and the transferential enactment may not be different points on a therapeutic and theoretical continuum, but rather may be two sides of the same coin. The distinctions Gill (1983) made may define analysts' doctrinaire and institutional loyalties; however, I suspect, even if sometimes outside of their awareness, most analysts utilize both sides of the interaction—language and behaviour—because that is inherently the nature of things.

References

Bateson, G. (1979). *Mind and Nature: A Necessary Unity.* New York: Dutton.

Bloom, H. (1973). *The Anxiety of Influence.* New York: Oxford University Press.

Bollas, C. (1999). *The Mystery of Things.* New York: Routledge.

Chalmers, D. (1996). *The Conscious Mind: In Search of a Fundamental Theory.* New York and Oxford: Oxford University Press.

Cooper, A.M. (2008). "American psychoanalysis today: a plurality of orthodoxies". *The Journal of the American Academy of Psychoanalysis and Dynamic Psychiatry.* 36(2): 235–253.

Damasio, A.R. (1994). *Descartes' Error.* New York: Grosset/Putnam.

Erikson, E. (1968). *Identity, Youth and Crisis.* New York: W.W. Norton & Company Ltd.

Fonagy, P. and G. Gergely, et al. (2002). *Affect Regulation, Mentalization, and the Development of the Self.* New York: Other Press.

Freud, S. (1905). Fragments of an analysis of a case of hysteria. *Standard Edition.* 7.

Freud, S. (1914a). On narcissism: An introduction. *Standard Edition.* 14: 69–102.

Freud, S. (1914b). On the History of the Psycho-analytic Movement. *Collected Papers*. London: Hogarth Press. 14.

Gill, M. (1983). "The interpersonal paradigm and the degree of the analyst's involvement". *Contemporary Psychoanalysis*. 18(2): 200–237.

Greenberg, J. and Mitchell, S. (1983). *Object Relations in Psychoanalytic Theory*. Cambridge: Harvard University Press.

Gregory, R.L. (1966). *Eye and the Brain*. Princeton: Princeton University Press.

Iacoboni, M. and Mazziotta, J.C. (2007). "Mirror neuron system: basic findings and clinical applications". *Ann.Neurol.* 62: 213.

Laing, R.D. (1967). *The Politics of Experience*. New York: Pantheon Books.

Levenson, E. (1972). *The Fallacy of Understanding*. New York City: Basic Books.

Levenson, E. (1983). *The Ambiguity of Change: An Inquiry into the Nature of Psychoanalytic reality*. New York: Basic Books.

Levenson, E. (1991). *The Purloined Self*. New York: Contemporary Psychoanalysis Books.

Levenson, E. (1998). "Awareness, insight and learning". *Contemporary Psychoanalysis*. 34(2): 239–249.

Levenson, E. (2001). "The Enigma of the Unconscious". *Contemporary Psychoanalysis*. 37(2): 239–252.

Menninger, K. and Holzman, P. (1973). *Theory of Psychoanalytic Technique*. New York: Basic Books.

Miller, J. (1995). Going unconscious. *New York Review of Books*. XLII: 59–65.

Popper, K. (1959). *The Logic of Scientific Discovery*. New York City: Basic Books.

Pulver, S. (2003). "On the astonishing clinical irrelevance of neuroscience". *J. Am. Psa Association*. 51: 755–772.

Ramachandran, V.S. (2000). "Mirror Neurons and imitation learning as the driving force behind 'the great leap forward' in human evolution". *Edge*. 69.

Richards, A. (2003). "Psychoanalytic discourse at the turn of our century: a plea for a measure of humility". *Journal of the American Psychoanalytic Association*. 51(suppl): 72–125.

Rizzolatti, G. and Sinigaglia, C. (2008). *Mirrors in the Brain: How Our Minds Share Actions and Emotions*. London: Oxford University Press.

Saporrta, J. (2008). "Digitalizing psychonalysis and psychotherapy". *American Psychoanalyst*. 42(2): 1–9.

Schore, A. (1994). *Affect Regulation and The Origin of the Self.* Hillsdale: N.J., Lawrence Erlbaum.

Searle, J.R. (1997). *The Mystery of Consciousness.* New York: Random House.

Sullivan, H.S. (1953). *The Interpersonal Theory of Psychiatry.* New York City: W.W. Norton.

PART II

THE KEYNOTE ADDRESSES

CHAPTER TWO

The nearness of you[1]: Navigating selfhood, otherness, and uncertainty[2]

Philip M. Bromberg, Ph.D.

In deciding how to write this Keynote Address I was helped by the two memorable Keynotes delivered by Adrienne Harris and Irwin Hoffman at the 2007 Division 39 Spring meeting in Toronto. I noticed while listening to them that the speaker is allowed remarkable personal latitude to write in whatever form and about whatever topic he or she chooses as long as it is germane to the theme of the conference. Harris (21 April, 2007) wrote autobiographically—and did it as though she were born to it—even though, as I discovered on my own, it is harder than it looks. In Hoffman's Keynote (22 April, 2007), I was equally struck by the speaker's freedom to write a position paper on whatever aspect of the theme he holds to be of most personal significance. In my own Keynote I have appreciatively drawn upon what they each did with this gift of freedom, by developing a perspective on "Knowing, Not-Knowing, and Sort-of-Knowing"

---

[1] Song title by Carmichael and Washington (1937).
[2] An earlier version of this chapter was presented 11 April, 2008 as a Keynote Address at the Twenty-Eighth Annual Spring Meeting of the Division of Psychoanalysis of the American Psychological Association, New York City.

that I believe speaks to the future of psychoanalysis in its relevance as a therapeutic process and in its value to society. I am going to begin autobiographically, using my relationship to writing as the point of entry.

More than thirty years ago, while I was a still a candidate at the White Institute, I published what was to be my first piece of analytic writing (Bromberg 1974). It wasn't actually a paper but rather a brief introduction to a 1972 symposium that I had organized and chaired as President of the Harry Stack Sullivan Society, the candidate organization. As my first official act, I decided it would be a really appealing idea to hold an "Inter-institute Candidate Symposium" where candidates from some of the major institutes in New York City would present short papers on what it was like to be in training, and then engage each other in discussion.

The word "appealing" didn't turn out to be the best way of characterizing it, but the experience definitely contributed to my later understanding of the advantages and disadvantages of dissociation. I had waded into a hidden swamp of psychoanalytic politics that I managed to feel had nothing to do with *me* because I just "knew" that my plan, including the name I chose for the symposium, could never stir up dozing alligators. I naively named it, if you can believe, "The Rational and Irrational in Psychoanalytic Training". Being me, I "knew" that once the leaders of each institute realized how valuable this meeting would be to candidates everywhere, they would all back it wholeheartedly. Amazingly, and despite some grouchy alligators, the meeting took place, with the participation of candidates from different institutes, including two that were affiliated with the American Psychoanalytic Association. That symposium marked the start of my psychoanalytic writing and with it the start of my reputation as someone who didn't seem to "get" the way things work.

The symposium got published, the gators seemed to go back to dozing, and there it was—in print—including my two-page Introduction which ended by my quoting Allan Wheelis's (1958: 154) famously challenging statement that "Without institutional protection, [although] the early discoveries of psychoanalysis might have been diluted or dispersed ... when the issue is an idea, the institution that protects the infant is likely to stunt the child".

I said that I learned a few things from the experience, but "getting" how things work didn't seem to be one of them. Happily unaware that I might have been lucky, I continued going pretty much my own way, more and more enjoying writing, and always puzzled by why I seemed to be raising the eyebrows, and at times the hackles, of some important folks at my own Institute. But I was never blocked from publishing in *Contemporary Psychoanalysis* (the journal published by the White Institute). If anything, I was made welcome by its then Editor, Art Feiner, to whom I will be forever grateful.

I am still not paying a lot of attention to "the way things work", and those who have read my writing over the years might have noticed how often I draw on something that could be considered a bit "edgy" for a psychoanalytic article. Just a few examples are Carlos Castaneda's work (1968, 1971); a Robert Parker (1983) "Spencer" novel; Theodore Sturgeon's (1953) sci-fi classic, *More than Human*; Arthur Conan-Doyle's Sherlock Holmes (Baring-Gould 1967); Mary Shelley's (1818) *Frankenstein*; George MacDonald's (1858) *Phantastes*; and Thane Rosenbaum's (2002) *The Golems of Gothem*.

I've always done it without anxiety because I feel a total compatibility between these authors and certain psychoanalytic authors with whom they share a home in my mind. In "Playing With Boundaries" (Bromberg 1999), I offered the view that the mind's fundamental ability to shift between different self states without losing self-continuity makes it possible for someone to use an other's self states as part of their own. I suggested that this process of self-state borrowing manifests itself within and between a reader and an author, and is what makes certain authors not just an author but *your* author. He or she becomes yours when the otherness of their words do not *feel* other to you—when the affective interplay among their self states allows the affective interplay among your own self states to join theirs. He or she then becomes *your* author, and you become *his/her* reader. In the words of Carlos Zafon (2001: 4–5), "Every book, every volume you see here, has a soul. The soul of the person who wrote it and of those who read it and lived and dreamed with it".

What I call, metaphorically, "playing with boundaries", overlaps dramatically at the neurobiological level with what Allan Schore (2003a: 96), writes about as a right-brain to right-brain channel of affective communication—a channel that he sees as "an organized dialogue", [that is, a dialogue that takes place through] "dynamically fluctuating moment-to-moment state-sharing". I believe it to be this process of state-sharing that not only allows an author to become your author, but also, in what we call "a psychoanalytically good match", it is what allows an analyst to become *your* analyst. Although I feel less secure in proposing that the *absence* of state-sharing is the thing that most accounts for so-called bad matches between patient and analyst, it seems plausible to me that this plays a role of no small significance.

This affect-based, right-brain to right-brain dialogue between self and other—if it lacks a cognitive context for too long a time—leads to what we are calling "sort-of-knowing", its quality of *uncertainty* being basic to the experience. In clinical work, the lack of cognitive context is what organizes the relational phenomenon that we label "enactment".

Sort-of-knowing

The terms "knowing" and "not-knowing" are relatively easy to think about as the experiences to which they refer are explicit. "Sort-of-knowing", however, is different. In its essence, it refers to something that is always at least somewhat *dissociative*; that is, our awareness of it is always more implicit than explicit. What I'm going to write about next is the difference between "sort-of-knowing" as a normal mind/brain process that helps us get through each day with the least amount of stress, and "sort-of-knowing" as a means of protecting oneself from what may be too much for the mind to bear.

In its everyday use, sort-of-knowing is not a defensive operation but rather an adaptive process in its own right—a process that among its other uses allows self–other boundaries to become sufficiently permeable to facilitate transition to knowing.

What I mean is nicely captured in a clinical vignette I presented at a 2002 conference that Richard Chefetz and I did together, called "Talking with Me and Not-Me". The conference was published in its entirety in *Contemporary Psychoanalysis* (Chefetz and Bromberg 2004).

It is a story told to me by a patient about an incident that took place while he was driving his fiancée to pick up her wedding dress. He had entered an intersection just as the light was changing from amber to red, and a police officer pulled him over. He of course told the cop that the light wasn't red yet, and he also asked to be given a break because they were about to get married. His fiancée suddenly took over and began chastising my patient at length, in front of the cop, about the light really being red and what a bad person he was to lie to a police officer. The cop listened quietly in amazement, and when he finally spoke he told my patient that he wasn't going to give him a ticket because if he was marrying *her* then he already had enough trouble. As they drove off, my patient said to her, furiously, "How could you have done that? How could you have been so mean to me?"

"You didn't get a ticket, did you?" she replied. He, in a state of total consternation, could barely get his words out: "You ... you ... you mean you did that on purpose?"

"Well ... I'm not sure—*sort of*", she mumbled.

"Sort of". If I had been a fly on the wall my guess is she would have been looking into space as she said "sort of". Eventually, when she was back to what she would call "herself", she acknowledged that she was terribly sorry and ashamed at what she had done, and that she hadn't done it on purpose. She also revealed that since a child she has always been terrified of police officers and "wasn't herself" whenever she was around one.

When she was with the cop, the self state that organized "me-ness" was dissociatively trying to control the affect that dysregula-tion caused by her hyperaroused fear, and in this sense it is accurate to say that her *brain* "did it on purpose" as an automatic survival response. The "purpose", however, has no cognitive representation in the *mind*. But later, when she responds to her irate boyfriend, "You didn't get a ticket, did you?", the hyperaroused fear of the cop had diminished enough for her to inhabit a self state that was *also* organized by attachment, making the *vituperousness* when the policeman was present, a "not me". At each point, what she did was "right", but in different ways.

To me, what is especially interesting is that in her effort to think about whether she "did it on purpose", her reply was not defined totally by *either* "knowing" or "not-knowing". Her ability to be confused and *to symbolize the confusion* by the term "sort of", speaks to a nascent capacity to experience intrapsychic conflict and hold it as a mental state long enough to reflect on what it is like—that is, to symbolize it cognitively. To avoid the mental confusion created by a question that required her to consider the possibility that *both* were "me", she was at least able to offer an "I'm not sure—*sort of*".

By my lights, that's pretty darned good. She didn't automatically switch self states dissociatively. She was able to *hold* both states (albeit with confusion) in a single moment of consciousness. Standing in the spaces between the states (Bromberg 1998) was not quite in place but she was able to hold both states long enough to experience their presence simultaneously. As a result, time, place, and motive became complex, and confusingly conflictual rather than dissociatively simplified. Because *resolution* of conflict was not yet possible for her, she used the term "sort of" in order to answer her boyfriend's question, a phrase that vividly captures the *uncertainty* that organized her unfamiliarly complex mental state and its immediate experience of unclarity.[3]

The reach of intersubjectivity

When you look at sort-of-knowing in its function as a normal brain process, it is not hard to see why the experience of uncertainty is so relevant as a conference theme. Mary Tennes (2007), in a paper titled "Beyond Intersubjectivity", linked the experience of uncertainty to what she called "a model of selfhood that resists the need for certainty" and, as have I, she proposes (p. 514) that "self and other, subject and object, both are and are not separate". Most centrally, Tennes argues that "as our clinical technique takes us further into intersubjective territory, we are encountering realities for which we have neither language nor context" and that "if we look more closely with less need to fit such experiences into our preexisting framework, we discover that they deconstruct in profound and perhaps destabilizing ways, our notions of self and other" (p. 508).

As with most radically new discoveries about the mind and its undiscovered realms, Freud had himself cast an eye in a similar direction, leaving its implications undeveloped. As far back as 1921 Freud offered the view that:

> "it no longer seems possible to brush aside the study of ...
> things which seem to vouchsafe the real existence of psychic

---

[3] Gratitude to Nina Thomas for recognizing that the presented version did not sufficiently develop this point, helping me to further clarify the relationship between dissociation and conflict.

forces other than the known forces of the human and animal psyche, or which reveal mental faculties in which, until now, we did not believe. *The appeal of this kind of inquiry seems irresistible.* (Freud 1921 in Devereux 1953: 56; my emphasis)

Freud, however, was overly optimistic in his prediction. It was quite resistible for the next seventy-five years, even among most Interpersonal and Relational analysts. Then, Elizabeth Lloyd Mayer (1996), in the *International Journal of Psychoanalysis*, published a groundbreaking article about the limitation in psychoanalytic thinking with regard to what we call intersubjectivity and about our anxiety in straying beyond the narrow range of what we hold to be "legitimate" clinical facts. A full two-thirds of her paper was devoted to hard research on energy fields—human and nonhuman—and their relationship to so-called paranormal phenomena that are always being encountered by analysts in their day-to day work with certain patients and subsumed under categories of experience such as intuition, empathic attunement, unconscious communication, and if those fail, then "coincidence". It is just such phenomena, Mayer argued, that most demonstrate "the enormous power of the human mind to affect—indeed to create ... what analysts have customarily called *external* reality" and that:

> "If we ignore research that significantly recasts our most important concepts, we may find ourselves in a position not unlike the Sufi sage Nasrudin, who searched for his keys at night under a lighted lamp-post not because he'd lost them there, but because there was more light there than where he'd lost them.
>
> We need to look wherever we're likely to find what we're actually looking for, whether or not it's bathed in the light of assumptions that are comfortably familiar". (Mayer 1996: 723–724)

Tennes (2007: 508) cites research by the biologist Rupert Sheldrake (1999, 2003) who developed, Tennes states, "a theory of the 'extended mind', which he links to already existing field theories in physics, mathematics, and biology. Our minds, he proposes, are not confined inside of our heads, but stretch out beyond them through morphic fields". Similarly, Neil Altman (2007: 529) in his commentary on Tennes's paper, suggests that holistic field theory is a potentially promising context for comprehending this heretofore unimaginable reach of the mind, and that Mayer's breathtaking report on Princeton's Anomalies Research Studies has cleared a path toward full acceptance of what we already recognize implicitly— that "people are able to obtain information from remote sources without having any conventional form of contact with the source of information".

Writing about self/other communication that transcends so-called normal channels has until now been pretty much limited to those who wrote about it as fiction, and to the rare breed of non-fiction authors (including a handful of analysts) for whom such things never were fiction. Thus the powerful link I have long experienced between the science fiction of Theodore Sturgeon, the research on dream telepathy by Montague Ullman and his colleagues (1973) at Maimonides Medical Center, and Sandor Ferenczi's (1930: 122) then edgy assertion that under the influence of shock, a part of the personality "lives on, hidden, ceaselessly endeavoring to make itself felt", and that sometimes we "persuade it to engage in what I might almost call an infantile conversation".

The reach of healing

I'm now going to get even more personal. I recently became aware that some of the "edginess" that infiltrates my blending of psychoanalysis and literature has always involved something else— something that although I "sort-of-knew", I did not in fact "know". The way that sort-of-knowing became knowing was amazing, but it is also so illustrative that I am going to tell you the story.

In the Fall 2007 issue of *Contemporary Psychoanalysis* there was a review of my book, *Awakening the Dreamer*, by Max Cavitch—a Professor of English at The University of Pennsylvania. The review was laudatory, but its biggest gift to me was something else. The review was titled "Dissociative Reading: Philip Bromberg and Emily Dickinson" (Cavitch 2007) and it was as illuminating about *me*, as it was about its formal topic, "dissociative processes and literature". The phenomenon of dissociation is an area of his special interest and a quite unusual one for a Professor of English. He is well read in the clinical literature although his special focus is on dissociation as a cultural phenomenon. Unknown to me, Emily Dickinson's verse happened also to be an area of his expertise and interest, which in itself would not be unusual were it not for the fact that, as a scholar, he saw these two areas of interest as profoundly related, and that as reviewer of my book he experienced this interrelationship as significant not only in my writing, but in the writer—that is to say, in *me personally*. He noticed that in Chapter Eight I had excerpted several lines from one of Dickinson's poems (poem #670) for use as an epigraph—her poem that begins "One need not be a Chamber—to be Haunted—" (Dickinson 1863/1960: 333). In my effort to make the relevance of her lines totally clear to *my* readers I had manifested an apparent lack of concern about the formal rules of literary scholarship by doing something that rendered them into (sort-of) prose so as to make my point clearer. In Cavitch's words:

> "He wants us to get the gist of the poem without having to wrestle too much with her linguistic contortions. Yet this also has the perhaps unconsciously intended effect of evacuating her poem of its uncanny resemblance, in its seemingly unbridgeable gaps and cognitive dissonances, to the very dissociative processes Bromberg wants Dickinson to help him illustrate. He mutes, in other words, the audibility to reflective thought of those places in the poem where dissociative gaps are created. One can point, for example, to his omission of all but one of Dickinson's famous dashes—*her most consistent and visible affront to linear narrative*". (2007: 686; my emphasis)

In fact, it was mainly my elimination of *her* unorthodox use of dashes that was my most manifest affront to Dickinson. As a Professor of English, Cavitch easily could have been critical of me—but he was not. What he did have to say was both non-judgmental and perceptive. It also was astonishing, and led to my highly personal reply to his review that was published in the same issue which is why I am writing about it now. Cavitch did not experience my obliteration of Dickinson's signature-style of versification as "mere sloppiness" or "unmotivated error" because in Dickinson, as he puts it, *"there may be no other writer in the English language who engages readers so relentlessly and so powerfully in the intersubjective experience of dissociative states"* (2007: 684; my emphasis). Cavitch continues:

> "Anyone averse to such biographical speculation need only turn to the poems themselves to encounter an imagination stamped with the imprint of all manner of violence: eyes gauged out, lungs pierced, brains trepanned, bodies subjected to extremes of heat and cold, soldered lips, gushing wounds, dismemberment, rape, torture, hanging, drowning, death in every form". (p. 684)

And on page 686 (my emphasis): *"To rend, reduce, and suture such a poem, as Bromberg does without comment here, is to seem to participate with the poet in a dissociative enactment"*—"a transferential encounter, of Bromberg's dissociative immersion in the enactment of the *poet's* traumatized relation to a flooding of affect in the process of being symbolized".

Cavitch's perceptiveness reached back to a trauma in my own past about which he could not have known but which in the idiom of the conference, was always "sort-of-known" by me. I am referring to the residue of an event that goes back to my days as a doctoral student in English Literature many years ago—an experience that was etched into my psyche when, without warning, I was deliberately shamed in front of the class by a professor who announced that I didn't belong in the field. *Why* did I not belong? Because I had used the assignment of writing an essay about Shakespeare's play, Henry IV Part I, as an opportunity to discuss Prince Hal's *personality*.

But the professor's *words* were not the core of the trauma. It was in *how* he did it. Cradling under one arm the class's completed essays, in the hand of his other side he held between thumb and forefinger a single essay. Silently, he walked slowly among the seated students and stopped at my desk, letting the solitary assignment fall onto it from above. It was then that he spoke his only words: "WE DON'T DO THAT SORT OF THING HERE".

This experience, both in spite of and because of its traumatic impact, played an explicit role in my finding a path that led me into the field of psychoanalysis, a field that I experience as my natural home. For many years I continued to use literature as part of my psychoanalytic writing—which I took as evidence that the trauma had been processed.

(Enter Max Cavitch, Stage Left.) Because of *him* I was able to recognize that a dissociated piece of it indeed had remained. I already knew that the trauma had allowed me to pleasurably immerse myself in literature by using it psychoanalytically, but what I had not seen was the dissociated presence of my determination to *never submit* to the arbitrary imposition of using literature in some "right" way. Cavitch intuitively sensed this from my interaction with Dickinson. In Max's eyes, Dickinson and I were comrades in arms. We each refused to bend to orthodoxy. In my use of her lines as an epigraph, I did not *simply* reduce her poetry to quasi-prose. Dissociatively, I did to her poetry my own version of what she did in writing it. I challenged the system (which for me, now included *her*) by obliterating, without acknowledgement, an important piece of what had been her own challenge to the system: her signature use of dashes— *her* violation of orthodoxy—a violation that, ironically, "the system" ultimately accepted.

Cavitch observed that I may have been participating in a dissociative enactment with Dickinson that was being played out as a power struggle, but for *both* Dickinson and me its origin was unknown to him—with Dickinson it was kept guarded from the world, and with me no prior personal relationship had existed through which I might have made it known either explicitly or through things "about" me that he might have unconsciously experienced. In Dickinson's case, Cavitch wrote, "There is much speculation as to what sort of traumatic experiences Dickinson may have endured that would help explain her famously extreme shyness and virtual self-sequestration in her family's Amherst home" (p. 684). *My* trauma with the other English Professor was likewise "unknown" to him until I shared it as part of my published response to his review.

By his not shaming me about my unscholarly behaviour, and even more by his appreciating what that behaviour represented as a way of understanding a mental process (dissociation) of interest to both of us, he helped me not only professionally, but also personally.

This is why my reply to his review was not only a professional expression of gratitude, but was also very personal. In it I recounted to him my experience as a graduate student in English and let him know how much I was benefiting from sharing with him a relational experience that was so personally healing. It was healing because it activated the shadow of the trauma with the other professor, while holding it in a relational context where I was being cared about as a person. What I call a "safe surprise" (Bromberg 2006) was created—and the creation of that safe surprise took place without any explicit interchange between us. *Uncannily,* without direct interchange, I was able to process a dissociated residue of past trauma—a residue about which I had "sort-of-known" because I knew *about* it, but of which I now *knew,* because I knew it personally. I knew it because I had *relived* the original traumatic scenario, but relived it in a manner that did not simply repeat the past. The reliving with Max allowed a new outcome to be part of the reality that defined me in relation to others.

Did trauma begin for me as a graduate student in English? Of course not! Like everyone else, I too had my share of developmental trauma. My history of not "getting" how things work predates that event and shaped my "naïveté" when, in organizing the Inter-institute Candidates Symposium, I believed that senior psychoanalysts could never allow the grinding of personal axes to infiltrate their devotion to fostering the autonomy of their "children".

The fly truffler

In the remainder of this chapter I am once again going to draw on literature. When I made that decision, a part of me was saying "Maybe Cavitch let you off easy; maybe you shouldn't push your luck". However another part of me was arguing that I should go for it. That latter part prevailed, and so I'm now going to address the theme of "knowing, not-knowing, and sort-of-knowing" through sharing self states with the author of an extraordinary novel, *The Fly Truffler* (Sobin 1999), a piece of writing that I hope will enrich your clinical perspective as it enriched mine.

It is a book that pulls a reader into the chaos of love, loss, and madness. It allows the reader to feel not just the increasing presence of mental destabilization, but the simultaneous voice of a potential for relatedness that is always moving along with it.

Written by an expatriate American poet, Gustave Sobin, the story is set in the rural countryside of Provence where, until his death in 2005, Sobin resided for forty years. It is the story of a man in love, a man named Philippe Cabassac, whose mind, slowly but agonizingly, loses the boundary that separates loss of an other from the traumatic loss of self—and loses the boundary that separates creative dreaming from autistic thinking. His mind could not hold the reality of the death of his beloved wife Julieta—a young student who disappears from his life as mysteriously as she entered it. To paraphrase Jennifer Reese's (2000) *The New York Times* book review, Julieta, out of nowhere, suddenly appears in Cabassac's classroom, taking voluminous notes. Cabassac is a professor of a dying language—Provençal linguistics—and she, an orphan who has been wandering aimlessly through the fading world of Provence has now, with Cabassac, found words that mystically connect her with her ancestral roots. Julieta moves into Cabassac's farmhouse, conceives a child, marries him, and miscarries. Shortly thereafter she dies. Unable to bear the loss, Cabassac's dreams become increasingly indistinguishable from waking reality.

Cabassac has hunted for truffles all his life by searching for the swarms of tiny flies that hover over the ground where the truffles are buried in order to lay their eggs in the aromatic earth beneath. Through this miracle of symbiosis, the truffles can then be found, and are indeed found by Cabassac, who fries them, sips herbal tea, and later, when he sleeps, has powerful dreams in which his wife returns to him.

To Cabassac, who was an emotionally isolated man even before Julieta's death, dreams become gradually more real than life itself. In them Julieta is about to tell him a profound secret—but he always awakens before it is revealed. He loses interest in his job as a professor of Provençal linguistics—a job that begins to die just as verbal language itself increasingly dies for him as a medium of communication. He becomes more and more isolated from human relationships and sinks gradually into a state of autistic madness, signing away piece after piece of his family home—the only thing that still connected him to the external world—until all that remained was to search out the flies that would lead him to the truffles and in turn to his lost beloved.

The Fly Truffler can be read from many different frames of reference, including as an allegorical portrayal of the Orpheus myth in which the doorway that leads to reunion with a lost beloved is beneath the ground—the doorway to Hell. But what I want to speak of is its ability to evoke the *affective* experience that makes us aware, sometimes disturbingly aware, of the link between trauma and dissociation and the potential *loss of self*.

Sobin's book raises the issue of how to think about people like the protagonist, Cabassac, who was unable to restore himself as he slid into madness, and how what we term "knowing" and "sort-of-knowing" might be viewed in the context of annihilation dread. Because "knowing" is dependent on thinking, and thinking is dependent on the degree to which one's capacity for mental representation has been compromised by trauma, it is worth reflecting on Laub and Auerhahn's famous observation that it is the primary nature of trauma to "elude our knowledge because of both *defense and deficit*" (1993: 288; my emphasis). The deficit is a dissociative gap, by virtue of which, "sort-of-knowing" is recruited from its everyday function into the service of the mind's evolutionary need to protect its stability (thus their term *"defense"*).

Cabassac's connection to Julieta became tied more and more concretely to his being able to experience her as a person who continued to exist as alive; and this Julieta, as even Cabassac sensed, was connected to his dead mother in an ineffable way.

With regard to the subtitle of my chapter, "Navigating Selfhood, Otherness, and the Experience of Uncertainty", Sobin's work of fiction is simultaneously a work of non-fiction. Certain people for whom the early development of intersubjectivity has failed to take place or been severely compromised are, in times of crisis, especially vulnerable to "uncertainty" of the boundary between selfhood and otherness, and can become unable to navigate this boundary. They become unable to sustain the loss of a needed person as a separate "other". It is these people for whom the potential for *annihilation dread* is often greatest. For them, the experience of loss can become such a threat to the experience of self-continuity that it results in what we know as insanity.

Self-continuity of course feels threatened in a lesser way even without annihilation anxiety (which is what makes trauma, "traumatic", rather than just a form of anxiety). However, when the inability to separate self and other—total depersonalization—is a genuine possibility, the function of dissociation as a protection against out-of-control affect dysregulation becomes a last-ditch effort to survive as a self. It can no longer assure that one or more parts of the self will continue to engage with the world in a way that is functional though limited. Dissociation becomes, instead, the means through which the mind/brain tries to avoid self-annihilation by protecting the inner world from the existence of the outside—gradually eliminating it as a *personal* reality by living more and more completely in a nonpermeable, self-contained "dream". One may still know *about* the outside world but is no longer "of" it.

When the original maternal object is insufficiently differentiated from the self to become a comforting internal "other" that can be remembered later in one's life, a person may appear in one's life—often after one's actual mother has died—a person who frequently embodies a likeness to the mother in some physically concrete way and who seems to be totally consumed by him. A passionate attachment to that person then develops a life of its own. In Cabassac's case, partly fueled by Julieta's death, this attachment became (borrowing the title of Jules Henry's 1965 classic) a "pathway to madness" that led to a final act done without self-reflection—the act of obliterating what remained of his outside world and his attachment to it. He sold, literally out from under himself, the land and home in which he and his family had lived for generations—a place that until then had been not just his, but *him*. As was made clear by the author, there was an eerie resonance between the increasing loss of personal meaning held by the outside world and a similar withdrawal into himself during his childhood.

What was the clincher for Cabassac? What pushed him over the edge? My answer would be that he had no one to talk to and no one to listen. Sobin portrays him as having been a loner all his life, and thus especially vulnerable to the horror of self-loss when Julieta disappeared from his external world as suddenly as she had once appeared in it. His struggle to "stand in the spaces" was unable to prevent his increasing isolation inside himself because he couldn't use the mind of an other to share what he felt. He not only was unable to use a real other, but was unable to use an imagined other as imagination requires the simultaneous existence of a separate self that is stable enough to remember a lost other without merging with that other.

Cabassac's external environment became more and more undifferentiated from his internal object-world, and could not be sustained as a reality that was *his*. The outside world became grimly limited in what it could offer as a potential anchor to sanity and literally had to be sold—to be rid of—because it was already starting to take on the presence of a now "malevolent other", threatening to disintegrate the boundary between self and object. *Sobin offers a portrayal, both inspiring and chilling, of what trauma can do when there is no one with whom to share it.* And to anyone who might see this novel as representing the consequences of substance abuse (mushrooms and herbal tea), I can only say, "Sorry folks—I don't think so!"

But read on. It's not over yet. There is another message embedded in this novel that is just as important to the theme of the conference and perhaps even more so. In this remote, sequestered environment of Provence, humans and animals share a relationship that is almost as vital to the evolutionary survival of both species as it was during the Middle Ages; thus the title of the novel. The inescapable power of the interrelationship between animal and human in this story touches directly on the way in which we are starting to understand the dialectic between thought and affect, between left and right brain, and between self states of the patient and self states of the analyst. And it relates in an especially interesting way to the recent discovery of mirror neurons, the postulation of which, if you will recall, came about through a researcher's fortuitous relationship with a monkey—or more accurately, an ape (see Gallese and Goldman 1998).

The rapport between art and science is something I remain of several minds about, but as it applies to psychoanalysis it has never been captured better than by the brilliant and troubled Italian poet Alda Merini (2007: 15) in the aphorism:

> Psychoanalysis
> Always looks for the egg
> In a basket
> That has been lost.[4]

For over a hundred years, psychoanalysts were trained to talk to their patients about an *inferred* egg, through associations and interpretations, because the basket (an entity called the unconscious) was believed "lost" (inaccessible) to here-and-now existence. At this point in the evolution of psychoanalysis it is increasingly recognized that the "egg" can *manifestly* be brought into palpable existence by accepting that "the unconscious" (the basket) is not a mental entity but rather a *relational process* that is accessible through enactment.

---

[4] I wish to thank Kristopher Spring for bringing Merini's aphorism to my attention.

The interdependence of mind/brain systems reflects the evolutionary status of the interdependence between what is most human and what remains most animal. A "truffler", as we know, is someone who devotes himself/herself to the solitary activity of hunting for truffles, but apart from certain environments—such as this area of Provence—it is an activity that has most famously been done with the aid of a pig. Pigs have been used because of both their great sensitivity in being able to sniff out where truffles are hiding beneath the ground, and their voracious craving for them which makes a pig fanatical in its search. The problem is that, if more civilized animals (such as us) are to get the prize, the truffler needs to be always on vigilant alert so that the pig does not scarf down the truffles before them. It is not hard to see why the flies in that respect were an improvement. It is clearly an easier, less fraught way to find truffles than by using a hyper-aroused pig.

In the passage with which I'm going to end, Sobin bridges the gap between the internal worlds of human life and "sort-of-human" life. The passage relates to the breeding of *silkworms*—an enterprise that for hundreds of years was done in this part of Provence by women, enabling them to survive economically. I quote:

> [T]he silkworms, as if on some magical signal, rose into their brushwood uprights and began spinning their cocoons. Rotating their heads continuously so that a thin, spittle-like secretion would run free of a pair of matching glands located on either side of their thorax, these creatures would each spin over a kilometer of precious, opalescent fiber in less than three uninterrupted days of labor. Nothing stopped them either. Nothing aside from *unwanted noises*. A single thunderclap, for instance, could break the thread, bring their spinning to an end, destroy a whole season's harvest.
>
> When a thunderstorm was seen approaching, the women—in preparation—would gather, begin ringing bells—goat bells, sheep bells—or beating, *gently at first*, against shovels, frying pans, cauldrons in an attempt to *prepare* their little nurslings for *the far more invasive sounds of the thunderstorm itself. They'd increase the volume of those cacophonous medleys with each passing minute. In response, the silkworms wove all the faster, and their thread,*

as a result, went unbroken throughout the ensuing thunderstorm.
(pp. 83–84; my emphasis)

When I first read this my mouth dropped open. *Silkworms? Really?* It seems that even invertebrates can get affectively destabilized—left unable to function—when they are subjected to shock—in this case, a sudden noise that is loud beyond their tolerance to bear. At that stage of their development, beyond infancy but still pretty vulnerable, it means they stop spinning silk. So the women do what a good therapist would do. To support the continuity of the silkworms' developmental maturation, they create conditions that they believe will raise their threshold for affect dysregulation. For a silkworm, developmental maturation at that phase means being able to spin thread, supporting a survival capacity (the creation of a cocoon) that is necessary to their existence. This survival capacity is helped along through a human/animal relationship that, at an affective level, is a plausible analogue of what Schore (2003b: 144) calls a conversation between limbic systems—even though, here, one party in the conversation might be seen as all limbic system. It matters not that the women, like therapists, also reap an economic benefit. A good therapist does what he does not just because of that benefit but with the benefit being always a *part* of it.

Is it a stretch to see the *initial* part of the relationship between the women and the silkworms as similar to an early maternal phase of human infancy? Consider this description by Sobin that begins with their caring for the eggs—the eggs which the women poured into little sachets that they'd sewn for the very occasion:

Wearing those sachets underneath the warms folds of their skirts or snug between their corseted breasts, they'd incubate those nascent silkworms on nothing more nor less than the heat of their own bodies.

For ten days running, then, women actually served as agents of gestation for these silkworms-to-be ... [T]he women would then deposit the freshly hatched larvae in nurseries—kindergartens of sorts—that they'd have meticulously prepared in advance. Temperate, airy, well-lit, these cocooneries became the silkworms' abode, now, as they passed through four successive moltings in as many weeks. Growing from delicate little caterpillars no more than a millimeter long to pale voracious

creatures a full sixty times that length, the silkworms required
continuous nursing. And nursing they received. (pp. 81–82; my
emphasis)

It was *after* infancy that the silkworms-to-be, now silkworms-that-
arc, bccamc part of an *interactive* process. In June "began the moment
in which ... the women responded to a need to protect them from
thunderstorms" (p. 83). I am offering the view that like the natural
presence of thunderstorms in the relationship between a silkworm
and its caretaker, the relationship between a patient and a psychoanalyst has its own natural disruptions. But unlike thunderstorms
created by the external environment, their psychoanalytic counterparts are not *exterior* events that intrude into an otherwise "safe"
treatment frame. Because our therapeutic work always involves
reliving areas of experience where developmental trauma has left
its residue to one degree or another, the analytic relationship is a
process of collision and negotiation. It is *both* the source of potential destabilization and the source of its healing. What patient and
analyst do together will always include collisions between subjectivities, some of which will *inevitably* feel too "loud" to the patient,
and it is part of the analyst's job to be alert to signs of this and to
address it with genuine personal involvement. Threatening "noise"
is inherent to the analytic relationship itself—a part of the optimal
therapeutic context that I call "safe but not too safe". The therapist's
commitment to helping a patient distinguish what is "disruptive but
negotiable" from the dissociated "truth" that all ruptures in attachment are "relationally irreparable" is an essential part of the work.
The therapist cannot prevent interpersonal "noise" from becoming
too loud no matter how *non*-intrusive he or she tries to be. Letting a
patient know in an ongoing way that his or her internal experience
is being held in your mind *while* you are doing "your job" is what
provides the safety—even though you are not doing it perfectly.

In humans, the ability to strengthen one's readiness to face potential trauma without transforming life itself into an act of intermi-
nable vigilance, depends on a relationship with an important other
who relates to your subjective states as important to him or her—and
to whose mental states you can reciprocally relate. Cabassac's capacity to feel that he existed in the mind of an other was so tenuous
that the death of his beloved became a loss of selfhood. There was

no longer a bridge that could link a stable mental representation of her to a self sturdy enough to maintain self-continuity without her concrete existence being part of that self. And he had no one with whom to talk.

The conference brochure asked: "How do we come to tolerate the ambiguity inherent in not-knowing or, more confusing still, sort-of-knowing?" I guess I would say it has to do, SORT-OF, with the wiring of the brain; SORT-OF with how much our caretakers were able to affirm the rights of all parts of us to exist; and SORT-OF being lucky to have someone to talk to at the right times—including someone who can think about you as a silkworm when you most need it.

I'll close by finally making reference to the title of my chapter, which I've not mentioned explicitly even though it is probably clear by now why I chose it. The link between the legendary 1937 song *The Nearness of You*, and what some of us now call implicit relational knowing, needs few words to explain it. And even though I love Allan Schore's concept of conversations between limbic systems, Hoagy Carmichael and Ned Washington when they wrote *The Nearness of You* already knew that "It's not your sweet conversation/That brings this sensation, oh no/It's just the nearness of you".

References

Altman, N. (2007). "Integrating the transpersonal with the intersubjective: Commentary on Mary Tennes's 'Beyond Intersubjectivity'". *Contemporary Psychoanalysis*. 43: 526–535.

Baring-Gould, W.S. (ed.) (1967). *The Annotated Sherlock Holmes: The Four Novels and the Fifty-Six Short Stories Complete by Sir Arthur Conan Doyle*. New York: Clarkson N. Potter.

Bromberg, P.M. (1974). "Introduction to 'On Psychoanalytic Training: A Symposium'". *Contemporary Psychoanalysis*. 10: 239–242.

Bromberg, P.M. (1998). *Standing in the Spaces: Essays on Clinical Process, Trauma and Dissociation*. Hillsdale, NJ: The Analytic Press.

Bromberg, P.M. (1999). Playing with boundaries. In: *Awakening the Dreamer: Clinical Journeys*. Mahwah, NJ: The Analytic Press, 2006, pp. 51–64.

Bromberg, P.M. (2006). *Awakening the Dreamer: Clinical Journeys*. Mahwah, NJ: The Analytic Press.

Bromberg, P.M. (2007). "Response to reviews of 'Awakening the Dreamer: Clinical Journeys'". *Contemporary Psychoanalysis*, 43: 696–708.

Castaneda, C. (1968). *The Teachings of Don Juan: A Yaqui Way of Knowledge*. New York: Ballentine Books.

Castaneda, C. (1971). *A Separate Reality: Further Conversations with Don Juan*. New York: Simon & Schuster.

Cavitch, M. (2007). "Dissociative reading: Philip Bromberg and Emily Dickinson". *Contemporary Psychoanalysis*. 43: 681–688.

Chefetz, R.A. and Bromberg, P.M. (2004). "Talking with 'Me' and 'Not-Me': A dialogue". *Contemporary Psychoanalysis*, 40: 409–464.

Devereux, G. (1953). *Psychoanalysis and the Occult*. New York: International Universities Press.

Dickinson, E. (1863). Poem 670. *The Complete Poems of Emily Dickinson* (ed.) T.H. Johnson. Boston: Little Brown, 1960.

Ferenczi, S. (1930). "The principles of relaxation and neo-catharsis". In: M. Balint (ed.) *Final Contributions to the Problems and Methods of Psychoanalysis*. New York: Brunner/Mazel, 1980, pp. 108–125.

Freud, S. (1921/1941). Psychoanalysis and telepathy. In: G. Devereux (ed.) *Psychoanalysis and the Occult*. New York: International Universities Press, 1953, pp. 56–68.

Gallese, V. and Goldman, A. (1998). "Mirror neurons and the simulation theory of mind-reading". *Trends in Cognitive Science*. 2: 493–501.

Harris, A. "You must remember this." Keynote Address, Spring meeting of the Division of Psychoanalysis (39), American Psychological Association, April 21, 2007, Toronto, CA.

Henry, J. (1965). *Pathways to Madness*. New York: Random House.

Hoffman, I.Z. "Therapeutic Passion in the Countertransference". Keynote Address, Spring meeting of the Division of Psychoanalysis (39), American Psychological Association, April 22, 2007, Toronto, CA.

Laub, D. and Auerhahn, N.C. (1993). "Knowing and not knowing massive psychic trauma: Forms of traumatic memory". *International Journal of Psycho-Analysis*. 74: 287–302.

Mayer, E.L. (1996). "Subjectivity and intersubjectivity of clinical facts". *International Journal of Psycho-Analysis*. 77: 709–737.

MacDonald, G. (1858), *Phantastes*. Grand Rapids, MI: Wm. B. Eeerdmans, 1981.

Merini, A. (2007). From "Aphorisms" (Trans. from Italian by Douglas Basford). *Poetry*, December.

Parker, R.B. (1983). *The Widening Gyre: A Spenser Novel*. New York: Dell.

Reese, J. (2000). Black magic. *New York Times*, 11 June, p. xx.

Rosenbaum, T. (2002). *The Golems of Gotham*. New York: Harper Collins.

Schore, A.N. (2003a). *Affect Dysregulation and Disorders of the Self.* New York: Norton.

Schore, A.N. (2003b). *Affect Regulation and the Repair of the Self.* New York: Norton.

Sheldrake, R. (1999). *Dogs Who Know When Their Owners Are Coming Home.* New York: Three Rivers Press.

Sheldrake, R. (2003). *The Sense of being Stared At.* New York: Crown.

Shelley, M. (1818/1991). *Frankenstein.* New York: Bantam Books.

Sobin, G. (1999). *The Fly Truffler: A Novel.* New York: preceding 2000.

Sturgeon, T. (1953). *More Than Human.* New York: Carroll & Graf.

Sullivan, H.S. (1953). *The Interpersonal Theory of Psychiatry.* New York: Norton.

Tennes, M. (2007). "Beyond intersubjectivity: The transpersonal dimension of the psychoanalytic encounter". *Contemporary Psychoanalysis.* 43: 505–525.

Ullman, M., Krippner, S. and Vaughn, A. (1973). *Dream Telepathy.* New York: MacMillan.

Wheelis, A. (1958). *The Quest for Identity.* New York: Norton.

Zafon, C.R. (2001). *The Shadow of the Wind* (Trans. from Spanish by Lucia Graves). New York: Penguin, 2004.

CHAPTER THREE

The unconscious as a knowledge processing centre

Arnold H. Modell, M.D.

The theme of this meeting, "knowing and not knowing", challenged us to reconsider a fundamental aspect of human nature, the relationship between our unconscious and our conscious mind. Psychoanalysis from its inception has focused on the connections between unconscious knowledge and conscious awareness. We can approach a definition of unconscious knowledge by asking the following questions: how can we know something without being aware of it? And how can we be aware of something that we don't know? In either case let us assume that the unconscious mind knows–that the unconscious retains in memory a lifetime of emotionally significant experiences and emotionally salient fantasies. This would include the memory of those experiences with one's caretakers that occurred prior to the age of two or three, prior to the age of retrievable memories. We may unable to recall such memories because prior to that age the hippocampus, that structure in the brain that is necessary for the recall of a memory, has not yet matured. These memories remain as unthought knowns (Bollas 2007). Such memories have also been referred to as somatic memories, indicating that our body remembers even if we can't remember. All of this is to indicate that the unconscious is a source of knowledge, but as

I plan to illustrate, the unconscious is the area of the psyche in which knowledge is processed.

With regard to the theme of knowing and not knowing, we need to be reminded that this subject was implicit in Freud's initial understanding of symptom formation in the hysteric patient. The hysteric patient's defences against unwanted thoughts and feelings are never completely successful; that which is repressed only returns in another form. In the case history of Elizabeth von R. (Freud 1893), Elizabeth knew and she didn't know that she was in love with her brother-in-law. Similarly in the case of Dora (Freud 1905), Freud interpreted her nervous cough as the expression of the wish to have oral sex with Herr K; as Freud noted, Dora knew about the sexual practice, but didn't know that she knew. Freud explained that an unconscious process cut off one psychical group from another so that at the same time one knew and one didn't know.

The idea of the unconscious as the area of the mind in which knowledge is processed is explicit in Freud's explanation of the formation of dreams as he outlined in *The Interpretation of Dreams*. There he stated that unconscious processing is a solidly established fact and that the unconscious must be assumed to be the basis of all psychical life. In *The Interpretation of Dreams* (Freud 1900) he posited an unconscious processing of symbolic and metaphoric elements that are combined by means of condensation and displacement. The result is the dream that we remember when we are conscious and awake. As you know the dream makes use not only of the knowledge contained in unconscious memory, but also the knowledge of recent experiences, those residues of the past twenty-four or forty-eight hours which are woven into the dream process to combine with memories extending from the present back to early childhood. This unconscious process continues after we wake up, determining our associations to the dream and possibly affecting our mood. The manifest associations that Freud reported in response to his dream of the Botanical Monograph, was, in Freud's (1900: 283) words, "like finding ourselves in the factory of thought". We know that dream thoughts penetrate our waking thoughts, and the unconscious can be viewed as the factory from which these thoughts emerge.

This insight of Freud's, that symbolic processing occurs unconsciously and extends into our waking experiences, has had a profound but largely unacknowledged influence on cognitive science.

It is now widely assumed in neurobiology and cognitive science that information is processed unconsciously. Neurobiologists and cognitive scientists have been for various reasons unwilling to recognize Freud's seminal contribution to the science of the unconscious. They are more likely to recognize that they have been influenced by Chomsky's theory that an unconscious symbolic process interprets the syntax of spoken language. Whether Chomsky (2002) was in turn influenced by Freud we do not know, but others have recognized this parallel between Chomsky's theory of language and Freud's theory of the unconscious mind.

The Freudian unconscious is not customarily viewed as a knowledge-processing centre. This is due to the fact that Freud radically altered his initial vision of the unconscious as described in *The Interpretation of Dreams*, because of his later commitment to instinct theory. Freud never disclaimed his description of unconscious processing in dreaming, but he viewed it as a special instance and put it aside when he re-characterized the unconscious not as an area in which knowledge is processed, but as a place of conflict between instincts seeking discharge and the forces of repression that prevents instinctual derivatives, thoughts, feelings and fantasies from becoming conscious. The primary function of this revised unconscious was not the processing of knowledge but to prevent unacceptable impulses, wishes and fantasies from becoming conscious. In his introduction to his 1915 paper *The Unconscious*, Freud states that everything that is repressed must remain unconscious, but he also noted that the unconscious has a wider compass, that the repressed is only part of the unconscious and does not cover everything. But Freud does not say what this other part consists of. Freud writes in that paper "the nucleus of the unconscious consists of instinctual representatives which seek to discharge their cathexes; that is to say, it consists of wishful impulses". In the 1915 paper Freud further states that "the content of the unconscious may be compared with an aboriginal population of the mind. If inherited mental formations exist in the human being–something analogous to instincts and animals–these constitute the nucleus of the unconscious". At the end of his life, when Freud (1940) wrote *An Outline of Psychoanalysis* he now viewed the unconscious not as potentially adaptive but as a danger to the self. The id was seen as the ego's internal enemy. This unfortunate revision of his early understanding of unconscious process has contributed, I believe, to a turning away from psychoanalytic theory.

We see that Freud's initial brilliant insight regarding the unconscious processing of symbolic elements was obscured and obfuscated by his later commitment to instinct theory. By this, I am not suggesting that we abandon Freud's concept of the dynamic unconscious, but as I shall later discuss, we need to radically revise our understanding of repression and the other so-called defense mechanisms.

Had Freud not replaced his earlier conception of the function of the unconscious he might have seen an analogy between the adaptive, synthetic function of the unconscious processing that occurs when we dream and the adaptive function of unconscious process that is present while we are awake. For I believe that an unconscious metaphoric process, analogous to dreaming is continuously operative while we are awake (Modell 2003). I visualize this waking metaphoric process as a kind of unconscious scanning that attempts to match current emotional experiences with old memorial categories.

Let me now provide two clinical anecdotes to illustrate how this unconscious process operates, how the memory of trauma unconsciously interprets ongoing experience in the here and now. These illustrations can be viewed as examples of the transference of everyday life with which we are all very familiar. In one example the memory of trauma is retained and fully conscious while in the other the memory of trauma cannot be retrieved. I believe that whether one does or does not unconsciously remember a traumatic experience has little or no influence upon the unconscious process itself. What is salient is the unconscious process; consciousness is a mere bystander.

When this woman was a little girl she had a loving relationship with her father that was irrevocably lost when her father became brain-damaged as a result of an industrial accident. As an adult she was compulsively driven to uncover defects in men almost as if it were a matter for survival. These presumed defects were then selectively perceived to the exclusion of whatever other virtues might be present. For example, she noted that her husband was driving slowly, overly cautiously, and in her judgement incompetently. She then wondered whether he was developing brain damage or becoming precociously senile. She became enraged at him, and then felt guilty because of the irrationality of her reaction. The intensity of her rage frightened her. She thought she was going a bit crazy, as if she had momentarily fallen into a time warp. For driving with her husband re-created in her imagination a similar scene from childhood when she was a five-year-old little girl sitting next to her father in the family car. As a result of his illness, her father was visually impaired and could barely see the road, and she was terrified that they would be killed.

This clinical fragment illustrates that the memory of a traumatic experience when matched metaphorically with an analogous experience in current time sets in motion an unconscious and involuntary interpretation of the meaning of that particular experience. The unconscious is timeless and she perceived no difference between the past and present. An unconscious metaphoric process created an identity of meaning, an example of the transference of everyday life. The fact that the memory of this traumatic relationship with her father was fully conscious had no effect on the unconscious processing of meaning.

In the following example the memory of trauma could not be recalled as the traumatic experience occurred before the hippocampus had matured. This is an example of an unthought known. A man, who happened to be a psychiatrist, became intensely frightened if he noted in his wife any indication of irrationality or what he feared to be a sign of craziness. This state of affairs was in contrast to the ease and comfort he felt when dealing with irrationality in his patients. He did quite well with very sick patients, especially schizophrenics. The meaning of his intense anxiety in response to his wife's presumed irrationality could be traced to the fact that at the age of two or three, the time is uncertain, he inferred that he was a witness to his mother having a spontaneous miscarriage. He was unable to remember the event but he did reconstruct that in all probability his mother became "hysterical" and was emotionally distraught for an undetermined period of time. He supposed that he felt as if his mother had suddenly and inexplicably gone crazy. When this man then became panicked as a response to his wife's presumed irrationality, we can infer the presence of an unconscious metaphoric process that melded or blended this childhood memory with his current perceptions and found a correspondence. An unconscious process equated his wife and his mother. He could tolerate craziness in his patients, upon whom he was not dependent, because they clearly were not his mother. In contrast to the woman with the brain-damaged father, this man could not recall the memory of his mother's miscarriage. I believe, however, that even if he had been able to recall that memory this would not have had any effect upon the unconscious process that I have described.

We should not overestimate the importance of conscious awareness; again what is salient is the unconscious process that continues to operate whether or not memories can be recalled. We must assume, and I believe that our clinical practice reinforces this assumption, that an unconscious interpretive process informs conscious experience. We are all aware of the extent to which unconscious fantasy interprets conscious experience. It is this unconscious process and not consciousness that is the determining factor. In this regard it seems to me that we may have overestimated the significance of whether or not a fantasy is conscious or unconscious; the unconscious effects of certain fantasies that are crucial to the self will become manifest whether or not these fantasies are conscious or remain unconscious. For in a fundamental sense unconscious thought precedes conscious thought and it is the unconscious thought that is determinant. In these two examples an unconscious thought process scanned current conscious experience to find a metaphoric equivalence between present and the past. This process was aided by the fact that unconscious perception synergistically combined with the memories of the affectively salient experiences. Unconscious perception and unconscious interpretation are seamlessly linked.

In a letter to Fliess in 1898 (Masson 1985) Freud states: "consciousness is only a sense organ; all psychic content is only a representation; all psychic processes are unconscious". And later Freud (1915: 171) states: "in psychoanalysis there was no choice for us but to assert that mental processes are in themselves unconscious and to liken the perception of them by means of consciousness to the perception of the external world by means of the sense organs". The crucial phrase is: "mental processes are in themselves unconscious". A radical view, to which I subscribe, is that all mental processes originate in the unconscious, and that an unconscious process precedes all conscious thought and feeling. Unconscious thoughts and unconscious emotional processes are the determining forces in mental life. Consciousness is only an observational faculty; and in itself does not cause anything.

A striking confirmation of this conception of the independence of unconscious thought from consciousness was recently provided by an investigation using functional magnetic imagery. This experiment demonstrated that complex mental processes, such as the comprehension of language and the use of the imagination, can occur unconsciously in the waking state without the participation of conscious awareness. In 2006, Owen, Coleman et al., a group of British researchers, report in the journal *Science* the results of the functional magnetic resonance imaging study of a twenty-three year-old woman who suffered extensive brain damage following a car accident. She was judged to be in a vegetative state. However, the cycle of sleep and wakefulness was preserved and the patient was awake while the study was performed. Although she appeared to be completely unresponsive, she was asked to imagine playing tennis and also was asked to imagine moving around her house. Surprisingly, after these instructions, identical motor areas of her brain were activated as compared to normal controls.

Although the woman remained unconscious her brain was able to process and understand the verbal instructions of the researchers and to imagine very specific motor activities, such as moving around her house and playing tennis, which in turn activated corresponding motor areas of her cortex. The research group that reported this finding could not believe that this process occurred entirely unconsciously and suggested that the patient's brain must have preserved some degree of conscious awareness although there was no evidence for this. This paper sparked a debate, and other research groups (Parashkev and Husain 2007) published responses that took issue with the author's conclusion that the patient retained some degree of conscious awareness. These critics believed, as I do, that complex mental processes such as speech comprehension and imagination occurred entirely unconsciously. The study again demonstrates that consciousness is only a sense organ, and is not necessary for the processing of knowledge. Imagining a scene and comprehending speech are indeed extremely complex processes which in this patient occurred entirely unconsciously.

We have long recognized that the unconscious metaphoric process that occurs in dreaming has great synthetic powers. One prominent example that is often quoted is that given by the chemist Friedrich August Von Kekule of how his discovery of the closed carbon ring structure of organic compounds was suggested to him in a dream in which a snake seized hold of its own tail (cited in Modell 2003). Many scientists report that what is essential for their creative discoveries is a process in which they turned away from linear declarative thought. They found it necessary to put consciousness to one side. When Einstein (cited in Hadamard 1945) was asked to describe the psychological aspect of his creative thinking he said that it was necessary for him to engage in what he described as "combinatory play" before there is any connection with logical construction and words.

Artists have also been aware that their unconscious self contains unknown knowledge and great synthetic powers. Conscious discursive, linear thought was seen as an obstacle that stood between their conscious self and a deeper source of more authentic unconscious knowledge. Some writers and painters, as we know, use alcohol and drugs to anaesthetize their conscious mind to enable them to contact this unconscious knowledge. As psychoanalysts we use the more benign method of free-floating attention. We avoid linear thinking through free association and nonlinear thinking can be enhanced by approaching dreamlike reveries, such as Bion recommended. We do all we can to facilitate the powers of unconscious perception. As psychoanalysts we train ourselves to listen with what Theodore Reik (1948) some years ago described as our third ear. We hope to enable our unconscious mind to perceive our analysand's unconscious communications.

Turning aside the conscious mind is a method that is also used by experts in other fields as well. This was illustrated in the recent bestselling book *Blink* written by the New Yorker journalist Malcolm Gladwell (2007). He described how a marble statue, a grave marker, dating from the sixth century B.C. was judged by experts to be a fake. This statue, previously authenticated by scientists who used rational, secondary process thinking, was about to be purchased by the Getty Museum. However, the museum was rescued by a group of art experts who immediately, within the blink of an eye, as it were, recognized the statue to be a fake. One expert Thomas Hoving, the former director of the Metropolitan Museum, immediately felt an "intuitive repulsion". Another expert, who habitually used free association when examining art, came up with the word "fresh". These experts unconsciously used their decades of professional knowledge to overrule the conclusion of scientists who relied only on linear, logical, thought. Gladwell described how successful politicians and sales people also train themselves to use unconscious perception in judging the other's intention, by watching the other's body language and facial expressions. Of course politicians can be mistaken, as when Bush looked up into Putin's eyes and thought that he had found his soul.

If the unconscious is the area of the mind that processes knowledge, how then do we understand the dynamic unconscious that Freud believed to be the consequences of repression? How does the dynamic unconscious fit into the processing of knowledge? We know that belief in a dynamic unconscious is a fundamental assumption of classical psychoanalysis, a theoretical assumption that distinguishes psychoanalysis from other forms of psychology. I don't question the existence of a dynamic unconscious but I view it as a particular kind of knowledge processing. The dynamic unconscious is that area of the unconscious mind that specializes in the negation of knowing and feeling that is linked to conflict. In Freudian theory the dynamic unconscious is the product of repression but, as I shall shortly discuss, we need to fundamentally revise our concept of repression itself.

In order to see how the dynamic unconscious can be integrated into this broader conception, we need to consider how Freud's dedication to instinct theory influenced his understanding of the process of repression. Again, Freud had it right before he developed instinct theory. Freud's thinking underwent a transformation from considering repression as a highly individualized process unique to the individual to conceptualizing repression as an impersonal process, something analogous to a physiological response, an automatic tropism. Such automatic responses do exist but I believe them to be a special case. Freud had it right in 1896 in his letter to Fliess (Masson 1985) when he understood that repression was directed against memory. This letter shows an uncanny insight into the nature of repression and memory. He introduced the concept of *nachtraglichkeit* that is fully consistent with contemporary neuroscience's understanding of memory. In this letter he described how memory was constantly recontextualized in accordance with later experience. He was thinking especially of the memory of sexual pleasure from the excitement derived from specific erogenous zones, pleasures that later, with the subsequent moral development of the child, would be felt to be unacceptable. Pleasure then became un-pleasure, and the un-pleasure itself became a signal for defence.

Freud also spoke of abandoned erotogenic zones. Repression organized memory in accordance with developmental epochs. What is acceptable at one stage of development may evoke disgust in a later stage. He wrote (cited in Masson 1985: 205) "at the boundary between two such epochs a translation of psychic material has taken place. I explain the peculiarities of the psychoneurosis by suppos-ing that this translation has not taken place in the case of some of the material which has certain consequences". He explained and defined repression as a failure of this translation. Repression, the negation of knowing and feeling, was correctly understood by Freud as a highly individualized unconscious selective process. To maintain our preferred self-image, at each developmental stage, the self unconsciously selects and forgets unacceptable memories, wishes and fantasies. In this fashion an unconscious process reor-ganizes memory. If repression serves to maintain a preferred image of the self, this process would also take into account the impact of culture. For culture also becomes the arbiter of what is acceptable or unacceptable. For example, Freud interpreted Dora's nervous cough as a displacement of her unconscious knowledge of oral sex. Such a displacement would be unthinkable in today's teenager, whose knowledge of oral sex far from being unconscious may be superior to that of her analyst.

By 1915, some twenty years after the Fliess' letters, Freud had an entirely different view of repression. Repression was no longer viewed as a process directed against memory but as a process directed against instincts and their derivatives. Instinctual derivatives con-sist of thoughts, feelings and fantasies. Freud no longer referred to his metaphor of repression as a failure to translate memory in accordance with subsequent experience. What was of significance was not individual experience as contained in memory. In Freud's later view repression was not directed against memory but directed against the instincts. The prohibition against incest was thought to be universal and the fantasies and wishes derived from the Oedipus were automatically brought under repression. As Freud believed these instincts to be the common inheritance of all of humanity, Freud now viewed repression largely as a universal, impersonal process in response to the vicissitudes of internal economic forces. Repression therefore became de-individualized. One cannot be certain of Freud's motives that underlie his unwavering commitment to instinct theory, but I suspect that he supposed that in doing so he was furthering the establishment of psychoanalysis as a scientific discipline. He believed that by placing instincts at the centre of his theory of the unconscious he was aligning psychoanalysis with what he thought to be contemporary evolutionary theory. He viewed the unconscious id to be the repository of what we would now describe as humanity's collective DNA.

In his attempt to be scientific, Freud made what philosophers might describe as a category mistake. He substituted a uniform, impersonal, quasi-physiological concept for the idiosyncratic, highly variable experience of the individual. Minds differ but bodies are (more or less) the same. When compared to the enormous range of individual differences that exists between minds, physiological processes are fairly uniform. Although Freud did not dwell on the term "mechanism" he did refer to the mind as an "apparatus". Freud's category error was perpetuated by ego psychologist who enshrined the term "defense mechanisms". The term "mechanism" belongs to the domain of physical objects and when applied to mental life it is a thoroughly misleading metaphor. Machines have no individuality; they are all stamped from the same mold. This is the opposite way of how we should think of repression. Repression is not a uniform mechanism; it is the outcome of an unconscious selective process that is unique to each one of us. Repression is one expression of the organization of our unconscious self.

We retain a magical belief that if we give something a name, it forms a category, and what we then label as such always refers to the same thing. We have come to think of "denial" and "repression" as if these terms represent some kind of uniform process. As I said, I believe, however, that each one of us responds to undesirable thoughts, upsetting memories and painful feelings in our own unique fashion. We each have our own style and method of dealing with painful experience, interpreted from the perspective of our entire life history. What we fail to remember and what we are unable to feel is also part of our imagination. Memory and imagination are thoroughly intertwined as we construct changing images of ourselves.

This same individualized construction is also true for denial, negating something that is real. Here too as with repression, denial is informed by the needs and requirements of the self. We all maintain a preferred image of ourselves whatever that image may be. For example, a man who believed in his nearly omnipotent capacity for solving problems thought that divorce was unthinkable. If he gave up on his marriage, this would conflict with his preferred self-image as a problem solver and represent failure. He needed to believe that he was capable of resolving any trouble which beset him. He therefore denied what was obvious to his friends and family, that his wife had never loved him and in fact was entirely self-serving.

Unconscious knowledge may be negated by repression and denial but unconscious knowledge may also be unavailable to consciousness because of an inability to select what is of value to the self. We select a value through self reference; if one loses self feeling that reference point is also lost. This is a very different process from that of repression.

Feeling oneself to be alive and in the world is something that we usually take for granted. This inner feeling of vitality is analogous to the feeling of the existence of our body when we pinch ourselves and feel the sensation of that pinch; we affirm that we are alive. This inner feeling of vitality and aliveness of the self becomes noticed only in its absence. We all are acquainted with analysands who describe themselves as dead, empty or, in extreme cases, feeling as if their sense of self is like a black hole. Some might take desperate measures and do dangerous things in order to artificially restore a sense that they are alive. By experiencing danger they know that they feel and hence know that they exist. This absence of self feeling, and absence of a sense of aliveness, is not necessarily accompanied by an inability to feel anxiety, anger or sexual excitement or guilt. That is to say, self feeling is something apart from other customary emotions. This absence is more like the absence of a sensation as if one touched one's skin and felt nothing. It as if the self has become anaesthetized.

When this occurs the consequences can be disastrous, for the individual has lost touch with all that they value. I can think of one young man in his twenties who suffered from this condition. He went on holiday with his girlfriend, who he did not particularly like, and had sex with her repeatedly without using contraception. The thought that she could become pregnant simply didn't occur to him. As he recalled, at the time he felt completely out of it–as if was not living in the world. He had no contact with what he would normally be expected to know. Of course his girlfriend did become pregnant and he entered into what became a miserable marriage. In addition to not knowing what he knew, he could not project the consequences of his actions into the future. Losing contact with himself meant that he couldn't simulate a future.

Another young man also felt dead inside and had no feeling of psychic aliveness. He allowed himself to accumulate $300,000 of credit card debt. He knew and didn't know the serious consequences that this debt burden would have on his future life. As in the other example, the absence of the sense of aliveness made him unable to simulate the future consequences of his present actions. An essential function of the self was lost. In order to select what is of value to ourselves and to anticipate the future consequences of our present actions, our selves must be invested with feeling. The absence of self feeling makes it impossible to know what is of value to the self and makes it impossible to model and anticipate future expectations. When self feeling is lost, there is not only an inability to select what is of value to the self but there is also an inability to create a virtual reality by means of imagination.

As psychoanalysts we are clinically acquainted with this phenomenon, but the importance of self feeling has not been sufficiently recognized by academic psychologists or philosophers. The phenomena of self feeling should not be confused with consciousness taken as a whole. Self feeling to be sure is an aspect of consciousness but it is not the same as consciousness itself. This neglect of self feeling by philosophers and academic psychologists may be due to the undue influence of Descartes who believed that thinking rather than feeling was proof of one's existence. It is not that I think therefore I exist but that I feel therefore I exist. In this regard I was very interested to learn that Aristotle and the ancient Greek Stoic philosophers did recognize the importance of self feeling, and awareness of the aliveness of the self. They believed that this sensation transcended the classical five senses and they referred to it as a kind of inner touch. They further believed that self feeling also existed in animals because animals know that they are alive. They did not confuse self feeling with consciousness because the concept of consciousness was yet to be formulated. These ancient philosophers recognized the importance of feeling the vitality of the self, an idea that was later lost probably through the influence of Descartes who deemphasized feelings in favour of thinking.

This lack of knowing due to the absence of self feeling was illustrated in the two foregoing anecdotes: The man who didn't know that he could get his girlfriend pregnant and the man who didn't know that having $300,000 in debt would have serious consequences. As I noted, not knowing through lack of feelings is quite different from lack of knowing due to repression. The young Freud understood that repression was the failure of the reorganization of memory, a failure of translation. In these anecdotes illustrating the loss of self feeling, the failure is not of memory but the consequence of an inability to select what is of value to the self. The psychological process is quite different from that of repression and denial. One man undoubtedly knew that if he did not use contraception his girlfriend could become pregnant, and the other man also knew that massive debt would be ruinous. But these pieces of knowledge were not invested with feelings and therefore had no value to the self. In addition, when the self lacks a sense of its own vitality, a sense of its own aliveness, it is also unable to simulate or imagine the future consequences of one's actions. One loses knowledge of the future. Our unconscious self interprets the meaning of the present moment in order to anticipate the future; this process fails if the self lacks feelings.

It is nearly self-evident to state that the unconscious self determines what we know. The unconscious self includes the salient memories of our entire life. These memories are subject to an unconscious metaphoric process that scans current experience searching for similarities and dis-similarities. This aspect of our dreaming mind is going on all the time while we are awake.

If these unconscious processes are the determining forces in mental life, if consciousness is only a bystander, why do we believe that knowing is better than not knowing? What then is the value of insight? Does self-knowledge lead to a degree of freedom from involuntary and uncontrollable unconscious processes? My answer would be yes. Insight, conscious self-awareness, extends the feeling of the agency of the self. Recall Freud's aphorism "where it was there shall ego be"; I would modify this slightly to read "where it was I shall be". This is to say, one aim of psychoanalysis is to transform the realm of involuntary processes into the domain of conscious self-awareness. To state it differently: One aim of psychoanalysis is to expand the agency of the self, which in turn increases the freedom of the self. The distinguished neurologist Kurt Goldstein (1995: 167) said "there is only one transcendent motive by which human activity is initiated: the tendency to actualize oneself".

To actualize oneself means that one expresses what is unique about one's self. Again, this expression requires a feeling of agency. We expand the agency of the self through the creation of new meanings. We do this by means of the freedom of the imagination. As I have been emphasizing, meaning construction is primarily an unconscious process and it is this unconscious process that causes things to happen. As I believe that unconscious processes are causal there is therefore no absolute freedom for the agency of the self but only degrees of freedom. We are here confronted with the ancient problem of free will and determinism. Some may argue that the agency of the self is only an illusion but it is an illusion without which we cannot live.

As I noted, the agency of the self does not represent an absolute freedom but only a relative freedom. If the agency of the self is enhanced through the creation of new meanings, we know how the creation of new meaning is impaired in the presence of trauma. Trauma results in a constriction of the freedom of the imagination. As we know, one of the consequences of traumatic events or traumatic relationships is a restriction in the ability to create new meaning. Transference, taken in its broadest sense, whether it occurs within the treatment relationship or in everyday life, constricts the degree of freedom of interpretation of experience in the here and now. This can be illustrated in the example I gave of the man who interprets his wife's presumed irrationality as if he was seeing his mother's craziness. This interpretation was involuntary and lacked any measure of uncertainty and complexity. If he had been self-aware his interpretation of his wife's behaviour would have included a measure of uncertainty that would allow for alternative interpretations and would have represented a greater degree of freedom. We can say that the agency of the self is enhanced through the unpredictable combinatory power of thought that creates new meaning.

In summation, I hope that I have convinced you that we need to revise our theory of the unconscious and the notion of defence mechanisms. My thesis that the unconscious is the area of the mind in which knowledge is processed is not new or particularly original as this was Freud's initial insight that he expressed in his letters to Fliess and was explicit in his masterpiece *The Interpretation of Dreams* (Freud 1900). I believe that these ideas were also implicit in Freud's earlier understanding of hysterical symptomatology. Unfortunately, as I have repeatedly noted, his later adherence to instinct theory obfuscated and hid this initial insight.

If the unconscious is viewed as the area of the mind in which information is processed, the unconscious can no longer be defined simply as that which is repressed. While we need to retain the idea of repression as a descriptive term, I also suggested that repression can no longer be thought of as a defense mechanism. Indeed, I believe the idea of defense mechanisms to be an antiquated concept in itself. To be sure, repression is an unconscious process, but I view repression as a highly individualized selective process that is the expression of individual selves. Repression is not a uniform process as if it were a physiological mechanism. As I noted earlier, Freud made what philosophers describe as a category mistake regarding repression when he substituted an impersonal, uniform process for the idiosyncratic unconscious selection of the self. This paper then represents a plea to recognize the transcendence of individuality. In a profound sense our selves sculpt our unconscious minds.

References

Bollas, C. (2007). *The Freudian Moment*. London: Karnac.
Chomsky, N. (2002). *On Nature and Language*. Cambridge University Press.
Freud, S. (1893). Fraulein Elisabeth von R. In: *Standard Edition 2*.
Freud, S. (1900). The Interpretation of Dreams. In: *Standard Edition 4, 5*.
Freud, S. (1905). Fragment of an analysis of a case of hysteria. In: *Standard Edition 7*.
Freud, S. (1915a). Repression. In: *Standard Edition 14*.
Freud, S. (1915b). The Unconscious. In: *Standard Edition 14*.
Freud, S. (1940). An outline of psychoanalysis. In: *Standard Edition 23*.

Gladwell, M. (2007). *Blink*. Boston: Back Bay publishers.

Goldstein, K. (1995). *The Organism*. New York: Urzone distributed by The MIT Press.

Hadamard, J. (1945). *The Psychology of Invention in the Mathematical Field*. Dover Press.

Masson, J.M. (1985). *The complete letters of Sigmund Freud to Wilhelm Fliess*. Cambridge: Harvard University Press.

Modell, A.H. (2003). *Imagination and the meaningful brain*. Cambridge: MIT Press.

Owen, A. and M. Coleman, et al. (2006). "Detecting awareness in the vegetative state". *Science*. 313: 1,402.

Parashkev and Husain, M. (2007). "Comment on detecting awareness in the vegetative state". *Science*, 315(5816): 1,221–1,222.

Reik, Theodore (1948). *Listening with the Third Ear*. New York: Farrar, Straus And Co.

PART III

DISSOCIATION—CLINICAL,
DIAGNOSTIC, AND CONCEPTUAL
PERSPECTIVES …
FROM MURDER THROUGH ABUSE TO
MASOCHISM

CHAPTER FOUR

Shooting in the spaces: Violent crime as dissociated enactment[1]

Abby Stein, Ph.D.

When Philip M. Bromberg (1996) coined the phrase "standing in the spaces", he fashioned a brilliant theoretic toggle. His word string demoted the minable, linear Freudian subject who had epitomized the late nineteenth and early twentieth centuries, and instead privileged the myriad internal characters that both cantilever and sabotage subjectivity. In clinical papers throughout the decade, Bromberg deftly and convincingly conjoined the unitary and continuous self with its more evanescent and excursive overlords: those divided selves, untethered from the constraints of temporal perspective, who demonstrated that consciousness was a corrugated continuum and not, as had been averred, a simple Freudian divide: conscious, unconscious, preconscious.

What gave Bromberg's assertions clinical power was that he managed to address the way that people dropped defensive anchor in a protean internal sea, even as they responded to shifting externalities

---

[1] Portions of this chapter are reprinted from *Prologue to Violence: Child abuse, dissociation, and crime,* © 2007 by Taylor and Francis. Reprinted with permission.

that revealed their own fractionation. Bromberg (1998) engaged core linearity ("staying the same") respectfully, while distinguishing multiplicity as the potential site of change.

Bromberg was following in the footsteps of Ferenczi (1980), Sullivan (1953), Laing (1960), and others who had front-burnered dissociation as a primary organizational tool of the psyche. At the same time, his work reflected postmodern sensibilities in philosophy, epistemology, linguistics, and neuroscience. Older theories regarding the impact of trauma, ripened in this newly sophisticated context, have had a tremendous influence on psychodynamic practice throughout the 1990s and into the current century.

Bromberg and other contemporary psychoanalysts were writing while I was a student intern at Bellevue Hospital, evaluating violent felons on the prison ward. I had never heard of him, nor of Donnel Stern (1997), whose writings illume how the raw data of traumatic experience are not attended in the first place and, consequently, remain unsymbolizable phenomena, condemned to be enacted without reflection in the whimpers and bangs of interpersonal life.

Worlds apart, the three of us were all struggling with the same conundrums: How are the paradoxes of multiplicity reconciled with an analytic project that still favors concordance, and narrative through-lines? How is forward movement made in a land where recursion is queen, and amnesia the coin of the realm? Bromberg's phrase constituted a clinical call to arms: help people "stand in the spaces" and view the disparate parts of themselves clearly enough to surface meaningful connections and, from that understanding, promote historical continuity and facilitate change.

His words would have had great clinical relevance to me had I known them at the time. Among the inmates, so many of whom had endured childhoods rife with neglect and abuse, dissociation reigned as both a default defensive operation and as a strategy for the conscious preemption of impending traumata. Clinical presentations ran the gamut from schizoid detachment, to sociopathic disavowal, to full blown Dissociative Identity Disorder (then called Multiple Personality Disorder). Harry Stack Sullivan, whose work I did know, had written eloquently about the suaveness of dissociative processes in malevolent transformations and the emergence of "not me" personifications who impose harm but have no sense of agency for their acts. I met these "not me" characters on the prison ward each day, although I often felt at a loss about how to engage them.

I stood with my population of murderers, rapists, and thieves and heard in the spaces only crossfire. Offenders had a scorched earth policy that rendered inaccessible the pieces from which we together might quilt a narrative. But, as the Chinese say, *wen ju*: a crisis is a dangerous opportunity. I decided to stand in the spaces with them, even if it meant getting shot.

At Bellevue, I worked with a team headed by pioneering forensic psychiatrist, Dorothy Otnow Lewis. Our offices were located on the child and adolescent ward, where we were often called in to do abuse and neglect evaluations. Simultaneously, we had funding to do research in the prison that comprises the nineteenth floor of the hospital. Inhabiting these two worlds, the world of abused children and the world of aggressive adults, provided a perfect perch from which to gather evidence regarding the transgenerational transmission of violent behaviour.

In the United States, forensic practitioners have believed for years that violence in parents begets violence in kids, but we have lacked a compelling explanation for how exactly that happens. And we need one because so many violent offenders come from childhoods of complex multiple traumas.

My own explanation is based on an analysis of the narratives of violent criminals that I have interviewed and worked with, both at Bellevue and in other places, men who committed a range of crimes including arson, rape, and serial homicide. The vast majority, roughly eighty percent were horrifically abused in childhood: suffering broken bones, loss of consciousness, and/or attempts made on their lives by parents or parental surrogates. About a third of those I have interviewed were sexually abused, often by more than one caretaker. This is a relatively common historical portrait of violent offenders.

So, are children just modeling the aggressive behaviour of their caretakers? Are they sustaining central nervous system injuries that make them more impulsive, unable to control their aggression? Is there any credence to modern day "bad seed" theories, explanations that posit a genetic inheritance for underlying vulnerabilities that predispose subjects to violence? Is it just a matter of "trickle down" trauma: the father belts the mother, who smacks the kid, who kicks the dog, who bites the caseworker from children's services?

What I first saw in the prison at Bellevue Hospital and in my later work—particularly on some FBI cases—led me to believe that there are, in addition to these things, processes that strongly facilitate the streaming of an unprocessed violent past into the present.

During early, intense, and repetitive trauma, there is a kind of adaptive disengagement—a form of dissociation—from any meaningful assessment of fear, or pain, or horror. To be fully present for it—and to process its implications—would simply overwhelm the brain.

This dissociation may help one survive the initial traumatic situation but because information about the threatening experience has remained unformulated, the experience cannot be reflected upon or learned from. For those who have been abused, fear and anger are difficult to mediate and are frequently impossible to diffuse. Dissociated violence is almost destined to be replayed in an endless, and thoughtless, loop.

The nature of crime

This may seem obvious but I find it worth saying because maybe you never thought about it quite in this way before: *A crime is nothing more nor less than an interpersonal event*. A stranger jumping out of the bushes and attacking may be the stuff of which our nightmares are made but such attacks are not very common. The vast majority of crimes are between people who have been in some sort of relationship, be that relationship anywhere from four hours to twenty years. Even what are labelled as stranger-on-stranger crimes generally occur between people who have been hanging out together at a bar all night; between the next door neighbour and the child he's been babysitting. A crime is the titanic culmination of a process that begins somewhere in childhood and ends long after the bodies have been taken away by the police. Think about it this way: *A violent crime is a kind of interpersonal enactment*.

Having put this out there, I doubt that anything I write from here on in will surprise you. In fact, I hope that you will recognize in my offenders the quite familiar outlines of your own patients:

their struggles with rage, grief, panic, separation, and—above all—attachment.

Like many of the traumatized patients you have probably treated, most perpetrators who shared with me their traumatic upbringings, took complete responsibility for the abuse they had suffered. One man told me that his father only beat him because he was too black; for punishment the father tied him up and left him in the closet for the KKK.

> *I had more welts from a garrison belt … my mother had to raise four*
> *kids by herself—she ran my father out with a knife. She once shoved a*
> *lit cigarette down my throat when she caught me smoking. My mother*
> *was a beautiful person, so lovely. If I said no, she beat me from one end*
> *of the house to another. I was only beaten if I did something wrong—*
> *like not eating.* (Stein 2007: 7)

When I asked this man about the origins of an old burn mark on his arm, he explained perfunctorily, "It's a *brand*—all babies got to get it to keep from being stolen". Maybe that's what he was told, or maybe that's the story he made up to explain why his parents put their cigarettes out on him. In his Orwellian narrative, being burned is a kind of security; the scar becomes a talisman against separation or abandonment.

Similarly, almost all of the offenders I have interviewed who have been sexually abused in childhood have reconfigured it as a consensual act, especially if the abuser was female. I have likened the slippery nature of sexual abuse by females to having an octopus in the bathtub with you (Stein 2006). Because women so often have intimate access to children's bodies, and because the contact is socially approved, it is that much easier to disguise the predatory caress as hygienic, as needed, as loving. For example, I often ask men how they were introduced to sex. Almost always, they claim to have instigated the contact themselves, even though they may have been only six years of age at the time.

Rewriting abuse as a self-initiated act confers the illusion of control; it is as if potential predators can be monitored and restrained through active choice. "If only I'd eaten; if only I wasn't so dark-skinned; if only I wasn't such a six-year-old sex maniac". These kinds of scripts, starring themselves as children, become templates for scripts that offenders employ during later crimes.

One sex offender explained to me quite earnestly how his four-year-old step-daughter seduced him. The image of a seductive child, asking to be raped, was an image which, I later discovered, developed in his own childhood to exonerate parents who used him for their own sexual pleasure. I read recently of a man who showed up for a lover's tryst with a six-year-old with an expensive doll and a promise to the child's mother that he was always gentle and loving when he had sex with children (Bunkley 2007). My sense is that these are not mere rationalizations, they are deeply believed in imaginings. The story of gentle, loving predators often echoes childhood narratives crafted to undo the reality of truly monstrous parents.

Sue Grand (2000) has described the insistence by victims that abusive violation is not really *real* or is not really happening to *me*. For those who later turn to violence or violation themselves, such massive denial becomes the starting point of an exercise in reality swapping: just like the abuse they suffered, they feel that the crime they commit is not really happening: I am not really doing this rape, the murderer is someone else … In a life filled with threats of potential violation, dissociation becomes the default defensive response.

The myth of the conscienceless criminal

This begs an important theoretical construction about offenders: it is often said that violent criminals operate without conscience. So how can we explain the fact that most offenders show abundant conscience and remorse in other areas of their lives? Quite a few I've spoken with claim to have attempted CPR on their own victim after committing their assaults. Almost all I work with describe themselves as peaceful; their violent selves feel like what Sullivan (1956: 361) called "not me":

"I'm not that type of person. I would never hurt anybody". (The victim was bound and gagged. The baseball bat on the bed was covered in blood, which had also sprayed the ceiling.)

"I'm a peaceful person". (The victim was decapitated.)

"I couldn't even picture myself doing it". (The victim was stabbed in both eyes, before a knife was plunged into her chest.)

Matias Reyes, the real killer in the Central Park jogger case, capped a career of robberies and serial sexual assaults by raping and stabbing a pregnant woman to death as her children listened from the next room. A short time later, he left another woman for dead, the victim of a rampage so brutal that NYPD detectives had a hard time accepting that a single offender perpetrated the crime. Yet, this attacker steadfastly rejects portrayals of himself as aggressive. "I always say no to violence" he claims. As if to punctuate the assertion, Reyes shared with his defense team's psychologist that he once surreptitiously called 911 to get help for a victim of his own sexual sadism. Such seemingly contradictory behaviour is not incompatible with reports that Reyes was known to take showers with his rape victims, apparently so that he could imagine their intimacies as consensual (Flynn 2002). If you speak with this man about his childhood, or read his case file, you will not feel the need to consult the human genome project about the causes of his violence or his attempts to remake violent rapes into romantic interludes. The scenarios are all there in Reyes' early biography. The violence he endured as a child has become the signature of his criminal activity.

Why exactly do so many violent offenders—abused in childhood—claim not to remember their crimes but confess to them anyway, only to recant later and vehemently state that they are not even capable of hurting a fly?

Those who study brain development and physiological responses to trauma have discovered fascinating things about the way that the brain formats abusive experiences. These researchers posit that the perceptual-affective flood engendered by a traumatic encounter is configured mainly as an autonomic response to danger; individuals may experience lasting hormonal and neurochemical changes, as well as deformations of neuroanatomical structure, following intense or prolonged exposure to threatening stimuli (van der Kolk 1996: 220). Of particular interest are regions of the brain that are implicated in the ability to reflect upon mental contents, first by attaching emotional significance to them and then by representing intentions symbolically, as a rehearsal for action. These areas have been shown to be compromised during trauma, leading to a disabling of normal integrative function. Severely abused children are like war veterans with post-traumatic stress disorder who become disturbed by vivid flashbacks of their war experiences. Bessel van der Kolk writes:

> *The experience is laid down, and later retrieved, as isolated images, bodily sensations, smells and sounds that feel alien and separate from other life experiences. Because the hippocampus has not played its usual role in helping to locate the incoming information in time and space, these fragments continue to lead an isolated existence. Traumatic memories are timeless and ego-alien.* (van der Kolk 1996: 295)

So, in addition to the variety of defensive deployments triggered by ongoing maltreatment, child abuse may *literally* crack the chronograph that laces temporal dimensions into meaningful spheres. Maltreated children are characteristically frozen in the traumatic moment, with no real demarcation among past, present, and future. Devoid of historical perspective, and absent of the learned link between cause and effect, the abused child grown up proceeds without true premeditation. Indeed, often *the bad act itself announces the intention to commit it.*

One man that I interviewed, Matty, had been forced to have sex with his mother as a young adolescent As an adult, Matty often became lost in reverie while looking at young women on the subway and subsequently "fantasized" that he would be invited to go home with them for sex. As it turned out, Matty was following women home and committing push-in rapes on their doorsteps, a version of events that only became consciously embraced by Matty when the police confronted him with evidence of the assaults. Up until that time he remained convinced that he had only "dreamed" about the sexual encounters, which, in his imagination, were consensual.

An attachment theory of crime

Now, the most popular explanation of this type of crime in the forensic literature is that criminals, behaving in a self-interested and rational way, get bored masturbating to their perverted fantasies and hit the streets to test them out on unwitting victims. But think of Matty and the man I mentioned earlier, Matias Reyes, who showered with his victims after raping them, so as to reinforce the idea that they were truly a "couple". Think of another perpetrator I know who wrapped his victim's braid around her throat after slitting it, apparently so he and the victim could watch television together. In encounters so sur-real, is it descriptively accurate to say that the perpetrator was acting out a conscious fantasy in real time? As James Gilligan (1996: 84), the former head of Bridgewater State Hospital for the Criminally Insane once said, "The only problem with a rational self-interest theory of crime is ... that it's completely wrong!"

First, although sexual predators have some rather bizarre fanta-sies, so do most college students (and even a few psychoanalysts). Studies (Crepault and Couture 1980) have shown that the major-ity of men have fantasies about raping women and a pretty robust percentage say they would do it if they could get away with it (Szymanski et al. 1993). To say that people who behave deviantly have deviant fantasies is seriously missing the point.

What I have learned during my own work with offenders regard-ing their dissociated histories of child maltreatment, leads me to ques-tion the linearity of the premise that sexually deviant fantasy—once it has somehow exhausted its physiological usefulness—blossoms into sexually deviant, criminal behaviour. Deviant sexual fantasies are within everyone's purview; my interviews with violent felons suggest that it is *not the perversion quotient of their sexual fantasies, but the underlying deviance of their early attachments that makes the interper-sonal landscape so toxic.* It is the tendency for symbolization processes to rapidly deteriorate in the face of perceived threat, coupled with a lust for symbiotic merger, which lays a foundation for the perverse, violent re-enactment of unintegrated traumata.

I believe that many offenders' so-called fantasies are really highly ritualized re-enactments of early abuse scenarios that they keep returning to, as one would to the scene of a bad accident. For example, one convicted child rapist described to interrogating offic-ers his "fantasy" (a memory, it turned out) of his brother anally sodomizing him. At three junctures of the interview, the offender represents this mental idea in three different ways: first, as a tool he consciously employs to reach orgasm while penetrating a little girl; then as an unwanted "flashback" that comes during a molesta-tion, triggered by his victim's tears. Finally, he describes a ritualized elaboration of the real assault by his brother-during which his hands were sometimes bound-into a full blown bondage scenario that he acts out with his own victims. To call these things "fantasies" is to miss something fundamental about their nature; it ignores the difference between a liberating flight of fancy and a perpetual enslavement to reality.

Indeed, it is the *absence* of fantasy that fuels violent crime. As Arthur Hyatt-Williams (1998), a British psychoanalyst who worked with murderous juveniles over many decades, showed: when people can be taught to imagine violence or sexual aggression they are *not* driven to blindly enact it; quite the opposite, they are relieved of the need to rid themselves of amorphous tensions through rape and murder.

In a recent and quite famous case, a man was caught and convicted of a dozen sexual murders that he had committed over the course of thirty years, all the time completely evading detection by the police (Dateline/NBC 2005). Dennis Rader—nicknamed BTK (Bind, Torture, Kill) for his preferred method of homicide—kept hundreds of index cards with pictures of men, women, and children accompanied by detailed biographies into which he inserted himself. He had seven three-ring binders, twenty-five hanging file folders, numerous floppy discs labelled "fantasy world", dozens of multi-coloured index cards depicting women bound and gagged, a Master File labelled "Communications" which housed "The BTK Story" (his autobiography), and poems about his victims, both before and after he killed them.

At his trial he spoke at length about the similarities between himself and his victims; he even said that he thought that they would be reunited in the afterlife. To me, these data reveal obsession, compulsion, delusion. They don't point to mere sexual fantasies as you or I would colloquially define them in the course of our work with patients. For BTK, for the man who showers with the women he rapes, for the man who watched television with his nearly decapitated girlfriend, it is not a matter of sexual fantasy.

It is almost more like hallucinating an attachment in order to keep the emptiness at bay.

For BTK, as for many serial killers, there is perhaps no conventionally recognized psychosis outside the one involving attachment. But there *is* evidence of the kind of stark dissociation that characterizes so many violent men that I have interviewed. BTK, it turns out, was the president of his local church and a steadfast family man. In the same third person narrative voice that serial killer Ted Bundy used to describe "the entity" that visited itself upon him during killing binges, BTK wrote that an "X factor" drove the homicides that shadowed an otherwise normal life: a life so ordinary in its suburban Kansas routines that, over thirty murderous years, it attracted absolutely no one's attention. BTK, you'll remember, in the end simply could not stand having gotten away with his crimes and so re-emerged from obscurity after many years of inaction to kill again and—more importantly—to taunt the police with clues until they captured him. This is how much he needed to be seen, to be known, to attach.

Conclusion

Of course, I do not mean to imply that all abused children become violent criminals or that child abuse is the only antecedent of violent crime. We all know people who have survived terrible childhoods but have not gone on to kill or maim or rob.

However, in the largest and most statistically sophisticated study of its kind ever done in the US, the National Bureau of Economic Research (NBER) has just published the results of a seven-year examination of the effects of child maltreatment on crime (Currie and Tekin 2006). The landmark report, based on a survey of 90,000 adolescents, over 15,000 of whom were personally interviewed at three year intervals, concludes that people maltreated in childhood are at least twice as likely to commit a crime as their non-abused counterparts.

Michael Stone, analyzing the life histories of two hundred and seventy-eight murderers, found that seventy-five had been horribly abused in childhood. The NBER study tells us that battered boys are especially at risk of committing crimes when they grow up, and that this effect is magnified by poverty. Moreover, the authors posit a hierarchical relationship between types of maltreatment and unfavourable outcomes: having suffered particularly severe maltreatment, or multiple types of abuse simultaneously, increases the propensity for criminal behaviour, with sexual abuse having the largest deleterious effect. We don't know much about BTK's childhood but I have heard him say on tape that his bondage "fantasies" developed during intense and lengthy spankings by his mother when he was a preteen.

In working with both criminals and non-criminals, or "normal" people as we like to call them, my observation is that the regular people I see have deviant, ugly, contemptuous, violent, disgusting thoughts at least as often as the offenders with whom I've worked, maybe more. But it is my impression that whatever their ability to recognize—rather than to dissociate—this aggression, correlates strongly with how well they manage anger in their everyday affairs. Or don't. What strikes me most about the difference between offenders and regular folk is not so much the quality and quantity of aggression, but rather the way that it is processed, if indeed it is processed at all.

References

Bromberg, P. (1996). "Standing in the spaces: The multiplicity of self and the psychoanalytic relationship". *Contemporary Psychoanalysis*. 32: 509–535.

Bromberg, P. (1998). "Staying the same while changing: Reflections on clinical judgment". *Psychoanalytic Dialogues*. 8: 525–536.

Bunkley, N. (2007). Prosecutor Tries to Kill Himself After Arrest in Pedophile Case, *The New York Times*, 21 September.

Crepault, C. and Couture, M. (1980). "Men's erotic fantasies". *Arch. Sex. Behav.* 9: 565–581.

Currie, J. and Tekin, E. (April 2006). Does Child Abuse Cause Crime? *NBER Working Paper*. No. W12171.

Dateline/NBC (12 August, 2005). *31 Years of the BTK Killer*. Correspondent E. Magnus, 8pm ET.

Ferenczi, S. (1980/1919). Technical difficulties in the analysis of a case of hysteria: Including observations of larval forms of onanism and onanistic equivalents (Trans. J.I. Suttie). In: J. Rickman (ed.) *Further Contributions to the Theory and Technique of Psychoanalysis*. New York: Bruner/Mazal, pp. 291–294.

Flynn, K. (7 December, 2002). Suspect in rape absorbed pain and inflicted it. *The New York Times*, p. 1, Section A, Column 1, Metropolitan Desk.

Gilligan, J. (1996). *Violence: Our Deadly Epidemic and Its Causes*. New York: Grosset/Putnam Books.

Grand, S. (2000). *The Reproduction of Evil: A Clinical and Cultural Perspective*. Hillsdale, NJ: The Analytic Press.

Hyatt-Williams, A. (1998). *Cruelty, Violence and Murder: Understanding the Criminal Mind*. Northvale, NJ: Aronson.

Laing, R.D. (1960). *The Divided Self: An Existential Study in Sanity and Madness*. London: Tavistock Publications.

Stein, A. (2006). "An octopus in the bathtub: The slippery nature of female sex Offending". *Sex Offender Law Report*. 7(6), 81–82, 94–95. Civic Research Institute.

Stein, A. (2007). *Prologue to violence: Child abuse, dissociation, and crime*. Mahwah, NJ: The Analytic Press.

Stern, D. (1997). *Unformulated experience: From dissociation to imagination in psychoanalysis*. Hillsdale, NJ: The Analytic Press.

Sullivan, H.S. (1953). *The Interpersonal Theory of Psychiatry*. New York: W.W. Norton.

Sullivan, H.S. (1956). *Clinical Studies in Psychiatry*. New York: W.W. Norton.

Szymanski, L.A., Devlin, A.S., Chrisler, J.C. and Vyse, S.A. (1993). "Gender role and attitudes toward rape in male and female college students". *Sex Roles: A Journal of Research*. 29 (1/2).

van der Kolk, B.A. (1996). The body keeps score: Approaches to the psychobiology of Posttraumatic Stress Disorder. In: B.A. van der Kolk, A.C. McFarlane and L. Weisaeth (eds) *Traumatic Stress: The Effects Of Overwhelming Experience On Mind, Body And Society*. New York: Guilford Press, pp. 214–241.

CHAPTER FIVE

Dissociative identity disorder: The abused child and the spurned diagnosis

The case of Yolanda[1]

Sheldon Itzkowitz, Ph.D.

For the past fifteen years I have been working with patients suffering with Dissociative Identity Disorder. During that time, I have encountered clinicians who have accepted this diagnosis as legitimate, others who ran the gamut from skeptical to critical, disbelieving, and shaming of patients and therapists who work so hard to help them. I chose to present the work with my patient, Yolanda, in the hopes of informing and enlightening clinicians about the reality of this disorder. To that end, a panel, and now chapter, entitled "Dissociative Identity Disorder: The Abused Child and the Spurned Diagnosis" was created.

After a brief description of my patient, Yolanda, are two discussion Chapters (six and seven) by Elizabeth Howell, Ph.D. and Elizabeth Hegeman, Ph.D. At the Div. 39 conference, a video clip from a session with Yolanda was presented. The video documents the transition of Yolanda from adult woman, to Carlos, a young boy around the age of six, and back to her adult self again. The audience saw

---

[1] Please note: The case of Yolanda that is being discussed in this chapter can be found in greater detail in Chapters six and seven.

the striking and dramatic shifts in self states from adult to child with the accompanying changes in body posture and movements, tone and timbre of voice, and rate and rhythm of speech, that accompanied her shift in cognition.

The following is a brief history of Yolanda and an introduction to the alters who make up her system.

Background

Yolanda is a twenty-eight year-old Hispanic woman who was born and raised for a brief while in the Caribbean before her mother moved the family to the United States. She was born into a chaotic family and to a very troubled mother. Yolanda has an older sister, a younger brother and a sister who is fourteen years her junior. Yolanda characterized her home life as disorganized. Her mother is described as selfish, and unstable. Yolanda reports that the children were often left to take care of each other while their mother would go out. Beatings, vile and crass language, threats, and strange men coming in and out of the home were regular occurrences. Expressions like "I hate you"; "I brought you into this world so I can take you out of it"; "You no fucking good you bitch" and "You stupid" were common to hear.

Experiences like seeing her mother trying to drown her brother in the bathtub, frequently waking up as a child by the sights and sounds of sexual intercourse between her mother and strange men and having plates and glasses thrown at her or broken over various parts of her body further contribute to the sense of the home being characterized by the expression of un-modulated aggressive affect.

System of alters

Carlos

Carlos is the youngest of the alters in Yolanda's system. He identifies himself as being 6 years old. He holds many of the memories of early traumatic experiences. He recalls watching "The bad mommy" drowning Yolanda's younger brother in the bathtub. Carlos also recalls and recounts scenes from childhood where a "bad man is on top of the bad mommy and hurting her. He's doing like this (she demonstrates pelvic thrusting) and he's making her scream. Yolanda recalls hearing her mother yell at her "What the fuck you looking at, turn around and go to sleep!"

Other memories held by Carlos include being repeatedly beaten with the buckle end of belts, regularly being locked in closets as a form of punishment by his older sister and "the bad mommy", and having dishes and glasses thrown at him.

Raymond

Raymond describes himself as a nine-year-old boy whose function in the system is that of a "superhero" and his job is to protect Rachel. He almost never makes eye contact and always talks in a soft, low, voice just above a whisper. He is not supposed to be detected.

Rachel

Rachel always presents in the same manner. Rachel speaks so softly that it's almost impossible for me to hear her. Carlos explains that she is sad, depressed and wants to die. Yolanda's family believes that evil spirits possess her and they have taken her to several Santeria sessions during her childhood and adolescence. Rachel and Mary are the ones who hold these experiences, and it was Rachel who was taken into the homes of her uncle and neighbors; to have the ritual of Santeria performed. In a drawing that she produced, she depicted a hand and a decapitated chicken. The decapitated chicken with a bloody head, which terrifies her, is what she recalls of the Santeria ritual. The hand belongs to a man and is the last thing Rachel recalls before dissociating. She explains that after regaining consciousness she saw that the room she had been in had now been totally destroyed. The violent destruction was done by Mary (another alter) without Rachel's awareness.

Savana

Savana is described as the sexy, hot, sexually acting out alter. Yolanda on more than one occasion has been in session and said, "That bitch [Savana] she was fucking my husband again last night. I'm gonna fucking kill her".

Given Yolanda's description of her I had been expecting to encounter a hot, Latin woman. However, Savana presented as a soft spoken, shy, demure woman who bares a similarity to a Southern

Belle. She is very competitive with Yolanda for her husband's time, attention, and love.

Mary

Mary is a perpetrating alter who presents as an identification with the abusive and aggressive parts of Yolanda's mother. She is a woman of few words, is angry most of the time and is very critical of Yolanda and her efforts at growing and getting better. She is cynical and sarcastic and is the first alter that emerges in the body to protect it. At the same time she is also the alter who emerges when Yolanda is threatened in any way. For example, last spring a classmate of Yolanda's was looking at her in what felt to Yolanda to be a peculiar way. Words were exchanged across the classroom. Yolanda lost consciousness and woke up in the school's disability office and was told about a physical altercation that took place between her and the other student. On another occasion, Yolanda was washing dishes while on the phone with her mother. She heard something from her mother that enraged her and Mary stepped in and crushed a ceramic mug. She had to be rushed to the ER and required surgery on her dominant hand to repair several tendons that were severed.

CHAPTER SIX

Dissociation and dissociative disorders: Commentary and context

Elizabeth Howell, Ph.D.

In this chapter I discuss the personality organization of highly dissociative individuals as well as the dissociative organization of our culture. Not only does the first mirror the second, but there are also profound interactions, based largely on shame and shaming and victim/aggressor dynamics. These dynamics increase the dissociation between contradictory cultural beliefs, such as the enacted belief in the ownership of children and the right to abuse them (for example, manifested in the extremely high prevalence of child sexual abuse), existing side by side with the even greater rate of its denial. These dissociatively based contradictions in cultural knowledge also further isolate those people who are highly dissociative.

First, I am going to comment on Dr. Itzkowitz's case of Yolanda and introduce some generalities about Dissociative Identity Disorder (DID). Then, I will offer a response to Dr. Itzkowitz's observations regarding the spurned diagnosis.

Studies of 719 DID patients indicate that they spent 5.0 to 11.9 years in the mental health system before they were diagnosed as having DID (The International Society for the Study of Trauma and Dissociation's *Guidelines for Treating Dissociative Identity Disorders in Adults*, 2005). More generally, the average amount of time that a patient with DID spends in the mental health system before being correctly diagnosed is about seven years. Of course many are never correctly diagnosed. It seems that Yolanda spent more than the average amount of time in the system before finding Dr. Itzkowitz, a therapist who was willing and able to listen to her alters' experiences, to understand them and their interrelationships, and in this way to help her to get better. Like so many of the patients in the mental health system who have DID but have been misdiagnosed, Yolanda previously bore diagnoses of schizophrenia, borderline personality disorder, and bipolar disorder. Many never recover from these diagnoses, never receiving any treatment that will enable them to get better.

DID generally starts at a young age, usually by the age of five, and rarely beyond the age of nine or ten (Loewenstein 1994). It is initially a useful coping response to an environment which is very difficult to endure. The problem is that dissociative responses—such as switching, blanking out, or going into a trance—become automatic, and, once the original abusive environment has been left behind, are of little use in life and may be detrimental.

A traumatically abused and terrified child may deal with overwhelming affect and pain by distancing herself from the experience to such a degree that she dis-identifies with the experience and becomes an observer (rather than an experiencer) of the event. In this depersonalized state, she then pseudodelusionally (Kluft 1984) views this as happening to another child. This "other child" then "holds" the affects and memories that would be unbearable to the host, thereby protecting the host from being continually overwhelmed and safeguarding the ability to function. Highly dissociative persons may also create internal protectors and guides, often modelled on a person with whom they had positive interpersonal experiences, as well as dissociated "identifications" (Howell 2002) with aggressors.

Like most severely dissociative people, Yolanda's system of alters mirrors the violent, dominant–subordinate, and neglectful family system in which she grew up. Understanding the relationship between and among the parts of the system is vital for understanding the dynamics of her system of alters, as it is in groups and families. Yolanda was severely neglected, abused, and unprotected. Several of her alters serve as protectors, but in different ways.

Mary is a part of Yolanda who does Yolanda a great service by "holding" the enormous anger resulting from so much abuse, unrequited longing, and chaos. This protects Yolanda from experiencing affect that would otherwise be overwhelming and that she does not know how to regulate. If Yolanda herself had expressed this anger as a child she might never have survived a drowning, or similar disaster of malevolence, like that from which her younger brother was luckily rescued.

Like many aggressive alters of persons with DID, Mary may well have started out as a protector. However, the function of protection merges into one of persecution. On the inside, Mary prevented Yolanda from being and feeling visible and angry when that could endanger her to violence from her mother or her mother's cohorts. One of her functions is that of a powerful personified internal model that pre-emptively keeps Yolanda in line to protect her from worse danger on the outside. Unfortunately, this involves inhibiting, restricting, cutting, and in other ways punishing Yolanda. One reason that protectors become abusing persecutors is that there has been more persecution than protection from the outside. An imitation cannot be better than the original, and it only has the original's methods at its disposal.

It is likely that Mary enacts and embodies a traumatic procedural identification with the aggressor (Ferenczi 1949; Frankel 2002; Howell 1999, 2002). To deal with the abuser, the child must get inside the head of that abuser. The result of dissociative identification, however, is that the abuser is now in the child's head (Frankel 2002). I have suggested that in this kind of traumatic identification, the abusive "part" of the self arises from the child's automatic mimicking of the abuser's omnipotent, devaluing behaviour. Terror often fosters a hypnoid narrowing of attention to only the most relevant stimulus; in this case, the abuser. The child who may need to calm or please the aggressor, focuses on the abuser's postures, facial expressions, and words, and automatically mimics them as enactive procedural dyadic learning.

If the abuser is a parent or close relative, the child is often much more intensely attached than if there has been no abuse. The abuse increases fear, and inasmuch as the attachment system reduces fear (Lyons-Ruth 2001), the need for the attachment object is greatly increased. With respect to dissociation, in order to preserve attachment to the abuser and the part of the self who loves the abuser, the child must be unaware of the terrifying experiences at the abuser's hands. These self–other experiences are split off and often personified. In addition, we often find one particular internal dyad: One part of the self, usually the host, is unaware of the abuse, while another part mimics the abuser's behaviour as a form of enactive, procedural, dyadic learning (Howell 1999, 2002, 2005). Once the abuser is inside the child's head, in addition to punishing the host, she can also take executive control and lash out violently at others. As it was in her family, for Mary, violence is often an automatic procedural way of handling things.

While Mary holds rage from the perspective of a hostile self in a hostile world, Carlos holds terrifying and painful memories of physical abuse, even torture, such as being thrown into a closet. Carlos witnessed his mother attempting to drown their younger brother, a sight that must have been terrifying in and of itself as well as carrying the additional message of, "You misbehave, you may be next".

Alters are often quite concrete and highly stereotyped in their thinking. Carlos is six years old, an age at which gender stereotyping is high. Having one or more male alters is very common for females with DID. Because males are thought of as strong, and not weak and vulnerable like girls, the creation of male alters provides a sense of protection. Since there is generally no real protector on the outside, and because some sense of protection is necessary for sanity, as a bulwark against being overwhelmed by feeling helpless and knowing that one is alone in an incredibly dangerous and potentially annihilating world, protectors are created on the inside and pseudo-delusionally viewed as real persons. The existence of these protective male alters often does provide a sense of protection, such that fear is lessened. It is amazing how some male alters can have great strength—much, much more than the host could have in the same situation. In addition, a male alter is often a stereotyped response to having been anally raped. Persons intuit the learning theory model of gender identity: "If I was anally raped, I must be a boy".

Raymond, the nine-year-old is a superhero who has to hide and whisper. He is a protector to Rachel, and he also has to whisper. This is an appropriate response to an environment in which hard objects are flying, may even be hurled at you and may hit you; in which you are always being told to shut up, or something similar; and are frequently reminded that Bad Mommy, like the Great Mother arche-type, not only gives life, but can take it away (Neumann 1959).

Rachel feels helpless and wants to die. Raymond does not feel sui-cidal because his job is to protect Rachel, but this then leaves Rachel with the suicidality. It seems that something happened to Yolanda/Rachel in the Santeria sessions, but, if it did, so far these memories have been kept from the alters who have presented themselves.

Savana, the sexy one, is also quiet. Like Raymond, she probably had to be. One also has to wonder why she exists. Often the sexy ones have evolved as a response to sexual abuse, but neither she nor Yolanda has said anything about such experiences. In fact, none of the alters have reported sexual abuse, but that does not necessar-ily mean that it did not occur. Nor am I suggesting that it did. Like Carlos and Raymond, Savana does not appear at all angry. As far as we know, Mary is the only angry one.

The spurned diagnosis

Shame

By shame, I have in mind the terrible, at times unfathomable, feeling of being outcast from human society, of being shunned and spurned, of being wanted by no one, and having no one who empathizes with you (Lynd 1958). Part of this experience of shame is the focus on the inadequacies of oneself in the eyes of others and oneself, and of feeling mortified, wanting to disappear, to hide inside a crack in the wall (Lewis 1971). Shame focuses on the *overall badness* of the self, rather on the bad things one has done, as in guilt (Lewis 1971). Another aspect of shame that many abused people express is a deep feeling of worthlessness, resulting from being treated as expendable, degraded and often as not even human. It can be very difficult to shake off or escape from such feelings of shame.

Most likely, Yolanda has suffered the intense shame of being spurned in the family, of rarely having anyone to care about her, protect her, or listen to her. Any one of these latter would probably have been highly reparative and would have helped her to connect the traumatic moment with some comfort and to put it in the context of ongoing events.

In addition, having DID in itself creates intense shame. A person continually has to deal with not remembering what one has said or done. Thus, the person with DID must be quick with inferences and cover-ups. Unfortunately, this often convinces her, as well as others, that she is a liar. The person with DID is also beset with intrusions from other parts, such as flashbacks, thoughts being taken away and thoughts being inserted, as if from an outside source. She experiences "made" actions, such as an arm or a leg feeling as if it is being made to do something (as if from some external source) that she did not intend, and voices telling her that she is bad, worthless, and undeserving of life. Thus, it is a balancing act of trying to look normal but fearing one is crazy, and of trying to hide all of this for fear of being judged crazy or because one has been threatened with dire consequences. For instance, adults with DID often report that they were told as children that if they tell about the abuse, the abusers will come and kill them and/or their family. Or, they may be made to witness the death of a loved pet, inculcating in them the fear that this could happen to them as well. Or, in some ways more pernicious—they may have been told that knowledge of the abuse would be so unbearable as to kill a loved mother or other family member if they were to tell. Thus, the child is made to believe that she would be the agent causing a loved one's death. As she understands it, the price of love is the necessity to never tell about the abuse. All of these, which may be compounded by race, poverty, or disability, contribute to a sense of being alone and outcast.

In many ways, however, the most shaming aspect of DID may be that this extremely painful and disorganizing problem of living is so often viewed as not existing. There seems to be a public phobia of knowing about DID and child sexual abuse. Ironically, this phobia exists in a culture in which it is known that child abuse is frighteningly common.

Dissociatively based contradictions in public knowledge

Estimates of prevalence of contact sexual abuse of girls below the age of eighteen average about twenty-five per cent. One study of nine hundred women found a rate of thirty-eight per cent (Russell 1986); and Richard Gartner (1999) estimates a sexual abuse rate of approximately seventeen per cent for boys. By far the majority of patients with DID have been severely abused, usually sexually abused. Current epidemiological research sets the prevalence of DID are 1.1% of the population, and of dissociative disorders at 17.3% for women (Sar, Akyuz and Dogan 2007, cited in Sar 2008).

Despite the fact that stories about the abduction and sadistic sexual torture of little children are often on the news, the denial of child abuse is rampant in our society. In my view, the spurning of DID is highly connected with knowing and not knowing about child sexual abuse. Side by side with the denial of childhood trauma and of severe dissociation, is an unmistakable cognizance of dissociative processes as they are embedded in our language. We regularly say things such as, "pull yourself together", "he is coming unglued", "she was beside herself", "don't fall apart", "he's not all there", "she was shattered", and so on.

The dissociative consequences of sexual and physical abuse are told in some well-known myths. For example, in the Greek and Roman myth, Persephone was abducted and implicitly raped by the god of the underworld, Hades. As a consequence of eating some pomegranate seeds while in the underworld, she would have to spend four or six months per year (depending on the version of the story) in Hades. Colin Ross (1989) has noted the correspondence between dissociative disorders and the myth of Osiris, the Egyptian god of the Nile who was dismembered by his brother Set, and then revived by his sister and wife, Isis, who put his dismembered parts back together and gave him new life.

Not only is dissociation implicit in our language and some of our myths, but the psychological problem that we now call DID has been with us for a long time, even if in current, educated, middle-class culture we are generally not so familiar with this. What we understand as DID has long been, and often still is, understood as demon possession (Ellenberger 1970)—as it was for Yolanda's family. When they are manifest, these "demons" speak in the first person, as they do in DID. It is quite common for people with DID to have parts named The Devil, Satan, Lucifer, or some other supernatural deity or entity of rage and destruction. In DID the demon part, when in executive control, refers in the third person to the "host"—and generally in contemptuous terms, for example, "She's a wimp", "She's an idiot", and "She deserves her punishment".

With the Enlightenment the dissociative symptoms of demon possession became medicalized (Ellenberger 1970). The dissociative symptoms were classified under the rubric of "hysteria", a term that was used to cover a range of problems (primarily in women) including what we would now call dissociative disorders, somatoform disorders, borderline personality disorders (BPD), post-traumatic stress disorders (PTSD) and reactive psychosis. Generally the central problem for people with hysteria was dissociation.

DID: Then and now

The current spurning of DID is in many ways repetitive of the way dissociation earlier lost favour in psychoanalysis. There are many similarities between the current situation for trauma and dissociation studies and Freud's situation in the late 1800s/early 1900s. As we know, psychoanalysis began with the study of hysteria and dissociation. *Studies on Hysteria* (Breuer and Freud 1893–95) and some of Freud's early writings focused on the traumatic etiology and dissociative features of hysteria. Breuer's patient, Anna O (Bertha Pappenheim) with her switching of languages and her amnesia for occurrences in other states, probably had DID (Ross 1989). As we know, in 1896 Freud presented his first theory of hysteria, the seduction theory that linked the symptoms of hysteria with child sexual abuse. He felt that his colleagues spurned him for this theory (Freud 1896; Ellenberger 1970). For a variety of reasons stated by him and hypothesized by others, he changed his mind. Brothers (1995), Kupersmid (1993), Masson (1984), and others have suggested that Freud's abandonment of his seduction theory was more the result of his own internal conflicts than of his officially stated reasons. Among these might well be fear of professional shame in his social circle, which was part of a patriarchal culture that implicitly permitted child sexual abuse.

Freud's theory of infantile sexuality replaced his seduction theory. Ironically, the Oedipus story that Freud presented left out much of its original context in child sexual abuse (Devereux 1953; Miller 1983; Ross 1982). King Laius, Oedipus's biological father, had abducted and raped the teenage son of a neighbouring king, thereby bringing on himself the curse that he would be murdered by his own son. In an attempt to avoid this curse, he arranged for his baby son to be left to die with a stake driven through his ankles (Oedipus in fact means "swollen foot"). The little Oedipus was brought up by another neighbouring king, as his own son. And you know the rest of the story, in which he enacted the prophesied drama. How is it that Freud's "blind eye" to such an important part of this story has been so largely unnoticed?

Early work about dissociative disorders

Although Freud was for the most part contemptuous about the usefulness of theorizing about dissociation after *Studies on Hysteria* (Bromberg 1998) some of his contemporaries, such as Pierre Janet, Carl Jung, and Eugen Bleuler continued to write about dissociation. Janet was the first to explicitly link trauma and dissociation, starting in his 1889 doctoral thesis (van der Kolk and Van der Hart 1989). He noted that traumatic experiences and the "vehement" emotions they evoked could not be mentally and emotionally assimilated, and became split off from ordinary consciousness, operating "subconsciously" and autonomously (Janet 1907, 1925). These "fixed ideas" then intrude into consciousness as behaviour, emotions, and thoughts. Janet's word to describe the separation of aspects of experience such that some of it was rendered subconscious was *désagrégation*, "disaggregation", which meant dissociation.

Although Janet's work was largely eclipsed by Freudian theory, his influence has been considerable. Jung's concept of "complex" was highly influenced by Janet's concept of fixed ideas (Ellenberger 1970). And he also used Janet's term dissociation, in his descriptions of complexes. Bleuler (1911/50) who was influenced by Jung, used the term as well.

In his 1911 book, *Dementia Praecox*, Bleuler introduced the term "schizophrenia", drawn from the Greek, meaning "split mind". He chose this term to replace the earlier more inexact term, "dementia praecox". In this book, Bleuler stressed the importance of dissociation, even noting, "the patient appears to be split into as many different persons or personalities as they have complexes" (Bleuler 1911: 361). Thus, he is also writing about what today we call DID.

To a large degree then, dissociative disorders became subsumed under the category of schizophrenia. Writers such as Harold Searles and R.D. Laing who wrote on schizophrenia in the 1950s and 1960s describe many cases of "schizophrenia", as involving overt switching of identity states, clearly cases of DID. Perhaps the literal translation of schizophrenia ("split mind") has remained lodged in the public subconscious such that the earlier assumptions of dissociativity continually re-emerge.

Meanwhile, across the Atlantic, William James and Morton Prince, among others, were highly interested in Janet's ideas and in multiple personality disorder (MPD). For the first few decades of the twentieth century MPD, now termed DID, was accepted and familiar. According to Hilgard (1977), three forces contributed to the waning of its familiarity. One was the rise of behaviourism, which eschewed anything unconscious or subconscious. Another was the rise of psychoanalysis with its focus on incestuous wishes. The last was the treatment of DID in academic studies in the United States that had the effect of significantly lessening interest in dissociation.

After around the 1920s and until recently, dissociation has been largely dissociated in psychoanalysis. Even theories that explained the dynamics of dissociation, such as those of Fairbairn and Ferenczi, generally used the word "splitting" rather than dissociation. In the 1950s Thigpen and Cleckley published *The Three Faces of Eve*; however, the description of this case was not linked to child abuse, and besides, by then this disorder was considered extremely rare.

Since the end of the Vietnam War and the advent of feminism, the idea of psychological trauma has become more acceptable. Yet, severe dissociation has not. To me this is somewhat illogical because, as I see it, the word "trauma" implies dissociation. I have proposed that trauma might be best defined as "the event(s) that cause dissociation", and that "thinking of trauma this way puts the focus on splits and fissures in the psyche rather than solely on the external event" (Howell 2005: ix). If an event cannot be assimilated, it cannot be linked with other experience, causing fissures in memory and experience, that is, dissociation. This conceptualization bypasses the confusing discussions about "objective" trauma (which does not result in post-traumatic stress to all of those exposed to it) versus "subjective" trauma (which can run the risk of categorizing anything that is distressing as traumatic).

Just as Freud's social environment was one in which child sexual abuse was common, so is ours. Just as Freud may have feared professional shame and becoming a social outcast, and just as academia played an important role in the diminution of interest in dissociation, today it is not so different. Many of us learned in the education system, and/or subsequent training, that multiple personality disorder, now DID, is extremely rare. And many of us learned in our textbooks, as well as from Ernest Jones and Peter Gay that Ferenczi, who in his later work, wrote of profound dissociative states resulting from child abuse was crazy. And perhaps, most importantly, we know what happened to him!

Going against the tide, especially a strong ideological one, and one which is also academically supported, is never easy. Even without the issues of DID and child sexual abuse, it is understandable that clinicians might have a fear of professional shame. One issue that does not directly have to do with child sexual abuse is that some psychoanalysts, academics and senior mental health faculty have taught their students that DID does not exist. And this teaching has been passed on from teacher to student, and so on.

Another powerful viewpoint, often picked up by the media, is that symptoms of DID are the result, not of child abuse, but of misguided therapy. The suggestion made to the public is that the dissociated self states, the alters, are an iatrogenic result of psychotherapy, specifically, that therapists have suggested the alters into being. A related suggestion is that patients' memories of abuse are not real but have been "implanted" in their minds by their therapists. These stances have often been presented by the false memory syndrome foundation (FMSF), implying that such a diagnostic "syndrome" involving suggestion and implantation of false traumatic memories, is recognized and used by the mental health profession. There has been a small but powerful group of academics, some connected with this group, whose writings, supportive of these themes, have been published in major journals. Of course, bad therapy, in which the therapist's assumptions or beliefs may be stated as fact, do exist, for example, "You were abused by your father", or "You were not abused by your father, but have simply mistaken your desires for their enactment". It is also true that patients can be psychotic or vindictive toward their parents. However, I think that the people who have been abused and who have doubted their own experience as a result of the implantation of these ideas into the media far outnumber the victims of poor therapists who wrongly infer abuse. All of the foregoing contributes to shame that is experienced by both patients and their therapists.

Shame is multi-levelled

Shame becomes a multi-levelled issue, involving the patient, the therapist, and the larger society. As the DID patient is shamed, often by not being believed, the therapist may be professionally shamed for some of the same reasons: She or he may not be believed and may therefore be thought to be nuts, they may be accused of imagining a disorder (DID) where none exists, or be accused of implanting false memories. The repercussions of professional shame, as well as the effect on one's sense of safety and livelihood, can be very powerful and often contribute to burnout. In a larger society that is phobic of knowing about child abuse, therapists who treat DID have been disproportionately sued, reported to ethics boards on made-up charges, and worse.

Seeing is believing

Despite beliefs in iatrogenesis, seeing is believing. How can you deny it when a patient who is talking to you, suddenly glazes over, and asks, "Where am I? Who are you?" In one case the patient thought I was a school counsellor and that she was thirteen years of age. She used the name that she used then, not the one she does now. For me to have created this alter, whose memories (unavailable to the host) were not previously known by me and were corroborated by corresponding memories of other parts, would have been, at the very least, highly complex. How do you understand it when someone begins to speak like a child, asks to play on the floor, and as she is playing tells you of rapes and other horrors that she regularly suffers. Then she suddenly "comes to" as it were and says with great embarrassment, "What am I doing on the floor?" Or, as sometimes happens, a patient is sitting in front of you, frequently turning her head to the side and saying apparently to someone, "Shut up".

What do you make of it when someone screams in terror and pain on the phone and tells you that "she" is hitting her but no one else is actually there with them? In fact, the first time something like this happened to me, I didn't know what to make of it, and so I didn't make much of it—I didn't spell it out, it remained unformulated (Stern 1997). While in one sense I intuitively knew what was happening, I didn't try to pursue what to make of it for a while. This was knowing and not knowing. Probably it would have been different if I had seen it.

I am reminded of an almost identical series of events, told to me recently by two different colleagues about two DID patients who were hospitalized for suicidal behaviour. In both cases the patients told the hospital staff that they had DID. In both cases they were disbelieved: DID does not exist. In one case the therapist who called the hospital was told by the attending that DID did not exist because he had never seen it. In both cases the patients soon began to floridly switch. In one case the patient was quite educated about her condition, and had attempted to explain to the staff what DID is and what the symptoms are. As a consequence, the staff members were able to recognize and understand her switches. After the visible switches of both patients the staff believed that DID existed and that these particular patients had DID. But the next response was rather chilling. Now it was requested of these vulnerable, suicidal patients that they consent to being filmed. Fortunately both patients refused.

Of course, not all switching is obvious. However, there are some things to be alert to. If a patient markedly changes expression, posture, or tone of voice, or sometimes speaks in a child-like voice, one might inquire about these occurrences and subsequently ask something such as, "Do you remember when we were talking about such and such?" The result might be the discovery that the patient does not remember, or that there are large chunks of the sessions and of her daily life that she does not remember. Without inquiry into such memories or into such experiences as pleasure and joy, one may never discover that the patient lives life for the most part in a depersonalized state. It is important to be alert to changes in affect, posture, facial expression, voice tone, body language, glazed over eyes, and so on, and to ask your patient if she is aware of them.

In sum, while DID may be spurned, close investigation renders it undeniable.

References

Bleuler, E. (1911/1950). *Dementia Praecox or the group of schizophrenias* (Trans. J. Zinkin). New York: International Universities Press.
Breger, L. (2000). *Freud: Darkness in the Midst of Vision*. New York: Wiley.
Breuer and Freud (1893). On the psychical mechanism of hysterical phenomena: preliminary communication. *Standard Edition*. 2. London: Hogarth Press.

Breuer and Freud (1893–95). Studies on Hysteria. *Standard Edition*. 2. London: Hogarth Press, 1955.

Bromberg, P. (1998). *Standing in the Spaces: Essays on Clinical Process, Trauma, and Dissociation*. Hillsdale, NJ: The Analytic Press.

Brothers, D. (1995). *Falling backward: An exploration of trust and self-experience*. New York: Norton.

Chu, J.A., Loewenstein, R., Dell, P.F., Barach, P.M., Somer, E., Kluft, R.P., Gelinas, D.J., Van der Hart, O., Dalenberg, C.J., Nijenhuis, E.R.S., Bowman, E.S., Boon, S., Goodwin, J., Jacobson, M., Ross, C.A., Sar, V., Fine, C.G., Frankel, A.S., Coons, P.M., Courtois, C.A., Gold, S.N. and Howell, E. Guidelines for Treating Dissociative Identity Disorder in adults. *Journal of Trauma & Dissociation*. 6(4): 69–149.

Courtois, C. (1999). *Recollections of sexual abuse: Treatment principles and guidelines*. New York: Norton.

Devereux, G. (1953). Why Oedipus killed Laius—A note on the complementary Oedipus complex in Greek drama. *Internat. J. Psycho-Anal.* 32: 132.

Ellenberger, H. (1970). *The Discovery of the Unconscious*. New York: Basic Books.

Ferenczi, S. (1949). "Confusion of tongues between the adult and the child". *International Journal of Psycho-Analysis*. 30: 225–231.

Frankel, J. (2002). "Exploring Ferenczi's concept of identification with the aggressor: Its role in everyday life and the therapeutic relationship". *Psychoanal. Dial.* 12: 101–140.

Freud, S. (1896). The aetiology of hysteria. *Standard Edition*. 3. London: Hogarth Press, 1962.

Gartner, R. (1999). *Betrayed as Boys: Psychodynamic Treatment of Sexually Abused Men*. New York: Guilford.

Hilgard, E.R. (1977). *Divided Consciousness: Multiple Controls In Human Thought And Action*. New York: Wylie.

Howell, E.F. (1999) "Back to the States: Victim Identity and Abuser Identification in Borderline Personality Disorder," presented at the Sixteenth Annual Conference of the International Society for the Study of Dissociation, 12 November, 1999, Miami.

Howell, E.F. (2002). "Back to the 'states': Victim and abuser states in borderline personality disorder". *Psychoanalytic Dialogues*. 12(6): 921–957.

Howell, E.F. (2005). *The Dissociative Mind*. Hillsdale, NJ: The Analytic Press.

Janet, P. (1907). *The major symptoms of hysteria*. New York: Macmillan.

Janet, P. (1925). *Psychological Healing*, Vol. I. New York: Macmillan.

Kluft, R. (1984). "Treatment of multiple personality disorder". *Psychiatric Clinics of North America*. 7: 9–29.

Kupersmid, J. (1993). Freud's rationale for abandoning the seduction theory. *Psychoanalytic Psychology*. 10(2): 275–290.

Lewis, H. (1971). *Shame and Guilt in Neurosis*. New York, NY: International Universities Press.

Loewenstein, R. (1994). "Diagnosis, epidemiology, clinical course, and cost effectiveness of treatment for dissociative disorders and MPD". *Dissociation*. 7(1): 3–11.

Lynd, H.M. (1958). *On shame and the search for identity*. New York: Harcourt, Brace & World, Inc.

Masson, J. (1984). *The assault on truth*. New York: Signet.

Miller, A. (1983). *For Your Own Good*. New York: Farrar, Straus, Giroux.

Neumann, E. (1959). *The Great Mother*. Princeton, NJ: Princeton University Press.

Ross, C. (1989), *Multiple Personality Disorder*. New York, NY: John Wiley and Sons.

Ross, J. (1982). "Oedipus Revisited-Laius and the 'Laius Complex'". *The Psychoanalytic Study of the Child*. 37: 169–174. New Haven, CT: Yale University Press.

Russell, D. (1986). *The Secret Trauma: Incest in the Lives of Girls and Women*. New York: Basic Books.

Sar, V. (V2008). "Trauma and personal life in context: Personal life, social process, and public health". *Journal of Trauma and Dissociation*. 9(1): 1–8.

Sar, V., Ayyuz, J. and Dogan, O. (2007). "Prevalence of dissociative disorders in the general population". *Psychiatry Research*. 149(1–3): 169–176.

Thigpen, C. and Cleckley, H. (1957). *The Three Faces of Eve*. New York: McGraw-Hill.

van der Kolk, B. and van der Hart, O. (1989). "Pierre Janet and the breakdown of adaptation in psychological trauma". *Amer. J. Psychiatry*. 146: 1,530–1,540.

CHAPTER SEVEN

Multiple personality disorder and spirit possession: Alike, yet not alike

Elizabeth Hegeman, Ph.D.

First I will compare my views of Multiple Personality Disorder (MPD) and Spirit Possession, and then talk about how I see them overlap in the patient, Yolanda, presented by Dr. Itkzowitz (see Chapter five). Both MPD the diagnosis and Spirit Possession as a widespread cultural tradition, challenge the Western definition of the self as highly bounded, individual, and autonomous. In fact, Western cultures are in the minority in doubting and pathologizing self states: ninety per cent of the world's 488 non-Western cultures accept some form of altered state experience, and at least fifty per cent have a structured belief in Spirit Possession as a valued and valid aspect of self. Second, and most salient to the case presented in Chapter five and the discussion in Chapter six, I believe that MPD definitely, and Spirit Possession potentially, serve to deny and disguise trauma, simultaneously hiding it and representing it in a disguised form. MPD is a 'spurned' diagnosis first, because unlike other cultures, Western culture valorizes a highly bounded self, and second, as Elizabeth Howell, Ph.D. (Chapter six) has shown, because the abuse of power that engenders it is still (and perhaps always will be) disavowed. Disbelief is the universal Western affective counter-transference both to the abuse, and to shifts in identity. To illustrate this devaluation: try noticing your own reactions to the diagnosis as you think about it—can you track disbelief, subtle contempt, skepticism, even if you think you 'believe' in the importance of understanding dissociative processes? I still feel those feelings when I talk about MPD. Fragmentation of the unitary self makes us anxious. Lawyers long ago abandoned dissociation as a defense in criminal trials because of the knowledge that juries dismiss it as simply an attempt to evade responsibility. So, we pathologize this form of human experience both from our ethnocentrism and from our need to deny and ignore the injustice of illegitimate dominance/subjugation.

The internal states—the 'parts' of a multiple personality, or the person with DID (Dissociative Identity Disorder)—each represent a facet of the incompatible internal experiences of the abused child, compartmentalized and segregated from each other so that the contradiction is not experienced as conflict. One way to understand MPD is as the attempts of a child to make sense of the confusing relational meanings of the abuser's motivation—the child is trying to form a "theory of mind" of the abuser—"Why is he doing this?" And, the child is struggling to find some internal stance. As Colin Ross has said, "What is MPD but a little girl pretending that the abuse is happening to someone else?" In the "inner cast of characters", the "protector" parts are identified with the strength and determination to resist abuse; the "persecutor" parts blame and punish the self but often have the disguised aim of resisting as well. Sometimes protector parts present as invulnerable to pain or death; suicide can be disguised euthanasia in reaction to the despair and helplessness surrounding the torture or abuse. Child parts are more varied: they may be identified with the abuser and clinging to the idea of being loved, or in despair, or in complete denial of malevolence, or struggling with other theories to try to understand what is happening in the relationship. As Jody Davies' three-year-old daughter said, when the doctor repeatedly kept trying to find a vein to take a blood sample, "I must be a very bad little girl for this to be happening" (Davies and Frawley 1994). In the face of being told not to tell, the child may split into a part that knows and keeps the secret, and a part that does not know. In brief, that is a description of the "knowing and not knowing" of trauma on the individual level.

Let us now consider how it works in other cultures. I believe that in a culture which has recognized spirits or gods who each represent some emotional/moral stance, the person who experiences the contradictions of being abused may well appropriate these spirits as concrete ways of representing the rage, hope, magical renewal, desolation, and omnipotent denial that arise from the experience of trying to make sense of having one's love and loyalty exploited in an intimate relationship. In other words, the spirits, like the inner parts, represent defenses against the horror and annihilation of knowing what is happening. I also think that the spirit world can also represent the normalized, but violent and unjust, power relationships of colonialism and conquest. I will try to show the connections between Yolanda's internal states or parts, and the ways in which spiritism can be adapted to personify these experiences.

Any pantheon of gods/goddesses/spirits is likely to include an array of emotionally defined relational reactions which correspond to the feelings of the betrayed, exploited child; these codify the internal stances of the child of abuse and the re-enactments not of the abuse, but of the *internal* experience of it—what the child makes of what happens is what gets labelled with a spirit name, or an internal name, and re-enacted. These parts, or spirits, become the vehicle in language of emotions taken up by the parts of the person, spread out and independent of each other so that the child can experience simpler feelings that can be processed by an immature cognition. A toxic projection by the abuser is too complicated to grasp: "I love you and I am hurting you", or "This is for your own good", or "Your body belongs to me so I can get rid of my fear of weakness by attacking it", or "You are the one who should feel the shame, not me", or "I can't stand your innocence and seductiveness and I want a new chance to feel good about myself so I am killing you off in my mind and in your body", or "You have to carry all the pain and humiliation and degradation I experienced in the Holocaust, or in my own abuse, so I won't have to feel it and can start a new life". These are actual statements that patients have come to formulate as they recognize the meaning of their own split-off states.

These hateful configurations (between abuser and abused) are too overwhelming and contradictory for a young child to understand. So in the culture which has religious figures who represent different moral positions, these figures will be appropriated by the child who is struggling to represent her experience and find healthy internal identifications. Santeria is a religion of ancestor worship and blood sacrifice which originated in Cuba during the period of slavery. It is a combination of African and Christian beliefs. The orishas, or gods, from Yoruba tribal culture were given the names of Christian Saints to disguise them from the slave owners and to protect the secrecy of the worship. For example, Ogun is associated with St. Peter or John the Baptist, but in Yoruba tradition he is a blacksmith—the maker of weapons, the symbol of all the pain and horror caused by war and violence. Worshippers propitiate him so he will protect them. Other Orisha figures come into play to make the emotions of abuse both concrete and legitimate, so the sufferer can feel understood and held by the other believers who participate in the ceremonies.

Like other worshippers, the abused child hopes to be cleansed and healed, but unless she feels supported by a family and culture of believers, she may be only further traumatized, as Yolanda was. She didn't understand the frightening rituals because the religion and culture are not really hers. The sacrifice of the chicken that Yolanda probably witnessed—(where the bird's head would have been pulled off by the medium conducting the ceremony, and its blood smeared on Yolanda)—was supposed to get rid of an ancestral spirit that was haunting her body and causing her misery. Her relatives may have had the best of intentions: if people live close to the land and to the lives of animals, they may feel differently about the violent death of a chicken—but for a city girl it probably felt like another terrifying threat that her family exposed her to. Her personality and defenses had already formed in an abusive, derogating setting; her alter Mary destroyed the room in which the ceremony took place, suggesting that she was lashing out in rage and terror.

Because they are mostly Westerners, anthropologists too are resistant to interpretations of altered states that involve individual suffering, such as MPD. They readily accept the notion of altered states and possession being connected with trauma or abuse of power, but mostly when the issue is framed in terms of *collective* violence and suffering. Anthropologists have long understood the apocalyptic revitalization religions which sweep through conquered lands as a response to the violent genocidal assault on Native Americans and subjugated colonies. Collective movements such as cargo cults in New Guinea during World War II, the Sun Dance of the Great Plains native peoples during the end of the nineteenth century, going into battle as a berserker, magical amulets protecting against bullets—each represents the attempt to make sense of a strange conquering culture, the disappearance of the old culture, and the emotional stances of denial, omnipotence, and despair. When one culture dominates another to the point of extermination, it seems natural for people to keep hope alive in some magical way. These collective responses are alternatives to anguish, as MPD is an alternative to individual despair in relationships.

To illustrate the social structural approach taken by anthropologists, which I feel colludes with the dissociative disguise of trauma, I will describe how anthropologist Janice Boddy interpreted possession states when she studied the zar cults of Northern Sudan in her field work in 1976 and 1983. In this culture, women undergo the most extreme form of genital operation without anaesthetic, as latency-age girls. As adults, those who become spirit-possessed join in a collective ceremony. Women gather in the afternoon, play drums and feast. As the day wanes, each woman becomes possessed of her own particular spirit and speaks in the voice of that spirit. If the spirit is not given the perfume and clothing it demands, the possessed woman will be infertile, a terrible curse for her husband, and for his patrilineage that needs children to continue. Boddy (2007) interprets the meaning of the zar cults in terms of the impact of colonialism—the need to coerce men to participate in the labour economy, to earn money to placate the spirits possessing their wives, rather than as representation of the women's suffering and need for spiritual comfort, even rebellion. The clothing and objects the spirits demand truly make the possession rituals seem like a farcical satire of the colonial officials, whom the women have never seen—a pith helmet, jodhpurs, a British officer's uniform, a cane, cigars. The women must be inspired by what they have heard from their husbands about these English officials; either they are acting out a mischievous pageant, or they pitifully envy the symbols of power, or both. We are left to infer the connection between the ritual practice of possession-trance by adult women, and the individual girl child's experience of shock, pain and betrayal.

However, the zar cults just happen to exist in the part of the world where the genital operation is performed on girls by their female relatives. Not only are all the external genitalia (labia, clitoris, and vulva) surgically removed, but the vaginal opening is sewed almost closed, making menstruation difficult and childbirth impossible without another unsanitary surgery. The physical shock, infections and suffering that come with this form of operation are probably obvious to us, but they are normalized by both the culture and most anthropologists. Boddy (2007) spends only a few words describing the customary operation, and dismisses it as "not very painful". She, and other anthropologists, make no connections between the pain, the intrusion to the body, the sense of betrayal by female relatives, and the later predisposition to Spirit Possession. To connect those would mean recognizing the individual girl's experience of agony and betrayal and the child's need to dissociate from them, rather than accepting the cultural suppression of those meanings. We are left to infer the connection between the ritual practice and the individual child's experience of shock, pain and betrayal, which she must suppress in the absence of cultural support for her feelings. This example is only one of many in which we could connect the capacity for altered states with individual trauma. The structural explanations based on Colonialism, such as Boddy makes, are not invalid, just operating on another layer of discourse—the collective layer of experience, rather than the individual.

I am not arguing that all Spirit Possession is dissociation arising from trauma, but rather, I am trying to show how self states, and a more variable definition of self, are far more accepted in other cultures, where they provide a structured form for individual expressions of identity and defenses, including the creative response to trauma. When I first encountered altered states of consciousness and Spirit Possession in the course of anthropological fieldwork in Puerto Rico, Colombia and Panama, I was fascinated by the emotional power of the possessed person to simultaneously communicate surrender, ecstasy, and supernatural authority. The espiritista healers who were able to induce trance at will in the service of diagnosing a client, the participant in a religious ceremony who becomes "born again" and speaks in tongues, the devotee of vodoun who is "ridden" by a spirit, all resemble each other in the powerful demonstration of a self that is starkly different from the familiar social identity of the person.

When I met multiple personality patients, I remembered the possession states I had witnessed before—the sudden shift into a different self, the sharp presentation of a different identity, were familiar. But with the multiple personality, or DID patients, there was something else: the facets of the person held the vivid experiential knowledge of some forbidden part of our culture—incest, criminal violence, sadism, torture, neglect, or abandonment. MPD/DID was different from possession states in that with Spirit Possession there is in the culture an accepted formal belief system to support the shift in identity. In contrast, MPD/DID patients know and speak or act out something hidden that they know they are not supposed to know or talk about, and in a way they have invented their own dissociation. The "person within the person" of the alter persona in the United States breaks the social rules of identity by differing from a conventional, accepted public self; the content of what she knows breaks the rules of what we are not supposed to know about in our culture, the misuse of power. MPD represents the attempt of a child to make sense of the impossible contradictions of abuse—"How could he be doing this to me if he knows how it makes me feel?" but at the same time, "He must know how this makes me feel, and that is why he is doing it". These contradictions are held by separate parts, rather than existing in conflict with each other. But when the experience is represented this way in the self, some part does not deny or disavow it. Both sides of the relationship are represented. As one DID patient suggested, "We have the ability to become the Other—if more people could do that, we wouldn't have wars".

I think each of the parts of Dr. Itzkowitz's patient Yolanda (see Chapter five) represents one aspect of her internal response to the confusing relational abuse she has experienced. Mary, the protector/persecutor, identifies with those who have hurt Yolanda and yet strikes out to protect her; Savana represents the sexualized child; Rachel feels the despair and terror; Raymond, the superhero, represents the grandiose effort to protect the self through invisibility; and Carlos tries to comfort the other selves despite what he knows.

Unfortunately, Yolanda lives at the edge of a Caribbean culture which accepts Spirit Possession, but as her family has tried to assimilate and has moved to the United States, she and her family are not really part of a cultural group that really believes in the religion. So, when Yolanda's family took her to be cured, because she did not understand what was happening or believe in its effectiveness, she experienced it as a terrifying assault rather than drawing comfort from an external structure that could contain and offer a valid way to express and transcend her suffering and degradation. Yolanda's self states were demonized by her family, who think she is possessed of evil spirits, and pathologize her further on that basis, even though they were the ones who introduced her to Santeria. The Santeria rituals that were meant to cure her, ironically further terrified her. If the family were more grounded in the Santeria, or even in the Catholic tradition of saints, Yolanda would have more social backing for her personal experience of self and the contradictory attitudes she has incorporated. But this family, trying to make it as economically marginal immigrants, tried (as we all do) to belong in American culture, through distancing from the culture of origin and by condemning that which it is forbidden to know in this culture—the abuse she experienced.

If Yolanda were a part of an Espiritista circle and met regularly with them, she could be apprenticed to learn to become a healer herself, after learning to "work her spirits" under the direction of an experienced healer. There she would find support, friends and colleagues in the frequent meetings and ceremonies devoted to making sense of internal ecstatic experience. She would develop her own spirit helpers, who would give her the power to control her own internal system, and help her to cure others. Instead, she and her husband are working to assimilate more to mainstream American culture—she is becoming more educated, is being acculturated into a world that rejects her spirits and her alter states, is participating in the Western medical system and is coming to psychotherapy.

So Spirit Possession is similar to MPD in its presentation of a strikingly different identity than the usual social self, yet it is unlike it in that MPD is diagnosed as an illness in cultures that impose a strict definition of the bounded, responsible individual. The spirits that possess people in an accepting culture are generally recognized by others in the culture, so the possessed person is using a shared language that makes for acceptance and recognition, even of pain and affliction. In contrast, in the United States, the MPD "patient" still carries the stigma, and has to invent her own names and symbols, which would have to be explained to others, and will be idiosyncratic. So potentially, the cultural surround of Spirit Possession *integrates*, and the diagnosis of MPD *isolates* the person by pathologizing symptoms and separating the patient from cultural supports. Yolanda has the misfortune to be an immigrant deprived of those supports, and also a patient whose body was further invaded and assaulted by inappropriate drugs before she found her therapist, Dr. Itzkowitz, who wanted to understand and help her heal.

In summary, both MPD and Spirit Possession involve altered states of consciousness and dramatic shifts in identity that correspond to internal self states; however, MPD is pathologized by Western culture because of the insistence in Western culture on a bounded, consistent self—outside the kind of psychotherapy that allows for different selves, our culture tolerates no creative play or expression of different internal states, especially when they represent traumatic experience. This pathologizing serves to conceal atrocity and suppress resistance to it, thus having political as well as psychic functions. Personally I have found that my clinical understanding of self-state dynamics has been deepened by cross-cultural knowledge. If we could be more open to learning from DID patients, we would learn a great deal about the psychic representations of self that master the fear of death and the feeling of being hated.

I would like now to explore possible similarities between a psychoanalytic understanding of unformulated traumatic experience, and ethnic syndromes and possession states in other cultures. Fundamental to this task is the daring stance that some elements of the dissociative response to traumatic experience are universal. This has not generally been an idea acceptable in the anthropological tradition, where imposing a Western idea or framework on other cultures is considered naïve, ethnocentric or even colonialist. Anthropologists have argued that the experience we assume is traumatic may not be so considered by the cultures under study. A second reason is that the practices I am calling traumatic are indeed normalized by the cultures described; they are part of the routine imposition of authority and the process of socialization within that culture. So, if they are not seen by the people themselves as disturbing, the anthropologist may not see them as traumatic even if they involve severe body injuries, pain, disturbances of attachment, and betrayal. Many if not all of the twenty-five "ethnic syndromes" listed at the back of the DSM IV in Appendix 1 include dissociative symptoms: trance, possession, glossolalia—but the accounts given of these states are generally (universally) grounded in the terms of a particular culture, for example, "Puerto Rican syndrome". For an understanding of the states, anthropologists have turned to religious beliefs, practices around disease and cure, and other *conscious* elements of the culture.

A rare exception to this practice of concretizing and isolating each tradition, and ignoring unconscious interpretations, is the early work of Margaret Mead and Gregory Bateson, who recorded community ritual of the trance dance in Bali on film, and connected the yearly ritual with the culturally normalized but emotionally brutal practice of weaning. In Balinese culture, anyone and everyone is expected to have the capacity for trance; it is neither pathologized nor normalized. This ceremony involves every member of the community: some play costumed parts in the ritualized killing off of a wicked witch; others go into a trance as bystanders while watching the lengthy ceremony; still others care for the trance dancers, ensuring that they do not hurt themselves, binding their hair up and giving them drinks of water as they come back out of trance. (Drinking water and combing hair are also ways that some MPD patients have of bringing themselves back to the host state.) This culture is one in which anyone and everyone can trance; other cultures such as the Kalahari K'ung have a tradition of specialization in which only designated people become spirit possessed, usually as part of a healing ceremony.

Mead and Bateson connect the trance dance with the customs of weaning. When the Balinese child is two to three years of age, there are several normal ways of handling weaning: the mother may go away for two weeks, or she may smear hot pepper on her nipples, or she may pick up another child, a doll, or a piglet and pretend to nurse it in front of her toddler. Mead and Bateson film the mother laughing maniacally while the child screams in anguish at the sudden betrayal. This continues for several minutes until the overstimulated child suddenly enters a protective trance state, and with a blank, loose-lipped face he or she begins to make the wrist-bending, choreiform hand-circling gestures associated both with neurological soft signs and with the stylized gestures of the classical Balinese dance.

Psychoanalytic theory has ways of understanding this behaviour as deviant that have confirmed Mead's insights. The "frightened or frightening" mother has been described by Karlen Lyons-Ruth (cited in Wallin 2007: 58) as engendering disordered attachment style. But what does it mean about a culture if this behaviour is the norm? Can Western psychological theory handle the idea that all the people of a whole culture can have disordered attachment?

As Mead points out in the voiceover to this dramatic film, the plot of the trance dance pageant is based on the gathering of soldiers (played by male members of the community) to kill a dangerous witch who is spreading disease and plague. The witch strides around in platform shoes and extra-long fingernails and headdress, cackling loudly like the weaning mother. As the witch turns her back on the assembled crowd, they sneak up on her carrying weapons. When she turns around, waving her wild hair and long fingernails and turns her terrifying, toxic gaze on the crowd, the people fall down in trance and act paralyzed until she looks away. When she turns away, they sneak up again and the same thing is repeated. (The performance is like the American version of the childhood game "Red Rover, Red Rover, will you come over?") The unconscious connections between the feelings of the anguished child and the wish to kill the brutally betraying and frightening witchy mother are clear to us as outsiders as a reference to the weaning situation, as if we were interpreting the Balinese a shared tradition as a kind of dream. The physical/neurological predisposition to entering trance, which most members of the community do at one time or another during the yearly ceremony, may also be conditioned by the early experience of needing dissociative relief from the overwhelming emotions of the weaning episode. We could speculate that these weaning practices are not the only child-rearing customs that teach children to dissociate. If mothers are routinely accustomed to taking pleasure in having the power to make their toddlers suffer, they probably make their toddlers suffer in other parenting situations. The toddlers will thus need to dissociate as a way of escaping intolerable emotions.

Examples of cultural content such as the story of the Balinese trance dance, which is so easy to connect with its cultural antecedent in the weaning process, or the zar cult which seems to empower and relieve women who split off their autonomy in the face of pain and betrayal, are not hard to find if we accept the connection between trauma and dissociation. The implications of this kind of connection are far-reaching—they mean that dissociated feelings and events can carry over even from early childhood and actually become embodied in cultural rituals for adults. Margaret Mead might have taken for granted that dissociated or repressed experience from childhood would reappear as cultural content in the context of ritual or ecstatic behaviour, since the connections between child rearing and personality were taken for granted by social science intellectuals of the 1930s to 1940s. But this kind of cultural analysis has lost ground in the last forty years; the dark and shocking connections between childhood experience and personality as shown in the extensive Rorschach studies, drawn by Cora Du Bois and Abraham Kardiner in *People of Alor* and *The Mark of Oppression*, a study of African Americans in the 1950s, took for granted that the political implications of the destruction of the culture of Alor, an island in the South Pacific, and the crushing impact of American slavery and racism, have now largely been dismissed as "unscientific" in that they are difficult to replicate or compare from one culture to another. The issue of childhood trauma and its connection to adult dissociative defenses has never been fully investigated because the ethos of the social sciences has changed; culture and personality have now ceded ground to cognitive science and perceptual measurements rather than psychodynamic formulations.

An exception to the unpopularity of psychodynamic interpretation is the 2003 work of Patricia Gherovici, a Lacanian analyst who has worked to understand *attaque de nervios*, or Puerto Rican syndrome, in the social context of hidden rage at racial and economic discrimination and gender oppression, Gherovici presents an analysis of *attaque* as the surfacing of the consciousness of exploitation through her practice of fieldwork and therapy in South Philadelphia. Without a community tradition as strong and united as that in Bali, the dissociative ritual may become fragmented and individualized, under the influence of Western Espiritista healers who have thrived alongside Western medical practice for many years. But on the fringes of Asian cities frantic to get hold of Western technology, the ties with the supernatural become furtive and devalued: often a Japanese or Korean husband who is economically successful will forbid his wife to consult the shaman rather than more formal established religious authorities. But his wife may secretly defy him and sneak off to have the rituals performed by a shamanic healer, out of fear that he has not been as obedient a son or grandson as he should. These individualized practices are even further fragmented by regional variations in the practice of a ritual, and arguments among shamans and apprentices as to how it should be performed, but the shamanic rituals (often by women healers) are very widespread. Anthropologist Vivian Garrison (1974) described the practice of Rosa, a healer who led her own "meeting" (reunion) of disciples who were apprenticed to become healers themselves, having received the call of Spirit Possession and having been treated themselves by Rosa who teaches them to master their affliction of trance by following her lead to master the spirits and learn from them about the emotional state of the patient.

A typical case described by Garrison is of a likely borderline middle-aged woman who was struck by her attaque while working on the floor of a sweatshop. Foaming at the mouth, speaking in tongues, her clothing in disarray and her arms and legs jerking, the woman is taken to Bellevue and evaluated. She is given Librium and discharged; Garrison is told by the woman psychiatrist who evaluated her that the patient is not a suitable candidate for psychotherapy because she is "too angry" and her personality is based too heavily on defenses denial. The patient's family then takes her to a healer named Rosa, who elicits that the patient is angry because she is married to an older man who promised to support her economically but has recently been diagnosed with cancer and cannot work. She now has to work in a sweatshop to support the family. In addition, the patient's adolescent son has been put on probation at school and has been arrested; she is worried because she cannot control him and her husband is no help. On top of these problems, many of his relatives have been visiting because of his illness and she is expected to cook and clean for them.

Rosa, the healer, goes into trance in her meeting of community members and followers, and her initial diagnosis is made with the guidance of her personal guardian spirit: the patient's anger and attaque episode are caused by the spirit of a 16th century village leader (*cacique*) who is inhabiting her body and causing her distress. This interpretation makes the patient comfortable by externalizing the causes of her anger. Rosa prescribes ritual cleansing for her body and her apartment, rituals of social support, engages the patient in a relationship with the congregation, and gradually begins to interpret her defenses. First, she conducts couple sessions with the patient's husband and explores the angry grievances against each other. Rosa confronts the patient with her evasion of responsibility for her feelings while supporting her parenting and her family connections by prescribing rituals the family must participate in. Over the course of a dozen sessions of combined rituals, spirit-possessed diagnosis, and social support, Rosa shifts her stance from totally supportive of the patient's hidden anger to confrontation of her rationalizations, and essentially, turns the patient into a patient.

So we can see that an episode of the "return of the dissociated" can serve many functions: it can gratify a need for attention and dependency, transform the social support system and community to recognize someone's distress, and in some cases lead to empowerment—if the patient had continued attending the meeting and working her spirits under Rosa's guidance, she might have reached the status of healer herself and formed her own congregation. (The parallel to analytic training is strong, except for the financial cost!) In the instance of *attaque*, the drama of the ritual is private and individually scripted rather than communal, and mediated by verbal tradition and myth as in Bali, but still the symptoms and the trance state are shared sufficiently in the belief system for everyone in the community to diagnose and respond.

One key difference between the trance dance and *attaque de nervios* is whether the dissociated action, feelings and events come back as *collective* pageantry or individual. The patient of the espiritista healer is following a kind of script, non-verbal, though she may never have personally seen an episode herself. There is no shared mythic plot, no narrative like the killing of the dangerous witch mother. In our secular culture, people are reduced to writing their own plays, and they may go unrecognized—in fact one of the important functions of the acted out dissociated material is *not* to be understood. I once worked with a woman who had been raped as an adolescent—she had been tied up, drugged, and humiliated. In recent years, she reported tearfully, she had been unable to get any professional help: whenever she became frantic and disconsolate she would go to an emergency room, where she would be interviewed by a psychiatrist. Inevitably she became angry at feeling dismissed and misunderstood, became abusive to staff, and ended up in restraints and injected with drugs. She saw no connection between her earlier rape and these events; she had repeated the scenario with eight different emergency rooms. Her experience demonstrates the tragedy of the enactment of dissociated trauma which is not recognized, and so cannot be transformed or addressed; instead of being relieved by the enactment, the sufferer stays unaware of the connections between the earlier emotional experience and what is being re-experienced in the present.

One of the problems in tying adult dissociation to childhood trauma cross-culturally is the lack of reliable data describing childhood experience of adults who later become dissociative healers. When I asked Piers Vitebsky, an expert on Siberian and South Asian shamanic traditions, what he thought of the formulation, he made a face and said, "Who is to say what is traumatic? People do all sorts of things to their children and to each other, yet it might not be designated painful or traumatic because it is accepted". How do we determine what is unbearable? The tradition of Siberian shamans (widespread outside of Siberia), however, includes an initial period in adulthood of severe mental illness lasting from a few months to over a year. In the Korean tradition this is called *hwa-byung* (included as one of the ethnic syndromes in the DSM IV) during which the person (usually a woman) loses a great deal of weight, stops bathing and grooming, sits staring silently, speaks incoherently, appears to be in a trance, bursts out in rages, stops working, or stops caring for her children. Only the diagnosis that she is called to the post of shaman and the apprenticeship to a senior woman shaman brings her back to a normal life. Like the victim of *attaque de nervios*, to become a healer she must serve her teacher for years, learning how to do different forms of divinations and ceremonies, to contact and control her spirits through trance, and to lead day-long rituals and feasts in honour of her clients' ancestors.

Is this lengthy episode which resembles psychosis brought on by trauma? In Youngsook Kim Harvey's (1979) study of the lives of six shamans, *hwa-byung* came on immediately after the death of an infant (which is not regarded as a serious tragedy since it happens so often), abandonment by a husband, or a severe reversal of economic security which demanded relocation from the city to a much poorer area. In each case the woman assumed markedly gender-deviant roles, supporting the extended family through the fees from her ritual work while her husband drank, gambled, and gave money to concubines. The successful shaman takes on apprentices of her own and wields great informal power within her lineage, despite the automatic power given in the culture to males by tradition to marry off daughters and control the lives of women.

But can we safely connect the adult trauma of these lives with the dissociative aspects of Korean shamanism, which involves exhausting performances of many hours in the spirit role, predicting the future and speaking in the voice of dead relatives to guide the family decisions and demand penance for omissions of duty? It is very hard to tell from the accounts of lives described by Youngsook Kim Harvey (1979) and even by Laurel Kendall, who did her work later, in 1987, because of the deprivation and violence of the Korean war which raged while these women were adolescents and newly married, and the starvation and chaos after it.

The losses and anguish which preceded each of these women's entry into shamanism may be indistinguishable from the ordinary suffering Piers Vitebsky refers to. We cannot know much specific about their childhood experience that sets them off from other children that might predispose them to the primary use of dissociation as a defensive structure. Rather than trauma, it may be "constitutional" or biologically based factors, towards which the pendulum is swinging towards these days. What I am struggling to understand is whether this pattern, based on dissociation, is universal, and why it takes the different forms it does in different cultures.

References

Boddy, J. (2007). *Civilizing Women: British Crusades in Colonial Sudan.* New Jersey: Princeton U. Press.

Davies, J.M. and Frawley, M.G. (1994). *Treating the Adult Survivor of Childhood Sex Abuse.* New York: Basic Books.

Du Bois, C. and Kardiner, A. (1960–61). *People of Alor.* Volumes 1 and 2. New York: Harper and Bros.

Garrison, V. (1977). The "Puerto Rican Syndrome" in Psychiatry and Espiritismo. In: V. Crapanzano and V. Garrison (eds) *Case Studies in Spirit Possession.* New York: Wiley-Interscience.

Gherovici, P. (2003). *The Puerto Rican Syndrome.* New York: Other Press.

Harvey, Y.K. (1979). *Six Korean Women: The Socialization of Shamans.* American Ethnological Society monograph #65. New York: West Group.

Kardiner, A. (1967). *The Mark of Oppression: Explorations in the Personality of the American Negro.* New York: Meridian Books.

Kendall, L. (1987). *Shamans, Housewives, and Other Restless Spirits.* Honolulu: U. of Hawaii Press.

Mead, M. and Bateson, G. (1938). *Trance and Dance in Bali.* Educational video produced by Museum of Natural History, New York, NY.

Vitebsky, P. (2003). Personal communication.

Wallin, D.J. (2007). *Attachment in Psychotherapy.* New York: Guilford Press.

CHAPTER EIGHT

Masochistic relating, dissociation, and the wish to rescue the loved one: A view from multiple self-state theory

Peter Lessem, Ph.D.

In working with Ned I was amazed and often frustrated by his willingness to allow himself to be repeatedly exploited and maligned by his wife. I was struck by his acquiescing to her numerous and usually unfair criticisms, her many outrageous and exploitive demands, and her remarkable sense of entitlement towards him. Yet, Ned maintained that she was entitled to act this way particularly because of his inadequacy and his being undeserving. I was impressed to see that he held this view tenaciously for a very long time despite my best efforts to question it, connect it with his relevant childhood experience, speculate about the functions it served for him, and point out how he was recurrently hurting himself in the process. I do not think that this is an unfamiliar scenario for us to hear about in our offices.

Use of the term "Masochism"

In this paper I will use the term "masochistic" in a particular, restricted way. I will use it solely to refer to a style of relating in which, in the analyst's opinion, the patient winds up being repeatedly mistreated. I want to be clear that I am not subscribing to a drive theory conception of masochism as seeking pain as a necessary precondition for, or accompaniment of, sexual pleasure. Also, I am not using the term to refer to particular sexual practices or to the practice of inflicting pain on oneself in order to shore up self-cohesion or to stimulate a sense of aliveness, or to assuage a sense of guilt.

Multiple Self-State Theory

Multiple Self-State Theory (MSST) holds a view of mind that differs from the singular, unitary view of mind that has characterized psychoanalytic thought and practice for most of its history. Based on Janet's (1907) conception of different centres of the mind and the primacy of dissociation and Fairbairn's (1952) idea of the multiplicity of ego states, MSST views mind as frequently shifting between different self states characterized by different senses of self. Davies (1996: 562) has analogized this model of the organization of the mind to the working of a kaleidoscope: "patterns, varied but finite, conflating and reconfiguring themselves from moment to moment". Slavin and Kriegman (1992: 278) speak of "multiple versions of the self {that} exist within an overarching synthetic structure of identity".

The process of dissociation is central to the multiple self-state model of mind. It considers the human mind as fundamentally dissociative. According to it, dissociation is regarded as one of the normal processes of mind. Dissociation is thought to function so as to provide a sense of subjective consistency between different self states. In most normal human functioning, Bromberg (1998) asserts that self-state switches are not emergency reactions; they take place without the presence of trauma but in response to the more usual stresses and strains and pleasures of living. Switches usually allow each self state to express itself while remaining part of a coherently experienced self that is felt as "me". Also, in usual functioning, each self state is experienced as "me" even when replaced by another.

Bromberg (1998) conceives of the unconscious in terms of dissociated self states. He writes: "What we call the unconscious we might usefully think of as the suspension or deterioration of linkages between self-states, preventing certain aspects of self—along with their respective constellations of affects, memories, values and cognitive capacities—from achieving access to the personality within the same state of consciousness" (p. 182). More generally, he states, "a noticeable shift has been taking place ... away from the idea of a conscious/preconscious/unconscious distinction per se, towards a view of the self as decentered, and the mind as a configuration of shifting, nonlinear, discontinuous states of consciousness in an ongoing dialectic with the healthy illusion of a unitary selfhood" (p. 270).

With regard to treatment, Bromberg (2006: 172) asserts that dissociation becomes an interpersonal process, a dynamic element in the patient–analyst relationship; moreover, he believes that "therapeutic action depends on the freedom of the analyst to make optimal use of dissociation as an interpersonal process that includes the analyst's dissociative experience as well as the patient's". Bromberg (1998: 278) avers that because of how dissociation functions interpersonally, "unsymbolized aspects of the patient's self are often enacted with the analyst as a separate and powerful channel of communication in the clinical process".

Stern (1997), writing from this perspective, has argued that dissociated self states are largely maintained as unformulated experience. According to Stern, making unconscious experience conscious not only involves expanding the patient's awareness of disavowed, repressed, and undeveloped aspects of his experience, but it also involves assisting him with developing a language to express thoughts and feelings that have never been articulated. Increasingly the patient is then able to be open to "unbidden experience" or, in Bromberg's terms, is more open to experiencing different self states.

Therefore, from this MSST perspective, the primary goal of treatment is self-expansion as the result of articulating and integrating disavowed or dissociated self states or senses of self and the consequent ability to move flexibly between different self states while continuing to experience oneself as "me". With regard to masochistic relating—as in the case I am describing—it is crucial to help the patient articulate and integrate vulnerable senses of self that have been disavowed and unconsciously identified with the loved one. Doing so, I will illustrate, is instrumental to helping some patients change a masochistic pattern of relating.

Relevant masochism literature review

There is a large literature on the problem of masochism. I do not have the space here to summarize it. Rather, I will only point out some highlights and trends in the theorizing about masochism that are relevant to my focus.

The concept of masochism was originally formulated by Krafft-Ebing (1895). He used the term to refer to a sexual perversion in which sexual pleasure was gained from the active seeking out of or the passive submission to cruel and/or humiliating behaviours performed by a beloved other. Building on Krafft-Ebing's formulation, Freud (1905, 1919, 1924) formulated two theories to explain masochism. In the first theory—his more influential one—he posited that masochism resulted from the person's own sadism being turned back against the self. He viewed anxiety and unconscious guilt as strong motivators of this behaviour. In time, Freud theorized, the masochistic person conscripts another to assume the sadistic role and so assuage the masochist's sense of guilt. Thus, he viewed masochism as the neurotic disposition to suffering in response to the demands of the superego. Freud's (1924) second theory of masochism conceptualized masochism as an expression of the death instinct. The aim was the satisfaction of unconscious guilt over forbidden impulses via "a need for punishment from an authority figure" (p. 166). This second theory has been far less influential than Freud's first theory of masochism.

Berliner and Menaker are two post-Freudian theorists of masochism whose works are germane to my focus because they both moved away from the Freudian drive theory view of masochism; instead understanding masochism through a more object-relational theoretical lens and with more of a focus on masochistic relating. Both theorists understood masochism as motivated primarily by the need to cling to a vitally needed love object, to keep intact a crucial attachment.

Berliner (1940, 1942, 1947, and 1958) took issue with Freud's view that masochism results from the patient turning his sadism against himself. Instead, Berliner (1947) theorized that it is not the sadism of the masochist himself that is turned upon his ego, but rather the experienced sadism of another, an important love object. In his view at the core of the masochistic person's experience is the painful dilemma of "loving a person who gives hate and ill-treatment" (p. 459). Berliner characterized masochism as "a disturbance of interpersonal relations, a pathological way of loving" (ibid.). He observed that the masochist relives and re-enacts in his relationships a submissive devotion to and felt need for the love of a rejecting or hating love object. This love object is experienced as a later edition of the rejecting parent or preferred sibling. Therefore, Berliner argued, what looks on the face of it to be a need for punishment or self-punishment is more accurately seen as a "bid for affection". It is, he asserts, the need for the love of the person who punishes. Berliner (1958) also characterized masochism as "the means to attempt to save love through suffering" (p. 42). Suffering, he said, serves to provide the masochist with an increased sense of love-worthiness or deservingness of love. In addition, Berliner (1940) pointed out that the masochist has repressed the anger and hatred with which he reacted to his love object's rejection.

Esther Menaker (1953), who was strongly influenced by Berliner's work, agreed with him that suffering is not the goal of masochism; rather, suffering is a means to the goal of clinging to a vitally needed love object. She theorized that masochistic self-devaluation is: 1) the result of traumatic deprivation and, 2) also functions as a defence against experiencing this deprivation with its concomitant anxiety and anger and so is a means of protecting the bond to the mother. I think she stated this well when she wrote: "Faced with insufficient love, the ego survives on the illusion of love—the potentiality for which is vested in the mother—and simultaneously accounts for its absence in reality by the conception of its own worthlessness" (p. 220). Attachment is safeguarded by the embracing of unworthiness.

Berliner and Menaker's view of masochism is congruent with attachment theory. Bowlby (1988) and those who have followed him in the attachment theory tradition have argued that the human infant is programmed for attachment for the purpose of survival. Proximity to an attachment figure is crucial both to safety and a sense of safety. This paramount attachment need persists throughout the life span. Regarding the overwhelming felt necessity of maintaining vital attachments, Bowlby observed—as did Fairbairn (1952) before him—that children who are abused by their parents cling even more tightly to them. Crucial to their being able to do so is their self-protective reflex to dissociate intolerable emotional states, to say, in effect, the child to whom my parent is doing these awful things is not me.

More recently, Howell (1996) has theorized that masochism is an adaptation to trauma based on the dissociation of painful experience. Howell asserts:

> *Viewed through the lens of trauma theory, masochism is the result of post-traumatic dissociation. Contrary to appearances, which might suggest that the masochist seeks pain or finds it pleasurable, the situation is quite the opposite. The masochist has dissociated the unbearable pain to which he or she was exposed as a helpless victim. These pain cues, then, are not available to consciousness, and the masochist is deprived of a vital source of information needed for self-defense and self-management. (p. 432)*

Translating Berliner and Menaker's ideas as well as Howell's into multiple self-state terms, we can say that the masochistic person copes with the primary painful experience with caregivers—whether deprivation, abuse, rejection or some combination of these—by dissociating and defensively segregating particular self states. Specifically, the masochist's painful sense of self as rejected and/or abused and/or abandoned stemming from the original experience of rejection or abuse is dissociated along with his reactive angry-healthily entitled sense of self. These self states are dissociated in the service of maintaining a crucial attachment. Usually, what becomes the masochistic person's dominant self state is a devalued, self-blaming one, for example, "I'm so unworthy, so undeserving", as is Ned's. Therefore, in order to alter this masochistic pattern I think it is crucial that these patients be helped with identifying and integrating these disowned self states.

Case vignette

Ned, aged thirty-five, entered therapy wracked by anxiety, suffering with an intense sense of precariousness, fearing and expecting catastrophe. A few years into his second marriage and father to a young child, he worried that his life was in danger of falling apart and that he needed to be at his absolute best to have any chance of preventing this from happening. He feared that he was doomed to fall into ruin, that his efforts were destined to be futile. He was frightened that a negative, escalating domino effect would take place whenever he suffered a setback so that the anticipated setback would lead to another and so on and so forth until he reached a place of complete failure and isolation. His sense of precariousness was so intense that often when one of the higher ups at work did not smile at him he would immediately get scared that he would be fired on the spot. Similarly, when one of the bosses walked past his office, he automatically imagined that he would be criticized for not doing what he was supposed to be doing and would soon be out looking for work. His main doomsday scenario was of himself all alone in the world, having been rejected and abandoned by all of the important people in his life, living in a dingy room with one naked light bulb hanging down from the ceiling, drinking himself into oblivion.

Accompanying his sense of awful precariousness was a tendency to be relentlessly self-critical. From his view, almost any situation with which he was involved that did not work was his fault. Also it was a telling reflection of his deficiencies as a person, demonstrating his inadequacy and undeservingness. I was impressed that Ned, when speaking of himself, focused almost exclusively on his perceived shortcomings. He was particularly self-critical about not being better disciplined. He believed that the variety of self-soothing activities he employs such as smoking and drinking were testament to his lack of self-discipline, betraying an overall inferiority of character. Also, I noticed that his self-criticalness often activates his intense sense of precariousness, for example, "I drank too much last night. I'm an undisciplined fuck-up and I'm going to screw things up at work and get canned for it".

Unfortunately for him and his relationship with his wife, his tendency to be self-critical was complimented by her predilection for externalizing and blaming. She came across in his recounting as being as critical of him as he was of himself. During the first few years of our work he was desperate to please her but usually felt unable to do so. She frequently found reason to criticize him for not being involved enough with her and their child and for not being sufficiently reliable. In time he told me that his wife's family was abandoned by her father when she was a youngster. She and her mother were strongly allied in their feelings of betrayal, abandonment and anger over having been left. Appreciating his wife's transference to him was of some help in his understanding how she viewed him and lessening his tendency to blame himself for not pleasing her.

The first phase of the treatment was mainly concerned with delineating the organizing themes of Ned's subjective world, for example, "Nothing works out for me", "I'm not deserving", "It's crucial that I always please others", and so on, and beginning to understand how he came to have arrived at them. Ned began to reflect on and begin to own, probably for the first time, many of the difficulties in his life experience. They began at birth. Under circumstances that remain somewhat unclear, Ned knows that he was given up for adoption in the first few months of life.

In adulthood he learned that his biological parents were both extremely troubled people; that his mother has had multiple psychiatric hospitalizations and his father was severely alcoholic throughout his life. We appreciated how this history contributed greatly to his belief that he is damaged goods and that he is destined for disaster, and also to his conviction that he is lucky that his wife is willing to put up with him. A second major source of difficulty was that when he was at an early age his adoptive parents split-up. With his emotionally devastated adoptive mother he moved to a different part of the country, seeing his adoptive father only for a winter weekend and for a few weeks usually during summer vacations (his adoptive father made little effort to contact him between visiting times). The split-up had a variety of problematic and painful consequences for him. One was that it left his adoptive mother in a deeply depressed state from which she was slow to emerge. We have done some imagining and speculating about what that time might have been like for him, emphasizing the likely change in his experience of his relationship with his adoptive mother. From that time he has an image of her lying on her bed crying. We've wondered if one of the main ways he understood his experience at that time was that he felt he was unable to please his adoptive mother, obtain her interest and enthusiasm, that it was his fault that he could not make her happy.

Regarding his adoptive father, some of the effects of the split-up were, first, to idealize his adoptive father as the superior parent whom he most needed to please; and, second, to believe that his adoptive father was someone whose interest and approval were very hard to obtain. Nevertheless, for the remainder of his childhood, adolescence, and early adulthood he tried extremely hard to do so. He says that this desire for his adoptive father's approval is primarily what pushed him to become an achiever in school and in college, becoming a high ranking student and outstanding athlete. When his achievements were not rewarded with his father's interest and approval, he concluded that it was because he had not done well enough—reinforcing his negative self-image and resolving that he just needed to do better. He must be more disciplined and hardworking (his adoptive mother's emphasized values). Again he protected his attachment to his parent by blaming himself, believing he was not good enough to please them.

I used our knowledge of his painful history to tell him in different ways how his fear of disaster could be understood as his memory of the disasters that had already occurred in his life, along the lines of what Winnicott (1963) theorized in his "Fear of Breakdown" article—that the breakdown a patient fears is the breakdown that has already occurred. Increasingly, this has made sense to him and over time appears to have made some small dent in his reflexive pessimism and fear of catastrophe.

Another line of understanding that over time has been useful to him has involved understanding his relentless, automatic self-criticalness according to Fairbairn's (1952) concept of the moral defence, that is, how children will insist on their own badness in order to preserve their parents needed and wanted goodness. In our discussions he has felt that the hope-maintaining function of his self-blame has been of paramount importance to him.

Going back to the chronology of the treatment, in the third year of our work his marriage worsened and his wife ultimately asked for a separation. This threw him into an awful state involving panic alternating with deep depression characterized by an intense sense of abandonment as well as an intensification of his characteristic self-blame; "She left me because I am a pathetic excuse of a husband", was a typical thing for him to say at this time. He felt devastated, desperate, and totally at sea. "The bottom has fallen out of my world", he would say. Also, "I defined myself by her", and "I could only feel ok if I made her happy". The extent to which he was oriented towards trying to please and accommodate his wife became even clearer to him. In addition, at this time he saw himself as a total failure and felt very guilty towards their child. He was drinking heavily. I was very concerned about him. For the first time he was willing to come in twice a week.

In retrospect the progression of this phase of treatment was his moving from a state of shock, grief, and desperation to one of intense conflict about his increasingly divergent feelings about his wife and whether he wanted to try to maintain the marriage. Frequently I would point out to him how he would become self-blaming at times that I/most people would probably have been furious at his wife. Later on in this period when he began to allow himself to feel and express anger towards his wife he would often quickly shift to self-criticism, a sequence I would repeatedly observe and remark on to him. At these times I would tell him that I thought that perhaps he was accustomed to hiding his anger at loved ones from himself by becoming self-critical.

During this time he came to appreciate his identification with his wife as rejected and abandoned. In order to achieve this we first needed to examine his tendency to idealize her. When I pointed out in this context that his idealization of his wife was reminiscent of his idealization of his father, it immediately made a lot of sense to him. He could see that in idealizing his wife as his adoptive father he is repeating the pattern of idealizing a critical, hard-to-please, loved one. Also, that maintaining this pattern has involved his disregarding and disavowing uncomfortable feelings and perceptions about his wife as he did for so long with his adoptive father. Interestingly, we learned that one of the qualities he most admired his wife for was her unabashed pursuit of her self-interest, a quality he finds very lacking in himself. He talked about how much he enjoyed doing things for his wife, making her happy for brief periods, more achievable early in their relationship.

Exploring his strong need to do things for his wife was illuminating for us. In doing so it became evident that he felt deeply for his wife in large part because of her having been rejected and abandoned by her father. (And in an even more abrupt, clear, and dramatic way than he had been by his own father). He appreciated how deeply identified he felt with her in this very powerful way. In his words, "I see her as this hurting child whom I'm responsible for. When I married her, her mother said please take care of her, she needs it. And I promised I would. This became my life's mission". We discussed how he would deny and minimize his wife's proclivity for being unreasonable, demanding, and exploitive while instead focusing on her as a victim of rejection and abandonment by her father in identification with this disavowed sense of himself as rejected and abandoned. I emphasized that his own sense of himself as rejected and abandoned was a self state that he rarely allowed himself to recognize. Also we discussed how it was much more comfortable for him to recognize it and respond to it in his wife from a position of being centered in the rescuer–protector self state than to recognize and feel his own rejected–abandoned sense of self.

We had many sessions focused in large part on his allowing himself to more fully explore this uncomfortable sense of himself including painful memories throughout his relationship with his adoptive father, in his relationship with his adoptive mother after the divorce, and his feelings regarding being adopted. This exploration went on at the same time as his discussing his increasingly conflicted feelings about whether to resume living with his wife. A couple of months after announcing she wanted a separation his wife decided she wanted to resume the marriage. He was torn, saying things now such as: "She's like a drug. I know she's bad for me but I crave her nevertheless". At times he would accede to her unfair demands about different things and afterwards feel angry with himself for having done so. In his usual self-critical style he chastised himself for performing for her "like a monkey with an organ grinder". He now began to be able to feel and express anger about her, talking about her selfishness and unfairness.

While continuing to be in intense conflict about what he wanted to do about the marriage, he was beginning now to allow himself to occupy a more healthily entitled, angry self state. About six months into the separation, Ned, quite by chance, met a woman he quickly hit it off with. Against what he said was his better judgment (he felt it was too soon for him to begin another relationship) he began to spend time with her. She came across in his descriptions of her and their interactions as a mature, reasonable, loving adult woman. This is not to say that she didn't have some areas of vulnerability and issues, but she seemed to be a very different kind of choice for him than the two women he had previously chosen to marry. The contrast between his relationship with his estranged wife—even at its best—and with this new woman was very striking to him as well as to me.

This relationship helped the treatment in several important ways. First, as mentioned, it helped him greatly with gaining a different perspective on his relationship with his wife. It had the effect of validating many of his perceptions and feelings about his relationship with his wife that he did not as yet have full confidence in. Second, he felt he did not deserve to be treated so well and to be with a woman as good as his girlfriend. Frequently when being treated lovingly he found it difficult to accept, hard to take in. At these times we noticed he would strain to find some reason to devalue his girlfriend. Third, his girlfriend, unlike his two former wives, did not need or want emotional rescuing. Thus, the relationship soon became psychologically disorienting for him but again in a highly useful way. During this phase he appreciated that he had a pattern of not staying with more nurturing women. Instead, he was in the habit of leaving them for needy, self-absorbed women such as his former wives. He often worried that he would disappoint his girlfriend or hurt her at times when he felt the pull to go back with his wife to whom he continued to feel attached. In addition, he was, of course, scared about getting emotionally involved again after his very disappointing experiences in his two marriages.

Perhaps as important as anything else for our work this relationship allowed him to have greater perspective on key painful assumptions that have done so much guiding of his conduct and shaping the way he has felt about himself and his life. In brief these assumptions are: that he is a defective, undeserving person who does not deserve to be treated well, who needs to be continually proving himself worthy to a critical, hard-to-please loved one whose love he needs to earn through achievement, sacrifice, suffering, and submission. Questioning this framework of guiding assumptions has been disorienting and anxiety-provoking for him. It threatens his sense of the "me" he knows. More recently, sessions are mainly focused on this process, the disorientation and anxiety he is sometimes aware of and on his tendency to retreat from it into the felt security of what he calls his safe "cocoon of unhappiness". Also, there are times now when he reports feeling happy, probably happier than he has ever felt. However, this is only for a few days at a time at best, he reports. And when his mood returns to its customary dark, anxious place, he says, it feels as if these happy times never happened. I tell him he's understandably conflicted—understandably scared of the change he so very much wants. This is where we are now.

Transference–countertransference

Now I want to say a bit about our relationship and the transference–countertransference configuration. Ned has been understandably slow to trust and depend on me. In the first couple of years especially I made comments to the effect that this was to be expected given his very painful experiences of rejection with his biological parents, his adoptive father and step-father. During this period his demeanour was quite compliant and eager to please. Also, particularly in the first few years we dealt a fair amount with his expectations that I was feeling critical of him but doing a good job of hiding it. He thought he was doing poorly in therapy and found it hard to believe that I did not agree with his negative assessment. During this time he generally gave the impression that I was of no importance to him and sometimes would indicate that given his financial strains maybe he should go to a low cost clinic. I felt somewhat hurt and rejected and braced myself for abandonment. In time I wondered to myself and later to him if among other things he was letting me get a sense of what he so often felt. I have also experienced feelings of being forgotten and abandoned in small ways such as his sometimes not returning my phone calls when these have been calls he has requested I make to him about alternate scheduling arrangements.

In our relationship I see many examples of Bromberg's contention that in treatment dissociation becomes an interpersonal process, a dynamic element in the therapeutic relationship. I will mention two of the more striking examples. First, for a long time I was the one of us who felt angry, who carried his warded-off anger towards his wife for mistreating him. Second, I find myself often moving into the rescuer role with him as I find my rescue reflexes stirred up more by him than most people with whom I work. I go more out of my way for him—extend myself more (rescheduling appointments, financial arrangements, and so on)—than with most other patients. On that score, I have allowed him to build up a balance during a time of severe financial stress when he was divorcing his second wife and seeing me twice a week. He has been paying me back consistently but more slowly than promised. I have just started trying to get him interested in our looking at what this may mean for him and between us. I do wonder if in time this will allow us to have his angry-healthy-entitled self state be a more recognized participant in our relationship. I suspect this disavowed sense of self may be embedded in the slowness of payment issue because lately I find myself feeling angrier with him than I usually do. Also, I wonder and hope that this may represent—among other meanings—his beginning to allow himself to reveal the part of him that does not want to do what he thinks he is supposed to do with me. If so, it would be a welcome advance from his usual reflexively compliant posture. To return to the rescuer role, sometimes I suspect that our shared, usually unstated recognition that we both tend towards occupying this role and self state has been one constituent of the bond that has grown between us.

In the past few months I have become aware of a change in our relatedness. I feel more seen and recognized by him as a person as opposed to solely being the therapist or analyst. I feel a much stronger sense of connection between us. I have been pleased to see that Ned can allow himself to be openly vulnerable with me. On a few occasions he has cried in response to things I have said to him that have touched him. This is something that would have been unthinkable in the first few years of treatment.

Discussion

In treating patients such as Ned who have a masochistic pattern of relatedness with loved ones I've found it useful to include the MSST model in my clinical approach. I believe that there are certain divisions in self-experience that perpetuate masochistic relatedness and so are crucial to address. I have found that addressing dissociated areas of vulnerability that are identified with and selectively responded to in the loved one, such as Ned's dissociated sense of himself as rejected and abandoned, has resulted in considerable therapeutic benefit.

One of the reasons I decided to write this paper was that my clinical experience was at variance with much of the literature on masochism and masochistic relating. The literature on masochism, especially the large segment of that literature written from a drive theory perspective, has focused almost exclusively on the role of sadism and anger in understanding and treating masochistic relatedness. While I do not dispute that addressing sadism and anger—or the dissociated angry self state in MSST terms—is a crucial component in the treatment of these patients, I have found that there are other critical areas that require considerable therapeutic focus such as disowned self states characterized by a high degree of personal vulnerability that are often unconsciously identified with and selectively responded to in the loved one.

The approach I am suggesting is derived from the more relational theoretical perspective on masochism and masochistic relating that I find best exemplified in the work of Berliner, Menaker, and Howell and consistent with attachment theory. Central to this perspective is viewing masochism as a complex characterlogical adaptation employed to maintain a vitally needed attachment bond in the face of deprivation, abuse, or neglect, or some combination of these experiences. As we know, in order to maintain a vitally needed positive tie to a parent or caregiver, children resort to dissociating the resulting painful self states such as rejection and abandonment as well as self states characterized by the anger that is reactive to suffering privation and abuse. These painful self states remain unformulated and are enacted in subsequent relationships—as Ned did with his wife. These self states, experienced as threatening to the essential positive tie and to a sense of emotional safety and security, nevertheless exert considerable influence on the personality. Moreover, Ned safeguarded his tie with his parents by means of adopting and maintaining his dominant sense of self as inadequate and undeserving, a psychic operation that took a terrible toll on his self-esteem and self-confidence.

Also I want to emphasize that the dynamic I have described and illustrated in the overview of Ned's treatment is an extremely potent one. For example, it was very emotionally compelling for Ned to want to rescue his wife from her pain, to help her heal from her rejection and abandonment by her father. His unrecognized identification with his wife in this way created in him a powerful sense of connection with her. This is understandable when we consider that finding in her what he did not allow himself to know and feel in himself probably is like finding someone who felt like a perfect fit with himself (which indeed in this way it was) or perhaps it's more accurate to put it in terms of finding someone who feels like completing himself. In addition, as discussed, it served at the same time to keep this most vulnerable sense or part of himself dissociated, out of awareness. Appreciating this dynamic helped Ned and I understand why, for so long, he found it inconceivable to consider dissolving his marriage. For him, ending his mission to rescue his wife from her pain had felt tantamount to giving up on his hope of being healed himself.

References

Berliner, B. (1940). Libido and reality in masochism. *Psychoanalytic Quarterly*. 9: 322–333.
——. (1942). The concept of masochism. *Pschoanalytic Review*. 29: 386–400.
——. (1947). On some psychodynamics of masochism. *Psychoanalytic Quarterly*. 16: 459–471.
——. (1958). The role of object relations in moral masochism. *Psychoanalytic Quarterly*. 27: 38–56.
Bowlby, J. (1988). *A Secure Base*. London: Routledge Press.
Bromberg, P. (1998). *Standing in the Spaces*. Hillsdale, New Jersey: The Analytic Press.
——. (2006). *Awakening the Dreamer*. Hillsdale, New Jersey: The Analytic Press.
Davies, J.M. (1996). "Linking the 'pre-analytic' with the postclassical: integration, dissociation, and the multiplicity of the unconscious process". *Contemporary Psychoanalysis*. 32: 553–576.
Fairbairn, W.R.D. (1952). *Psychoanalytic Studies of the Personality*. London, England: Routledge & Kegan Paul.
Freud, S. (1905). Three Essays on the Theory of Sexuality. *Standard Edition*. 7: 125–245.
Freud, S. (1919). A Child is Being Beaten. *Standard Edition*. 17.
——. (1924). The Economic Problem of Masochism. *Standard Edition*. 19.
Howell, E. (1996). Dissociation in Masochism and Psychopathic Sadism. *Contemporary Psychoanalysis*. 32: 427–453.
Janet, P. (1907). *The Major Symptoms of Hysteria*. New York: MacMillan.
Krafft-Ebing, R.F. (1895). *Psychopathia Sexualis*. London: F.A. Davis.
Menaker, E. (1953). "Masochism—a defense reaction of the ego". *Psychoanalytic Quarterly*. 22: 205–220.

Slavin, M. and Kriegman, D. (1992). "Why the analyst needs to change: Toward a theory of conflict, negotiation, and mutual influence in the therapeutic process". *Psychoanalytic Dialogues*. 8: 247–284.

Stern, D. (1997). *Unformulated Experience: from dissociation to imagination in psychoanalysis*. Hillsdale, New Jersey: The Analytic Press.

Winnicott, D.W. (1963). *The Fear of Breakdown in Psychoanalytic Explorations*. C. Winnicott, R. Shepherd, and M. Davis (eds). Cambridge, MA.: Harvard University Press, 1989.

PART IV

WHEN EXPERIENCE HAS
A MIND OF ITS OWN

CHAPTER NINE

Things that go bump in the night: Secrets after dark

Jean Petrucelli, Ph.D.

hen I was five years old, one of my favorite experiences was to have a sleepover at my Italian grandmother's house. It was a house filled with magical things—silk sheets, delicious smells of pasta, coffee and garlic—and I could always count on Tony Bennett or Frank Sinatra to be singing in the background. There was just one thing I wasn't so crazy about. My Grandmother, although well-meaning, was insistent that when it was bedtime, it was bedtime. So instead of singing me a lullaby or lulling me to sleep, she'd tell me her version of a bedtime story. It went something like this: "*From ghoulies and ghosties to four legged beasties ... Giovonna Maria Theresina Petruccelli [as she would call me], rememberrr ... there are thingsa that go bumpa in the nighta*". Out of the corner of my eye I would see her wink as she said it, trying to only "sort-of" scare me so I wouldn't get out of bed. And on one level ... it sort-of worked. I stayed in bed. However, my mind travelled to many a scary place. I never told her that I was afraid of these "thingsa". Pretending to be brave and being the good grandchild, I had to hold the secret that I was scared. Appearing brave allowed me to believe the fantasy that my grandmother admired my bravery. Not acknowledging my fear relegated this experience to a more private domain.

One could say that I had the luxury or burden of choosing to keep a secret. But keeping secrets is not always a conscious decision. Many powerful internal and external forces often prevent the truth from surfacing. For example, dissociation, experienced as the numbness or psychic closing off that so often accompanies trauma and follows in its wake, can facilitate and contribute to the silence of secrets. The defense that helps people to cope at one point ultimately complicates their lives at another. Dissociation is not-knowing that there is a secret you are keeping, and this secret-keeping is often an attempt to protect both an aspect of self, as well as sometimes, those around the self. Secrets kept by dissociation exist between two worlds—with one world not acknowledging the uncomfortable existence of the other. Something which is dissociated in a person necessitates the existence of that other world.

With secrets and secret lives there is a split, a "this" (before) and a "that" (after)—two parallel existences. In a certain way, this split allows one to bury a part of oneself alive. Kwawer (2005) has suggested that, for some, the purpose of a secret life arguably is to bring a livelier, intimate, and energized part of oneself out of the dark. This parallel existence, the experience of living in two worlds, is often perpetuated in the realm of addiction by a relationship to a substance, be it food or drug. The use of a substance helps facilitate the process of dissociation by narrowing one's range of self-experience. In analytic treatment I believe the best way to address an addiction is to coax it out of hiding by introducing the patient to his multiple addresses, the various places he lives, unaware. In order to do this the therapist has to visit these places herself, losing and finding her way along with the patient.

Working with patients suffering from various addictions, one quickly discovers the deep level of entrenchment that the addiction and the compulsive behavior have over their lives. What you also see is how the addictive behavior or symptom is an "adaptive" attempt at a solution to a much deeper psychic issue. If, as Adam Phillips (1993) suggests, phobias are where the wild things are, perhaps addictions are where the wild things go to get high. If secrets and secret keeping are a part of this "adaptive" response, then one's personal truth is also embedded in the secret. This ultimately plays a role in shaping one's life.

What happens when one struggles to not-know cognitively what one knows affectively? Does a secret life begin in desperation? As analysts, we need to be mindful that secrets may need to be allowed their own place in time and in our work. What happens when secrets are revealed that feel like a tsunami in their attempts to break through non-consciousness? Being conscious of balancing our own emotional experiences with those of our patients may help them to develop secure attachments and a sense of agency. This is crucial because when attention is focused in one arena, the real action often is in what is *not* being seen—the secret—because it is not being expressed in words, but is being felt through enactment.

I would like to explore the role of secrets and the different effects of secrets revealed with two of my patients, both of whom live double lives.

Stella

Twilight foreshadows darkness, and danger slinks in darkness. Darkness for twenty-year-old Stella is cloaked in a layered secret life, whether it be the secrecy of her bulimia at home and in school growing up, or now in her young adult life. Stella was a women's studies major at an Ivy League School by day and a professional dominatrix by night—although she prefers the title "Adult Entertainer in the fetish industry". When I asked how she got the job she replied simply, "Oh, I went on Craig's list, answered an ad and the money was good". She added quickly though, "I'm not a mean dominatrix though; I don't work with needles". I responded nonchalantly and knowingly, "Oh". And we nodded as if we were talking about her working at Starbucks.

Overweight as a child, by junior high school Stella weighed 198 lbs at 5'7". Her bulimia began when she was 14; initially she lost 40 pounds. She began her story by revealing the following shameful secret. Craving attention and feeling that boys didn't pay attention to her, she performed oral sex on an unpopular older boy on the football team. In a matter-of fact manner, she told me how she had read about how to give a blow job in *Cosmo* and then simply followed the instructions. This boy also hurt her while forcing himself on her with all his might. He was unable to penetrate her and she experienced excruciating pain, but he disregarded her pleas for him to stop. Needless to say, she broke up with him. He, then, bragged to the guys about the blow job. She called him a liar in front of people. He cried. She later discovered when she could not insert a tampon that she had an imperforate hymen that required surgery. After learning about mutual consent, she felt this boy had sexually assaulted and abused her, but Stella was dissociated in telling this story to me.

Desperate loneliness and feelings of worthlessness prompted Stella to engage with others who confirmed for her, by gut-wrenching betrayal, that people seduce and then betray. For Stella "love sucks". This issue of the transmission of pain and the concept of physical and mental penetration became a poignant dynamic to explore in terms of Stella's work as a dominatrix. In her history, the male causes her pain, she shames him, and he cries. In her adult work, she causes the male pain, shames him, and he begs for more. She feels contempt throughout, but having grown up in a deadened depressed family she also feels her vitality through the expression of her contempt. Being a dominatrix offered her an outlet to express her contempt for herself and her clients—men.

This is a complex case and in keeping with the theme of this chapter I have chosen to focus on a specific issue in our clinical work, namely the impact of the revealing of Stella's secret life. Over time as our work developed, Stella was secretly hoping for an opportunity to be able to give up living with secrets but was trapped financially—this job paid for her college, living expenses and vacations. All of which she paid for with a hefty emotional price.

Then … the unexpected happened. Stella's mother was anony-mously sent a picture of Stella as a dominatrix with the word "pros-titute" written on it, and Stella was given the "opportunity" to reveal her secret. She willingly embraced it as an opportunity to give up this line of work. Her experience was one of "orgasmic" relief. She was busted, the "game" was finally over, and the layers of denial in the family were, at last, being disrupted. Stella used the revelation of her secret life as an entrée into embracing the possibility of freeing herself from the psychic prison she had inhabited.

Stella had dissociated the many ways in which she had always felt bad about herself as a kid, from her low energy level to her bod-ily shame and disgust. She began to tie these ideas to why being a dominatrix itself was on some level, a maladaptive attempt to be in control and cause bodily pain to another—to bring *them* to their knees. At least *she* was in charge.

Stella's concern with being seen and judged, coupled with her desire to be the "good girl" growing up and the "good patient" with me, fosters the need for secrets to be kept, with secrets being a form of rebellion, the safe and hidden way she can be more real. Stella, being the "good girl" growing up, had now found a way to be naughty. For Stella, secrets are an expression of anti-compliance (Canarelli 2008; personal communication). As Stella is getting better at discriminating/regulating what to take in from me, there is less of a feeling of her placating me or worrying about my response. She is getting better at being openly her own person in treatment.

Recently, Stella has been discovering family secrets related to a history of mental illness, suicide, depression and addiction; all things that were kept hidden. Some of these things she "sort-of-knew" but could not let herself *know* she knew. She is angry at being left in the dark and feels that this information could have been useful to her understanding her depression earlier on. She also feels anger and contempt for her father who would come to her for help with problems with her siblings rather than go to her mother, saying, "Now don't tell your Mom". Stella does not want to be the secret keeper anymore.

When Stella was able to express all that was within her, especially the more self-destructive, "disgusting" parts of herself, the process between us started to feel very different. Stella was able to risk investing more in her relationship with me. She could tolerate more uncertainty within her and as a result our exchanges began to feel more alive, genuine and honest. Telling her secret allowed Stella to live in a more integrated way, something she had wanted but could not get to. Her family's involvement initiated the process. This then allowed access to other disgusting shameful aspects of self which freed her up emotionally in the treatment and in her life. Opening up one secret in the family took the lid off Pandora's Box.

However, it is not the revealing of the secrets that in and of itself produces the therapeutic outcome. Why? Because when the mind deals with unbearable affective overload through dissociation and creating double lives, it needs to make sure that its secrets are surrendered only when they are truly ready to be heard. This requires an other who *truly* wants to hear them. Let me tell you about Anthony.

Anthony

Twilight foreshadows darkness, and danger slinks in darkness. Darkness, for twenty-one year-old body builder and personal trainer by day, was the arena for his other life. Anthony was having a clandestine taboo love affair filled with anticipation fueling excitement, intimacy enveloped in secrecy, and the experience of guilt and remorse when it was over. In the middle of the night, several nights during the week, Anthony engaged in a secret "love" affair which sometimes led to roaming the streets of Manhattan or to his parent's kitchen. This secret love affair took the form of night bingeing and this was ... the single most, important thing in his life. If he was hanging out with the boys or on a date with a girl, he still eagerly anticipated coming back to his "secret love", and no person seemed to have as great a pull on him as did food. He openly acknowledged that sadly, whatever girl he was out with didn't stand a chance. He compared his first sexual experience to "doing laundry"... only engaging in it to lose his virginity. Anthony added that sex doesn't last long—he's not interested in giving or receiving oral sex, gets bored quickly and never has had a long relationship. In fact, he consistently loses interest at about the one month mark.

However, his interest in his "secret love" does not wane. This nightly ritual structures his daily routine, taking precedence over family, social activities, hobbies and work. Once in this state, "the food zone", he would describe the experience itself as having a mind of its own. To Anthony, night bingeing felt more "pleasurable and safe" than the possibility of real human contact.

Anthony has lived with a childhood fear that things could happen to him when he is asleep. As a kid he would sleep with a blanket over his head—like a hood. He feared that little warriors would attack him. He would get up and then sleep in his parent's bed.

At 5'8" Anthony's weight fluctuated from 142–170 lbs over the course of our work, but he was basically all muscle. Even with all of the night bingeing, one couldn't detect an ounce of fat on him. He's a good looking athletic type, a sort of dark haired, introverted Mark Walberg meets Derek Jeter meets Jake Gyllenhaal ... a little shy, mild-mannered, impishly charming, equipped with a good sense of humour, and seemingly outwardly motivated.

During the day, Anthony maintained a healthy food plan, although it sometimes bordered on being deprivational given his level of physical exercise. At night, like clockwork, after being asleep for an hour or two, Anthony would wake and binge for hours, sometimes going out to one delicatessen after the next. His caloric intake could range from 2,000–3,500 calories at a pop. The signal that "allowed" him to stop was reaching a state of anaesthetized numbness and insuring that his stomach hurt. Anthony would eat all of the forbidden foods that he wouldn't allow himself during the day. The next day's food hangover left Anthony feeling disgusted, debilitated, and despairing. He felt tortured by his guilt, remorse, and shame.

While symptomatic change is a significant goal for someone with an eating disorder or an addiction, just as important is the therapist's attempt to enter the dissociated world of the alienated self and to allow it entry into the world of the therapeutic relationship. Finding a way to gain access into Anthony's secret life, this ritualized, tangled and unique relationship with food felt like vying for the role of "mistress" to his affair. But it would only be through the process of knowing Anthony through *direct relatedness* to those aspects of self that cannot speak on their own, that they would ever find a voice. Anthony responded to experiences with action more than through the process of talking and understanding. The action of his night bingeing was a vehicle for both the expression and the containment of his unmeasured, unmastered and sort-of-known experience and emotion. The secret night bingeing concretized and embodied the danger inherent in any intimate exchange.

It terms of symptom alleviation, we were at a standstill. Under good enough circumstances a child develops both a mind of his own and the ability to accept the mind of another person without surrendering his own mind (Bach 2006). I wondered if Anthony feared that giving up the night bingeing might leave him vulnerable with me because vulnerability would require openness to new experience. Was he worried that this would be a potential place for him to "lose his mind", or that a new shared experience might bring intense, painful and threatening feelings of shame? As I saw it, in trying to provide a good enough environment where information could flow easily and negotiation would be possible, I was offering a variety of ways that this might happen by paying attention to what happens not only when suggestions are followed, but also when they are not.

I wanted to be a nurturer and it seemed that he wanted to be nurtured. But I felt some disguised immediate resistance. This resistance was not a clear vision because it was the articulation of a part of him we could not yet know. It was an "affective" truth that had no cognitive formulation. I experienced Anthony's emptiness with his hunger. At the same time, I wondered if the trigger for Anthony numbing himself was the awareness of a wish to be more connected.

Anthony was a difficult non-difficult patient. On the surface he appeared "easy" in that he did not provoke uncomfortable reactions in me; he posed no threat to my organizing principles; our work proceeded without stormy ruptures or rage-filled demonstrations of my failures as a containing object. In fact, in the first year of treatment, our work was often so even-tempered and uneventful that it lacked a sense of vitality and tended to be very slow. Yet it was this combination of the lack of vitality in him and my overworking to "enliven" him that became my warning sign that something else was going on. His vitality was not to be shared.

I tried, through self-reflection, to understand what felt like a stuck treatment process. There were sessions when I felt exhausted after seeing him, as though I had worked much too hard, yielding less than fruitful results, even though his intentions always seemed well meaning. In some way the harder I worked, the more the symptom seemed to worsen, even though, he was, over time, more engaged in the room. I struggled to find ways to connect with him, common areas of interest, trying to discover what he might feel passionate about, and yet I always came up empty handed. He continued, politely, to tell me that the only thing he was truly interested in was the food at night. Day in and day out, he felt ashamed about it and upset with himself after every binge.

As time went on and he continued to talk only about food, I became aware of how my attention would wander, and I began to experience him as numbing me so that I too would not feel anything or think anything. Was I protecting myself from the lack of attunement in the room? If so, I was beginning to wonder if his bingeing numbness was a protection against the painful loss of an attunement to an other. Was our mutual goodness predicated on falsehood, on the illusion of feeding, and of being fed? Anthony was not about to give up this secret affair for me or anyone.

It was about 5:30 pm ... twilight ... when I received an urgent message from Anthony's mother, Maria, on my answering machine. Maria said, "I need to tell you something about Anthony's behavior that is worrying me". Immediately after telling Anthony that I had received this concerned message from his mother, he gave me permission to speak with her. And he did this without batting an eye. I asked if he knew what this was about, and he said he wasn't sure but he didn't mind if I spoke to her. So I did.

Anthony's mother was concerned that he had stolen some of her Ambien, and possibly some codeine, and that he had denied the charge, something which seemed abnormal to her. She was afraid that he had become a really good liar because he was denying it so convincingly. I listened wondering if Anthony was feeling the need to numb himself more. Or was the food anesthesia not doing the trick in the same way any more? What was going on that he felt he needed to up the ante? If it wasn't true, then what was his mother's real concern at this point ... and why now?

Maria also mentioned that it would be helpful for me to speak with her therapist, with whom she had worked with for over thirty years, in order to understand more of the family dynamics. There was just one piece of information that would have to be kept a secret from Anthony but it might help. At the time, this stipulation didn't strike me as being central to what was going on, but once I found out the family information I felt differently. I sort-of-knew I had let myself be pulled into the family system and its web of secrets and I wasn't sure how to extract myself.

Every family lives with secrets. However, Anthony's family was built upon a foundation of secrets and double lives. Anthony's parents had been married for thirty years and had four children—and many secrets. Secret number 1: Anthony's father is homosexual. The four children (ages 28, 26, 24, 22) don't "know". Secret number 2: This marriage is Anthony's mother's third. She had two brief marriages when she was very young. During that time she was also morbidly obese. Secret number 3: Throughout many years of her present marriage, Anthony's mother has had a long-term affair with a man who lived in another part of the world, and so she travelled a lot. This was part of the parent's arrangement. Secret number 4: Anthony's mother is currently very ill. Non Secret Fact: According to Anthony's parents, they love each other very much and have a close, connected relationship.

Knowing this information pulled me into the family system. I was caught in an enactment where I now had to keep secrets. Even having Anthony's permission to speak to his mother's therapist, I was uncomfortable knowing something about his life that he didn't know I knew and, to make matters worse, it was something he himself did not know. It was not until I began writing this paper that I was able to see the extent of my own dissociation in the enactment we were in. I had dissociated the fact that by having the information, I had compromised our "family of two" in what I told myself was Anthony's best interest. While I have to admit it has been central to the way the case has unfolded, and while family involvement with an eating disorder case is often the norm, it has been extremely helpful for me to think about the complexities of my involvement. In this case, I became the temporary holder of family secrets and temporarily had to live a double life. I felt my disease in knowing something that I couldn't reveal I knew, and I couldn't escape my disease by dissociating. Being caught up in this way showed me how valuable dissociation can be. In an odd way, I sort-of envied Anthony, because, unlike him, I didn't have the luxury of dissociating what I knew.

At the same time as I was feeling uncomfortable with "the knowing", I also felt excited and hopeful. I wondered if this was the "missing piece" that might finally shake up the treatment so we could stop dancing in the dark. With Anthony's permission, his parents had asked to come in for a session, their second in three years. They had begun to wonder if secrets and secret keeping might have taken a quiet toll on the family, particularly on Anthony.

Secrets had been sanctioned consciously and unconsciously, barters and bargains had been made, all in the service of maintaining a surface illusion that they were just like other families. In this family, everybody's sexuality is dissociated. In such a system, each member dissociates the part of himself or herself that doesn't "fit" the family. In the session with Anthony's parents, we talked about how and when secrets are sanctioned in the family system, how each member learns, in different ways, that having a secret life (or another life) keeps them connected to the family system. For example, Anthony's brother was secretly addicted to online poker and computer games such as *Second Life*. Additionally, it is interesting to note that one of Anthony's sisters, undoubtedly the healthiest of the siblings, has made a career choice as an actress.

Anthony's parents had a very positive response to talking about this. As soon as they walked out of my office, Maria left the following message: *"Thank you for this session. It was very helpful to us. It was really amazing that as we were walking down the street it popped right into my head why I had wanted you to know the whole story because of course, my therapist and my husband's therapist, were also in on the secret and you weren't. Thank you for putting the pieces together to help our son. We are thinking that we may want to finally tell our kids"*.

And so they did. Outwardly, Anthony seemed remarkably "fine" with the news. He said he was very surprised. He didn't know at what age people stopped having sex and it had always seemed like there was simply no lust in his parent's marriage. He said that they seemed like "old people" to him. Anthony said his father just came out and said, "I'm gay". He explained that around the time Anthony was seven or eight his father had revealed this to his mother and that they had decided that since they were best friends they would remain together. Interestingly, it was at this same time that Anthony saw a child therapist for another matter. He had started acting "like a baby" speaking baby talk all the time. In hindsight, clearly this was Anthony's unconscious reaction to his parent's dynamic and perhaps his unspoken attempt to "ensure" they stay together to take care of "baby".

Anthony's father told him that only three people in the world knew. Anthony asked his parents with genuine love and concern, "Have you guys been OK?" and his father replied, "It was rough before your mother knew and then a great relief".

I kept trying to focus on Anthony's experience of that moment. He said his heart had started racing, that he had felt shocked. His parents asked him if he was mad. He told them no, that he was extremely grateful for them staying together for the sake of the kids and the family, that he respected them even more for that. Anthony told me that he felt bad for his Father. It made him sad and he imagined his father was unhappy, that he had had to live his whole life suppressing his true feelings. I commented that he, too, knows all too well what it feels like to live a double secret life. He agreed and continued by saying that he was glad that they waited to tell him at this age. He emailed his father that night to tell him how much he loved him because he didn't want him to feel bad.

Anthony's response felt pretty genuine and selfless, but that speaks to the heart of his problem. He cannot allow himself to feel his full range of feelings, be it anger, desire, or disappointment. He cannot allow himself to feel anything that might place his feelings and interests before that of his family's welfare. Anthony can only hunger in private. Anthony's intellectual understanding that secrets are sanctioned in the family and part of the family system, as well as the fact that he too plays his part in having a secret life, served to enable him to flee rapidly from "knowing" his complex affective experience. In the room he was pensive, thoughtful, scared, and confused.

I suggested that we meet twice a week for a couple of weeks to try to process this before it went underground. He agreed, and then proceeded to cancel the next six sessions calling me each time to cancel and, of course, asking that I call him back to make sure I had received his message. Sometimes we would speak on the phone, and I addressed how his difficulty in showing up might be a reaction to the news and that maybe I had pushed him too quickly. He, of course, said he was "fine with this family news" but couldn't understand why his bingeing had suddenly become worse. I persisted in reaching out to him, and he finally came in.

On some level, Anthony enacts the "not me" sexy guy who feels passionately and thereby keeps his rage and anger out of the room. The "nasty stuff" needs to be kept in the closet. He is invested in being the sweet nice boy with me and with his parents. When he can't tolerate seeing me, Anthony sometimes misses sessions—but he always calls to let me know. Not wanting to fully "break off" the relationship, Anthony always asks for a call back, just to be sure that I received the message. I believe he is making sure that I hold him in mind when he isn't there. He may be phobic of seeing anybody that "knows". Our further work will be to find a way to talk about what *remains* to be talked about, including his "not-so-nice" feelings about my involvement. I am the one now trying to talk about what must not be spoken. So when Anthony misses his sessions he is trying to stay away—trying to change what he can in his *outside* world, which is his only defense. It is for now the only way he can maintain the dissociation.

We talked about my putting a demand on him to deal with this information by encouraging him to come more frequently. I expressed my concern that I had, after learning of the new information, missed something in my zeal—and suddenly I could feel what it was: I'd been excited, and he'd been saying, "Hold your horses, I'm not ready". I kept trying to help him connect the dots, but the more I tried the less he did.

My need to "figure it out" was unintentionally exacerbating the interpersonal danger of intrusion and coercion. In the face of such interpersonal tensions, Anthony would retreat to food. The intensification of his symptom could also be thought of as an opportunity to know, and that his darker self aspects were hovering in the room. Paying attention and staying attuned to the shifting feeling states in the room, bodily or otherwise, can often give us clues that something is happening.

While believing in the value of bringing light to things not fully or sort-of-known, we often fail to respect a person's fight to keep meaning *obscured*. Perhaps it is a more difficult struggle for a patient suffering from addiction. If so, the connection between addiction and secrets necessitates having to be especially careful handling those secrets once they are discovered.

Inviting both the night-eating aspect of Anthony's self-experience and his feelings about his father into the room, allows him access to a part of himself, which was previously contained and dissociated, expressed only through consistent unpremeditated and premeditated secret behavior. Like his parents, Anthony had learned that he could only experience his confusion, hunger and self-interest in secret. Inviting him to share these parts of himself, with me, and mine with *him*, will involve him in being more safely in touch with his aggression and his darker side. Maybe then he could grasp life and feel passionately about others rather than food.

With secrets revealed in the family, Anthony was forced to experience an over-stimulating world of too many new truths which proved to be too much for him. He now needs more access to the role of "aggressor"—by deciding just how much and when he can tolerate taking in new information. As evidenced by a recent dream, it is a process that has already begun. In this dream, he was able to express his dissociated rage—towards me, in part, as the instigator of revealed secrets. This dream occurred after his parents revealed their secret to his brother and the boys talked together about it.

The dream: "My brother and I had killed two people ... no, three random people—it had something to do with my mother. She was deciding if she was going to turn us in". He adds as an aside: "I had watched the prison show *Oz* that day. Then, in the dream, we were in the car, and I was trying to convince her how bad it would be to turn us in ... how bad it would be for us to be in jail". Anthony went on to say, "It was a long strange dream, pretty dramatic, scary and intense. I think one of the people I killed was the doorman in my building. I remember feeling that I had to do it—but I didn't want to—so I suffocated him". I playfully asked Anthony if I should be worried. He laughed and said, "No ... I really like my doorman; I talk with him about sports all the time. The other two people— I don't remember ... but it was me, my mom and my brother in a boat and we buried some of the bodies there".

Thinking that the doorman is the gatekeeper of all secrets, I asked him, "Why the doorman? Did he see something? Was he in on the secret? Or your secret?" Anthony said, "You know, I thought about that but he never worked at night so he never witnessed my comings and goings".

I wonder if the comings and goings in the treatment enacted Anthony's experience of me as the gatekeeper to his secret life, the place where the bodies were buried.

Summary

We could speculate why undoing the secret had a better outcome initially with Stella than with Anthony. Stella owned her secret—it was her narrative of truth. She was in a state of readiness and longing to rely less on dissociative behaviors. Stella was more ready to integrate the dissociated aspects of self into her current life. Anthony needed a different process. Although he had his own secret and secret life, his narrative truth about his family and himself was shattered with the revelation of family secrets that was forced upon him. Putting together the old and the new was too much for him. He was given a binge of information and, in a way, the treatment underwent a trauma. To regulate his trauma he had to purge me, the therapy, and his family ... for awhile. His night bingeing remains the essence of his vitality.

Some of the ways that the mind deals with experience is by keeping secrets and creating double lives that seem to have lives of their own. These secrets may need to be revealed only when they are truly ready to be known. Sometimes, however, as Anthony's case highlights, the systemic way of working with patients in the eating disorder realm means that the therapist learns things before the patient is ready to hear them.

Revealing her secret freed Stella and helped her move from dissociation to a true coherence of the many parts of her self-experience. I revealed Anthony's secret and by discovering it the way I did, I gave him another of those things that go bump in the night—those wild creatures—his ghoulies and ghosties that represent his darker, more primitive side but also his passion and vitality. For now, this not–me part can only be maintained in secret. In their family, Anthony's parents may have felt more immediate relief from the burden of keeping the secret. For Anthony it will take more time for his life to grow increasingly dimensional. I am hopeful.

References

Bach, S. (2006). *Getting from Here To There: Analytic Love, Analytic Process.* Hillsdale, NJ: The Analytic Press, p. 57.

Cannarelli, J. (2008). Personal communication.

Kwawer, J. (2005). As quoted in The Secret Lives of Just Everybody. B. Carey (author), *The New York Times*, 11 January, 2005.

Phillips, A. (1993). *On Kissing, Tickling and Being Bored: Psychoanalytic Essays on the Unexamined Life.* Harvard University Press: Cambridge, Massuchusetts.

CHAPTER TEN

Psychoanalytic treatment of panic attacks[1]

Mark J. Blechner, Ph.D.

Panic attacks are a major mental health problem in the United States today. It has been estimated that between 1% and 3% of the general population experience panic attacks during their lifetimes (Schuman et al. 1985; Katon 1996). Patients with panic attacks use up a lot of time in medical practices and emergency rooms, when they show up repeatedly, thinking they are having a heart attack or a stroke or some other medical crisis. Of course, tests have to be run to make sure that they are not really having a heart attack or a stroke, so a lot of time and money is wasted. I think that psychoanalytic therapists should be the first line of treatment for patients with panic attacks, but that is not the case today. The conventional wisdom is that such patients should be sent to a cognitive-behavioural therapist or a psychopharmacologist. This is not good for the patients, and it is not good for psychoanalysts. I will explain why.

I will describe three patients I have seen in treatment. I will summarize what I observed with them and then discuss the theoretical implications of this data. After presenting my own data, I will summarize some of the generalizations that have been made about panic

---

[1] An earlier draft of this chapter was published in Blechner (2007).

patients and then evaluate them in terms of my own clinical data. I will suggest some ways in which we might revise our theory of panic attacks and test out a newly formulated theory.

When I was first referred a patient with panic attacks twenty-two years ago, I realized I had learned next to nothing specific during my training about how to work with panic attacks. It meant that I had no special plan to help my patient, whom I will call Mr. A, but in a way, I was fortunate. It also meant that I could listen to Mr. A with an open mind and try something original with him. This was fine with him, since he had already been seen by a number of experts, and he was not happy with the result. Mr. A had his first panic attack when he was twenty-eight years of age. He felt chest pains and shortness of breath, thought he was having a heart attack, and was rushed to the emergency room. There, all tests on his heart function were normal. He was told he had a panic disorder and was referred to a psychiatrist who prescribed Xanax (alprazolam). About a month later, he had another acute episode and again was rushed to the emergency room. The findings were the same, and they increased his medication dose. That is when he decided he wanted another approach; he was afraid there would be yet another attack, plus he did not like the wooziness he felt from the medication. He was referred to me.

He was a young, vigorous man, extremely ambitious and already quite wealthy. I asked Mr. A if there was anything going on in his life that could actually be making him afraid. He told me there was nothing that he knew of, but during our initial consultation, I discovered that he was involved in a rather elaborate, corrupt scheme in his business, in which profits were being hidden and customers were being misled. He seemed rather blasé about it. He said, "Dude, lots of people do what I do. You gotta chill. I know what I'm doing, and I won't get caught". Then, as I explored his history, I discovered that his father, who was now retired, had been brought to trial for similar corrupt business practices, and had been nearly ruined financially by that experience. Although Mr. A had not seemed worried about his own business practices, he became very distraught when we were discussing his father's professional downfall. I told Mr. A that, considering what had happened to his father, it would be quite normal to fear getting caught for what he was doing in his business. I told him that anyone doing what he was doing and whose father had been nearly ruined by similar behaviour, would probably be very afraid. It was not surprising to me that he was feeling panic; what was surprising to me was that he was not feeling fear much more consistently. He did not like hearing me say that, but the panic attacks stopped.

He continued in treatment for a number of years. He had no more panic attacks. He soon stopped all medication, and the panic attacks still did not return. In my view, I had replaced discontinuous panic with a more steady-state of fear appropriate to the situation. I had undone the dissociation between his horror about what has happened to his father and his awareness of how similar was what he was now doing in his own business. In subsequent sessions, I could feel the pressure in him to reinstitute the dissociation and hope the whole thing would go away, and I had to constantly work against that process. Eventually, however, those pressures gave way in the treatment to his facing the reality of what he was doing and changing it.

The second case, Mr. B, was a thirty-one year-old gay man referred to me by his internist. During the day he would sometimes have severe shortness of breath, and he would wake up in the middle of the night in terror. Unlike many other referrals of patients with panic attacks, Mr. B had had no previous psychiatric care and had not tried any psychotropic medications, neither benzodiazepines nor Selective Serotonin Reuptake Inhibitors (SSRIs). He claimed to be aware of no reason for his feeling of panic and his disrupted sleep. I asked him if he was dreaming when he awakened. He told me that the last time it happened, he was dreaming that he had AIDS. This was in the early 1990s, when the AIDS epidemic was at its worst. There were no really effective treatments, and many people were dying. I asked Mr. B if he had been tested for HIV. He had been tested about a year before, and he was HIV-negative. However, as I spoke with him some more, I discovered that he was involved in a relationship of two-years standing with a man, Leo. Leo's prior lover had died of AIDS, yet he never told Mr. B, who found out three months into the relationship from someone else. He mentioned it to Leo who had a lame excuse for keeping it secret. Mr. B rationalized away his immediate suspicion and then forgot about it (except in his dreams). Leo himself had not been tested for the HIV virus; in fact, he refused to be tested. I said to Mr. B that anyone in a gay relationship at that time would be concerned about AIDS, that anyone would be especially concerned if their partner had had a long-standing relationship with someone who had died of the disease, even more so if the partner had *concealed* this fact, even more so if their partner *had not been tested*, and even more so if the partner *refused* to be tested. Mr. B seemed startled by these thoughts; however the panic attacks stopped.

The third case, Mr. C, was a seventy-year-old man, also referred by his physician. He complained of dizziness and blackouts, but a medical workup could find no physical cause. He led an active life, and the most recent attack had been while he was playing tennis. He suddenly became dizzy and fell to the ground on the tennis court. With a man of that age, I was especially cautious about presuming a psychological cause to his panic attacks, and I encouraged him to follow through on any possible further medical investigations. Nevertheless, as I then proceeded with the initial interview, I discovered that he had been married for twenty-six years to his first wife. He had had multiple affairs during that marriage, but when his wife discovered the last affair, she divorced him. Their divorce was one of the bitterest I have ever heard about. Mr. C was publicly humiliated, the scandal compromised his career, his children barely spoke to him any more, and the divorce damaged him financially. Yet after this dreadful event, Mr. C had not given up. He was now remarried to a woman about twenty years younger, a great woman, according to him—intelligent, beautiful, supportive, and kind. So I asked him, "Are you being faithful to her?" His face twisted up, he hemmed and hawed, and then confessed to me that no, he was actually having two affairs, but they were both out of state. He felt sure he would not be caught. To me, the situation seemed quite close to his first marriage. It brought to mind a twenty-year-old young man who had recently explained the "zip-code rule" to me: if you sleep with a girl who is in a different zip code to that of your girl-friend, it is not considered cheating. I said to Mr. C, "After the horrible divorce you have been through, which was presumably caused by your infidelity, you have managed to find a wonderful woman to be your wife. Yet, by cheating on her, you are risking having your whole life fall apart. For you, such a fear is not a hypothesis. You have been through the wringer in one divorce, and now you are risking another. No wonder you are having panic attacks—anyone who had been through what you have been through, and was risking it again, should be very, very afraid". Mr. C argued with me that he really was safe this time, that the situation was different.

His defenses were not convincing. He left the first session quite disturbed; however panic attacks stopped.

To summarize: With each of these patients referred to me because of panic attacks, my procedure was fundamentally the same. I first inquired in detail about their lives. Usually I started with an inquiry into the symptom: when it happened, what were the immediate circumstances preceding the panic attack, and what function the panic attack had in shifting their current lives. I would then look more closely at their general life situation. While each person's circumstances were unique, I found, to my surprise, that they all had something in common. Each patient had a life circumstance which I thought *should* cause him or her to be very afraid. Each of them had consciously diminished the seriousness of what could for anyone be a fear-causing situation. In each case, I was able to tell the patient: "The situation you describe in your real life would make anyone very afraid. For the most part, you are ignoring the normally fear-causing situation, and so, the fear that you feel is real; what is abnormal is that you don't know where the fear is coming from, that you do not connect the emotion with the situation in your life. Because of that, it feels like an attack that comes out of the blue. But it is not. You have very good reason to feel a lot of fear, and, if you want the panic attacks to stop, you must change this fear-causing situation".

Such interpretations had a very striking effect. Most of the patients did not like them; it forced them to pay attention to something disturbing in their lives and put them in a state of continuous elevated anxiety. Yet in every case the panic attacks stopped. My hypothesis was that I had replaced an erratic eruption of intense fear, disconnected from any content, with a continuous high state of fear, connected with its cause. It was very unpleasant but relatively steady and stable, and the patient could then work with the situation consciously.

It was surprising how quickly my interventions stopped the panic attacks. Psychoanalysts are not ordinarily known for quick results. In subsequent sessions, I could feel the patients trying to re-establish their dissociation, and I had to work vigorously to interrupt that process. As George Orwell (1946) said, "To see what is in front of one's nose needs a constant struggle".

This is not a large scale study; we need a much broader sample and more controlled conditions to make any definitive conclusions from my clinical data. If you are a practicing clinician, I encourage you to try my approach and see if it works with your panic disorder patients.

Nevertheless, based on these clinical experiences, my view of panic attacks differs in several ways, and one major way, from many current writers on the subject. Alexander, Feigelson, and Gorman (2005: 132) wrote:

> "During a panic attack, a patient perceives danger, but no danger actually exists. In this case, anxiety is inappropriate".

We hear something similar from LeDoux, the expert on the neurobiology of fear, who wrote in *The Synaptic Self* (2002: 294):

> "Fear in panic patients has no apparent relationship to any actual threat and often involves abnormal sensitivity to uncomfortable somatic sensations".

And David Barlow, a leader in the field of Cognitive Behavioural Therapy (CBT) of panic attacks, also believes that panic attacks are not based on any real threat (Barlow 2002). They all agree: if you have panic attacks, there is no rational reason for you to be afraid. For most of us, if we hear something stated authoritatively often enough, we tend to believe it, and so most clinicians today believe that panic attacks are not based on any real threat. I think that may be wrong, at least with some panic patients. However, if you do not probe deeply and persistently enough, you may never discover the real danger, if there is one.

This may help explain the dismal long-term results of medication and CBT treatment of panic (Barlow et al. 2000). Six months after CBT treatment has stopped, there is a relapse of panic attacks in 68% of the patients. That means more than two out of three patients will go back to having panic attacks. The relapse rate six months after medication treatment is even worse: the panic attacks come back in 80% of the patients.

This finding suggests a basic conceptual error in psychiatry today concerning panic attacks. The general view in psychiatry today is that the pathological symptom is the panic reaction. I am saying that the pathological symptom is not just the panic reaction, but also the denial and dissociation of fear when no panic attack is happening, and you have to treat both. If you give someone Xanax, it may control the symptom of fearful panic, but it will do nothing to the denial.

This one-sided focus on the panic reaction informs most of the prominent theories of panic attacks today. They propose that there is an increase in sensitivity of some neurobiological alarm system. Klein's account suggests increased sensitivity of the suffocation alarm system. Gorman, LeDoux, and others suggest increased sensitivity of the fear network. Panksepp (2005) suggests increased sensitivity of the separation-distress system.

A theory of erratic dissociation

What I am proposing is something different. I am proposing *erratic inhibition and dissociation of fear as important factors in panic attacks*. The situation in the brain with panic attacks is more erratic than hypersensitive. My clinical interventions, so far as I know, did nothing to change the general sensitivity of my patients' neurological fear systems. It is not likely that an interpretation could reverse such a neural tuning; if it could be achieved by psychoanalysis, that would take a much longer time. I think instead that what my clinical interpretation did was quickly undo the dissociation between idea and affect that had allowed my patients to suppress realistic fear, but only erratically.

The dissociation between ideas and affects brings up an interesting connection between panic attacks and obsessional neurosis. In *Inhibitions, symptoms, and anxiety*, Freud (1926) described the defense of isolation, which he thought was basic to obsessional neurosis. In obsessional neurosis, Freud wrote "the experience is deprived of its affect, and its associative connections are suppressed or interrupted so that it remains as though isolated and is not reproduced in the ordinary processes of thought" (p. 120). The obsessional patient experiences the idea without the accompanying emotion.

Panic attacks may be the converse of the separation of affect and idea that Freud described. In obsessional neurosis, the person experiences the idea without the accompanying emotion. In panic attacks, the person experiences the emotion without the accompanying idea. The person feels enormous fear, but it does not seem connected to any actual ideas or experiences—at least consciously.

Therefore, we could also hypothesize that panic attacks are the opposite of obsessional thoughts: in one, the patient has pervading thought without affect, in the other, pervading affect without thought.

The dissociation of affect and idea in both processes seems analogous, and it is tempting to wonder if there is a related neurological underpinning between the two kinds of isolation, of affect from idea, and idea from affect. (See Blechner [2007] for a further discussion of the neurobiology of dissociation in panic attacks.)

Comparison with another psychoanalytic approach

Milrod and her colleagues have studied a traditional psychoanalytic approach to panic disorder. They have written a manual (Milrod et al. 1997) of what they call "Panic-Focused Psychodynamic Psychotherapy" and have received large grants from the government to study their approach. Their focus in treatment is on irrational psychodynamic factors, originating in early experience, of which the patient is unconscious, such as fears of separation, loss, and anger. They do not seem to consider that the patient's panic may be due to a real but dissociated danger situation in the present. While their approach has much merit and has been shown to be effective in a clinical trial (Milrod et al. 2007), it is my view that the best clinical approach would be first to rule out real but dissociated dangers in the present before speculating on the involvement of irrational fantasies. Like me, they report that with effective intervention, the patient's panic attacks may stop abruptly (for example, the cases of Ms. P and Ms. S in Milrod et al. 1997; see also Milrod and Shear 1991). A more precise comparison of their cases and mine would not be possible without interviewing the actual patients, although it seems possible that some of their patients may have real, dissociated dangers in their lives, and that interpretation of conflictual fantasies may have inadvertently affected dissociated real dangers in the patient's life.

Varieties of dissociation

It is difficult to describe precisely how conscious was the inhibition of fear and the denial of danger in my panic patients. None of my patients described a process of denying fear deliberately. Mr. C did not say, "I want to stay married, but playing around with other women gives me pleasure and satisfies other needs. And so, in order to have my cake and eat it too, I will simply act like I am not afraid of the consequences of my infidelity, and everything will work out for the best". Yet I cannot say that his denial and dissociation were totally unconscious either; when I pointed it out, he did not deny what he was doing. It might be more accurate to say that the knowledge is unformulated, in the manner described by Stern (1997). Various clinicians and researchers continue to suggest refinements in our terminology, such as whether there is a difference between "implicit, non-conscious" and "repressed" memories (for example, Shevrin 2002; Anderson et al. 2004).

Had I not spelled out for Mr. C what the situation was, I am not sure he would have spelled it out himself. This is the tricky thing about dissociation; it is not repressed in the Freudian sense, pressed so powerfully out of awareness that it is not accessible when first interpreted—with my patients, one session of interpretation was enough to dislodge the dissociation. Yet the dissociation was not so available to awareness that the patient could simply undo it by himself with enough will.

We could also describe the situation, perhaps more accurately, with what Harry Stack Sullivan (1953: 170) called "selective inattention". Selective inattention is a subspecies of dissociation in which something that will cause anxiety is inattended. The patient avoids noticing the obvious, and he avoids letting the psychoanalyst find out the obvious, although the patient does not know that he is doing so. We need to clarify the neurobiological mechanisms of all these types and gradations of inattention and dissociation if we are really going to understand panic attacks.

Summary

Most theories have presumed that during a panic attack a patient perceives danger but no actual danger exists, so the anxiety is inappropriate. I am reporting that, at least with some patients, the anxiety is appropriate. The patient really does have something to fear, but the cause of this fear has been dissociated. When the clinician identifies to the patient the real danger situation, occasional sudden panic is replaced by a more consistent state of intense fear. The patient may then feel worse overall, but the panic attacks stop. The long-term resolution of the patient's anxiety then requires a realistic change in the danger situation, which results in lasting cure.

I want to stress what I am *not* saying. I am not saying that I know this to be true of all panic patients. I have had a relatively limited number of panic patients, and although they mostly have been treated successfully, that cannot be generalized to all patients with panic attack. Only a much larger and systematic study can establish how frequently dissociation of real danger is involved in panic attacks.

I am also not saying that we should dismiss any of the earlier research on panic disorder, although we may want to reinterpret the significance of some earlier findings. For example, Donald Klein, as mentioned above, has argued that panic attacks are triggered by suffocation alarm. He has noted that heavy smokers are more prone to panic attacks. My patient, Mr. A, was a very heavy smoker, about three packs a day. However, I do not think his smoking was the cause of the panic attacks. After the attacks stopped, he was still smoking just as much. It could be that suffocation anxiety does not itself cause panic attacks, but it may determine which *kind* of panic attack the patient will have. Patients with suffocation anxiety may have attacks with shortness of breath and fear of heart attack. Patients without suffocation anxiety may be more likely to have other forms of panic attacks, such as dizziness and loss of consciousness. Without a real but dissociated psychological fear, the same person might not have the panic attack, no matter how much he or she smokes.

I am also not ruling out that patients who have panic attacks may have had an early modification of their fear response due to trauma, as argued by Gorman et al. (2000). In particular, there are studies showing that panic attacks are more likely in patients who have experienced early losses, such as parental divorce or death of a parent (Stein et al. 1996; Tweed et al. 1989). My patient Mr. A had two of the main experiences connected with panic attacks: his parents divorced when he was a child and his mother dropped dead of a heart attack before his eyes, right after he had a big argument with her. Mr. C spent much of his youth in Auschwitz, experiencing and witnessing terrible suffering. I have no knowledge of such childhood trauma in Mr. B, although most gay men who lived through the 1980s and 1990s experienced multiple traumas as adults during the worst ravages of AIDS. The tuning of the neural system by trauma may well have *predisposed* each of my patients to panic attacks. My clinical experience, however, leads me to question whether such tuning is either necessary or sufficient to account for panic.

Also, if early trauma predisposes people to panic, it is an open question as to how it does so: Does early trauma make the fear system hypersensitive? Or does early trauma lead one to be more prone to rely on dissociation as a defense (van der Kolk 1987; van der Kolk et al. 1996)?

If I am correct that dissociation plays a major role in panic attacks, at least for some patients, then that may require a rethinking of the neurological underpinnings of panic attacks. We would want to pay more attention to the neurobiology of dissociation, which I do not think is well understood. We will want to understand how connections between thoughts and emotions can be kept separate in the brain, with more or less effectiveness. These separations may lead to instability in the suppression and expression of affect, which will lead to erratic outbursts of panic instead of more even, steady-state fear.

References

Alexander, B., Feigelson, S. and Gorman, J. (2005). "Integrating the psychoanalytic and neurobiological views of panic disorder". *Neuro-Psychoanalysis*. 7: 129–141.

Anderson, M., Ochsner, K., Kuhl, B., Cooper, J., Robertson, E., Gabrieli, S.,

Barlow, D. (2002). *Anxiety and its disorders: The nature and treatment of anxiety an panic*. 2nd Edn. New York: Guilford.

Barlow, D., Gorman, J., Shear, M.K. and Woods, S. (2000). "Cognitive-behavioral therapy, imipramine, or their combination for panic disorder: A randomized controlled trial". *Journal of the american medical association*. 83(19): 2,529–2,536.

Blechner, M. (2007). "Approaches to panic attacks". *Neuro-Psychoanalysis*. 9: 93–102.

Bromberg, P. (1998). *Standing in the Spaces: Essays on Clinical Process, Trauma, and Dissociation*. Hillsdale, NJ: The Analytic Press.

Freud, S. (1926). "Inhibitions, symptoms, and anxiety". *Standard Edition*. 20: 87–174.

Glover, G. and Gabrieli, J. (2004). "Neural systems underlying the suppression of unwanted memories". *Science*. 303: 232–235.

Gorman, J., Kent, J., Sullivan, G. and Coplan, J. (2000). "Neuroanatomical hypothesis of panic disorder, revised". *American Journal of Psychiatry.* 157: 493–505.

Gorman, J., Liebowitz, M., Fyer, A. and Stein, J. (1989). "A neuroanatomical hypothesis for panic disorder". *American Journal of Psychiatry.* 146: 148–161.

Katon, W. (1996). "Panic disorder: Relationship to high medical utilization, unexplained physical symptoms, and medical costs". *Journal of Clinical Psychiatry.* 57: 11–18.

Klein, D. (1980). "Anxiety reconceptualized". *Comprehensive Psychiatry.* 6: 411–427.

Klein, D. (1993). "False suffocation alarms, spontaneous panics, and related conditions: An integrative hypothesis". *Archives of General Psychiatry.* 50: 306–317.

LeDoux, J. (2002). *The Synaptic Self.* New York: Viking.

Milrod, B., Busch, F., Cooper, A. and Shapiro, T. (1997). *Panic-focused Psychodynamic Psychotherapy.* Washington, DC: American Psychiatric Press.

Milrod, B., Leon, A., Busch, F., Rudden, M., Schwalberg, M., Clarkin, J., Aronson, A., Singer, M., Turchin, W., Klass, E., Graf, E., Teres, J. and Shear, M. (2007). "A randomized controlled clinical trial of psychoanalytic psychotherapy for panic disorder". *American Journal of Psychiatry.* 164: 265–272.

Milrod, B. and Shear, M.K. (1991). "Dynamic treatment of panic disorder: A review". *Journal of Nervous and Mental Disease.* 179: 741–743.

Orwell, G. (1946). In Front of Your Nose. *London Tribune.* 22 March, 1946.

Otto, M., Gould, R. and Pollack, M. (1994). "Cognitive-behavioral treatment of panic disorder: Considerations for the treatment of patients over the long term". *Psychiatric Annals.* 24: 307–315.

Panksepp, J. (2005). Commentary on "Integrating the Psychoanalytic and Neurobiological Views of Panic Disorder". *Neuro-Psychoanalysis.* 7: 145–150.

Schuman, R., Kramer, P. and Mitchell, J. (1985). "The hidden mental health network: Treatment of mental illness by nonpsychiatric physicians". *Archives of General Psychiatry.* 42: 89–94.

Shevrin, H. (2002). "A psychoanalytic view of memory in the light of recent cognitive and neuroscience research". *Neuro-Psychoanalysis.* 4: 131–139.

Stein, M., Walker, J., Andersen, G., Hazen, A., Ross, C., Eldridge, G. and Forde, D. (1996). "Childhood physical and sexual abuse in patients with anxiety disorders and in a community sample". *American Journal of Psychiatry*. 153: 275–277.

Stern, D.B. (1997). *Unformulated Experience: From Dissociation to Imagination in Psychoanalysis*. Hillsdale, NJ: The Analytic Press.

Sullivan, H. (1953). *The Interpersonal Theory of Psychiatry*. New York: Norton.

Sullivan, H. (1973). "Dissociative processes". In: *Clinical Studies in Psychiatry*. New York: Norton, pp. 166–181.

Tweed, J., Schoenbach, V., George, L. and Blazer, D. (1989). "The effects of childhood parental death and divorce on six-month history of anxiety disorders". *British Journal of Psychiatry*. 154: 823–828.

van der Kolk, B. (1987). *Psychological Trauma*. Washington, DC: America Psychiatric Press.

van der Kolk, McFarlane, A. and Weisaeth, L. (1996). *Traumatic Stress: The Effects of Overwhelming Experience on Mind, Body, and Society*. New York: The Guilford Press.

CHAPTER ELEVEN

On getting away with it: On the experiences we don't have

Adam Phillips[1]

If guilt is the psychoanalytic word for not getting away with it, what is the psychoanalytic word for getting away with it? In the psychoanalytic story people are ambivalent and transgressive, whatever else they are; and these predispositions raise, by implication, the issue of getting away with something, of avoiding what are deemed to be the inevitable consequences of certain actions. So it needs to be said right at the start that if the human subject, as described by psychoanalysis, is a split subject, in conflict, by definition, with himself and others, then getting away with it—acts of harming those you love, desiring forbidden objects, letting yourself and others down, sacrificing your desire—is not an option. There is no truthful, no realistic description in the language of psychoanalysis, for getting away with it. And yet, of course, psychoanalysis also urges us to take our wishes seriously, to read them as disguised formulations of unconscious desire. And there is perhaps no stronger wish—beginning, of course, in childhood—than the wish to get away

---

[1] An earlier draft of this paper was published in Phillips, A. (2009). "On Getting Away With It". *Psychoanalytic Dialogues.* 19: 98–102.

with things. It is worth wondering what the wish to get away with it is a wish for; and of course it may be different in each instance.

One of the most interesting things about wishful fantasies and the narratives they provide is where they stop. Of course they couldn't include all the possible consequences of the gratified wish, but they are often surprisingly abbreviated; curtailed all too soon, as if to say, where will it all end? In the wishful fantasies of getting away with the prohibited thing we seem to know about the experience we won't have, the experience avoided by the act of getting away with it. If I get away with it, it is as if I know somewhere in myself what it is that I have got away with. I seem to know a great deal about an experience I haven't had. I remember asking a seventy year-old man who had come to see me whether he had children and he smiled and said, "No, I managed to get away with it". When I asked him what he imagined he had got away with, he gave me an elaborate and not unfamiliar account of the general inconvenience of having children. He seemed, in a certain sense, immensely authoritative and informed about just how difficult children can be. When I asked him how he knew so much about an experience he hadn't had, he said—I thought rather shrewdly—"Only people who don't have children know what it's really like". When he said this I was reminded of Winnicott's remark that only a man knows what it's like to be a woman, and only a woman knows what it's like to be a man. There is, clearly, a kind of knowledge borne of the absence of experience. It often tends towards cliché and omniscience—there is no language more clichéd than the language of the omnipotent—but there is also a freedom to imagine in it.

So we might imagine, for example, that a child who gets away with stealing something from a friend—the child, that is to say, who is not caught—knows more about punishment than the one who is found out. And what he knows more about is his super-ego, the language, the severity, the obscenity of the self-punisher he calls up by his act. What he doesn't know about is the experience of being punished and whatever else by the adults, by his peers, by his friend. He might say—I think probably would say—that he knows more about the experience he hasn't had, because he has been able to imagine it. Reality hasn't muscled in and pre-empted the immediacy of his fantasy life.

Getting away with it, in other words, provides us with the opportunity to consider the senses in which we know more about the experiences we don't have than the experiences we do have. I know more about being punished by not being punished; I know more about sexuality by never having sexual experiences with other people. What is the more that I know? In the masturbation of adolescence in one description, it is as if one got away with having sex without having to have sex. Perhaps we should take more seriously than we often do how long we spend in our lives not having sexual experiences but being, as we say, full of fantasies; knowing more about what we might want than about what we can have. An adolescent state of mind is one in which we get away with being a child and get away with being an adult. Getting away with it—at least in fantasy—may be about not having to face the consequences; but how can you face the consequences if you don't and couldn't know what they are.

The phrase "getting away with it" makes us face what the phrase "facing the consequences" might mean. It is realistic to think that if you have unprotected sex you may conceive a child or get a sexually transmitted disease, but you can't know, in the omniscient sense of knowing, what that eventuality would actually be like for you. The fantasy of getting away with it, I want to suggest, is not only an excessive knowingness, it can also be a way of phrasing the possibility that you don't know the consequences of your actions; a wish not to assume what the gratification of your wishes might entail.

"Don't wish too hard or you'll get what you want" means don't be the false prophet of your own desire. Don't get bamboozled by your culture—by your upbringing and education—into being an expert in cause and effect. When I think, calmly or feverishly, I could get away with this, I am not only giving myself permission, I am also imagining that one thing doesn't always lead to another that I know about. When I imagine getting away with it I am not assuming, consciously, that my act will have no consequences. I am, at best, just assuming it won't have the predictable consequences. It is worth wondering whether some desires are only made possible, only made riskable, sponsored by the fantasy of getting away with it.

"I won't be punished" is a fear and a wish. Because the other thing getting away with it brings up, or brings on, is the authorities; if you get away with it does that mean the authorities don't really love you, don't really care about their rules, are in fact quite unable to enforce their rules, are secretly complicit with your breaking them; in short, are not all that they are cracked up to be, by you and yours?

If you get away with it, is God impotent, absent, or negligent? Or is he just biding his time, letting you sweat and boast, but leaving you unsure? After all, when do you know, when do you really know, you actually have got away with it and that you can finally relax? If getting away with it is just the illusion of getting away with it, then you *haven't* got away with it—you have just protracted the torture, deferred the moment of (punitive) truth.

Or perhaps God is merciful, or sympathetic, or thinks you deserve time out, or time off. Or whatever he can do with time to make it kinder. Whichever it is, getting away with it is going to make you think, perhaps like nothing else, about the authorities. They are never more present than when you seem to have slipped their attention. When I am having the all-too-common fantasy of getting away with it I am thinking about the rules, and how they work and if they work, and what happens to me if they don't.

Sartre tells that story about the young married couple who each morning have breakfast together, then the wife kisses her husband goodbye and sits by the window all day crying until he returns; then she perks up. The psychologically minded, Sartre intimates, would say that this young woman is suffering from a form of separation anxiety; that she is, as some of us might say now, anxiously attached. But in Sartre's view they are wrong because this woman is suffering from a fear of freedom.

When her husband goes out she can do, in a sense, whatever she wants and it is this possibility that terrifies her. The thought of being able to get away with it, the possibility of that, paralyzes her. What Sartre doesn't say—probably because it is a mixture of being too banal, too bourgeois, and too psychoanalytic—is that she may be terrorized by her guilt; her husband's absence leaves her at the mercy, one might say, of her super-ego. From a psychoanalytic point of view—in psychoanalytic language, as it were—we have to wonder not whether it would be possible not to feel guilty. But how is it possible, what would it sound like, not to be stifled by guilt? If it didn't sound too pragmatic, too anti-psychoanalytic, the question might be, what, if anything can be done with (or to) guilt? Getting away with it, as a wishful fantasy, is a way of imagining doing something to the super-ego that would make desire seem bearable, that would make pleasure seem pleasurable. Phrases like "modifying the super-ego" only sound plausible because they sound reasonable.

The super-ego as we have construed it may not be the kind of thing, the kind of voice, that can have things like modification done to it. What is to be done that getting away with it might be pointing us in the direction of, consciously and unconsciously?

If the question is what it is about your life that interests you, and if symptoms, as it were, take the matter out of your own hands by *forcing* your attention, a symptom being whatever it is that you can't stop thinking about but would prefer not to, then the symptom of not having been punished is of particular interest. If you are troubled by not having been punished for something, then you might say that you *are* being punished because it preys on your mind as guilt. And yet it is surprisingly common for patients to remember from childhood several misdemeanours that went unpunished. These incidents, many of which at face value seem even to the person confessing, rather minor, seem to have acquired a disproportionate amount of guilt. Of course a lot of the mischief and delinquency of childhood and adolescence goes unpunished; and yet, for some people, it is the unpunished acts that stay to haunt them.

The irony of these predicaments is that punishment, of course, is no longer really available; and yet something is being sought in their being kept as secrets, and their being confessed to in analysis. And often these apparently trivial confessions will be prefaced by the admission that the patient has never told anyone before. It seems to me that often what is being reported on in these moments is an uncompleted action. There was an experience the patient missed having, and it is called punishment. I think we need to bear in mind that punishment is also the word we use, and the thing we do, that brings certain acts to their supposed conclusions; it gives them a sense of an ending. It confirms a cause and effect story; it narrows the consequences of actions. If you get away with it, for however long, you are on the open road of unpredictable consequence.

As we know people, including ourselves, can speak with immense conviction about what is missing in our lives, about the experiences we haven't had or aren't having, and what our lives would be like were we to have them. What is unusual about these not-having-been-punished experiences from childhood—those times when we got away with it, and that stayed with us; these miniature death-of-God experiences when we were abandoned to our transgressions—is that people often have a very limited sense of how their lives would have been better if the requisite, appropriate thing had happened. If I could get the house, the job, the woman of my dreams I can speak at length about how my life would be better. And over time people begin to have a sense, in psychoanalysis, of how their lives might have been different without the deprivations of their childhood.

The memories of getting away with it, in childhood and adolescence, are, I want to suggest, more bluntly enigmatic. If you get away with it, what exactly is the experience you haven't had, given that the experience you have had over all these years is a more or less severe private guilt? Indeed in this scenario guilt might be construed, might be experienced as, a refuge, a retreat, a substitute, a something you had instead of another experience you might have had.

On the straightforward confessional model, or the less straightforward sado-masochistic model, you could say that external punishment, or at least external acknowledgement—being found out—would have freed you from the burden of guilt and enabled you to void it, to evacuate it by some kind of penitence and reparation. It was a mistake, an error, a falling short of an ideal, and it could have been in some sense recognized as such, and corrected. When someone admits to such things in analysis they want to bring their getting away with it to an end.

A patient describes in quite lurid detail as a ten-year-old child stealing a friend's gloves and burying them in the back garden: she describes it with such trepidation and terror that you might think—and we, as analysts would think—that she had, at least unconsciously, committed some terrible crime. But the terribleness of the crime has been subsumed for her by the terribleness of having never been caught. She left a mystery in the world; her friend's gloves were lost unaccountably and even though the world may have mostly forgotten, this sixty-three year-old woman has not. The world went on making sense for her because she knew how it had happened; but everyone else involved was left with what she called "a hole in the net". I said to her that whatever else was going on she had wanted other people to have the experience that she had had of things (and people) unaccountably disappearing. She replied, "Yes, but I got away with it, because the gloves hadn't unaccountably disappeared, I had disappeared them!"

The experience she couldn't let herself have, the experience we might say she could not bring within the orbit of her omnipotence, was of nobody making things happen; of some things, perhaps the most significant things, happening beyond human agency. When you get away with it, only you know that the world has changed; you have changed the world without letting it know. Indeed if you had let it know, it wouldn't have changed. Getting away with it, as a child and as an adolescent, is a form of radical privacy; and even if it is with accomplices that you get away with it, you are living a version of a private language. You know the crucial thing, the essential fact; you are not the person supposed to know, you are the person who knows.

Getting away with it, in other words, is an experiment in privacy. It is, one might say, a conscious solitude with an unconscious backdrop. The person who gets away with it is hyper-conscious of one thing—as in most symptoms—but unconscious of much else. What I am interested in is the person's unconscious experience of getting away with it; how, one might say, it makes them live. Because whatever else they are doing, or have been doing, they have been living as if they have got away with something. They are living with an experience—the possibility of an experience—that they have never had. Bringing these things up in analysis is an attempt to find out what the missing experience is assumed to be. The person has a completed narrative—a set of potentially completed narratives—that they are unconscious of. Their imaginations have had to do the work that reality failed to do for them. If reality had intervened, if they had been caught—in itself an interesting phrase—something might have been pre-empted or foreclosed. Or to change the emphasis slightly, does the young person who gets away with it know more or less about guilt than the person who doesn't?

We will, of course, never know, at least in their lifetimes from those who were determined to get away with it, what the guilt experience was like for them. Did getting away with it make them bolder or more timid, more ruthless or less? Did it make them fans of honesty, or secretly amused by the authorities? We will never know unless they tire of getting away with it; unless, for some reason, as with the patients I mentioned, a time comes when it seems essential to speak about the experience of getting away with it which, in itself, brings that experience to an end, in its terminal and irrevocable breach of a hard-won and often hard-worn privacy.

What does the adult in analysis, in so far as one can generalize, want from such belated admissions? What is being asked for? That, certainly, is one of the questions being asked in such confessions; and partly because, as the patient usually knows in some part of his or her mind, the analytic setting is neither a toilet, nor a confessional, but something else altogether.

One of the things that has usefully reconfigured our writing of psychoanalytic theory now is our unavoidable acknowledgement that we can't confidently, anymore, make generalizations across cultures, religions, genders, or even perhaps families. All psychoanalytic theorizing has to have now, as a coda, the question: for whom could these sentences be pertinent or useful? Of course this cuts both ways: because we never know exactly who we are talking about now we can also be more wildly speculative, and just see who, if anyone, picks it up. I raise this here because getting away with it is so particularly pertinent to immigrant experience, or people trying to live lives they want in oppressive political regimes. The question for these people is, or for some of these people some of the time, is, "What can I get away with?" which is a question we are more likely to associate with adolescents or criminals. How can I get away with living according to the things I believe in a society which either outrightly outlaws these practices—Muslim children in France, for example, have to, by law, obey secular dress codes—or is prejudiced against them. In these contexts what we might call "getting away with it" can be a matter of life or death; or a matter of ethical life or death. As honourable psychoanalysts in Germany in the thirties we would not presumably be turning our Jewish patients and colleagues in to the Nazis.

In other words what we, in a psychoanalytic way, would think of as the childhood wish—or the wish beginning in childhood—to get away with it, turns out, obviously, to have complicated, and sometimes untraceable repercussions. What is going to be the fate of someone who, broadly speaking, feels unable, or unwilling, to get away with things? For whom the whole notion of getting away with things—which might, by displacement, seem to be rather trivial things—is unbearable, something they would prefer not to have in their personal repertoire?

By way of an answer to my question—What are people asking for in analysis by making their belated admissions of often minor misdemeanours?—there is one obvious consideration, though it is not often obvious to the person making the admission; and that is, what has made guilt so unbearable to them, what is their personal history of this essential feeling such that they need to invite in another person to their predicament? And then there is my question—the answers to which arc partly unconscious and will differ in each case, and at each time—what is wanted from the analyst? What is the experience they haven't had—the missing experience, as it were—that, it is imagined, will complete or at least continue the story of the crime?

What is being asked for is the provision not of the missing experience necessarily, but of an account of what the missing experience might have been felt to be. There was something they got away with, and something they got away without. What can be done in analysis—and it will of course partly be guess work, the best kind of work psychoanalysts do—is to consider the possibilities and what they might have led to. You cannot of course supply missing experiences, but you can describe what they might have been—what might have been wanted, or feared, or both—and how that might have made the person's life different. And something in all this describing may be useful material for a possible future. We can never be quite sure when the possibility for an experience is over; wanting to mourn missed opportunities is sometimes an attempt to foreclose this unknowable future. "Getting away with it", whatever else the phrase portends, is a way of talking about unexpectable experience.

PART V

HOW DO WE KNOW AND HOW DOES IT CHANGE? THE ROLE OF IMPLICIT AND EXPLICIT MIND/BRAIN/BODY PROCESSES

CHAPTER TWELVE

The right brain implicit self: A central mechanism of the psychotherapy change process

Allan N. Schore, Ph.D.

After a century of disconnection, psychoanalysis is returning to its psychological *and* biological sources, and this re-integration is generating a palpable surge of energy and revitalization of the field. At the centre of both theoretical and clinical psychoanalysis is the concept of the unconscious. The field's unique contribution to science has been its explorations of the psychic structures and processes that operate beneath conscious awareness in order to generate essential survival functions. In the last ten years implicit unconscious phenomena have finally become a legitimate area of not only psychoanalytic but also scientific inquiry. Writing to the broader field of psychology, Bargh and Morsella (2008: 73) now conclude, "Freud's model of the unconscious as the primary guiding influence over every day life, even today, is more specific and detailed than any to be found in contemporary cognitive or social psychology".

An important catalyst of this rapprochement is the contact point between modern neuropsychoanalysis and contemporary neuroscience. Current neurobiological researchers now conclude, "The right hemisphere has been linked to implicit information processing, as opposed to the more explicit and more conscious processing tied to the left hemisphere" (Happaney, Zelazo and Stuss 2004: 7). Indeed, over the last two decades I have provided a substantial amount of interdisciplinary evidence which supports the proposition that the early developing right brain generates the implicit self, the human unconscious (Schore 1994, 1997, 2003a, 2005, 2007, 2009b). My ongoing studies in regulation theory focus on the essential right brain structure–function relationships that underlie the psychobiological substrate of the human unconscious, and they attempt to elucidate the origin, psychopathogenesis, and psychotherapeutic treatment of the early forming subjective implicit self.

In this chapter I demonstrate that current clinical and experimental studies of the unconscious, implicit domain can do more than support a clinical psychoanalytic model of treatment, but rather this interdisciplinary information can elucidate the mechanisms that lie at the core of psychoanalysis. The body of my work strongly suggests the following organizing principles. The concept of a single unitary "self" is as misleading as the idea of a single unitary "brain". The left and right hemispheres process information in their own unique fashions, and this is reflected in a conscious left lateralized self system ("left mind") and an unconscious right lateralized self system ("right mind"). Despite the designation of the verbal left hemisphere as "dominant" due to its capacities for explicitly processing language functions, It is the right hemisphere and its implicit homeostatic-survival and affect regulation functions that are truly dominant in human existence (Schore 2003a, 2009b). Over the life span the early-forming unconscious implicit self continues to develop to more complexity, and it operates in qualitatively different ways from the later-forming conscious explicit self. Recall Freud's (1920/1943: 188) assertion that the unconscious is "a special realm, with its own desires and modes of expression and peculiar mental mechanisms not elsewhere operative". In essence, my work is an exploration of this "special realm".

With the emergence of modern neuropsychoanalysis and its direct connections with contemporary neuroscience, the right brain's dominance for an "emotional" and "corporeal" sense of self (Devinsky 2000; Schore 1994) is now common ground to both disciplines. This integration clearly demonstrates that evolutionarily adaptive implicit bodily based socio-emotional functions represent the output of the unique developmental, anatomical, and psychobiological properties of the right brain. Indeed the implicit functions and structures of the right brain represent the inner world described by psychoanalysis since its inception. From its origin in *The Project for a Scientific Psychology*, Freud's explorations of the deeper levels of the human mind have exposed the illusion of a single state of surface consciousness, and revealed the essential contributions of a biological substratum of unconscious states that indelibly impact all levels of human existence. The temporal difference of right implicit and left explicit processing is described by Buklina (2005: 479):

> [T]he more "diffuse" organization of the right hemisphere has the effect that it responds to any stimulus, even speech stimuli, more quickly and, thus earlier. The left hemisphere is activated after this and performs the slower semantic analysis ... the arrival of an individual signal initially in the right hemisphere and then in the left is more "physiological". (See Figure 1.)

Another reason for the strong attraction of psychoanalysis to the right brain is found in its unique survival functions, processes that are disturbed in various psychopathologies. Schutz (2005) highlights the adaptive functions uniquely subserved by this "emotional brain":

> The right hemisphere operates a distributed network for rapid responding to danger and other urgent problems. It preferentially processes environmental challenge, stress and pain and manages self-protective responses such as avoidance and escape ... Emotionality is thus the right brain's "red phone", compelling the mind to handle urgent matters without delay. (p. 15)

A more profound and comprehensive understanding of the organizing principles of this rapid acting and therefore non-conscious right brain "physiological" implicit core system can provide not only essential and relevant clinical and experimental data, but also a theoretical lens which can illuminate and penetrate the fundamental problems addressed by psychoanalytic science. Just as studies of the left brain, dominant for language and verbal processing, can never elucidate the unique non-verbal functions of the right, studies of the output of the explicit functions of the conscious mind in verbal transcripts or narratives can never reveal the implicit psychobiological

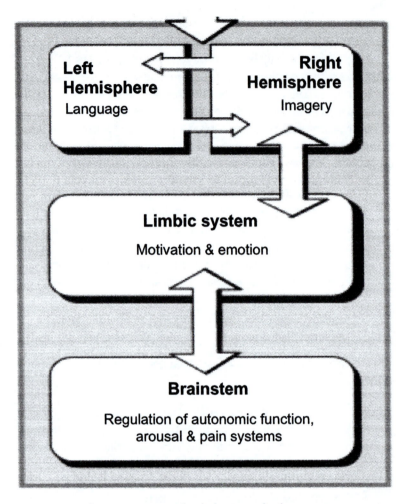

Figure 1. Implicit processing of right brain and subsequent connections into left brain explicit system.

dynamics of the unconscious mind (Schore 1994, 2002, 2003a; Schore and Schore 2008).

This neuropsychoanalytic perspective echoes Freud's fundamental assertion that the central questions of the human condition, which psychoanalysis directly addresses, can never be found in knowledge of how the conscious mind of the explicit self system works, but rather in a deeper understanding of the implicit psychobiological mechanisms of the unconscious mind. Other fields of study are currently appreciating the importance of this unconscious realm in all levels of human existence. Thus not only psychoanalysis but a large number of disciplines in both the sciences and the arts are experiencing a paradigm shift from explicit conscious cognition to implicit unconscious affect. In a recent editorial of the journal *Motivation and Emotion*, Richard Ryan asserts, "After three decades of the dominance of cognitive approaches, motivational and emotional processes have roared back into the limelight" (2007: 1). A large number of interdisciplinary studies are converging upon the centrality of these implicit right brain motivational and emotional processes that are essential to adaptive functioning.

Right brain implicit processes in contemporary psychoanalysis

In this section I describe a surface, verbal, conscious, analytic explicit self versus a deeper non-verbal, non-conscious, holistic, emotional corporeal implicit self. These two lateralized systems contain qualitatively different forms of cognition and therefore ways of "knowing", as well as different memory systems and states of consciousness. But I will argue that implicit (non-conscious) functions are much more than just learning, memory, and attention, processes highlighted by cognitive psychology. A psychological theory of cognition, even unconscious cognition, cannot penetrate the fundamental questions of development, psychopathology, and the change process of psychotherapy.

In addition to implicit cognition (right brain unconscious processing of exteroceptive information from the outer world and interoceptive information from the inner world) the implicit concept also includes implicit affect, implicit communication, and implicit self-regulation. The ongoing paradigm shift from the explicit cognitive to the implicit affective realm is driven by both new experimental data on emotional processes and updated clinical models for working with affective systems.

Freud (1915) stressed that the work of psychotherapy is always concerned with affect states. In my first book, I expanded upon this therapeutic principle, asserting that affects are "the center of empathic communication" and that "the regulation of conscious *and* unconscious feelings is placed in the center of the clinical stage"

(Schore 1994: 448–449). Consonant with these ideas, the essential clinical role of implicit affect is underscored in current neuroscience research reporting that unconscious processing of emotional stimuli is specifically associated with activation of the right and not left hemisphere (Morris, Ohman and Dolan 1998), and documenting a "right hemispheric dominance in processing of unconscious negative emotion" (Sato and Aoki 2006: 261) and a "cortical response to subjectively unconscious danger" (Carretie 2005: 615). This work establishes the validity of the concept of unconscious (and also dissociated) affect, a common focus of the treatment of pathological defences.

In this same volume I offered a model of implicit communications within the therapeutic relationship, whereby transference–countertransference right brain to right brain communications represent interactions of the patient's unconscious primary process system and the therapist's primary process system (Schore 1994, 2009c). Neuroscience documents that although the left hemisphere mediates most linguistic behaviours, the right hemisphere is important for the broader aspects of communication. This research also indicates that "the right hemisphere operates in a more free-associative, primary process manner, typically observed in states such as dreaming or reverie" (Grabner et al. 2007: 228).

Congruent with this model, Dorpat (2001) describes the implicit process of "primary process communication" expressed in "both body movements (kinesics), posture, gesture, facial expression, voice inflection, and the sequence, rhythm, and pitch of the spoken words" (p. 451). According to his formulation affective and object-relational information are transmitted predominantly by primary process communication, while secondary process communication has a highly complex and powerful logical syntax but lacks adequate semantics in the field of relationships. In light of the fact that the left hemisphere is dominant for language but the right is dominant for emotional communication, I have proposed that the psychotherapy process is best described not as "the talking cure" but "the communicating" cure (Schore 2005: 841). Chused (2007) now asserts, "I suspect our field has not yet fully appreciated the importance of this implicit communication" (p. 879).

With regard to implicit cognition, I have recently suggested that primary process cognition underlies clinical intuition, a major factor in therapeutic effectiveness (Schore and Schore 2008). Indeed, the definition of intuition, "the ability to understand or know something immediately, without conscious reasoning" (Compact Oxford English Dictionary) clearly implies right and not left brain processing. Bohart (1999) contends that in the psychotherapy context, "what I extract perceptually and intuitively from lived experience is far more compelling that thought information" (p. 294). In an important article on this theme, Welling (2005) concludes that the psychotherapist who considers his or her methods and decisions to be exclusively the result of conscious reasoning is most likely mistaken. He asserts that no therapist can reasonably deny following hunches, experiencing sudden insights, choosing directions without really knowing why or having uncanny feelings that turn out to be of great importance for therapy, and points out that all these phenomena are occurrences of intuitive modes of functioning.

The central theme in all of my writings is the essential function of implicit affect regulation in the organization of the self. Citing my work, Greenberg (2007) proposes:

> ... an issue of major clinical significance then is generating theory and research to help understand to what extent automatic emotion processes can be changed through deliberate processes and to what extent only through more implicit processes based on new emotional and/or relational experiences. Stated in another way the question becomes how much emotional change requires implicit experiential learning vs. explicit conceptual learning. (p. 414)

In agreement with current trends in modern relational psychoanalysis Greenberg (2008: 414) concludes, "The field has yet to play adequate attention to implicit and relational processes of regulation". Recall that an inability to implicitly regulate the intensity of emotions is a major outcome of early relational trauma, a common history of a large number of psychiatric disorders.

In the following I overview my work on the centrality of unconscious processes and right brain structures from the perspective of regulation theory (Schore 1994, 2003 a, b). I begin with a description of implicit affective processes in psychotherapeutic change processes. I then focus on the expression of right brain unconscious mechanisms in affect-laden enactments and in the therapist's moment-to-moment navigation through these heightened affective moments by not explicit secondary process cognition, but by implicit primary process clinical intuition. Direct access to implicit processes will be shown to be central to effective treatment.

Right brain implicit processes in psychotherapy

Over the course of my work I have provided interdisciplinary evidence to show that implicit right brain to right brain attachment transactions occur in both the caregiver–infant and the therapist–patient relationships (the therapeutic alliance). I suggest that not left brain verbal explicit patient–therapist discourse but right brain implicit non-verbal affect-laden communication directly represents the attachment dynamic embedded within the alliance. During the treatment, the empathic therapist is consciously, explicitly attending to the patient's verbalizations in order to objectively diagnose and rationalize the patient's dysregulating symptomatology. But she is also listening and interacting at another level, an experience-near subjective level, one that implicitly processes moment-to-moment socio-emotional information at levels beneath awareness (Schore 2003a). Just as the left brain communicates its states to other left brains via conscious linguistic behaviours so the right non-verbally communicates its unconscious states to other right brains that are tuned to receive these communications.

On this matter Stern (2005) suggests:

> Without the nonverbal it would be hard to achieve the empathic, participatory, and resonating aspects of intersubjectivity. One would only be left with a kind of pared down, neutral 'understanding' of the other's subjective experience. One reason that this distinction is drawn is that in many cases the analyst is consciously aware of the content or speech while processing the nonverbal aspects out of awareness. With an intersubjectivist perspective, a more conscious processing by the analyst of the nonverbal is necessary. (p. 80)

Studies show that sixty per cent of human communication is nonverbal (Burgoon 1985).

Writing on therapeutic "nonverbal implicit communications" Chused (2007) asserts that, "it is not that the information they contain cannot be verbalized, only that sometimes only a non-verbal approach can deliver the information in a way it can be used, particularly when there is no conscious awareness of the underlying concerns involved" (p. 879). These ideas are echoed by Hutterer and Liss (2006), who state that non-verbal variables such as tone, tempo, rhythm, timbre, prosody, and amplitude of speech, as well as body language signals may need to be re-examined as essential aspects of therapeutic technique. It is well established that the right hemisphere is dominant for non-verbal (Benowitz et al. 1983) and emotional (Blonder, Bowers and Heilman 1991) communication.

Recent neuroscientific information about the emotion-processing right brain is also directly applicable to models of the psychotherapy change process. Uddin et al. (2006) conclude, "The emerging picture from the current literature seems to suggest a special role of the right hemisphere in self-related cognition, own body perception, self-awareness and autobiographical memories" (p. 65). This hemisphere is centrally involved in "implicit learning" (Hugdahl 1995: 235), and implicit relational knowledge stored in the nonverbal domain is currently proposed to be at the core of therapeutic change (Stern et al. 1998).

Describing the right hemisphere as "the seat of implicit memory", Mancia (2006) observes that, "the discovery of the implicit memory has extended the concept of the unconscious and supports the hypothesis that this is where the emotional and affective— sometimes traumatic—presymbolic and preverbal experiences of the primary mother-infant relations are stored" (p. 83). Right brain autobiographical memory (Markowitsch et al. 2000), which stores insecure attachment histories, is activated in the therapeutic alliance, especially under relational stress. Cortina and Liotti (2007) point out that "experience encoded and stored in the implicit system is still alive and carried forward as negative expectations in regard to the availability and responsiveness of others, although this knowledge is unavailable for conscious recall" (p. 207). Such affective memories are transmitted within the therapeutic alliance. These affective communications "occur at an implicit level of rapid cueing and response that occurs too rapidly for simultaneous verbal transaction and conscious reflection" (Lyons-Ruth 2000: 91–92).

More specifically, spontaneous non-verbal transference–countertransference interactions at preconscious–unconscious levels represent implicit right brain to right brain face-to-face non-verbal communications of fast acting, automatic, regulated, and especially dysregulated bodily based stressful emotional states between patient and therapist (Schore 1994, 2009c). Transference is thus an activation of right brain autobiographical memory, as autobiographical negatively valenced, high intensity emotions are retrieved from specifically the right (and not left) medial temporal lobe (Buchanan, Tranel and Adolphs 2006). Updated neuropsychoanalytic models of transference (Pincus, Freeman, and Modell 2007) contend that "no appreciation of transference can do without emotion" (p. 634), and that "transference is distinctive in that it depends on early patterns of emotional attachment with caregivers" (p. 636). Current clinical models define transference as a selective bias in dealing with others that is based on previous early experiences and which shapes current expectancies, and as an expression of the patient's implicit perceptions and implicit memories (Schore 2003a, 2009c).

Right brain implicit processes in clinical enactments

The quintessential clinical context for a right brain transferential–countertransferential implicit communication of a dysregulated emotional state is the heightened affective moment of a clinical enactment. There is now agreement that enactments, "events occurring within the dyad that both parties experience as being the consequence of behavior in the other" (McLaughlin 1991: 611), are fundamentally mediated by non-verbal unconscious relational behaviours within the therapeutic alliance (Schore 2003a). These are transacted in visual-facial, auditory-prosodic, and tactile-proprioceptive emotionally charged attachment communications, as well as in gestures and body language, rapidly expressed behaviours that play a critical role in the unconscious interpersonal communications embedded within the enactment. This dyadic psychobiological mechanism allows for the detection of unconscious affects, and underlies the premise that "an enactment, by patient or analyst, could be evidence of something which has not yet been 'felt' by them" (Zanocco et al. 2006: 153).

In my book *Affect Regulation and the Repair of the Self* I offered a chapter entitled "Clinical implications of a psychoneurobiological model of projective identification" (Schore 2003a). This entire chapter on moment-to-moment implicit communications within an enactment focuses on phenomena which take place in "a moment", literally a split second. In it I offer a slow motion analysis of the rapid dyadic psychobiological events that occur in a heightened affective moment of the therapeutic alliance. This analysis discusses how a spontaneous enactment can either blindly repeat a pathological object relation through the therapist's deflection of projected negative states and intensification of interactive dysregulation, or provide a novel relational experience via the therapist's autoregulation of projected negative states and co-participation in interactive repair. Although these are the most stressful moments of the treatment, in an optimal context the therapist can potentially act as an implicit regulator of the patient's conscious and dissociated unconscious affective states. This dyadic psychobiological corrective emotional experience can lead to the emergence of more complex psychic structure by increasing the connectivity of right brain limbic-autonomic circuits.

Consonant with this conception of implicit communication (and citing my right brain neurobiological model), Ginot (2007) concludes, "Increasingly, enactments are understood as powerful manifestations of the intersubjective process and as inevitable expressions of complex, though largely unconscious self-states and relational patterns" (p. 317). These unconscious affective interactions "bring to life and consequently alter implicit memories and attachment styles" (p. 317). She further states that such intense manifestations of transference–countertransference entanglements "generate interpersonal as well as internal processes eventually capable of promoting integration and growth" (pp. 317–318).

In a parallel work, Zanocco et al. (2006: 145) characterizes the critical function of empathic physical sensations in the enactment and their central role in "the foundation of developing psychic structure of a human being". Enactments reflect "processes and dynamics originating in the primitive functioning of the mind", and they involve the analyst accomplishing a way of interacting with those patients who are not able to give representation to their instinctual impulses. These early "primary" activities are expressed in "an unconscious mental activity which does not follow the rules of conscious activity. There is no verbal language involved. Instead, there is a production of images that do not seem to follow any order, and, even less, any system of logic" (p. 145). Note the implications to implicit primary process cognition and right brain representations.

It is important to repeat the fact that the relational mechanism of enactments is especially prominent during stressful ruptures of the therapeutic alliance. Enactments occur at the edges of the regulatory boundaries of affect tolerance (Schore 2009b, 2009c), or what Lyons-Ruth (2005) describes as the "fault lines" of self-experience where "interactive negotiations have failed, goals remain aborted, negative affects are unresolved, and conflict is experienced" (p. 21). However, neuroscientists are describing "neuroplasticity in right hemispheric limbic circuitry in mediating long-lasting changes in negative affect following brief but severe stress" (Adamec, Blundell and Burton 2003: 1,264). Thus, an enactment can be a turning point in an analysis in which the relationship is characterized by a mode of resistance/counterresistance (Zanocco et al. 2006), but these moments call for the most complex clinical skills of the therapist.

This is due to the fact that such heightened affective moments induce the most stressful countertransference responses, including the clinician's implicit coping strategies that are formed in his/her own attachment history. Davies (2004) documents, "It seems to me intrinsic to relational thinking that these 'bad object relationships' not only will but must be reenacted in the transference–countertransference experience, that indeed such reenacted aggression, rage, and envy are endemic to psychoanalytic change within the relational perspective" (p. 714). It is important to note that enactments represent communications of not only stressful conscious affects, but also unconscious affects. Recall the "right hemispheric dominance in processing of unconscious negative emotion" (Sato and Aoki 2006). Very recent work in interpersonal neurobiology, attachment theory, and traumatology equates unconscious affect with dissociated affect (Schore 2007, 2009a, 2009b, 2009c, in press). Bromberg (2006) reports, "Clinically, the phenomenon of dissociation as a defense against self-destabilization ... has its greatest relevance during enactments, a mode of clinical engagement that requires an analyst's closest attunement to the unacknowledged affective shifts in his [sic] own and the patient's self-states" (p. 5).

On the other hand, Plakun (1999) observes that the therapist's "refusal of the transference", particularly the negative transference, is an early manifestation of an enactment. The therapist's "refusal" is expressed implicitly and spontaneously in non-verbal communications, not explicitly in the verbal narrative. A relational perspective from dynamic system theory clearly applies to the synergistic effects of the therapist's transient or enduring countertransferential "mindblindness" and the patient's negatively biased transferential expectation in the co-creation of an enactment. Feldman (1997) notes that, the fulminating negative state "may evoke forms of projection and enactment by the analyst, in an attempt at restoring an internal equilibrium, of which the analyst may initially be unaware" (p. 235).

Making this work even more emotionally challenging, Renik (1993) offers the important observation that countertransference enactments cannot be recognized until one is already in them. Rather spontaneous activity is expressed by the clinician's right brain, described by Lichtenberg, Lachmann, and Fosshage (1996: 213–214) as a "disciplined spontaneous engagement". These authors observe that such events occur "at a critical juncture in analysis" and they are usually prompted by some breach or miscommunication that requires "a human response". Although there is a danger of "exchanges degenerating into mutually traumatizing disruptions" that "recreate pathogenic expectations", the clinician's communications signal a readiness to participate authentically in the immediacy of an enactment. This is spontaneously expressed in the clinician's facial expressions, gestures, and unexpected comments that result from an "unsuppressed emotional upsurge". These communications seem more to pop out than to have been planned or edited, and they provide "intense moments that opened the way for examination of the role enactments into which the analyst had fallen unconsciously".

These "communications" are therefore right brain primary process emotional and not left brain rational logical secondary process communications. Thus explicit, conscious, verbal voluntary responses are inadequate to prevent, facilitate, or metabolize implicit emotional enactments. Bromberg (2006) refers to this in his assertion, "An interpretative stance … not only is thereby useless during an enactment, but also escalates the enactment and rigidifies the dissociation"

(p. 8). Andrade (2005) concludes: "As a primary factor in psychic change, interpretation is limited in effectiveness in pathologies arising from the verbal phase, related to explicit memories, with no effect in the pre-verbal phase where implicit memories are to be found. Interpretation—the method used to the exclusion of all others for a century—is only partial; when used in isolation it does not meet the demands of modern broad-based-spectrum psychoanalysis" (p. 677).

But if not an explicit analytic insight–directed response, then what type of implicit cognition would the therapist use in order to guide him or herself through stressful negative affective states, such as terror, rage, shame, disgust, and so on? What implicit right brain coping strategy could not only autoregulate the intense affect, but at the same time allow the clinician to maintain "an attunement to the unacknowledged affective shifts in his own and the patient's self-states"?

Right brain implicit processes and clinical intuition

In my introduction I proposed that the therapist's moment-to-moment navigation through these heightened affective moments occurs by not explicit verbal secondary process cognition, but rather by implicit non-verbal primary process clinical intuition. From a social neuroscience perspective, intuition is now being defined as "the subjective experience associated with the use of knowledge gained through implicit learning" (Lieberman 2000: 109). The description of intuition as "direct knowing that seeps into conscious awareness without the conscious mediation of logic or rational process" (Boucouvalas 1997: 7), clearly implies a right and not left brain function. Bugental (1987) refers to the therapist's "intuitive sensing of what is happening in the patient back of his [sic] words and, often, back of his conscious awareness" (p. 11). In his last work Bowlby (1991) speculated, "Clearly the best therapy is done by the therapist who is naturally intuitive and also guided by the appropriate theory" (p. 16).

In a groundbreaking article Welling (2005) notes that intuition is associated with pre-verbal character, affect, sense of relationship, spontaneity, immediacy, gestalt nature, and global view (all functions of the holistic right brain). He further discusses that "there is no cognitive theory about intuition" (p. 20), and therefore "what is needed is a model that can describe the underlying formal process that produces intuition phenomena" (pp. 23–24). Developmental psychoanalysis and neuropsychoanalysis can make important contributions to our understanding of the sources and mechanism of not only maternal but clinical intuition. With allusions to the right brain, Orlinsky and Howard (1986) contend that the "non-verbal, prerational stream of expression that binds the infant to its parent continues throughout life to be a primary medium of intuitively felt affective-relational communication between persons" (p. 343). There are thus direct commonalities between the spontaneous responses of the maternal intuition of a psychobiologically attuned primary caregiver and the intuitive therapist's sensitive countertransferential responsiveness to the patient's unconscious non-verbal affective bodily based implicit communications.

In the neuroscience literature, Volz and von Cramon (2006) conclude that intuition is related to the unconscious, and is "often reliably accurate" (p. 2,084). It is derived from stored non-verbal representations, such as "images, feelings, physical sensations, metaphors" (note the similarity to primary process cognition) (ibid.). Intuition is not expressed in language but rather is "embodied" in a "gut feeling" or in an initial guess that subsequently biases our thought and inquiry. "The gist information is realized on the basis of the observer's implicit knowledge rather than being consciously extracted on the basis of the observer's explicit knowledge" (ibid.).

With direct relevance to the concept of somatic countertransference, cognitive neuroscience models of intuition are highlighting the adaptive capacity of "embodied cognition". Allman et al. (2005) assert, "We experience the intuitive process at a visceral level. Intuitive decision making enables us to react quickly in situations that involve a high degree of uncertainty; situations which commonly involve social interactions" (p. 370). These researchers demonstrate that right prefrontal-insula and anterior cingulate relay a fast intuitive assessment of complex social situations in order to allow the rapid adjustment of behaviour in quickly changing circumstances. This lateralization is also found in a neuro-imaging study by Bolte and Goschke (2005), who suggest that association areas of the right hemisphere may play a special role in intuitive judgements.

In parallel psychoanalytic work, Marcus (1997) observes, "The analyst, by means of reverie and intuition, listens with the right brain to the analysand's right brain" (p. 238). Other clinicians hypothesize that the intuition of an experienced expert therapist lies fundamentally in a process of unconscious pattern matching (Rosenblatt and Thickstun 1994), and that this pattern recognition follows a non-verbal path, as verbal activity interferes with achieving insight (Schooler and Melcher 1995). Even more specifically, Bohart (1999: 298) contends that intuition involves the detection of "patterns and rhythms in interaction". But if not verbal stimuli, then which patterns are being intuitively tracked?

Recall, "transference is distinctive in that it depends on early patterns of emotional attachment with caregivers" (Pincus et al. 2007), and that enactments are powerful expressions of "unconscious self-states and relational patterns" (Ginot 2007). Indeed, updated models of psychotherapy describe the primacy of "making conscious the organizing patterns of affect" (Mohaupt et al. 2006: 243). van Lancker and Cummings (1999) assert, "Simply stated, the left hemisphere specializes in analyzing sequences, while the right hemisphere gives evidence of superiority in processing patterns" (p. 95). Thus I have suggested that the intuitive psychobiologically attuned therapist, on a moment-to-moment basis, implicitly tracks and resonates with the patterns of rhythmic crescendos/decrescendos of the patient's regulated and dysregulated states of affective arousal. Thus, intuition represents a complex right brain primary process, affectively charged embodied cognition that is adaptive for implicitly processing novelty, including object relational novelty, especially in moments of relational uncertainty.

Welling (2005) offers a phase model, in which the amount of information contained in the intuition increases from one phase to another, resulting in increased levels of complexity. An early "detection phase" related to "functions of arousal and attention" culminates in a "metaphorical solution phase", in which the intuition presents itself in the form of kinesthetic sensations, feelings, images, metaphors, and words. Here the solution, which has an emotional quality, is revealed, but in a veiled non-verbal form. These descriptions reflect the activity of the right hemisphere, which is dominant for attention (Raz 2004), kinesthesia (Naito et al. 2005), and the processing of novel metaphors (Mashal et al. 2007).

Phases of intuitive processing are thus generated in the therapists's subcortical-cortical vertical axis of the right brain, from the right amygdala to the right orbitofrontal system (see Figure A-2 in Schore

2003a). The orbital frontolimbic cortex, the highest level of the right brain would act as an "inner compass that accompanies the decoding process of intuition" (Welling 2005: 43). The orbitofrontal system, the "senior executive of the emotional brain" (Joseph 1996), is specialized to act in contexts of "uncertainty or unpredictability" (Elliott, Dolan, and Frith 2000). It functions as a dynamic filter of emotional stimuli (Rule, Shimamura, and Knight 2002) and provides "a panoramic view of the entire external environment, as well as the internal environment associated with motivational factors" (Barbas 2007: 239). It also formulates a theory of mind, "a kind of affective-decision making" (Happeney et al. 2004: 4), and thereby is centrally involved in "intuitive decision-making" (Allman et al. 2005: 369).

I have suggested that the right orbitofrontal cortex and its subcortical and cortical connections represent what Freud described as the preconscious (Schore 2003a). Alluding to preconscious functions, Welling (2005) describes intuition as:

> ... a factory of pieces of thoughts, images, and vague feelings, where the raw materials seem to float around half formless, a world so often present, though we hardly ever visit it. However, some of these floating elements come to stand out, gain strength, or show up repeatedly. When exemplified, they may be easier to recognize and cross the border of consciousness. (p. 33)

Over the course of the treatment the clinician accesses this preconscious domain, as does the free associating patient. Rather than the therapist's technical explicit skills the clinician's intuitive implicit capacities may be responsible for the outcome of an affectively charged enactment, and may dictate the depth of the therapeutic contact, exploration, and change processes.

Right brain implicit process central to change: Affect regulation

According to Ginot (2007), "This focus on enactments as communicators of affective building blocks also reflects a growing realization that explicit content, verbal interpretations, and the mere act of uncovering memories are insufficient venues for curative shifts" (p. 317). This clearly implies that the resolution of œ involves more than the standard Freudian idea of making the unconscious conscious. Not these explicit factors, then what implicit therapeutic experience is essential to the change process, especially in developmentally impaired personalities who are not psychologically minded? At the base the implicit change mechanism must certainly include a dysregulating affective experience that is communicated to an empathic other.

But in addition, the relational context must also afford an opportunity for interactive affect regulation, the core of the attachment process. Ogden and her colleagues (2005) conclude:

> Interactive psychobiological regulation (Schore, 1994) provides the relational context under which the client can safely contact, describe and eventually regulate inner experience ... [It] is the patient's experience of empowering action in the context of safety provided by a background of the empathic clinician's psychobiologically attuned interactive affect regulation that helps effect ... change. (p. 22)

It is the regulation of stressful and disorganizing high or low levels of affective-autonomic arousal that allows for the repair and re-organization of the right lateralized implicit self, the biological substrate of the human unconscious.

A cardinal principle of affective science dictates that a deeper understanding of affective processes is closely tied to the problem of the regulation of these processes. Affect regulation, a central mechanism of both development and the change process of psychotherapy, is usually defined as a set of conscious control processes by which we influence, consciously and voluntarily, the conscious emotions we have, and how we experience and express them. In a groundbreaking article in the clinical psychology literature, Greenberg (2007: 415) describes a "self-control" form of emotion regulation involving higher levels of cognitive executive function that allows individuals "to change the way they feel by consciously changing the way they think". This explicit form of affect regulation is performed by the verbal left hemisphere, and unconscious bodily based emotion is usually not addressed in this model. Notice this mechanism is at the core of insight, heavily emphasized in therapeutic models of not only classical psychoanalysis but also cognitive behavioural therapy.

In contrast to this conscious emotion regulation system, Greenberg (2007) describes a second, more fundamental implicit affect regulatory process performed by the right hemisphere. This system rapidly and automatically processes facial expression, vocal quality, and eye contact in a relational context. Therapy attempts not control but the "acceptance or facilitation of particular emotions", including "previously avoided emotion", in order to allow the patient to tolerate and transform them into "adaptive emotions". Citing my work he asserts, "It is the building of implicit or automatic emotion regulation capacities that is important for enduring change, especially for highly fragile personality-disordered clients" (Greenberg 2007: 416).

Even more than the patient's late acting rational, analytical, and verbal left mind, the growth-facilitating psychotherapeutic relationship needs to directly access the deeper psychobiological strata of the implicit regulatory structures of both the patient's and the clinician's right minds. Effective psychotherapy of attachment pathologies and severe personality disorders must focus on unconscious affect and the survival defense of pathological dissociation, "a structured separation of mental processes (e.g., thoughts, emotions, conation, memory, and identity) that are ordinarily integrated" (Spiegel and Cardeña 1991: 367). The clinical precept that unregulated overwhelming traumatic feelings can not be adaptively integrated into the patient's emotional life is the expression of a dysfunction of "the right hemispheric specialization in regulating stress—and emotion-related processes" (Sullivan and Dufresne 2006). As described earlier, this dissociative deficit specifically results from a lack of integration of the right lateralized limbic-autonomic circuits of the emotional brain (see Figure 1).

But recall Ginot's assertion that enactments "generate interpersonal as well as internal processes eventually capable of promoting integration and growth". Indeed, long-term psychotherapy can positively alter the developmental trajectory of the right brain and facilitate the top-down and bottom-up integration of its cortical and subcortical systems (Schore 2003a, 2007, 2009b, 2009c, in press). These enhanced right amygdala-ventral prefrontolimbic (orbitofrontal) connections allow implicit therapeutic "now moments" of lived interactive experience to be integrated into autobiographical memory. Autobiographical memory, an output of the right brain, is the highest memory system that consists of personal events with a clear relation to time, space, and context. In this right brain state of autonoetic consciousness the experiencing self represents emotionally toned memories, thereby allowing for "subjective time travel" (Kalbe et al. 2008: 15). The growth-facilitating expansion of interconnectivity within the unconscious system also promotes an increased complexity of defences, right brain coping strategies for regulating stressful affects that are more flexible and adaptive than pathological dissociation. This therapeutic mechanism supports the possible integration of what Bromberg (2006) calls "not-me" states into the implicit self.

Indeed, these developmental advances of the right lateralized vertical axis facilitate the further maturation of the right brain core of the self and its central involvement in "patterns of affect regulation that integrate a sense of self across state transitions, thereby allowing for a continuity of inner experience" (Schore 1994: 33). These neurobiological re-organizations of the right brain human unconscious underlie Alvarez's (2006) assertion, "Schore points out that at the more severe levels of psychopathology, it is not a question of making the unconscious conscious: rather it is a question of restructuring the unconscious itself" (p. 171).

Earlier I suggested that the right hemisphere is dominant in the change process of psychotherapy. Neuroscience authors are concluding that although the left hemisphere is specialized for coping with predictable representations and strategies, the right predominates for coping with and assimilating novel situations (Podell et al. 2001) and ensures the formation of a new programme of interaction with a new environment (Ezhov and Krivoschchekov 2004). Indeed, "The right brain possesses special capabilities for processing novel stimuli … Right-brain problem solving generates a matrix of alternative solutions, as contrasted with the left brain's single solution of best fit. This answer matrix remains active while alternative solutions are explored, a method suitable for the open-ended possibilities inherent in a novel situation". (Schutz 2005: p. 13)

The functions of the emotional right brain are essential to the self-exploration process of psychotherapy, especially of unconscious affects that can be potentially integrated into a more complex implicit sense of self. At the most essential level, the work of psychotherapy is not defined by what the therapist explicitly, objectively does for the patient, or says to the patient. Rather the key mechanism is how to implicitly and subjectively be with the patient, especially during affectively stressful moments when the "going-on-being" of the patient's implicit self is dis-integrating in real time.

References

Adamec, R.E., Blundell, J. and Burton, P. (2003). "Phosphorylated cyclic AMP response element bonding protein expression induced in the periaqueductal gray by predator stress; its relationship to the stress experience, behavior, and limbic neural plasticity". *Progress in Neuro-Pharmacology & Biological Psychiatry*. 27: 1,243–1,267.

Allman, J.M., Watson, K.K., Tetreault, N.A. and Hakeem, A.Y. (2005). "Intuition and autism: a possible role for Von Economo neurons". *Trends in Cognitive Sciences*. 9: 367–373.

Alvarez, A. (2006). "Some questions concerning states of fragmentation: unintegration, under-integration, disintegration, and the nature of early integrations". *Journal of Child Psychotherapy*. 32: 158–180.

Andrade, V.M. (2005). "Affect and the therapeutic action in psychoanalysis". *Internat. J. Psychoanal.* 86: 677–697.

Barbas, H. (2007). "Flow of information for emotions through temporal and orbitofrontal pathways". *Journal of Anatomy*. 211: 237–249.

Bargh, J.A. and Morsella, E. (2008). "The unconscious mind". *Perspectives on Psychological Science*. 3: 73–79.

Benowitz, L.I., Bear, D.M., Rosenthal, R., Mesulam, M.M., Zaidel, E. and Sperry, R.W. (1983). "Hemispheric specialization in non-verbal communication". *Cortex*. 19: 5–11.

Blonder, L.X., Bowers, D. and Heilman, K.M. (1991). "The role of the right hemisphere in emotional communication". *Brain*, 114: 1,115–1,127.

Bohart, A.C. (1999). "Intuition and creativity in psychotherapy". *J. Constructivist Psychology*. 12: 287–311.

Bolte, A. and Goschke, T. (2005). "On the speed of intuition: Intuitive judgments of semantic coherence under different response deadlines". *Memory & Cognition*. 33: 1,248–1,255.

Boucouvalas, M. (1997). "Intuition: The concept and the experience". In: R.D. Floyd and P.S. Arvidson (eds). *Intuition: The inside story*. New York: Routledge, pp. 39–56.

Bowlby, J. (autumn 1991). The role of the psychotherapist's personal resources in the therapeutic situation. In: *Tavistock Gazette*.

Bromberg, P.M. (2006). *Awakening the dreamer: Clinical journeys*. Mahweh, NJ: The Analytic Press.

Buchanan, T.W., Tranel, D. and Adolphs, R. (2006). "Memories for emotional autobiographical events following unilateral damage to medial temporal lobe". *Brain*. 129: 115–127.

Bugental, J.F. (1987). *The Art of the psychotherapist*. New York: W.W. Norton.

Buklina, S.B. (2005). "The corpus callosum, interhemispheric interactions, and the function of the right hemisphere of the brain". *Neuroscience and Behavioral Physiology*. 35: 473–480.

Burgoon, J.K. (1985). "Non-verbal signals". In: M.L. Knapp, and C.R. Miller (eds) *Handbook of interpersonal communication*. Beverly Hills CA: Sager Publications, pp. 344–390.

Carretie, L., Hinojosa, J.A., Mercado, F. and Tapia, M. (2005). "Cortical response to subjectively unconscious danger". *NeuroImage*. 24: 615–623.

Chused, J.F. (2007). "Non-verbal communication in psychoanalysis: commentary on Harrison and Tronick". *J. Amer. Psychoanal. Assn.* 55: 875–882.

Cortina, M. and Liotti, G. (2007). "New approaches to understanding unconscious processes: Implicit and explicit memory systems". *Internat. Forum of Psychoanal.* 16: 204–212.

Davies, J.M. (2004). "Whose bad objects are we anyway? Repetition and our elusive love affair with evil". *Psychoanal. Dial.* 14: 711–732.

Devinsky, O. (2000). "Right cerebral hemispheric dominance for a sense of corporeal and emotional self". *Epilepsy & Behavior*. 1: 60–73.

Dorpat, T.L. (2001). "Primary process communication". *Psychoanal. Inq.* 3: 448–463.

Elliott, R., Dolan, R.J. and Frith, C.D. (2000). "Dissociable functions in the medial and lateral orbitofrontal cortex: evidence from human neuroimaging studies". *Cerebral Cortex*. 10: 308–317.

Ezhov, S.N. and Krivoschekov, S.G. (2004). "Features of psychomotor responses and interhemispheric relationahips at various stages of adaptation to a new time zone". *Human Physiology*. 30: 172–175.

Feldman, M. (1997). "Projective identification: the analyst's involvement". *Int. J. Psychoanal.* 78: 227–241.

Freud, S. (1895). Project for a Scientific Psychology. *Standard Edition*, Vol. 1, 281–397.

——. (1915). The unconscious. *Standard Edition*, Vol. 14, 159–205.

——. (1920/1943). *A general introduction to psycho-analysis*. Garden City New York: Garden City Publishing Company.

Ginot, E. (2007). "Intersubjectivity and neuroscience. Understanding enactments and their therapeutic significance within emerging paradigms". *Psychoanalytic Psychology*. 24: 317–332.

Grabner, R.H., Fink, A. and Neubauer, A.C. (2007). "Brain correlates of self-related originality of ideas: Evidence from event-related power and phase-locking changes in the EEG". *Behavioral Neuroscience.* 121: 224–230.

Greenberg, L.S. (2007). "Emotion coming of age". *Clinical Psychology Science and Practice.* 14: 414–421.

Happaney, K., Zelazo, P.D. and Stuss, D.T. (2004). "Development of orbitofrontal function: Current themes and future directions". *Brain and Cognition.* 55: 1–10.

Hugdahl, K. (1995). "Classical conditioning and implicit learning: The right hemisphere hypothesis". In: R.J. Davidson, and K. Hugdahl (eds) *Brain asymmetry.* Cambridge, MA: MIT Press, pp. 235–267.

Hutterer, J. and Liss, M. (2006). "Cognitive development, memory, trauma, treatment: An integration of psychoanalytic and behavioural concepts in light of current neuroscience research". *J. Amer. Acad. Psychoanal. Dynamic Psychiatry.* 34: 287–302.

Joseph, R. (1996). *Neuropsychiatry, Neuropsychology, and Clinical Neuroscience.* 2nd ed. Baltimore: Williams & Wilkins.

Kalbe, E., Brand, M., Thiel, A., Kessler, J. and Markowitsch, H.J. (2008). "Neuropsychological and neural correlates of autobiographical deficits in a mother who killed her children". *Neurocase.* 14: 15–28.

LeDoux, J. (2002). *Synaptic self: How our brains become who we are.* New York: Viking.

Lichtenberg, J.D., Lachmann, F.M. and Fosshage, J.L. (1996). *The clinical exchange.* Mahwah, NJ: The Analytic Press.

Lieberman, M.D. (2000). "Intuition: a social neuroscience approach". *Psychological Bulletin.* 126: 109–137.

Lyons-Ruth, K. (2000). "'I sense that you sense that I sense …': Sander's recognition process and the emergence of new forms of relational organization". *Infant Mental Health J.* 21: 85–98.

———. (2005) "The two-person unconscious: Intersubjective dialogue, enactive representation, and the emergence of new forms of relational organization". In: L. Aron and A. Harris (eds) *Relational psychoanalysis,* Vol. II. Hillsdale, NJ: The Analytic Press, pp. 2–45.

Mancia, M. (2006). "Implicit memory and early unrepressed unconscious: Their role in the therapeutic process (How the neurosciences can contribute to psychoanalysis)". *Int. J. Psychoanal.* 87: 83–103.

Marcus D.M. (1997). "On knowing what one knows". *Psychoanal. Q.* 66: 219–241.

Markowitsch, H.J., Reinkemeier, A., Kessler, J., Koyuncu, A. and Heiss, W.D. (2000). "Right amygdalar and temperofrontal activation during autobiographical, but not fictitious memory retrieval". *Behavioral Neurology.* 12: 181–190.

Mashal, N., Faust, M., Hendler, T. and Jung-Beeman, M. (2007). "An fMRI investigation of the neural correates underlying the processing of novel metaphoric expressions". *Brain and Language.* 100: 115–126.

McLaughlin, J.T. (1991). "Clinical and theoretical aspects of enactment". *J. Amer. Psychoanal. Assn.* 39: 595–614.

Mohaupt, H., Holgersen, H., Binder, P.E. and Nielsen, G.H. (2006). "Affect consciousness or mentalization? A comparison of two concepts with regard to affecr development and affect regulation". *Scandinavian J. Psychology.* 47: 237–244.

Morris, J.S., Ohman, A. and Dolan, R.J. (1998). "Conscious and unconscious emotional learning in the human amygdala". *Nature.* 393: 467–470.

Naito, E., Roland, P.E. Grefkes, C., Choi, H.J., Eickhoff, S., Geyer, S., Zilles, K. and Ehrsson, H.H. (2005). "Dominance of the right hemisphere and role of Area 2 in human kinesthesia". *J. Neurophysiology.* 93: 1,020–1,034.

Ogden, P., Pain, C., Minton, K. and Fisher, J. (2005). "Including the body in mainstream psychotherapy for traumatized individuals". *Psychologist-Psychoanalyst,* XXV, No. 4. 19–24.

Orlinsky, D.E. and Howard, K.I. (1986). "Process and outcome in psychotherapy". In: S.L. Garfield, and A.E. Bergin (eds) *Handbook of psychotherapy and behavior change,* 3rd Edn. New York: Wiley.

Pincus, D., Freeman, W. and Modell, A. (2007). "A neurobiological model of perception. Considerations for transference". *Psychoanal. Psychol.* 24: 623–640.

Plakun, E.M. (1999). "Making the alliance and taking the transference in work with suicidal patients". *J. Psychotherapy Practice and Research.* 10f: 269–276.

Podell, K., Iovell, M. and Goldberg, E. (2001). "Lateralization of frontal lobe functions". In: S.P. Salloway, P.F. Malloy, and J.D. Duffy (eds) *The frontal lobes and neuropsychiatric illness.* London: American Psychiatric Publishing, pp. 83–89.

Raz, A. (2004). "Anatomy of attentional networks". *Anatomical Records.* 281B: 21–36.

Renik, O. (1993). "Countertransference enactment and the psychoanalytic process". In: M.J. Horowitz, O.F. Kernberg, and E.M. Weinshel (eds) *Psychic structure and psychic change: Essays in honor of Robert S. Wallerstein.* Madison CT: International Universities Press, pp. 135–158.

Rosenblatt, A.D. and Thickstun, J.T. (1994). "Intuition and consciousness". *Psychoanal. Q.* 63: 696–714.

Rule, R.R. Shimamura, A.P. and Knight, R.T. (2002). "Orbitofrontal cortex and dynamic filtering of emotional stimuli. Cognition, Affective, & Behavioral". *Neuroscience.* 2: 264–270.

Ryan, R. (2007). "Motivation and emotion: A new look and approach for two reemerging fields". *Motivation and Emotion*. 31. 1–3.

Sato, W. and Aoki, S. (2006). "Right hemisphere dominance in processing unconscious emotion". *Brain and Cognition*. 62: 261–266.

Schooler, J. and Melcher, J. (1995). The ineffability of insight. In: S.T. Smith, T.B. Ward, and R.A. Finke (eds) *The creative cognition approach*. Cambridge, MA: MIT Press, pp. 27–51.

Schore, A.N. (1994). *Affect regulation and the origin of the self*. Mahweh NJ: Erlbaum.

———. (1997). "A century after Freud's Project: Is a rapprochement between psychoanalysis and neurobiology at hand?" *J. Amer. Psychoanal. Assn*. 45: 841–867.

———. (2002). "The right brain as the neurobiological substratum of Freud's .dynamic unconscious". In: D. Scharff (ed.) *The psychoanalytic century: Freud's legacy for the future*. New York: Other Press, pp. 61–88.

———. (2003a). *Affect regulation and the repair of the self*. New York: W.W. Norton.

———. (2003b). *Affect dysregulation and disorders of the self*. New York: W.W. Norton.

———. (2005). "A neuropsychoanalytic viewpoint. Commentary on paper by Steven H. Knoblauch". *Psychoanal. Dial*. 15: 829–854.

———. (2007). "Review of Awakening the dreamer: clinical journeys by Philip M. Bromberg". *Psychoanal. Dial*. 17: 753–767.

———. (2009a). "Attachment trauma and the developing right brain: Origins of pathological dissociation". In: P.F. Dell, and J.A. O'Neil (eds) *Dissociation and the dissociative disorders: DSM-V and Beyond*. New York: Routledge, pp. 107–141.

———. (2009b). "Relational trauma and the developing right brain: an interface of psychoanalytic self psychology and neuroscience". *Annals of the New York Academy of Sciences*. 1159: 189–203.

———. (2009c). "Right brain affect regulation: an essential mechanism of development, trauma, dissociation, and psychotherapy". In: D. Fosha, M. Solomon, and D. Siegel (eds) *The hearing power of emotion: Integrating relationships, body and mind. A dialogue among scientists and clinicians*. New York: Norton, pp. 112–144.

———. (in press). "Relational trauma and the developing right brain: the neurobiology of broken attachment bonds". In: T. Baradon (ed.) *Relational trauma in infancy*. London: Routledge.

Schore, J.R. and Schore, A.N. (2008). "Modern attachment theory: the central role of affect regulation in development and treatment". *Clinical Social Work Journal*. 36: 9–20.

Schutz, L.E. (2005). "Broad-perspective perceptual disorder of the right hemisphere". *Neuropsychology Review*. 15: 11–27.

Soanes, C. and Hawker S. (2005). *Compact Oxford Dictionary of Current English*. Oxford: Oxford University Press.

Spiegel, D. and Cardena, E. (1991). "Disintegrated experience: the dissociative disorders revisited". *Journal of Abnormal Psychology*. 100: 366–378.

Stern, D.N. (1998). Bruschweiler-Stern, N., Harrison, A.M., Lyons-Ruth, K., Morgan, A.C., Nahum, J.P., Sander, L. and Tronick, E.Z. "The process of therapeutic change involving implicit knowledge: Some implications of developmental observations for adult psychotherapy". *Infant Mental Health J.* 19: 300–308.

——. (2004). *The Present moment in psychotherapy and everyday life*. New York: WW Norton.

——. (2005). "Intersubjectivity". In: E.S. Person, A.M. Cooper, and G.O. Gabbard (eds) *Textbook of psychoanalysis*. Washington, DC: American Psychiatric Publishing, pp. 77–92.

Sullivan, R.M., and Dufresne, M.M. (2006). "Mesocortical dopamine and HPA axis regulation: Role of laterality and early environment". *Brain Research*. 1076: 49–59.

Uddin, L.Q., Molnar-Szakacs, I., Zaidel, E. and Iacoboni, M. (2006). "rTMS to the right inferior parietal lobule disrupts self-other discrimination". *Social Cognitive and Affective Neuroscience*. 1: 65–71.

van Lancker, D. and Cummings, J.L. (1999). "Expletives: neurolingusitic and neurobehavioral perspectives on swearing". *Brain Research Reviews*. 31: 83–104.

Volz, K.G. and von Cramon, D.Y. (2006). "What neuroscience can tell about intuitive processes in the context of perceptual discovery". *J. Cognitive Neurosci.* 18: 2,077–2,087.

Welling, H. (2005). "The intuitive process: the case of psychotherapy". *J. Psychotherapy Integration*. 15: 19–47.

Zanocco, G., De Marchi, A. and Pozzi, F. (2006). "Sensory empathy and enactment". *Int. J. Psychoanal.* 87: 145–158.

CHAPTER THIRTEEN

The uncertainty principle in the psychoanalytic process

Wilma S. Bucci, Ph.D.

In his paper "The analyst's self-revelation", Bromberg (2006) says that change:

> ... "takes place not through thinking, 'If I do this correctly, then that will happen' but, rather, through an ineffable coming together of two minds in an unpredictable way". (p. 147)

I have referred to this as Bromberg's uncertainty principle; in this paper, I will try to deconstruct this principle and also extend it in some ways.

The concept of "ineffable"

At a conference in Rome in July, 2007, on Psychoanalytic Theories of Unconscious Mental Functioning and Multiple Code Theory,[1] two of the speakers, Giuseppe Moccia (2007), and Giuseppe Martini (2007), both members of the Italian Psychoanalytic Society, surveyed the

---

[1] Conference of the Italian Psychoanalytic Society and the International Psychoanalytical Association, Rome, 2007.

domain of implicit or unconscious processes from psychoanalytic and philosophical perspectives, starting with Freud's (1915) original insight concerning the nonrepressible part of the unconscious:

> "Everything that is repressed must remain unconscious; but let us state at the very outset that the repressed does not cover everything that is unconscious. The unconscious has the wider compass: the repressed is a part of the unconscious". (p. 166)

Since Freud's time, the fields of phenomenology and hermeneutics have "more deeply studied and valorized that wider compass", as Martini and Moccia pointed out, giving it many labels and emphasizing many different aspects. Thus Martini (2007) characterized this domain as the unrepresentable; the perturbing and ineffable sphere that escapes the clarifying ambition of interpretation. Heidegger (1959) referred to the reality that escapes the word; Gadamer (1989) referred to the enigmatic question; Ricoeur (1970) to the untranslatable. Jaspers (1963) discussed this domain as the incomprehensible, both on a psychopathological level as referring to delirium, but also in more general philosophical terms, as referring to bodily experience. Bion (1962) referred to the unthinkable, the unknown, unknowable, infinite without form; Bollas (1987), from a somewhat different perspective, referred to the unthought known. There are also related concepts in the writings of Ferenczi, Winnicott, Piera Aulagnier, Loch, Matte Blanco, Ferrari, and many others.

I believe that all of these writers, philosophers, and psychoanalysts are attempting to characterize the same epistemological domain, but that their characterizations are divergent and to some extent contradictory. The known that is unthought of Bollas is different from the unknown, the unknowable of Bion. And both are different from the incomprehensible of Jaspers, and the unrepresentable of Martini. The untranslatable of Ricoeur, and Heidegger's concept of the reality that escapes the word are similar to one another, but different from the rest.

I suggest that the conceptual struggle that we see here arises because all of these writers are still trapped in the implicit contradictions of the classical psychoanalytic metapsychology, while explicitly they may reject this framework. Freud's formulation of two distinct systems of thought within the psychical apparatus, including a system of thought outside the verbal categorical domain, was certainly one of his most profound insights. But in character- izing this system, Freud was caught in the inconsistencies of the energy theory that he himself formulated, as well as in his implicit valuing of language over non-verbal forms. On the one hand, he characterized the primary process as a systematic mode of thought, organized according to a set of principles that he specified as the laws of the dream work. On the other hand, he also characterized this system as the mode of thought associated with unbound energy, the forces of the Id, chaotic, driven by wish fulfilment and divorced from reality. This inconsistency can be seen throughout psychoan- alytic theory, as in the comments of the writers I have mentioned here. We need to work through some of these implicit assumptions so as to develop a more veridical understanding of emotional mean- ing and emotional communication.

In the context of the cognitive psychology and neuroscience of today, in the theoretical framework of multiple code theory, I have pointed to a world of complex thought that is non-verbal and even non-symbolic; that occurs in its own systematic and organized for- mat, primarily continuous and analogic; that is rooted in our bod- ies and sensory systems; and that can be consciously known and comprehended; but that is not directly representable in words. Such non-symbolic, or what I call subsymbolic, processes occur in percep- tion and as imagery, in motoric, visceral, and sensory forms, in all sensory modalities. Subsymbolic processing is required for a vast array of functions from skiing to musical performance and creative cooking—and for the interactions of ballroom dancing, especially the Argentine tango, of which more later. Subsymbolic processing in visual and other modalities is central in creative scientific and math- ematical work; research mathematicians and physicists understand this very well. Einstein (1949) referred to sensory and bodily, par- ticularly muscular, experiences as the basic elements of his thought.

Of greatest interest to psychoanalysis, subsymbolic processing is dominant in emotional information processing and emotional communication—reading facial and bodily expressions of others; experiencing one's own feelings and emotions. All of these functions call for processing that is analogic and continuous, not discrete, and that occurs in specific sensory modalities, not in abstract form. We know this processing as intuition, the wisdom of the body and in other related ways. The crucial information concerning our bodily states comes to us primarily in subsymbolic form, and emotional communication between people occurs primarily in this mode. Reik's (1948) concept of "listening with the third ear" relies largely on subsymbolic communication, as I have discussed in detail elsewhere (Bucci 2001).

In the context of the cognitive science of today, subsymbolic processes are understood as organized, systematic, rational forms of thought that continue to develop in complexity and scope throughout life. They are modelled by connectionist or parallel distributed processing (PDP) systems (McClelland et al. 1989), with the features of dynamical systems.

All processing, including symbolic as well as subsymbolic, may operate either within or outside of awareness. Subsymbolic processing often operates within awareness, but we cannot capture it. Most of us have not developed the skills of focusing attention on this processing mode, although one can perhaps begin to learn to do this in meditation and using certain feedback mechanisms, as in the devices used for self-regulation of blood pressure, where people learn to listen to their bodies. We are not accustomed to thinking of processes, including sensory, motoric, and visceral processes that cannot be verbalized or symbolized, as systematic and organized thought; the new understanding of subsymbolic processing opens the door to this reformulation. It changes our entire perspective of pathology and treatment when we are able to make this shift.

This formulation cuts the theoretical pie in a new way. Subsymbolic processes are lawful and systematic, not chaotic. They are not driven by wish fulfilment; they can be both thought and known, in the senses of Bion and Bollas. But the specific psychical terrain that we are trying to explore can be mapped only partially onto words; if we try to place the signposts prematurely—apply general mappings that have been used in other terrains—we will find ourselves either blocked or lost. The subsymbolic processes constitute the untranslatable, in the sense of Ricoeur; the reality that escapes the word, in the terms of Heidegger. They are not unrepresentable; but do exist in what Martini (2007) referred to as the "perturbing and ineffable sphere that escapes the clarifying ambition of interpretation".

The concept of "minds": The emotion schemas

Returning to Bromberg's uncertainty principle, I have formulated the concept of "ineffable coming together" as emotional communication, which is largely subsymbolic. For "minds", I refer to a more complex structure, the emotion schema, that includes components of all three processing systems: subsymbolic processes, symbolic imagery, and later language.

Emotion schemas are types of memory structures that constitute the organization of the self in the interpersonal world. They are formed on the basis of repeated interactions with caretakers and others from the beginning of life. The subsymbolic sensory, somatic, and motoric representations and processes constitute the affective core of the emotion schema—the source of the varieties of arousal, pleasure, and pain that constitute emotional experience. In each event of life, the processes of the affective core will be activated in relation to the people, places, and activities that figure in that event; thus we build memories of people and events that give us pleasure or pain, that activate happiness, or dread, or a wish to attack. Autobiographical memory is built out of such events; this is the basis for the organization of the self in the interpersonal world.

The emotion schemas develop in an interpersonal context; the baby who laughs and smiles and has feelings of joy can see and hear the other person also smiling and laughing and making the corresponding sounds; the expressions of the other becomes incorporated in the schema of joy. If the child who cries hears sympathetic sounds and sees a particular facial expression, along with feeling a soothing touch, the child's schemas of pain or fear will develop to incorporate responses of turning to others and expectations that others can help. If the caretaker typically responds to the child's cries with annoyance or withdrawal, schemas of negative expectations and associated responses will develop.

Dissociation within the emotion schemas

Every person has multiple emotion schemas, including schemas of self and schemas of others, integrated to varying degrees. Dissociations may occur within the schemas, and among them. Some degree of dissociation is normative and necessary to allow us to function smoothly in our lives; not every desire or expectation or response will be formulated in symbolic form (Bucci 2007 a, b). In some cases, however, dissociations occur in response to events that are extremely painful, experienced as threats to life or to the organization of the self. With such dissociation, it is not only that we haven't made a connection to symbolic forms, not only that the schema may never have been formulated, but that we avoid such integration. If the parent is herself or himself the source of the negative affect, acting in such a way as to elicit pain or rage or terror in the child, this type of avoidant dissociation will occur and will be crystallized and reinforced. We must avoid knowing who or what is the source of the extreme pain, in order to go on with life, to retain the connection to the caretaker that is emotionally and physically essential for survival, and to maintain a sense of self. The initial dissociation is a life-saving event; if the dissociation is crystallized so that new emotional information cannot be taken in, it becomes the problem that interferes with life and brings patients to treatment.

The concept of the unpredictable in the analytic interaction

Analyst and patient each come to the session with a set of emotion schemas, developed in the course of their lives, affected by events of life outside of the session as well as by events within it. The interaction is inherently unpredictable, as Bromberg has said. The meeting of the emotion schemas that have been activated is new and unique; this particular interaction with activation of these particular emotion schemas in each participant has never existed prior to the moment. The schemas that are activated are dominated by the affective core and in some cases will be dissociated, certainly for the patient, and also to a certain degree for the analyst. In such cases, the affective core of sensory and somatic experience is not connected to the source of the activation and the connection is avoided; thus both participants may be aroused in particular ways and may not know why. This interactive arousal, which is largely unsymbolized—feelings of rage, humiliation, or despair, the meanings of which are not known or are wrongly known—is the potential source and content of the therapeutic work; it is also the potential threat.

In a more general sense, the interaction is also unpredictable in that therapists today must negotiate this terrain largely without the explicit traditional guides of theory and technique. The analyst can no longer assume that there is a particular repressed scenario that is guiding the patient's experience, that he or she is avoiding, and that can be uncovered. The analyst can also not assume a set of rules and parameters that define the correct way to work. These changes bring freedom from theories and techniques that do not fit; they bring the uncertainty of freedom as well.

Subsymbolic experience is the guide to the uncharted terrain of the analytic interchange. Both participants must learn to follow this, to receive and send signals that are outside of the symbolic domain.

The uncertainty principle of tango

In tango, the leader and follower generally do not follow a specified sequence of steps; tango differs from other ballroom dances in that respect. Bodily communication is crucial; the leader needs to feel the follower's position at every moment to enable him or her to signal the next moves; the follower needs to be poised to receive and respond to the leader's signals. This involves a type of normative dissociation for both partners; the interaction occurs primarily in the subsymbolic bodily zone; verbal guidance is too slow, too limited, violates the flow of the dance. At every moment both participants need to be in an activated and open state that the tango dancer and teacher Dardo Galletto[2] calls "maybe". The leader tries to signal a move, maybe it will work, maybe it won't; each partner needs to continuously receive bodily information from the other and continuously test and shift the signals to produce a response. This is Dardo's uncertainty principle in tango, a true dynamical system in a technical sense, dependent on transmission of sufficient information to override uncertainty and exceed the response threshold. The state of 'maybe' involves the capacity to rely on analogic information without symbolic guideposts; to remain suspended—sometimes on one foot—in the zone of subsymbolic processing, without the usual support of symbolic images or words. Some people cannot bear the uncertainty; they want to repeat, fixed routines; the fear of losing one's balance, and the humiliation of miscommunication, feel too great; they do not get far in learning tango.

---

[2] Artistic Director and Choreographer, New Generation Dance Company.

The subsymbolic communication, the state of maybe, the capacity to endure a state of uncertainty, are necessary for tango, but it is also true that they are not sufficient. Tango dancers also need to bring at least two additional psychic supports to the milonga, the dance: one is basic knowledge of steps and techniques, the other is attitude. It is all very well to be open and suspended on one foot, but without some movement vocabulary, some knowledge of the positions, the communication cannot work. Here is one place where the symbol system must enter tango, as for any dance and sport. Teachers try to break down the sequences into their elements, to analyze the steps and techniques, to teach the names of the steps. They also analyze the ways to use the body and the feet: relax the hips, feel the upper and lower body separately, keep the upper body facing the partner. To a large extent, teachers work by showing their own movements as images. Dardo demonstrates a specific way of holding the body and of moving; the students watch and translate the moves to their own bodily systems. Dardo also emphasizes metaphor to characterize the movements, and then goes beyond that to characterize attitude and attunement as well. We do not only relax our hips and turn our upper bodies, we walk like Argentine woman (or Argentine man, which is quite different). We must delight in our partner as in a delicious meal of grilled meat; we must feel our partner, not just love and delight but a far more complex range of feelings including aspects of dominance and submission and their consequences.

The choreography of the analytic interchange

In psychoanalysis, as in tango, the subsymbolic exploration and the connection to the symbolic domain within the relationship, as well as within each participant's autobiographical memory are necessary for both participants. The patient is struggling to talk, or is not talking, or talking about not wanting to talk, or talking about how the analyst looks, or how the room smells, or whether the room is too cold or too hot. We can see the patient as beginning to enact a dissociated schema that represents a particular expectation about another person.

The analyst will be having his or her own struggles, determined, as the patient's are, by the emotion schemas that are activated. There is a flow of subsymbolic experience going on within the analyst, linked to symbolic representation to varying degrees.

With the synergy of the moment, an interaction will occur that is both old and new: old in that it is based on the emotion schemas with which each participant habitually interacts with the interpersonal world, and with which each has entered the session; new in that each is confronting a particular person, at a particular time and in a particular place, in a particular role, for the first time.

For both participants, it is necessary not only to be open to subsymbolic experience and to respond to it, but also to be willing to endure some degree of painful activation; the willingness to endure the activation in turn requires some capacity to contain it. As the arousal and the interaction proceed, both participants will be searching and exploring in their associations and responses, in their past lives, and in their present interactions; both will be examining their experience, to construct formulations that will enable them to explore together. The connections from the subsymbolic to the symbolic domain are necessary to enable sharing of experience, to put down signposts in the shared terrain, and to open new exploration.

The view of treatment proposed here, in which both participants enter with dissociated schemas, both engage in exploration of subsymbolic domains, both make new connections to symbolic experience, is very different from a model in which a patient is viewed as coming in with unconscious experience that has been previously formulated and then repressed, the analyst has a neutral affective stance, and the analyst interprets the patient's associations with the goal of insight and uncovering the repressed contents.

To work in the mode of uncertainty, the analyst, like the patient needs to develop the skills of operating in the implicit interactive domain. By virtue of experience and training and perhaps other factors, the analyst may develop this to a relatively high degree and may have a somewhat greater sense of safety in negotiating the troubled waters.

What does the analyst bring, what does the analyst need, to support work in this domain? Here are a few possibilities:

- In tango, the teacher or the experienced dancer has an advantage in symbolic vocabulary, not necessarily verbal. He or she knows a set of sequences and how to direct the moves. Similarly, the analyst has more symbolized emotional categories with which to identify what is occurring—not necessarily more categories with diagnostic names, not even more verbal categories, but more schemas, more meanings: this patient is like others I have seen, or others I have known or read about; this tangle is like others in which I have been caught.

- There are obvious differences in feeling states between therapist and patient on many levels, differences in degree of fear, of risk, and of pain with which they enter the therapeutic relationship. The modulation of affective intensity supports the analyst's capability to seek new zones of interaction, rather than to repeat past protective sequences.

- There is also a general difference in attitude that is not so obvious. As I have suggested elsewhere (Bucci 2007 a, b), analysts have developed, implicitly, a capacity for flexible shifting in self states, a capacity to find different parts of themselves that are genuine but context determined. This involves a particular analytic attitude that I characterize as a normative and adaptive dissociated mode, not unlike the mode of the actor who is immersed in a role, but with more uncertainty, without a script. The state that is activated in the therapist in the session, the love or hate or fear or shame, is fully genuine at the moment, necessarily open to some degree of risk, but in the context of a background knowledge that it is only one way of being, that there are other ways of being that will be activated in different contexts, and that they are all held within one overall autobiographical frame. It is that background knowledge, which is likely to be implicit, that allows the immersion in the moment that is necessary for analytic exploration.

- Beyond all this, to support the freedom of emotional exploration, I suggest that analysts also require a systematic general psychological theory that specifically accounts for the unique and unpredictable interactions of the analytic interchange—that makes the interactions, in fact, more predictable in certain respects. If clinicians do not have an explicit theoretical framework to guide them in a situation of uncertainty and risk, they will draw on an implicit one. The problem with implicit theories is that they may tend to lead clinicians in ways that are unrecognized, and unexamined, down the slippery slope of assumptions concerning specific repressed scenarios to be uncovered, or techniques involving interpretation of resistance, or from another perspective, recourse to projective identification defined in terms of the patient's intolerable affects somehow being placed in the therapist. In place of such implicit assumptions, we need a systematic psychological theory that provides an understanding of affect emerging in a complex way from the therapist's and patient's own emotional schemas in the context of their relationship—how each connects dissociated states within him/herself; how each person connects to the other on several levels; how each connects the events of the present to memories of the past; and how all these connecting processes can be used to bring about change.

Beginning with uncertainty and risk, we can try to increase the zone of the symbolic and the predictable, without losing the richness of the treatment situation. We need to address this goal both in the specific interactions of the treatment situation and in the development of the guiding principles of theory, and we need to build this knowledge from both clinical and research sources.

References

Bion, W.R. (1962). "The Psycho-Analytic Study of Thinking". *Int. J. Psycho-Anal.* 43: 306–310.

Bion, W.R. (1962). "A theory of thinking". *International Journal of Psycho-Analysis.* 43: 306–310.

Bollas, C. (1987). *The Shadow of the Object: Psychoanalysis of the Unthought Known.* N.Y.: Columbia University Press.

Bromberg, P.M. (2006). "The analyst's 'self-revelation': Not just permissible, but necessary". In: *Awakening the Dreamer: Clinical Journeys.* Mahwah, NJ: The Analytic Press, pp. 128–150.

Bucci, W. (2001). "Pathways of Emotional Communication". *Psychoanalytic Inquiry.* 21: 40–70.

Bucci, W. (2007a). "Dissociation from the perspective of multiple code theory: Part I; Psychological roots and implications for psychoanalytic treatment". *Contemporary Psychoanalysis.* 43: 165–184.

Bucci, W. (2007b). "Dissociation from the perspective of multiple code theory: Part II; The spectrum of dissociative processes in the psychoanalytic relationship". *Contemporary Psychoanalysis.* 43: 305–326.

Freud, S. (1915). The Unconscious. *The Standard Edition of the Complete Psychological Works of Sigmund Freud,* Vol. 14, p. 166.

Gadamer, H.G. (1989). "Hermeneutics and psychiatry". In: H.G. Gadamer (ed.) *The Enigma of Health: The Art of Healing in a Scientific Age* (Trans. by J. Gaiger and N. Walker). Stanford: Stanford University Press.

Heidegger, M. (1959). *On the Way to Language* (Trans. by P.D. Hertz). San Francisco: Harper & Row, 1982.

Jaspers, K. (1963). *General Psychopathology* (Trans. by J. Hoenig and M.W. Hamilton). Chicago: University of Chicago Press.

Martini, G. (2007). New prospects on unconscious mental functioning and their reflections on the clinical practice. Paper presented at Conference of the Italian Psychoanalytic Society and the *International Psychoanalytical Association*, Rome, 2007.

Moccia, G. (2007). Psychoanalytic theories of unconscious mental functioning and multiple code theory. Paper presented at Conference of the Italian Psychoanalytic Society and the *International Psychoanalytical Association*, Rome, 2007.

McClelland, McClelland, J.L., Rumelhart, D.E., and Hinton, G.E. (1989). "The appeal of parallel distributed processing". In D.E. Rumelhart, J.L. McClelland, and the PDP Research Group (eds) *Parallel Distributed Processing: Explorations in the Microstructure of Cognition* (Volume 1: Foundations). Cambridge, MA: MIT Press, pp. 3–44.

Reik, T. (1948). *Listening with the Third Ear: The Inner Experience of a Psychoanalyst*. New York: Pyramid Books, 1964.

Ricoeur, P. (1970). *Freud and philosophy; an essay on interpretation*. New Haven: Yale University Press.

CHAPTER FOURTEEN

Implicit and explicit pathways to psychoanalytic change

James L. Fosshage, Ph.D.

T heories of psychological development and therapeutic action require an understanding of how we learn, how we remember, how memory affects ongoing organization of experience, and how past learning, memory and psychological organization are transformed. Most contemporary cognitive science models differentiate between two, at times three, memory systems (Epstein 1994). The model that differentiates between two domains of learning and memory, the implicit/nondeclarative and explicit/declarative systems has recently received considerable focus in psychoanalysis with significant implications for therapeutic change.[1]

Focusing their work on the implicit and explicit systems, the Boston Change Process Study Group (Stern et al. 1998; BCPSG 2005) have proposed that therapeutic change occurs principally in the area of "implicit relational knowing" during moments of emotional connection between analyst and patient called "moments of

---

[1] This paper was presented at the Spring Meeting of the Division of Psychoanalysis of the American Psychological Association, 11 April, 2008, New York City. Some portions of this paper have been borrowed from a much longer manuscript entitled, "How Do We 'Know' What We 'Know'? And Change What We 'Know'?" In press.

meeting". These moments, they argue, occur typically at an implicit level. Changing implicit relational knowing through implicit moments of meeting underwrites the importance of new relational experience, often occurring outside conscious awareness. For the Boston Group, interpretation can contribute to a moment of meeting, but the moment of meeting is where the transformative action occurs.

Pivotal for understanding the pathways of therapeutic change is how the implicit/non-declarative and explicit/declarative systems connect. How these systems encode information for processing sheds light on their interconnection and transformation. The purpose of this chapter is to explore how these systems encode information, how encoding affects conscious accessibility of implicit processing, and the implications of encoding and conscious accessibility in delineating a theory of multiple pathways for therapeutic action (Fosshage 2003, 2005; Gabbard and Weston 2003).

Explicit/declarative and implicit/non-declarative affective/cognitive systems

Implicit processing, similar to dreaming, appears from registering, organizing, and logging into memory subliminally perceived information, to a more focused parallel processing of information that occupies our explicit/declarative efforts. These two parallel yet interpenetrating systems work in tandem. When creatively writing, for example, we speak of the need for periods of incubation, periods that accentuate unconscious processing during which time new creative organizations of material will spring into consciousness. Within the analytic exchange our implicit processing on occasion emerges spontaneously into consciousness in the form of affect-laden images and words powerfully capturing an aspect of an analysand or pattern of interaction.

Convergence of concepts from different fields of discourse

The concepts of implicit processing and implicit mental models that have emerged out of cognitive science, converge with the neuroscience concept of neural memory networks or maps (that is, those that are established at an implicit level) and with a number of psychoanalytic concepts. The psychoanalytic concepts that refer to implicit memory patterns include: internal working models (Bowlby 1973); principles or patterns of organization (Wachtel 1980; Stolorow and Lachmann 1984/85; Fosshage 1994; Sander 1997); pathogenic beliefs (Weiss and Sampson 1986); mental representations (Fonagy 1993); expectancies (Lichtenberg, Lachmann and Fosshage 1996), and implicit relational knowing (Stern et al. 1998). In other words, the convergence of implicit learning (from cognitive psychology), neural memory networks (from neuroscience), and patterns of organization (from psychoanalysis) offers further validation of these concepts across different fields of discourse.

Integrating these discourses, we can say that the continuity and intractability of organizing patterns is related cognitively to their long-term or permanent implicit and explicit memory status, neurologically to the establishment of primary neural memory networks, and psychologically to their past and current adaptive value. In contrast to the intrapsychic models in our field that privilege universal fantasy distortion of life's events, the concept of organizing patterns emphasizes learning through lived experience, occurring at implicit and explicit levels of awareness. In the clinical arena, models that emphasize implicit and explicit learning help us to hear, believe and, thereby, implicitly validate the patient's thematic lived experience. These models free us from an attitude of scepticism, anchored in models of fantasy and defensive distortion that traditionally has so dominated the analyst's perception of the patient's communications.

Once established, organizing patterns function in the following ways: 1) activation of expectancies; 2) selective attention to cues that correspond with the expectancies; 3) attribution of meanings that are in keeping with the expectancies; and 4) interacting in such a way as to confirm the expectancies (Fosshage 1994). How we construct our relationships, how we relate to one another in all of its intricacies, is anchored in implicit and explicit learning.

Encoding

How do we encode and log information into memory in the implicit and explicit systems? How do we change or transform implicit and explicit mental models?

Many years ago, I (1983, 1987) came to appreciate "imagistic thinking" in my work on dreams, recognizing that images register experience and meaning and that sequencing of images is a form of thinking. REM dreams especially utilize imagistic symbolic processing with images capturing meaning and experience, and a sequence of images creating a narrative. I differentiated, thus, between imagistic and verbal modes of processing. Imagistic processing refers to thinking in images based on any one of our sensory modalities—sight, hearing, smell, touch, and taste—as well as motoric and visceral information. Somatic memories, for example, refer to memories that are primarily comprised of bodily sensations and experience. I subsequently became aware of the developments in cognitive psychology, especially Paivio (1971, 1986, 2007) and Bucci (1985, 1997) who had developed a dual coding model, what Paivio referred to as imagistic and verbal, and Bucci as non-verbal and verbal, symbolic formats.[2]

Images refer to mental images or mental patterns. For example, my grandson, aged two and a half, had learned through watching his father how to lock his complex and, for me at that time, quite difficult to master car seat belt—an example when my grandson's implicit and explicit systems converged in focusing imagistically on resolving the puzzle. On several occasions when my grandson saw me struggling, he would take over saying, "Here Papere, I'll show you how". He knew imagistically and communicated his images through gestures; words played no part.

It is generally agreed that the imagistic symbolic format is available at birth and is utilized by both implicit and explicit memory systems. When language developmentally comes on board, beginning around eighteen months, thinking and encoding involves two distinct cognitive subsystems, an earlier functioning imagistic system involving sensorial-based perceptions and mental images and, now, a verbal system involving language. According to this dual coding model, both imagistic and verbal systems are generally involved

---

[2] I prefer the term "imagistic" to "non-verbal" to refer to this format of symbolic processing. "Imagistic" is more descriptive; "non-verbal" only says what it is not. In addition, I wish to avoid confusion with the use of the term "non-verbal" to refer to the whole realm of communication that involves gestures, tonality, speech rhythms, and so forth.

in thinking. "The verbal system dominates in some tasks and the imagery system in others. Thinking is a variable pattern of the interplay of the two systems" (Paivio 2007: 13). Imagistic thinking is more prevalent in emotionally based right-brain functioning and verbal processing dominates analytic left-brain functioning (Schore 2003; Paivio 2007). Emanating from the right brain, images—as compared to words—are more affect loaded.

Both the implicit/non-declarative and explicit/declarative systems symbolically encode information imagistically and verbally. The interpenetration of imagistic and verbal formats used in both explicit and implicit systems I have proposed, increases the interconnection bi-directional influence, and fluid interplay between these systems. For example, subliminal processing springs into consciousness in the form of intuitive "hunches" and of enlightening images of our patients. Spontaneous humour and interpretive remarks emerge from the interplay between these two systems that leaves us at times truly awed, questioning, "Where did that come from?" The interpenetration and fluid interplay between these two systems has important implications for therapeutic action, which will be addressed.

Some cognitive scientists postulate a third form of processing referred to as Parallel Distributing Processing (PDP), or what Bucci (1997), in her development of a multiple code theory, calls subsymbolic processing. It involves rapid processing that, for example, enables us to judge distances and not walk into walls. Bucci suggests that subsymbolic processing is involved in processing emotions and establishing "emotional schemas" (LeDoux 1996: 195).

In contrast to Paivio's dual coding model and Bucci's multiple coding model, some infant researchers have posited that an altogether different form of encoding occurs in the implicit system. They argue that this form of encoding occurs "at a presymbolic level, prior to the capacity to evoke images or verbal representations of the 'object'" (Lyons-Ruth 1999: 586), what Lyons-Ruth (1999: 579) calls "enactive representation" and what Beebe and Lachmann (2002: 78–79) refer to as "presymbolic representations". Whereas Beebe and Lachmann posit that the implicit system uses a presymbolic form of encoding prior to the availability of symbolic encoding, Lyons-Ruth, a member of the Boston Group, suggests that enactive representation remains as the primary form of encoding within the implicit memory system. These theorists, in contrast to the cognitive scientists, argue that symbolic processing is not available at birth. The infant researchers have well demonstrated the encoding of interaction patterns, the "how to" patterns of relating beginning shortly after birth. Assuming that imagistic symbolic encoding is not available at birth, these researchers posit another form of encoding, a presymbolic encoding, to account for establishing these patterns in memory. The particularities of presymbolic encoding, to my mind, have not been well delineated.

The Boston Change Process Group posits an altogether different form of encoding, the presymbolic format, to be primary for the implicit memory system in contrast to the verbal symbolic format of the explicit system. Positing different formats positions the BCPG to view the implicit and explicit systems as functioning in parallel. They argue that these memory systems, therefore, require different change processes in the psychoanalytic arena. The primary locus of change, in their view, is in implicit relational knowing, the "how to" patterns of relating.

Emergence of implicit and explicit processing

In the cognitive sciences it is generally agreed, however, that the imagistic symbolic format is available at birth and is utilized by both implicit and explicit memory systems. Controversy surrounds the issue, however, as to whether or not explicit/declarative processing is available at birth. While some infant researchers suggest that explicit memory begins around nine months, others (see Rovee-Collier, Hayne and Colombo 2000) suggest that both implicit and explicit memory are available at birth. The research finding that an infant within the first fifteen hours can focally attend and distinguish mother's voice, smell, and face to those of a stranger appears to suggest a combination of early forms of implicit and explicit processing.

Accessibility to consciousness and reflective capacity

Recognition of implicit processing, in my judgement, has catapulted the issue of conscious accessibility into the forefront in considering avenues of therapeutic action. By conscious accessibility I mean the capacity to recognize and reflect on. When implicit patterns of organization are accessible to consciousness, they can be addressed through analytic exploratory work, expanding conscious awareness of implicit patterns and their origins. Conscious awareness disrupts the automatic "flow" and gradually builds a reflective capability for intervening and suspending oneself from the grips of a procedural pattern. In turn, an individual can take in contrasting relational experience and gradually establish new patterns of organization. In contrast, if implicit patterns of organization are not consciously accessible, the only recourse for change is the co-creation of new implicit relational experience.

We are just beginning to explore how implicit processing varies as to its accessibility to consciousness (Fosshage, In press). I have suggested that conscious accessibility is partially related to how implicit procedures are formed. Similar to tennis strokes or driving, what, at first, begins as explicit/declarative learning becomes over time a procedural memory. For example, repeated parental warnings not to cross the street without looking gradually become implicit procedures. A formative sequence of explicit to implicit makes these procedures more available for conscious recollection.

A variety of other factors contribute to the variability of procedural knowledge to conscious access. They include: the age of onset when the procedure was being learned, frequency of repetition, intensity of affects, degree of emotional trauma, and the current analytic intersubjective context. An analytic context in which the analyst listens closely and resonates with the patient's affect from within the patient's frame of reference creates an atmosphere of safety that enhances fluidity between the implicit and explicit. For emotional trauma requiring dissociation for self-regulation, it is certainly more difficult to gain conscious access. In addition, when a severely traumatic relational procedure becomes accessible to consciousness, a person's reflective capability to intervene and deactivate the procedure usually remains difficult for some time.

Implicit and explicit domains: Two fundamental pathways of change

The two fundamental pathways of change, I propose, are the explicit learning that occurs through the more traditional psychoanalytic emphasis on exploration and expanded awareness and the implicit procedural learning that occurs through relational processes often out of awareness. While collaborative exploratory (not authoritarian interpretive) work and relational experience usually work in tandem, their relative balance varies from moment to moment.

Using both imagistic and verbal symbolic formats facilitates the interconnection and interplay between implicit and explicit systems. In other words, the task in bringing implicit learning into consciousness does not require overcoming different encoding formats and increases the potential for conscious access to implicit experience. These considerations have played a major role in what I believe are two fundamental, interrelated pathways of change involving explicit exploration/learning and implicit learning that occur in the psychoanalytic encounter (Fosshage 2003, 2004, 2005). Rather than change taking place primarily through exploration, the traditional focus, or primarily through implicit relational learning—the focus of the BCPG, I emphasize the ongoing interplay between the implicit and explicit systems for therapeutic action.

References

Beebe, B. and Lachmann, F. (2002). *Infant Research and Adult Treatment.* Hillsdale, NJ: The Analytic Press.

Boston Change Process Study Group (2005). "The 'Something More' than Interpretation". *Journal of the American Psychoanalytic Association.* 53(3): 693–729.

Bowlby, J. (1973). *Attachment and Loss. Vol. II Separation.* New York: Basic Books.

Bucci, W. (1985). "Dual coding: A cognitive model for psychoanalytic research". *J. Amer. Psychoanal. Assn.* 33: 571–607.

Bucci, W. (1997). *Psychoanalysis & Cognitive Science: A Multiple Code Theory.* New York: Guilford Press.

Epstein, S. (1994). "Integration of the cognitive and the psychodynamic Unconscious". *Amer. Psychol.* 8: 709–724.

Fonagy, P. (1993). "The roles of mental representations and mental processes in therapeutic action". *Psychoanalytic Study of the Child.* 48: 9–48.

Fosshage, J. (1983). "The psychological function of dreams: a revised psychoanalytic perspective". *Psychoanalysis and Contemporary Thought.* 6(4): 641–669. Also in: M. Lansky (ed.) *Essential Papers on Dreams.* New York, NY: New York University Press, 1992.

Fosshage, J. (1987). "A Revised Psychoanalytic Approach". In: J.L. Fosshage, and C.A. Loew (eds) *Dream Interpretation: A Comparative Study*. New York: PMA Publishing.

Fosshage, J. (1994). "Toward reconceptualizing transference: theoretical and clinical considerations". *Int J. of Psycho-Anal.* 75(2): 265–280.

Fosshage, J. (2003). "Fundamental pathways to change: Illuminating old and creating new relational experience". *International Forum of Psychoanalysis.* 12: 244–251.

Fosshage, J. (2004). "The explicit and implicit dance in psychoanalytic change". *The Journal of Analytical Psychology.* 49: 49–65.

Fosshage, J. (2005). "The explicit and implicit domains in psychoanalytic change". *Psychoanalytic Inquiry.* 25(4): 516–539.

Fosshage, J. (In press) How do we 'know' what we 'know'? And change what we 'know'? *Psychoanalytic Dialogues.*

Gabbard, G.O. and Weston. D. (2003). "Rethinking therapeutic action". *Int. J. of Psycho-Anal.* 84: 824–841.

LeDoux, J. (1996). *The Emotional Brain*. New York, NY: Touchstone, Simon & Schuster.

Lichtenberg, J., Lachmann, F. and Fosshage, J. (1996). *The Clinical Exchange: Technique from the Standpoint of Self and Motivational Systems.* Hillsdale, NJ: The Analytic Press.

Lyons-Ruth, K. (1999). "The two-person unconscious: Intersubjective dialogue, enactive relational representation, and the emergence of new forms of relational organization". *Psychoanal. Inq.* 19: 576–617.

Paivio, A. (1971). *Imagery and Verbal Processes.* New York: Holt, Rinehart & Winston. Reprinted 1979, Hillsdale, NJ: Lawrence Erlbaum Associates.

Paivio, A. (1986). *Mental Representations: A Dual Coding Approach.* New York: Oxford Universities Press.

Paivio, A. (2007). *Mind and Its Evolution: A Dual Coding Theoretical Approach.* Mahway, NJ: Lawrence Erlbaum Associates.

Rovee-Collier, C., Hayne, H. and Colombo, M. (2000). *The Development of Implicit and Explicit Memory.* Philadelphia: John Benjamins Publishing Co.

Sander, L. (1997). "Paradox and resolution". In: J. Osofsky (ed.) *Handbook of Child and Adolescent Psychiatry.* New York: John Wiley, pp. 153–160.

Schore, A. (2003). *Affect Regulation and the Repair of the Self.* New York: Norton.

Stern, D.N., Sander, L., Nahum, J., Harrison, A., Lyons-Ruth, K., Morgan, A., Bruschweiler-Stern, N. and Tronick, E. (1998). "Noninterpretive mechanisms in psychoanalytic therapy: The 'something more' than interpretation". *Int. J. Psycho-Anal.* 79: 903–921.

Stolorow, R. and Lachmann, F. (1984/85). "Transference: the future of an illusion". *The Annual of Psychoanalysis*. 12(13): 19–37.

Wachtel, P.F. (1980). "Transference, schema and assimilation: The relevance of Piaget to the psychoanalytic theory of transference". *The Annual of Psychoanalysis*. 8: 59–76.

Weiss, J. and Sampson, H. (1986). *The Psychoanalytic Process*. New York: Guilford.

CHAPTER FIFTEEN

Life as performance art: Right and left brain function, implicit knowing, and "felt coherence"

Richard A. Chefetz, M.D.

"Today Is A Day When It Is Hard To Keep Going. I Literally Got Through The Afternoon By Thinking About A Suicide Plan, Notes, A Sort Of "Make Shift" Will And I Even Picked Up My Room And Packed Another Box; As Though Tidying Up For Departure. But I Will See You Tomorrow Morning Though. J"

Ihave always marvelled at how understanding something, "getting it", feels so good and behaves so powerfully. It is not that there is suddenly an intellectual understanding and something changes, it is that something ineffable, something felt but not necessarily clearly known, changes. There is a place within us all that seems to "know" even when we aren't yet clear about "why" we know it—or sometimes even "what"—exactly. And when this happens, when we achieve this understanding, we feel better, relieved of tension, relaxed. This is a place of "felt coherence". Conversely, there are times in all our lives when we behave in ways that are clearly purposeful, though perhaps not consciously intentional, and may even leave us gasping, wondering, how and why we could ever have "done" or "said" what we did! There is a way in which we know how to enact what we don't even know we know or intend to communicate. Sometimes, we tell the story of the unbearable, the incoherent, with action. Perhaps at those times it's the only way we stand a chance of knowing what part of our mind can't bear to know, or is forbidden to know, but otherwise already knows, and in great detail.

When she was a child, J had the unpopular habit of taking perfectly good items that were regularly strewn about her room and throwing them in the closet as a way to "clean up". After a while, the collection was quite impressive, she said. Sometimes she spent several hours sitting quietly on the pile in the closet, door closed, in the dark.

When the pile got too much for her mother, J was ordered to clean it up. She attended to the command by dutifully taking a new black plastic garbage bag, filling it to the brim with the household goods that had collected in the closet, and dragging the heavy bag out to the curb where she put it next to the other trash. This prompted a family ritual of her parents rushing to the curb before their possessions were carted off. They regularly retrieved much of the useful goods that were in the bag. Her father used to say that J was "crazy".

It turned out that J wasn't crazy. She was not crazy at all. It's just that her manner of communication was necessarily embedded in action to an extent that nobody really appreciated, including J. Why would anybody put perfectly useful goods in the trash? Who would do such a thing? Why did she sit, for hours, on the pile of "trash" in the closet? What did she know then that I didn't know now? And, more importantly, what did *she* seem to know now in her actions that she didn't really know then, or now?

Dissociation

The unlinking of symbolic and sub-symbolic references (Bucci 1997) and the isolation of affect (Freud 1909) describe much the same unconscious phenomena: dissociation of one element of experience from another such that the context and meaning of experience is not discernable. How do references get linked to experience in the first place and what is it, specifically, that interferes with, or undoes that linking? If we use the term "isolation", then what exactly is isolated from what?

In Bucci's definition, the use of the word "unlinking" presupposes that something was linked. I don't think Bucci would regret or argue against the idea that there are situations where linking never takes place during experience. It's more like the elements of experience are vaguely and invisibly tethered to each other through a fog, tugging on each other from time to time, suddenly, and seemingly inexplicably, changing the trajectory of a life. You've heard that in your consultation room: "I had no intention of having a drink! The hostess came by with a tray loaded with champagne, and Jack took one glass and put another in my hand. He wouldn't let me say, 'No, thank you,' and I felt stupid just standing there with the glass. The first sip tasted so good. I don't remember what happened after that". Or: "Last night I ordered three large pizzas. I heard myself doing it. I wanted to just hang up the phone but my arms wouldn't work. I shovelled the slices into the maw that was my mouth until my belly hurt so much I couldn't stand it. I don't remember what happened next. I just woke up again on the floor of the bathroom hugging the toilet".

Enactive knowing, repetition, and implicit processes

While enactment may be understood in several different ways as involving countertransference responses and projective identificatory processes (Chused 1991) (McLaughlin 1991), I prefer a description of enactment that pays respect to the dissociative process (Bromberg 2006) that creates the fertile ground in which isolated elements of consciousness are buried and then influence whatever grows from that soil. Personality, according to Bromberg, as well as enactment, are grossly formed by the magnetic effects of dissociative (isolated) experience on the trajectory of motivation and meaning-making processes in all of us. It is the implicit nature of the isolation of experience that leaves us blind to the extent that our actions, thoughts, and feelings are unconsciously guided by the remains of emotionally invalidating and disconfirming experiences such as humiliation and the toxicity of shaming. However, not all action in a therapy, or in a life, deserves the technical label of enactment unless the dance (Baker 1997) of isolated experience in the therapist and patient occurs in some kind of meaningful synchrony.

Enactive knowing and the repetition of past experience are based upon implicit, procedural knowledge that is gathered through behavioural experience. While Bowlby emphasized internal working models that were fairly inclusive of affects, ideas, behaviour, and world view (Bowlby 1969/1982), and Tomkins was appropriately fond of an appreciation of affect scripts (Tomkins 1995), Ryle developed a model for understanding procedural elements of experience through a cognitive analytic therapy paradigm that makes use of the concept of behavioral scripts and expectancies (Ryle 1999). "Enactive knowledge is information gained through perception-action interactions with the environment. Examples include information gained by grasping an object, by hefting a stone, or by walking around an obstacle that occludes our view. It is gained through intuitive movements, of which we often are not aware. Enactive knowledge is inherently multimodal, because motor actions alter the stimulation of multiple perceptual systems. Enactive knowledge is essential in tasks such as driving a car, dancing, playing a musical instrument, modeling objects from clay, performing sports, and so on. Enactive knowledge is neither symbolic nor iconic. It is direct, in the sense that it is natural and intuitive, based on experience and the perceptual consequences of motor acts" (Bardy and Mottet 2006).

We can see from these perspectives that there is an implicit and dissociative quality to what is, as Christopher Bollas put it some years ago, "the unthought known" (Bollas 1987: 277). The clinical challenge, of course, is how to "smoke out" what isn't thought, but nevertheless regularly leaves tracks in the fresh snowfall on a distressed mind's inner landscape.

What's "under the hood"?

There are several neurological lines of evidence that make clear we can hold compelling, and sometimes conflicting, thoughts in mind without explicitly knowing it, and often without having any anxiety about it. A female patient who knew and liked Michael Gazzaniga, was studied in a split-brain experiment. V.P. was shown a movie of a violent murder, but because of her split brain, she experienced the movie as only a flash of light. However, after the movie, she said she felt kind of jumpy. In fact, she recognized that she was frightened of Dr. Gazanniga! She had a feeling, and she attributed the feeling to what she could perceive: the man right in front of her. Her emotionality was stirred, and she knew there was fear, but she didn't know why, and couldn't connect her affective experience with its source (Carter 1999).

A man with bilateral loss of both hippocampi (the famous case of H.M.) (Squire 1999) had the expectable loss of short-term memory and an inability to form new long-term memories. He could remember what he learned for several minutes, but then he could not explicitly recall his new knowledge. On one day, his neurologist reported to the patient what he had just learned from the patient's wife: the patient's mother was quite ill. On a return visit the next day, the neurologist asked the patient how he was. The patient reported that he was fine. After several minutes of conversation, the patient asked if he could borrow the doctor's telephone. Why? He wanted to call his mother. Why? He didn't know. He just had a strong urge to do it. He wanted to make sure that she was OK. He didn't know why he was concerned. While this man couldn't explicitly name the problem, implicitly he had a "sense" that he needed to do something. This feeling of "needing to do" is part of the implicit memory system that often guides our "intuitive" activities just because "I feel like it!"

Reinders and Nijenhuis used brain scanning to study the function of cerebral cortex in several individuals with dissociative identity disorder (Reinders et al. 2003). They compared scans of individuals who had "switched" from one identity to another in an effort to discern what neurologic substrate was operative, if any, between self states. They observed that the patterns of activation for each self state showed widely spread patterns across many areas of brain, left and right sides, and that between self states there were significant non-congruent patterns. Each of the different self states in dissociative identity disorder activated widely disparate areas of brain on both sides of the corpus callosum (the structure that is split in "split-brain" patients) consistent with the hypothesis of un-integrated experience existing between those self states. Split-brain experience is not a model for dissociative disorders, but it does teach us about implicit memory and dissociation of some functions.

A patient with a dissociative disorder was in intensive psychotherapy for five years when the valued, stable relationship with her husband ended due to his death from cancer. For several years afterward she was sexually promiscuous for the first time in her life. The behaviour resisted any analysis related to loss of her husband and there was no history of sexual abuse. Three years later, at the funeral of a beloved family member, she nearly fainted when she looked across the church and saw an uncle whom she suddenly remembered had severely abused her, emotionally, physically, and sexually, for a number of years in her mid-childhood. In the initial exploration of this experience her promiscuity ended.

Dissociation: The engine that drives enactment and enactive repetition

Experience that is too affectively charged and can neither be assimilated into existing internal working models of the world, nor accommodated by the expansion of those working models, is bereft of a framework upon which it can be understood. Moments like this go beyond watching the towers of the World Trade Center collapse and saying out loud or silently: "I don't believe it! I can't believe it!" Although for some of us it was enough to view the collapse of the buildings to trigger a post-traumatic reaction and peri-traumatic dissociation, for others it was in watching people leap from the towers, sometimes hand in hand together, choosing to fall to their deaths rather than be burned alive. Writing these words catapults me into moments of painful reverie, and I only watched from a distance! I felt compelled to visit the Pentagon in my home town and to travel to New York to see with my own eyes the aftermath of what had happened. For the victim of sadistic sexual abuse, there is no distance, no need to travel to the scene of terror, and while entering the obfuscating fog of depersonalization offers some respite, dissociation fails in sadistic abuse, when the pain, the intentionally inflicted miserable pain, drags us back into our bodies. And still, oftentimes, the blessing of amnesia comes even if depersonalization, derealization, identify confusion, or identity alteration have already combined to further isolate the pain from consciousness.

And yet our minds seek coherence when there are fragments and raw chunks of our lives that are un-tethered to our personal narratives of living, dissociative living, implicit in its quality. In this view it is this tendency to try to resolve the unfinished narrative that Mardi Horowitz called the completion tendency (Horowitz 1986) and Freud called the repetition compulsion (Freud 1920). *Coherence is a function of dissociative process in tension with associative process*, and we can clearly understand that in the context of infant attachment theory unresolved experience "doesn't make sense"! Sroufe first proposed that an additional goal of infant attachment went beyond the proximity seeking of Bowlby's behavioural model and included a sense of "felt security" (Fonagy et al. 2003: 89). We all seek to create an emotionally and linguistically coherent narrative of our lives. We seek "felt coherence", and relax when things finally do make sense. (Of course, we may be willing to accept incorrect narratives if they can make enough sense and also relieve us of the otherwise intolerable content of experience!) *I see the problem of repetition of trauma as less a compulsion to repeat what is unresolved and more a need to make sense out of disparate elements of experience using the only means available when thinking and feeling are blocked by dissociative process: action, enactive repetition.* Bucci correctly calls the unresolved elements unlinked, and I believe these also are inextricably bound to each other in their disrupted condition (Chefetz 2004), influencing behaviour. Thus, when meaning-making is deprived of explicit knowing and felt, emotionally alive sensing, then only action remains as a means of communication. In other words, what we only know implicitly is condemned to be told mostly with action until it can be made explicit and coherent. I have dubbed this tendency, and the preceding context the "coherence principle".

The coherence principle

The human mind is organized in such a manner as to facilitate the establishment of coherence. There is a primal division of function that is, for our purposes, best understood heuristically as the contrast between left brain logical, mathematical, linguistic, linear time and space defined boundaries versus right brain affective, sensory, motoric, rhythmic, non-linear operations that, for example, facilitate the dream operations of condensation, displacement, and symbolic substitution. It is useful shorthand (but a significant simplification) to think of left brain operations as "thinking", and right brain operations as "feeling". How do we integrate these linear and non-linear elements of experience?

Our minds live in the routine tension between associative and dissociative processes that predict the creation of coherent meaning for experience. Transfer of information between left and right brain helps to sort details of experience for salience, and creates symbolic and sub-symbolic links that move in complexity from the indexical, through the iconic and finally become discernable in the symbolic realm of spoken language (Keinänen 2006). It is important to note that spoken, not written, language engages both left and right brain processes in a compelling manner. Speech requires left brain logical and expressive organizational activity and right brain tonal and emphatic nuances. Speech also is supervised and observed for its accuracy and emotive quality, sometimes evoking from the speaker an: "I think it might be better understood if I say it this way" kind of statement.

Have you ever had the experience or simply observed the development of an inability to speak during a eulogy at a funeral? It is not that reading prepared remarks has not already happened, privately, it is that speaking them out loud completes the affective linking together of a coherent narrative that provides the full context of meaning for our words. Speaking is an action that contributes to coherence. Telling the story is a central part of creating coherence (Rynearson 2006). Performing a story is not the same as telling it even if the meaning is covertly, or even overtly, conveyed.

Left and right brain elements of experience are knitted into a coherent narrative by the left brain's ability to interpret what the right brain's emotionality generates but can't name. The right brain has a very limited capacity to interpret the nature of whatever emotion is being felt! It knows that there is intensity, and it knows the behavioural scripts that fit the intensity, but it can't actually name the feeling (Bermond et al. 2006). This conclusion is similar to that reached about how the left brain and right brain come to different conclusions about the meaning of an experience and the action required to resolve a situation (Gazzaniga et al. 1962, 1995). Additionally, our capacity to speak when on "emotional overload" becomes limited when high intensity emotion somehow provokes the amygdala to cause a reduction of blood flow in the area of the brain that generates expression of thought. A Broca's aphasia is a well-known stroke syndrome. Less well known is that we become speechless in fear, or intense pleasure, when emotional circuitry is overloaded. Our ability to generate narrative is impaired during highly emotional moments (Rauch et al. 1996).

Neurobiological reality provides additional interesting lessons for psychoanalytic clinicians: massive activation of one hemisphere inhibits activity in the other hemisphere, as a normal response (Bermond et al. 2006). Obsessional adaptations aside, "keeping busy" during an emotionally stressful time shuts down and modulates our ability to feel emotion. Action can have an additional function beyond that of telling a story or accomplishing a task. Action may be a distraction from feeling. It is also true that high levels of emotionality can pre-empt thoughtful approaches to a challenge. Hemispheric overloads work both ways as a modulator of affect: when either side of the brain is overloaded the production of coherent narrative suffers. We can see the influence of hemispheric overload in everyday language: "I'm too upset to think about it. We'll have to deal with it later!" "I'm sorry I was so blunt. I was so focused on what I was doing I forgot my manners!"

Healthy minds search for coherence. Coherence is most easily achieved in the context of optimal physiologic arousal; that is, in a safe relationship, or what has artfully been called a relationship that is "safe, but not too safe" (Bromberg 2006: 189). We must constantly sort what we perceive, inwardly and outwardly, to achieve coherence. We sort and unconsciously "decide" whether something is a "match" or not: "Should I exclude or include this element of experience from this scene?" "Should I associate or dissociate this element of experience?" Most sorting is outside awareness. Thus, coherence is a function that is dependent upon the tension between associative and dissociative processes. Maintaining coherence may trump reality testing if it eliminates intolerable anxiety over the meaning of a toxic event. The toxic event might be intrapsychic or in the world.

The tension between associative and dissociative processes

Normal orbito-frontal and medial prefrontal cortical inhibition of amygdalar activation is reduced in insecure attachment (Schore 2003). This is a partial restatement of the work of Rauch from an attachment perspective. However, what is normal creates unfortunate burdens in trauma, even when the event is only of an exquisitely painful emotional experience. We have seen how over-activation of hemispheres inhibits interpretation of experience and leads to the failure to assimilate or accommodate traumatic experience. The inability to integrate left and right brain cognitive/interpretive and emotional experiential elements leads to a *de facto* dissociation of intense experience. Nothing need be repressed to remain outside awareness; it simply never gets glued together via association. This is a dissociative process; the ghost of repression need not be conjured here. This is not quite the "weak dissociation" of Don Stern (1999: 129) the failure to know something for lack of effort. This is the dis-aggregation of Janet as seen in the failure to link implicit and explicit right and left brain functions, respectively. This is what I prefer to call a failure of formulation that leads to what Stern (1999: 51) called "unformulated experience".

What really happens in dissociation? Associative and inhibitory processes fail! The normal integrative functions of mind fail! The creation of a narrative of interpretable experience does not occur. Experience is incoherent: behaviour, affect, sensation, knowledge (Braun 1988) may not be linked together on a sub-symbolic or symbolic level. Affect may still be present but it is isolated from interpretability and may induce scripted emotional behaviour (Bermond et al. 2006). Higher cortical brain areas are not prepared to deal with the physiologic disarray of intense affects and cortical inhibition of sympathetic nervous system outflow fails (van der Kolk et al. 1996). We can't interpret our experience but it intrudes piecemeal, albeit incoherently, almost begging for understanding; and so we avoid/ withdraw, and with more intensity we get numb, and sometimes we get "triggered" and are gripped with fear that seems to make no conscious sense. We can even alternate from numbness to flooding and not know why!

Dissociation is not a banishing act that puts intolerable experience in orbit, completely isolated from reach. Dissociation is an odd binding-disruption where the "tag ends" of what ought to match are held in close proximity, but outside awareness, procedurally. These incomplete psychic constructions nevertheless influence behaviour and reactivity via implicit processes, including the scripted performance of actions with meaning.

We all seek coherence, both consciously and unconsciously. Both enactive repetition and enactment seek coherence through whatever mode of expression will finally, logically and emotionally, make sense out of what was incoherent, unbearable, and unspeakable.

Teaching the left brain to "dance": Building and re-building referential links to experience via safe relating

The recent emphasis in trauma studies has been on two main areas related to right brain function: the failure of medial prefrontal cortex to inhibit the emotional emergency centres in the amygdala, and the lowered threshold for adrenalin release secondary to resetting autonomic activity after the hyper-arousal of trauma (Schore and Schore 2008). In plain English, it is as if our minds still think we are about to get hurt (autonomics) and we can't reason our way out of that expectancy (prefrontal cortical influence on emotion fails).

In effect, a useful heuristic is that left brain logical, mathematical and linguistic functions can't control mid-brain emotional circuitry and doesn't understand what the right brain is upset about. The left brain is also clear that if the right brain is so upset, then the left brain will gladly pass up the opportunity to know what is making that right brain so frantic. Left brain avoidance strategies include: denial, disavowal, minimization, rationalization, disowning, obsessive preoccupation, ritual undoing, staying busy, working until exhausted, and ignoring the clues that something emotionally charged is going on by simply "not going there", isolation of affect. Avoiding intense affect becomes a necessity. Activating emotional strata of the brain results in flooding from pent up affective scripts that are ready to flow. Staying rule bound is a Shangri-la familiar to some of those people who make a career out of the practice of law or engineering, amongst other heavily left-brained careers. Some of these people watch their feet when trying to learn how to dance. Going with the flow of the music is tantamount to "losing control", a not so hidden reference to having intense feelings that actually flow! Teaching the left brain to dance is a way of reframing the relational aspect of intensive psychoanalytic therapy.

It is in the hard-earned safety of a relationship that the left brain of a patient begins to trust that the emotional aliveness in their therapist is something they might consider tolerating and then unconsciously emulate in their own processing of emotion. It is in the therapist's scrupulous attention to interpersonal boundaries that the right brain gains a tentative confidence that it will not be emotionally assaulted. The right brain develops a sense that if it feels threatened, then spoken language is enough to stop the action of the therapist. In the world of interpersonal abuse, words have lost their meaning, especially the words of the patient, and the only reliable source of information is through action. "No" has been stripped from the patient's lexicon of available expressions. Protest was brutally squashed. "Anger as protest" is dangerous and not a thought for the survivor of sadistic childhood abuse. The negotiation of the capacity for meaningful and emotionally alive communication in psychotherapy is an art form. It takes much longer than what Goldilocks and the Three Bears worked out in their negotiations. Regardless, negotiation is the name of the game.

Teaching the right brain to read music

It's troubling to appreciate that the left brain doesn't always understand what disturbs the right brain after traumatic experience. It's as if the left brain knows to be afraid, but doesn't quite know why, and that only makes things scarier. It's akin to the second fear phenomena described in panic syndromes (Weekes 1969/1990). We become frightened of being frightened and scrupulously avoid, only to become subject to an adrenalin surge bursting through into consciousness as a clue that there is still an unresolved emotional disturbance. Apparently neither the left nor the right brain has sufficient experience to be able to read right brain music and interpret its meaning when overwhelming emotional experience is writing the musical score. The right brain needs left brain cognitive appraisals of emotional meaning before it can understand what it is emotionally experiencing. The notion of emotional communication being almost all right brain to right brain (Schore 2003) ought to be conceptually expanded. The left brain interpreter mechanism noted is bereft of the skills/experience to understand trauma, and the right brain really has a hard time of making inferences about the "meaningful drift" of associations to "the emotional music" without an accompanying coherent narrative that interprets the somato-sensory symphony that is part of traumatic recollecting and remembering. The right brain doesn't know how to really "read" the music when the chaotic composition of traumatic experience is "playing in the body with 'surround-sound' that is wired to muscles and bowel, and so on". Secure parenting, in this view, must include the parent engaging the child in a process where there is active and implicit emotional communication, *and* the parent also names the feelings/emotions that they can see the child experiencing. It is this naming process, both behaviourally and affectively, that is so powerful in shaping the child's behaviour as well as self-image. The Circle of Security Project shows with clarity that Type D, A, and C parenting can revert to Type B when mothers learn to correctly intuit/observe the meaning of behaviour in their infant children. Most exciting is that this can actually alter infant attachment patterns as a parent learns these new skills (Marvin et al. 2002). The role of the clinician is clear in this situation: *provide affective containment that settles autonomic arousal and assists in constructing general and then more specific new narrative that actively names and assists both left and right brains to coherently interpret experience, assign affective valences, and fit the newly understood experience into an ever expanding autobiographical narrative.* The value of an emotion focused treatment is robustly clear.

An old script being enacted

My patient sent me an email on the day before her usual Monday morning session. Short, and not sweet, it was written with each word starting with a capital letter, for emphasis:

> "Today Is A Day When It Is Hard To Keep Going. I Literally Got Through The Afternoon By Thinking About A Suicide Plan, Notes, A Sort Of "Make Shift" Will And I Even Picked Up My Room And Packed Another Box; As Though Tidying Up For Departure. But I Will See You Tomorrow Morning Though. J"

How would you respond to this? What are the considerations for safety; the patient's need for freedom to have their thoughts and feelings; the need to not let the action "get out of hand"? I chose to think about these things, but not to engage in action. This was the third year of our work, we had been through many suicidal and para-suicidal crises, and she regularly sought out me or another trusted person when she was distressed—if not always. Sometimes she retreated to her bed for several days, un-showered, not eating, fully withdrawn from all but her beloved cats. She said she would see me tomorrow, and so I put the potential self-harming behaviours on a special shelf in my mind, and went on with my day.

The Monday session began with her silence. "There's really nothing to talk about", she soon said. I countered that it seemed as if there was so much to talk about it wasn't exactly clear where to start! "What have you been doing with your time, over the weekend?" I asked, trying to get inside the context of her email message. "You know, J, that was quite the email you sent to me yesterday. I'm concerned about what it meant".

"Oh, that, well, I've been puttering around my room, collecting things and putting them in boxes. I've nearly finished, at this point", she said, in a tone reminiscent of having gone about the day cleaning all the windows in a house, and now being nearly done.

"Why are you putting things in boxes, J?"

"I don't think I'm going to need them, and I don't want my landlady to be bothered with having to clear out my room if it's a mess. That's too much work for her, and she already does too much for me".

"I don't understand, J, why would she be clearing out your room? Where are you going?"

"I think it's about time that I just left this place, Dr. Chefetz", she said, as if I had totally failed to understand what was going on in her life. "There's nothing for me here, and I don't want to keep on being in pain", she said, as the tears started to run down her cheeks. "I'm just garbage, and it's time to put me out of my misery".

I asked her for more details about what was supposed to happen. She explained that she had not yet quite figured out how to kill herself, but she was working on it. She considered the possibility of hanging herself, as her fiancé had done near the end of her first two months of therapy. She was clear that she didn't want to be a burden for anybody, that nobody should be inconvenienced by her death. Her landlady would just put the boxes out on the curb with the other trash when J was gone. She would also probably be glad to take care of her cats.

There were times when in a period of relative well-being J would work with her sewing machine, making clothes for her cats, dressing them up playfully, like the cat in the hat, and so on. Now, she was planning her death, in honest detail. She was letting go of beloved relationships. She was taking the organizing steps I had seen in many other patients whose suicides I had interrupted over the years.

"J, it seems pretty clear that you are planning to kill yourself, and taking care of all the details so you don't put anybody out after you've done yourself in", I said plainly. "That's not OK, with me, J".

J was reassuring, in her own way. She said, "You know, Dr. Chefetz, with as much work as you've done with me, if I kill myself it has nothing to do with you and that you won't have failed me at all; it will be something I've done completely on my own and you would not have to feel bad at all, would you?"

"Of course I'd feel awful and that I've failed you, J".

"But, Dr. Chefetz, that's not logical! It would be me who had done this".

"It doesn't matter what's logical or not, J. Feelings don't have to be logical, they just are. It's how I feel, J. You said earlier that you know I've been really invested in helping you in the therapy. I have worked hard, but my investment is in You, not in the therapy, even if that's what we do together. And, if you killed yourself, then I would feel a miserable grief, and that I had failed you. Logical or not, that's what I would feel. What is all this about, J, and why might this be happening right now?"

"I really don't know, Dr. Chefetz". She clearly switched self states and emotionally stepped back from her nearly nonchalant reassurance that I'd done all I could for her and could feel guiltless if she'd killed herself. She spoke now with sadness in her voice. "I've been thinking a lot about when I lived back home and how I used to go around the house and collect the things I liked, putting them all over my room, and just sort of letting them accumulate. It used to eventually drive my mother crazy, especially when she could no longer walk in the room because of the clutter". She went on to tell me the story about putting perfectly good things in the trash, out at the curb. She reminded me about how her father had once again, on this occasion, repeated the lament he so often used, that she "was crazy!"

"I want you to know that I get it about the message you tried to send to your parents that they were throwing away a perfectly good daughter along with perfectly good things that were in that big black plastic bag. That's why you sat on the heap in your closet, I believe. It was a message. I don't want you to throw yourself away. It would be terribly sad if after having survived the horrors of the emotional abuse, and the sexual and physical abuse, that all these years later you might kill yourself as you finally become conscious of your life. It's one thing to know how you were abused, and how awful that was, but it's another thing to realize in the deepest ways, how little understanding, if any, your parents had about you, and how now you appreciate the pain of not really being related to or with them, in any of the ways in which you now value relatedness. I think that in some ways that's a bigger hurt than the grossly abusive things".

J had constructed a suicide fantasy that was a match for the way in which she felt she had been thrown away with "perfectly good stuff" that she had collected in a closet that she often sat in, and that her parents had retrieved from the curb. It was a way in which she had attempted to tell them they were throwing away a perfectly good child, their daughter, and that somebody needed to get her out of the trash. She was asking me to notice, and I knew I had to be explicit in naming what was going on.

"If you put yourself in the trash now, literally, then there is no way to get you back", I said. "I'm hoping we can talk about these feelings, and that you won't act on them".

"Tell me it's OK, Dr. Chefetz, that I don't have to do anything this week, that I can just do nothing, and that it's OK, please? Tell me that my job is just staying alive; tell me that's all I have to do? If that's all I have to do, then I think I can make it to the next appointment. I think I can do that. Just tell me it's OK not to do anything else, please?!"

"Yes, J., of course, that's the name of what needs to happen right now. That's all that needs to happen. Your job is to just stay alive, and that's good enough. OK?"

"Yes".

"Then, call me if you need to. I'll be here for you".

"I know, Dr. Chefetz. Thank you for helping me, Dr. Chefetz".

The next day, in a brief email exchange, J reminded me what she had been absent-mindedly thinking about, but had forgotten, as had I. A year ago, almost to the day, the daughter of her fiancé had also killed herself by hanging. Another perfectly good daughter had been thrown away. In the only way in which J could communicate what was unbearable and isolated (dissociatively held) from her aware-ness, she told both her own story, and the story of a major loss, via the implicit process of enactive repetition.

References

Baker, S. (1997). "Dancing the dance with dissociatives: Some thoughts on countertransference, projective identification, and enactments in the treatment of dissociative disorders". *Dissociation* 10(4): 214–223.

Bardy, B. and Mottet, D. (2006). *Enactive/06: Enaction & Complexity*. Third International Conference on Enactive Interfaces, Montpelier, France, http://www.enactive2006.org/Enactive_06_proceedings.pdf.

Bermond, B., Vorst, H.C.M. and Moorman, P.P. (2006). "Cognitive neu-ropsychology of alexithymia: Implications for personality typology". *Cognitive Neuropsychiatry*. 11(3): 332–360.

Bollas, C. (1987). *The Shadow of the Object: Psychoanalysis of the Unthought Known*. New York: Columbia University Press.

Bowlby, J. (1969/1982). *Attachment*. 2nd Edn. New York: Basic Books.

Braun, B.G. (1988). "The BASK model of dissociation". *Dissociation* 1(1): 4–23.

Bromberg, P.M. (2006). *Awakening the Dreamer: Clinical Journeys*. Mahwah, N.J: The Analytic Press.

Bucci, W. (1997). *Psychoanalysis & Cognitive Science*. New York: Guilford Press.

Carter, R. (1999). *Mapping the Mind*. Berkley: University of California Press.

Chefetz, R.A. (2004). "The paradox of 'detachment-disorders': binding-disruptions of dissociative process, Commentary on 'Cherchez la Femme, Cherchez la Femme: A paradoxical response to trauma (Penelope Hollander)'". *Psychiatry* 67(3): 246–255.

Chused, J.F. (1991). "The evocative power of enactments". *Journal of the American Psychoanalytic Association*. 39: 615–639.

Fonagy, P., Gergely, G., Jurist, E.J. and Target, M. (2003). *Affect Regulation, Mentalization and the Development of the Self*. New York: Other Press.

Freud, S. (1909). Notes upon a case of obsessional neurosis. *The Standard Edition*. J. Strachey. London: Hogarth Press. 10.

Freud, S. (1920). Beyond the Pleasure Principle. *The Standard Edition*. London: Hogarth Press. 18: 147–156.

Gazzaniga, M. (1995). Consciousness and the Cerebral Hemispheres. *Cognitive Neuroscience*. M. Gazzaniga. Cambridge, Massachusetts, MIT Press.

Gazzaniga, M.S., Bogen, J.E. and Sperry, R.W. (1962). Some functional effects of sectioning the cerebral commisures in man. *Proceedings of the National Academy of the Sciences* .15(48): 1,765–1,769.

Horowitz, M.J. (1986). *Stress Response Syndromes*. New York: Jason Aronson. Keinänen, M. (2006). *Psychosemiosis as a key to body-mind continuum: the reinforcement of symbolization-reflectiveness in psycho-therapy*. New York: Nova Science Publishers, Inc.

Marvin, R.C.G., Hoffman, K. and Powell, B. (2002). "The circle of security project: Attachment-based intervention with caregiver-pre-school child dyads". *Attachment & Human Development*. 4(1): 107–124.

McLaughlin, J. (1991). "Clinical and theoretical aspects of enactment". *Journal of the American Psychoanalytic Association*. 39: 595–614.

Rauch, S.L., van der Kolk, Bessel, A., Fisler, Rita E., Alpert, Nathaniel M., Orr, Scott P., Savage, Cary R., Fischman, Alan J., Jenike, Michael A., and Pitman, Roger K. (1996). "A symptom provocation study of posttraumatic stress disorder using positron emission tomography and script driven imagery". *Archives of General Psychiatry.* 53: 380–387.

Reinders, A.A.T.S., Nijenhuis, E.R.S., Paans, A.M.J., Korf, J., Wilemsen, A.T.M. and den Boer, J.A. (2003). "One brain, two selves". *NeuroImage* 20: 2,119–2,125.

Ryle, A., Ed. (1999). *Cognitive Analytic Therapy: Developments in Theory and Practice.* New York: John Wiley & Sons.

Rynearson, E.K. (2006). *Violent Death: Resilience and Intervention Beyond the Crisis.* New York: Routledge.

Schore, A.N. (2003). *Affect Regulation and Repair of the Self.* New York: W.W. Norton & Co.

Schore, J.R. and Schore, A.N. (2008). "Modern attachment theory: the central role of affect regulation in development and treatment". *Clinical Social Work Journal.* 36: 9–20.

Squire, L.R. and Kandel, Eric R. (1999). *Memory: From Mind to Molecules.* New York: Scientific American Library.

Tomkins, S.S. (1995). Script theory. *Exploring Affect: The selected writings of Silvan S. Tomkins.* E.V. Demos. New York: Cambridge University Press.

van der Kolk, B., MacFarlane, Alexander and Weisaeth, Lars (1996). *Traumatic Stress.* New York: Guilford Press.

Weekes, C. (1969/1990). *Hope and Help for Your Nerves.* New York: Signet.

CHAPTER SIXTEEN

Bridging neurobiology, cognitive science and psychoanalysis: Recent contributions to theories of therapeutic action

A discussion of Chapters 12, 13, 14 and 15

Sandra G. Hershberg, M.D.

C hapters twelve, thirteen, fourteen and fifteen explore the ways in which knowledge and research about the implicit and explicit domains, in the context of relational experience, reconfigures concepts of memory, learning and a sense of self in the developing brain and, furthermore, contributes to a theory of mind. These findings, particularly in the areas of attachment, infant observation, and neuroscience, emphasize the primacy of relational experience and inform our notions of how psychoanalysis leads to change.[1]

In an effort to achieve a sense of balance between coherence and chaos, Schore, Bucci, Chefetz, and Fosshage, have provided footholds of clarity and understanding as we consider various aspects of the implicit and explicit domains. Schore (1994, 2003a, 2003b, 2010),

---

[1] This paper was presented at the Spring Meeting of the Division of Psychoanalysis of the American Psychological Association, 11 April, 2008, New York City. Some portions of this paper have been excerpted from a longer manuscript entitled, "Interfaces Between Neurobiology, Cognitive Science, and Psychoanalysis: Thoughts about Implicit and Explicit Communication in Promoting Change" submitted for publication.

in his painstaking and creative endeavour to integrate the implicit self, psychoanalysis and neuroscience, focuses on the questions: Where in the brain do we locate the implicit self, that aspect of ourselves which is responsive to non-verbal expressions of emotions, the markers of attachment and emotional connection, and the seat of affect regulation, originally configured between infant and caregiver? What are the implications of these findings, from his perspective, for the therapeutic process?

Schore (2010), bringing together a wide range of data, posits a model which highlights the major importance of the developing infant and young child's right brain. Emerging from attachment experiences of child and caregiver, the right brain is the site of "the implicit self", which essentially encodes mainly imagistic symbolic and Bucci's subsymbolic processes. Affective non-verbal and paralinguistic communications of facial expression, posture, tone of voice, physiological changes and so on, are stored imagistically at a non-conscious level. These relationally emergent affective experiences influence the development of self and interactional regulation. Proposing ways in which these findings may lead to change in the therapeutic endeavour Schore highlights the importance of empathic immersion, sensing into the mind and state of the other, involving right brain to right brain communication. Transference/counter-transference exchanges and, often, enactments represent implicit co-constructed exchanges. In the revival of thwarted developmental longings the possibility exists for recovery of dysregulated right brain activity, or, put another way, a shift from disorganized to insecure or secure attachment experiences mediated through the non-conscious (or unconscious) implicit systems which regulate affective and body states.

The aim of the multiple code theory is to delineate the relationship between various kinds of psychological information and experience, organized in a range of forms, recorded as bodily experience, action and the images and memories of our lives which may function within and outside of awareness. Bucci's system, which I will discuss next, does not make the boundaries between these domains so distinct. Perhaps the focus on right brain processes, which in the past have been under-emphasized and less well understood, needs now to be better integrated with insight and interpretation, a point that Fosshage addresses.

Bucci (1985, 1997, 2001, 2010) has proposed a theory of psychological organization or theory of mind organized around the interaction of different forms of thought or representation: the multiple code theory. In Chapter thirteen, elaborating on this model and its implications, she addresses the following questions: How does the multiple code theory and referential process foster integration and communication? How is the understanding of the referential process useful in psychoanalytic treatment? How does the process of dissociation operate in this framework?

The aim of the multiple code theory is to delineate "the interplay between different kinds of psychic knowledge and experience, organized in different forms, registered as bodily experience, action and the imagery and memories of our lives, which may operate within or outside of awareness". Viewing the human mind as a multi-format, emotional information processor with only partial integration of formats, Bucci proposes two primary formats—subsymbolic and symbolic, further divided into symbolic verbal and symbolic non-verbal. The subsymbolic mode is characterized as "analogic, and processed as variation on continuous dimensions, rather than generated through combining discrete elements as in symbolic forms" (Bucci 2002: 769). Variably accessible to consciousness, subsymbolic processing functions at the implicit level (we are unable to capture it) although as Bucci explains, it is possible, with training and focused attention, to gain greater awareness of this realm. In the treatment situation, subsymbolic thinking plays out in enactments, feelings, and non-verbal communications. This arena, as we have seen, corresponds to the right brain locus in Schore's system, and, to be discussed, Fosshage's imagistic symbolic processing. The verbal symbolic mode is familiar to us language. Importantly, the non-verbal symbolic realm encompasses images in all sensory modalities—vision, touch, smell, and taste.

The referential process links the three systems—subsymbolic, symbolic verbal, and symbolic non-verbal, which are all linked to each other and to language. The foundational body elements of the emotion schemas constitute the affective core, consisting of subsymbolic sensory, somatic and motoric representations which accounts for the feeling of self across various emotional contexts. Emotion schemas are the memory building blocks which constitute one's sense of self and the range of self-with-other experiences.

From my reading, Bucci's expanded category of subsymbolic processes, comprising the "affective core" of emotion schemas, corresponds to what Fosshage and others refer to as organizing patterns. These organizing patterns are developed in relational contexts, through lived experience, and are experienced at implicit and explicit levels of awareness. Bucci (2010: 7) states that "subsymbolic experience is the guide to the uncharted terrain of the analytic interchange" and in comparing the dance of the tango with wonderful Dardo as guide to the analytic tango (and the state of *maybe*), the emphasis is again on the subsymbolic.

Finally, Bucci, following Bromberg (2006), speaks of the analytic understanding of dissociated schemas that may become triggered in the analyst or analysand. These dissociated schemas may have originally arisen as ordinary, protective responses, but, for various reasons, they have remained integrated—a change from the classical model where repression is the name of the game, with the use of insight and interpretation the curative treatment. She emphasizes the importance of a guiding theoretical framework as a protection against implicit, idiosyncratic attitudes foreclosing a more open meaningful exchange.

Fosshage's Chapter fourteen is an exploration of "how the explicit and implicit learning and memory systems encode information, how encoding affects conscious accessibility of implicit processing, and the implications of encoding and conscious accessibility in delineating a theory of multiple pathways for therapeutic action". Drawing upon the "revolutionary" finding of these dual systems, working at different levels of awareness, and, yet, in tandem, particularly the expanded role of unconscious processing at the implicit level, Fosshage mines their import in the analytic process and in understanding the persistent and often inflexible seeming nature of these problematic organizing principles.

Fosshage advances the notion of imagistic thinking, that is images generated in all sensory modalities—sight, smell, touch, taste, viscerally and motorically bodily sensations—as basic to all thinking, emphasizing the very early capacity of the infant for non-verbal symbolic processing, supported by the demonstration of rapid eye movement (REM) activity in utero and the Dr. Seuss study. Following Damasio (1999) and Paivio (2007), Fosshage underscores the role of non-verbal imagery, questioning the need to posit the separate category of subsymbolic processes, an important difference from Bucci's model. In addition, commenting on the idea of intuition, Bucci understands that phenomenon as a reflection of the subsymbolic, while Fosshage renders intuition as the "fluid interplay" of implicit and explicit systems at a subliminal level.

How can implicit devitalizing mental models be modified? How does one's understanding of relational procedural knowledge and its accessibility to consciousness inform a theory of therapeutic action? Fosshage answers these questions by juxtaposing two models of therapeutic action based on implicit and explicit processing and on the characteristics of implicit mental models. "Rather than change taking place primarily through explanation, the traditional focus, or primarily through implicit relational knowing, the focus of the Boston Group", Fosshage emphasizes, "the interplay between the implicit/explicit and imagistic/verbal systems for therapeutic action". In addition, he highlights the clinical import of understanding that relational procedural knowledge varies, depending on the process of formation and other variables, such as trauma, intensity of affects, and frequency of repetition, as accessibility to consciousness. In clinical situations when procedural knowledge is not accessible to consciousness, emphasis on "interactive intersubjective processes" or "non-interpretive processes" will be more productive. However, if procedural knowledge can come into consciousness, via an explicit declarative focus, increased awareness gradually contributes to a capacity to suspend momentarily intractable mental models to enable the registration and establishment of new models, based on co-creation of new relational experience within the analytic relationship, into long-term memory. Thus Fosshage posits two fundamental avenues for therapeutic action that work in conjunction, but vary in terms of which process is in the forefront in the moment-to-moment clinical exchange.

From my perspective, following Modell (2003), I would propose metaphor formation to be a bridging implicit/explicit cognitive linguistic concept, imagistically generated from multimodal bodily sensations, which both shifts meanings between disparate arenas and by means of innovative rearrangements can transform and spawn new perceptions.

One further point of discussion is Fosshage's view of dissociation, which provides a difference from Bucci. Rather than viewing dissociated states as "unsymbolized, unformulated, not me" states—tilted to function defensively—Fosshage argues that many of these states can be more parsimoniously explained as the activation of implicit procedures, that is learned patterns of interaction, symbolically encoded, which may or may not have a defensive slant.

Focusing on the importance of coherence and meaning-making, Chefetz, in Chapter fifteen, "sees the problem of repetition of trauma as less a compulsion to repeat what is unresolved and more a need to make sense of our disparate elements of experience using the only means available when thinking and feeling are blocked by dissociative process: action, enactive repetition". When thinking and feeling are unlinked, when subsymbolic and symbolic references are disconnected (Bucci), action is the only way of communicating implicit procedural knowledge. Chefetz sees the linking of the right and left brains in the act of speaking as a potentially potent bridge to linking affect and autobiographical narrative. This point is very similar to Fosshage's understanding of the variability of access of relational procedural knowledge to an explicit focus within a therapeutic relationship.

I wish to thank Schore, Bucci, Fosshage, and Chefetz for their contributions about the ways in which implicit and explicit domains are conceptualized cognitively, neurobiologically, and psychoanalytically and inform the manner in which we think about psychoanalytic change and therapeutic action.

References

Bromberg, P. (2006). *Awakening the Dreamer: Clinical Journey.* Mahwah, NJ: Analytic Press.

Bucci, W. (1985). "Dual coding: A cognitive model for psychoanalytic research". *J. Amer. Psychoanal. Assn.* 33: 571–607.

Bucci, W. (1997). *Psychoanalysis & Cognitive Science: A Multiple Code Theory.* New York: Guilford Press.

Bucci, W. (2001). "Pathways of Emotional Communication". *Psychoanalytic Inquiry.* 21: 40–70.

Bucci, W. (2002). "The Referential Process, Consciousness, and the Sense of Self". *Psychoanalytic Inquiry.* 22: 766–793.

Bucci, W. (2010). "The Uncertainty Principle in the Psychoanalytic Process". In: J. Petrucelli (ed.) *Knowing, Not-Knowing and Sort-of-Knowing: Psychoanalysis and the Experience of Uncertainty.* London: Karnac Books.

Damasio, A. (1999). *The Feeling of What Happens*. New York: Harcourt Brace & Co.

Fosshage, J. (2004). "The explicit and implicit dance in psychoanalytic change". *The Journal of Analytic Psychology*. 49: 49–65.

Fosshage, J. (2005). "The explicit and implicit domains in psychoanalytic change". *Psychoanalytic Inquiry*. Vol. 25, 4: 516–539.

Fosshage, J. (2010). "Implicit and Explicit Pathways to Psychoanalytic Change". In: J. Petrucelli (ed.) *Knowing, Not-Knowing and Sort-of-Knowing: Psychoanalysis and the Experience of Uncertainty*. London: Karnac Books.

Modell, A. (2003). *Imagination and the meaningful brain*. Cambridge, MA: MIT Press.

Paivio, A. (2007). *Mind and Its Evolution: A Dual Coding Theoretical Approach*. Mahway, NJ: Lawrence Erlbaum Associates.

Schore, A.N. (1994). *Affect regulation and the origin of the self*. Mahwah NJ: Erlbaum.

Schore, A.N. (2003a). *Affect Regulation and the Repair of the Self*. New York: W.W. Norton.

Schore, A.N. (2003b). *Affect Dysregulation and Disorders of the Self*. New York: W.W. Norton.

Schore, A.N. (2010). "The Right Brain Implicit Self: A Central Mechanism of the Psychotherapy Change Process". In: J. Petrucelli (ed.) *Knowing, Not-Knowing and Sort-of-Knowing: Psychoanalysis and the Experience of Uncertainty*. London: Karnac Books.

PART VI

HOW BODIES ARE THEORIZED, EXHIBITED AND STRUGGLED WITH AND AGAINST: GENDER, EMBODIMENT, AND THE ANALYST'S PHYSICAL SELF

CHAPTER SEVENTEEN

Lights, camera, attachment: Female embodiment as seen through the lens of pornography

Jessica Zucker, Ph.D.

She had dildos on a shelf and a tray of paraphernalia tucked under her couch including lighters for her endless round of cigarettes. She had whips and gas masks dangling from a hook in the living room, chains, and what looked like a leash. She veered from timid and reserved to very "out there" in the telling of her life story, her expressive body almost preaching at times.

She was mesmerizing, but I found myself preoccupied by my car. Was I caught in a red zone? Would I be stuck here? Turns out, my car was fine, but I wasn't sure that I was. "Good girl" researcher meets up with "bad girl" porn star—two sides of feminism, two sides of femininity. It was 2005, but in many ways, it was still 1975—we may have come a long way (baby), but we are still panicked by sex that is not embedded in relationships, especially when it is so obviously embedded in the market economy.

At the end of each of the interviews, I would typically ask if the interviewees had any questions for me. June took this opportunity to ask me what I fantasize about when I masturbate, what fetishes I have, and what my addictions are—turning the interview into something that felt like a desperate molestation. Was that the way I made her feel, despite my careful protocol of questions, many aimed at nothing more lurid than mother–daughter relationships? She pressed me, now squarely in her "out there" persona, to go to her sex show the following night, where she would be performing female ejaculation on stage—opining that it would be good for me and my husband. I politely declined (while internally I was roiling and frozen). She walked me to my car and I sensed that she wanted to get in and drive away with me. The trauma of her stories and history, while told with very little affect, were now lodged in me—an instance of projective identification I can understand in retrospect.

Women's bodies have always been a site of desire, pleasure, and of course objectification (see, for example, Bordo 1997; Davis and Vernon 2002; de Beauvoir 1952; Gilligan, Brown, and Rogers 1990; Lorde 1997; Moradi, Dirks, and Matteson 2005; Mulvey 1988; Person 1999). Moreover, female sexual subjectivity, in all its aspects, is typically construed as dangerous (for example, Fine 1992; Vance 1984). Feminist thought of the 1970s and 1980s grappled with the ways in which our culture viewed female sexual desire and longing as something to be sequestered and tamed inside the domestic and relational sphere, or perhaps worse, something that would be owned and operated by men. Debates between feminist sex radicals such as Ellen Willis, claiming women's right to sexual sovereignty in all manner, clashed with the cultural feminists such as Robin Morgan, in the campaigns against prostitution during the 1970s and 1980s— the "Take Back the Night" marches in New York, for instance.

But another perspective on female sexuality was also developing during this period, one which moved the debate out of a binary stalemate into the complications and paradoxes that continue to define issues of female sexuality and embodiment to this day.

In an early experiment in collective writing about bodies and health, which became the classic *Our Bodies, Ourselves* published in 1973, female sexual subjectivity was suddenly rendered from the inside out. Women spoke and shared and published their thoughts and experiences collectively and safely—there was no subject/object power relation in the investigations, no researcher/research subject, no doctor/patient, no sexual educator/compliant student opening up women's erotic lives—just women, working their way through to the second wave feminist principle "the personal is political".

Many books built on this foundation, including Barbara Ehrenreich's *Re-making Love* which in 1986 examined the sexual revolution from the perspective of women, while Muriel Dimen's *Surviving Sexual Contradictions* (published in 1986) broke out of the form by using her own erotic and psychological life to study, theorize and politicize female sexuality, including our active role in sexual objectification, what she called the position of the subject-as-object.

Locating myself in this still developing feminist conversation, I felt inspired to get an up close and personal understanding of how women think about their sexuality and their meaning-making processes with regard to it, by engaging with one group of women who inhabit a highly charged social location—pornographic actors. These women embody the subject-as-object paradox. Their sexuality is displayed and captured on film, but what is the relationship between those sexual performances and the interior experience of these actors who make it seem so real—well not so real, but who make us know that they are performing a fantasy made for us, the viewer?

My aim was to engage the enormous complexities of these women's self states, by asking them to reflect on how they made meaning of their lives vis-à-vis the choice to make sex an aspect of work through pornography. In that spirit, I did not set out to find the singular, "causal" factor that led these women to become pornographic actors. Rather I wanted to wade through their personal histories with them, in an effort to gain a deeper understanding about how they reflected upon their sexual choices, the pleasures and pains of sex work, the early sexual messages they absorbed in their families, especially from their mothers, and how they made meaning out of their ways of living out Dimen's position of the subject-as-object. The goal was not merely to know "them", but to connect their storylines to our own.

Sigel (2005) wrote "sexuality constitutes a large part of modern people's sense of self. Identities, dreams, and fears can be grounded in sexuality, and pornography allows for the examination of these issues. It exposes the culture to itself. Pornography is the royal road to the cultural psyche" (p. 3). Williams (2004) added, "As a cultural form that is as diverse as America, pornography deserves both a serious and extended analysis that reaches beyond polemics and sensationalism" (p. 6).

To achieve the extended analysis of which Williams speaks, I wanted to look beyond the sexual performances, beyond the cultural and economic organization of the pornography industry, and into the personal histories of the pornographic actors, especially into the texture of their relationships, what we might now call "attachment history". White (2005) wrote "within contemporary relational theories, sexuality has come to be seen as the central arena in which the dramas of attachment are played out—in which emotional connection and intimacy is sought, established, lost and regained" (p. 5).

Sexual knowledge and body understanding are cultivated contextually. Karin Flaake (1993) points out that mothers and daughters seldom discuss the full range of the daughters' sexual development, rendering it a silent and procedural crisis. Flaake stated that "mothers and daughters do not speak about emotions, or the sensations accompanying the daughter's development; about desires or fantasies, about shame or pride concerning the body" (p. 9).

Not surprisingly, this characterization fits the narratives of the women in my study, even though Flaake was not selecting out sex workers as being unique in this way. Many of the women in my study did, in fact, turn to their mothers with the hope of gleaning insight and clarity about bodily maturation, reproductive lessons, and sexual sagacity. Their mothers responded in many ways, running the gamut, as all mothers do—silence, confusing messages, anger, and personal sharing. But, in whichever way, compromised communication from mother to daughter around such issues as sexual confusion, pleasure, shame, choice, and safety get imprinted on a developing body/mind.

The following qualitative findings constitute a snapshot of twenty pornographic actors who reflected on aspects of their embodiment and sexual development, beginning with the onset of menarche, followed by an illustration of how experientially powerful interactions led to the incorporation of early sexual maternal messages, and concluding with examples of current sexual practices and beliefs.

I initially intended to use a clinical/research setting for each interview. However, hours before my first interview, I found myself in an emblematic quandary as twenty-one year-old Orlanda explained that her ulcer was creating physical pain and asked if I could travel to her home in the San Fernando Valley.

My resistance and anxiety built as I drove to her house, and considered all the methodological, personal, and theoretical dilemmas this change of venue would present to my "neat" and "tidy" academic dissertation. However, it quickly became clear that whatever my discomfort, this arrangement provided my interviewees far greater psychological ease—and comfort—and was much more consistent with a feminist methodology. Robert Stoller's landmark book *Porn: Myths for the 20th Century* (1991), which described his own ethnographic explorations in the porn industry, exalted the intersubjective messiness that resulted from conducting his interviews with sex workers outside of a standard research setting. My work builds on that tradition, while also bringing a feminist standpoint to the project. Ethnographic in form, all twenty interviews took place in the field.

***

Madison, age fifty-four, illustrates with dramatic force the emotional silence around bodies and embodiment that Karin Flaake (1993) has described. She recalled an influential moment of sexual quandary as she began to wonder about feminine flowering on her way toward puberty. Curious and on an inquisitive path of information gathering, Madison queried her mother about menstruation:

> And I remember I said, "Mom, what does menstruation mean?"
> And she about had a flippin' car accident. She ran off the road, slammed the brakes, and looked at me and said, "Why are you asking me this?"
> I couldn't believe it. "Why are you asking?" and I said, "Because we had a mmm ..." Well, you know, she was so flustered she just could not answer my questions. The thought of talking about sex ...

Gilligan, Brown, and Rogers (1990) have explored the ways that a mother's own unresolved conflicts around sexuality can result in complex double messages to daughters, who cope with these contradictions in various ways. Elle, for example, age forty-nine, craved validation from her mother as she embarked on her first sexual experiences. She received incongruous messages about how to traverse her nascent sexual feelings. Elle's mother authenticated her daughter's burgeoning sexual curiosity, and at the same time induced a sense of humiliation about Elle's sexual exploration as a blossoming adolescent. Elle reported:

> I took everything my parents said literally. My mother told me that no matter what you do, don't let a man touch you down

there. I don't know it was around puberty or something. So I would go with guys and they could fuck me but they couldn't touch me. Do you know what I mean? There was always like a shame about that part of my body.

By vacating parts of herself so as to privilege maternal messages over her own exploration or pleasure, we can speculate that Elle might be attempting to keep her mother with her—or at least not to lose her—as she engages her own sexuality. Orbach (2004) has written on this problematic struggle, and is not optimistic, writing that femininity, in the context of the mother–daughter relationship, is constructed with "emotional deprivation and a consequent feeling of unentitle-ment, a psychic receptivity to second-class citizenship" (p. 23).

Though some women received contradictory sexual modelling, others learned absolutely nothing, trying to make their way in a communicative wasteland. Jade, age twenty-one, recalled a deaf-ening silence looming in her home around sexual discovery and embodiment. "She (mother) really never talked about it (sexuality) to be honest. It was never—I never got the sit down birds and bees talk or anything like that".

The mothers' lack of sexual pride, pleasure or communication of the "normalcy" of sexual life must have had their impact on these daughters subsequent sexual decisions, exploration, and relational intimacy—although the routes to sexuality and its discontents are far too complex to show themselves in any obvious way.

A number of my interviewees did make some explicit connec-tions, however. Jade is one of many. She is one of many whose early maternal experiences around issues related to sex and the female body partly informed her decision to pursue pornography. "I know it might sound weird but I feel safe here (in the industry) because people just talk about everything—sex, body, whatever. This is really where I've come to learn about my sexuality. My mother's fears of her own body made me ashamed of mine, but now I feel a part of something important. Proud".

Relational complexities get illuminated further as we look at the exhibitionistic, attention-seeking, and people-pleasing draw to pornographic acting. Orbach (2004) asserts that "repeated experi-ences of recognition are the ways the baby comes to have a sense of self as generative and vibrant. The relational interchange is the emotional food which the baby internalizes in the development of the self" (p. 26). Perhaps metaphoric starvation is alive in some of these attachment relationships, leaving the daughter hungry for adoration. Mackenzie, age twenty-two, basks in the attention that accompanies working in porn and explained that she prefers performance over intimacy:

> I guess I'm an exhibitionist. Like I would totally go and have sex in front of a thousand people. I've done a sex scene where I've been in a club and I've done like a scene with the whole club watching, which was really cool. I don't know. It's just exciting.

Schwartz (2005) found that "anxious/insecure attachments where conflicted longings for closeness exist often lead to needs for bodily affect regulation. In all attachment difficulties there can be profound insecurity about inhabiting one's body" (p. 52) and negotiating intimate connections. Furthermore, Yellin (2005) noted a profound, common byproduct of an attachment breakdown, resulting in dissociation. "Dissociation is often precisely an experience of being disembodied, out of body, of physical non-existence" (p. 22). Mackenzie's example of valuing exhibitionism over intimacy speaks to the slippery sexual slope that may have resulted from the anxious, insecure attachments described in many of these interviews.

We know the need for connection can be sexualized, and sometimes we can intuit that a sexual scene is a site for enactments and re-enactments. Diamond and Marrone (2003) found that "in extreme forms of atypical sexual behavior involving sexualized ways of representing through re-enactments of childhood attachment traumas, the individual relives the traumatic situation but, this time around, as transformed into something sexually pleasurable" (p. 194).

Several women did emphasize their desire for aggressive sexual practices, for example, such as the desire to be "rough", preferring "hard" sex, and shared fantasies of being "raped". Mackenzie revealed:

> I don't know (laughter). It just feels better. It's more exciting. I think—I don't know. The rough stuff's exciting. The other stuff is kind of boring. I also watch a lot of porn. I'd rather see more excitement (laughter), you know, like even in my personal

> life I– like when I have sex, I like it rough. I like my hair pulled,
> I like being choked and whatever. I don't know if that has any-
> thing to do with my childhood or what, but that's what I like.

It was hard for me to discern whether Mackenzie's reference to her childhood was a moment where she chose to mock the interview(er) or if she was truly trying to make connections between her present sexual life and her history, which was rife with maternal insecurity and unpredictability. Later, Mackenzie shared that she has a "fuzzy" memory of being molested but wondered if it was actually a "dream and not reality". Afraid to upset her mother, she has never disclosed that she believes her step-brother took advantage of her sexually as a child.

Audrey, age thirty-six, however, talked definitively about her extensive sexual abuse history, which began with being coerced as a child to take nude photographs with other children. The photos began with sexual petting and later went on to being drugged and gang raped at seventeen. After sharing the horrendous details of going in and out of consciousness during the traumatizing gang rape across different settings and with different men, she talked about how much she enjoys doing gang rape scenes in front of the camera today. We can surmise that the repetition of these sexual scenes, in a form of play, are helping her master the early trauma—in bed and on screen, even if not in the consulting room, in words.

Tori, age thirty-six, spoke of a father who physically abused her and a mother who ignored these traumatic daily assaults. She now describes how she electively seeks being "roughed up" on and off camera:

> All those dicks I sucked, oh my God. But I've gotten gonorrhea,
> you know. And then I was into S&M, and I liked to get the face
> slapped. Oh my god, I got Fibromyalgia. I'm thinking, part of
> Fibromyalgia is if you have a head injury; maybe that was what
> I got it from.

Many years of "self-destructive" and "suicidal" gestures accompanied her to the porn industry, a place that now feels like "home", a place where she "belongs". Tori unequivocally stated, "Oh, I love this (referring to her work in pornography), I'm never leaving the porn world. Never".

Like Tori, many of the women I spoke with expressed an allegiance to the porn community, as a form of empowerment that awards the acting out of sexuality and of body exhibitionism in a structured—and remunerated—form. And yet, as we have seen, in many of the narratives, the choice to perform sexuality within the porn "family" yields mixed results—ranging from dissociative sexual encounters to the inability to navigate emotional intimacy, and in some cases, like Tori's, physical harm.

Through these discussions, my own feminist perspective on pornography was productively complicated. The title of an early feminist classic on female sexuality, *Pleasure and Danger* (1984) distills that paradox.

Though I employed feminist methodological and grounded theory perspectives, I too may have unconsciously yearned for a definitive turning point in these women's lives to elucidate *the* reason for their engagement in sex work, but the "truth" insisted on messier interpretations, and a plethora of conflicting conclusions about mother–daughter relations and their consequences in adult life.

And yet, haven't we all struggled to understand our co-constructed bodies, our sexualities, how we inhabit our skin? Haven't many of us as women asked our mothers about our bodies and sexualities, only to be met with awkward ambivalence, stilted confusion, or thunderous silence?

The developing sexual storylines of these twenty women are not so different from our own. Ultimately, their decision to make sex their livelihood places them on the fringe of our culture. However, their development with regard to embodiment can be seen on a continuum, in which we all can place ourselves. Porn stars or stars in our own personal dramas, all our sexual lives embody, repeat, repair, and transcend our histories of pain and pleasure.

References

Bordo, S. (1997). "The body and the reproduction of femininity". In: K. Conboy, N. Medina, and S. Stanbury (eds) *Writing on the body: Female embodiment and feminist theory*. New York: Columbia University Press, pp. 90–110.

Boston Women's Health Book Collective (1973). *Our bodies, ourselves*. New York: Simon and Schuster.

Davis, D. and Vernon, M.L. (2002). "Sculpting the body beautiful: Attachment style, neuroticism, and use of cosmetic surgeries". *Sex Roles: A Journal of Research.* 129–147.

de Beauvoir, S. (1952). *The second sex.* New York: Vintage Books.

Diamond, N. and Marrone, M. (2003). *Attachment and intersubjectivity.* Philadelphia: Whurr Publishers.

Dimen, M. (1986). *Surviving sexual contradictions: A startling and different look at the day in the life of a contemporary professional woman.* New York: MacMillan.

Ehrenreich, B. (1986). *Re-making love: The feminization of sex.* New York: Anchor Press.

Fine, M. (1992). "Sexuality, schooling, and adolescent females: The missing discourse of desire". In: M. Fine (ed.) *Disruptive voices: The possibilities of feminist research.* Ann Arbor, MI: The University of Michigan Press, pp. 31–59.

Flaake, K. (1993). "A body of one's own: Sexual development and the female body in the mother-daughter relationship". In: J.V. Mens-Verhulst, K. Schreurs, and L. Woertman (eds) *Daughtering and mothering: Female subjectivity Reanalyzed.* New York: Brunner-Routledge, pp. 7–14.

Gilligan, C., Brown, L.M. and Rogers, A. (1990). "Psyche embedded: A place for body, relationships and culture in personality theory". In: A.I. Rabin, R.A. Zucker, R. Emmons, and S. Frank (eds), *Studying persons and lives.* New York: Springer, pp. 86–147.

Lorde, A. (1997). "Uses of the erotic: The erotic as power". In: K. Conboy, N. Medina, and S. Stanbury (eds), *Writing on the Body: Female Embodiment and Feminist Theory.* New York: Columbia University Press, pp. 278–282.

Moradi, B., Dirks, D. and Matteson, A.V. (2005). "Roles of sexual objectification experiences and internalization of standards of beauty in eating disorder symptomatology: A test and extension of objectification theory". *Journal of Counseling Psychology.* 52(3): 420–428.

Mulvey, L. (1988). "Visual pleasure and narrative cinema". In: C. Penley (ed.) *Feminism and film theory.* New York: Routledge, pp. 57–68.

Orbach, S. (2004). "The John Bowlby memorial lecture 2003: The body in clinical practice, part one: There's no such thing as a body". In: K. White (ed.) *Touch: Attachment and the body.* London: Karnac Books, pp. 17–34.

Person, E.S. (1999). *The sexual century.* New Haven: Yale University Press.

Schwartz, J. (2005). "Attachment and sexuality: What does our clinical experience tell us?" In: K. White (ed.) *Attachment and sexuality in clinical practice.* London: Karnac Books, pp. 49–56.

Sigel, L.Z. (2005). *International exposure: Perspectives on modern European pornography: 1800–2000*. New Brunswick: Rutgers University Press.

Stoller, R.J. (1991). *Porn: Myths for the twentieth century*. New Haven: Yale University Press.

Vance, C. (1984). *Pleasure and danger: The politics of sexuality*. Boston: Routledge and Kegan Paul Books, Ltd.

White, K. (2005). *Attachment and sexuality in clinical practice*. London: Karnac Books.

Williams, L. (2004). *Porn studies*. Durham: Duke University Press.

Yellin, J. (2005). "Such stuff as dreams are made on: Sexuality as re/creation". In: K. White (ed.) *Attachment and sexuality in clinical practice*. London: Karnac Books, pp. 11–37.

CHAPTER EIGHTEEN

Purging as embodiment[1]

Katie Gentile, Ph.D.

Introducing patrice

Patrice enters my office at the college appearing agitated, but I am never sure because identifying her affect is like seeing turbulent water through a frozen glass surface.

"I'm pregnant and I'm getting married in two weeks", she says flatly. I'm stunned, panicked.

"Slow down", I say, with a lot of affect, acting as if *she's* racing when only I am. She is sitting as still as a boulder, just like usual. "Let's take one thing at a time. You're pregnant?"

"Yes".

"How far along?"

"A few weeks".

"Ok. What do you want to do about it?"

"What do you mean?"

---

[1] This chapter was part of the Gender Section panel organized by Virginia Goldner on the contributions of feminist psychoanalysts. I thank her for her important feedback on the presentation, and of course, for her seminal contributions to feminist psychoanalysis.

265

There are usually three to four young women who are mothers, most without partners, in the classes I teach. I typically sign withdrawal slips for some of these women who must drop the class. If not, I watch them struggle through it, juggling studying, at least one job, and parenting. I also see them succeeding, but I fear how Patrice will respond to these pressures. I witness how quickly she dissolves in the face of interpersonal conflict, and how she seems resigned to obey even the most outrageously ridiculous demands of her mother and her boyfriend, Anthony. When she utters those words—"pregnant" and "married"—her future flies before my eyes, my gut clenches and I melodramatically see only the tragedy of yet another a smart young woman stalled in reaching her educational and professional goals.

This background story is no excuse for my emphatic and complete collapse of potential space. And it was not just any collapse. With this one question my white, atheist body-mind that believes it has choices bumps up against her Christian South Asian body-mind where choices might be more complicated. My future for her involves graduate school—not a baby right now. I can physically feel a gaping space forming between us that is psychological and cultural, for these cannot be separated. As I sit there caught I can feel the historic split between different forms of feminism: white feminist theory that historically has identified the family as a site of oppression via the social reproduction of patriarchy, from Charlotte Perkins Gilman in the 1800s to Betty Friedan in the 1960s to Judith Lorber in the 1990s versus the womanist centered feminisms of women of colour such as Patricia Hill Collins (1990), Gloria Anzaldúa (1987), Uma Narayan (1997), and Chandra Mohanty (2004), who have challenged this absolutist assertion and identified family more complexly, and often as a site of social and cultural support. I also know that with my one comment I have become her mother, telling her what to do. I may have inserted my white values and fears so as to "rescue" her from her predicament (rescue me from my anxiety over her "predicament") but like her mother I have jumped in to take over her life before giving her any space to identify or create her own experience.

I change my focus and ask as neutrally as possible:

"Married?"

"It's what my mom will force me to do".

"She will force you? Do you have any say in the matter of your life?" Again, my anxieties spill out all over onto Patrice.

"No", she says with a little sarcasm, indicating that she sees my point, but she is stuck. "She will want the wedding as soon as possible so I don't show. She will be too embarrassed to have a pregnant daughter who isn't married. I wish I could turn back and do it different. Not get pregnant. Not be with Anthony. I want to get rid of it so I can break up with him".

I can feel myself feeling all the disgust and shame that Patrice predicts will be fostered by her body, growing with a baby that is not supposed to be, right now. I collude in trying to get rid of it—but not through marriage.

"Get rid of it?" I ask, without bothering to question the use of "rid" or "it" or any other desperate affects conveyed in this statement.

"Yes. I want to get an abortion".

"Ok. This is what you want. You have been telling me what your mother wants, what Anthony wants, this is what you want. This is your life" (and my agenda).

She says yes. She wants an abortion.

Later that week she goes to the clinical but walks out within minutes. She believes she made the mistake and it is her fault. She must live with the consequences. Within two weeks of our session she is married to a man she did not want to date, pregnant with a child she did not want to have, and deferring graduate school. I could not create the space and time necessary for a thoughtful decision, a "choice" for Patrice.

This session took place during our seventh week of treatment. At the time, Patrice was a twenty-five year old graduate student, referred to me by a South Asian professor, Tammy, who had been trying to help her stand up for herself and stop vomiting every time she ate. According to Tammy, Patrice would show up at her office and sit on her couch for hours at a time saying nothing in particular or, less frequently, talking about her mother. This professor was a confidante, a big sister for Patrice who did not feel she could trust her friends with the details of her life.

This brief snippet of a session had hallmarks of many of our interactions, most not quite this dramatic. But there was a common relational sequence: Patrice saunters in and presents a problem flatly with little to no affect. I pick up on some unspoken crisis dimension of it, or, like her mother, I manufacture it as a crisis based on my goals for her, and I panic. It takes every ounce of my energy not to tell her what to do and instead to create a space for reflection.

This is not an uncommon response to patients with eating disorders who can have difficulty differentiating and symbolizing their experiences such that much of the relating in a session occurs through bodies (Gentile, 2007; Petrucelli, 2008). The short time I spent with Patrice (three months during her pregnancy and about two months after the baby was born) left me feeling that I had horribly and seriously let her down, and the evidence was before us each week in her growing belly that unmistakably charted how quickly her life was devolving into one that she hated.

Given that the body was our medium of communication, sitting with Patrice was excruciating. From the beginning she made it clear she was there only because Tammy told her to come. Tammy is about my age, but is quite thin and tiny. She wears expensive clothing and jewellery. I am thin, but not tiny and I tend toward a thrift-store casual. With Patrice, I feel I am always compared to Tammy and coming up short as a cheap substitute for her, even though she is not a clinician and even though none of this is ever spoken. Still, after a few sessions Patrice began sharing tale after tale of her mother and her husband controlling her every move—what times she could go to classes, what foods she ate, what clothes she wore, and when she would have sex. Anthony had not wanted to wear a condom, so she got pregnant. She had no agency in her stories. The only person not dominating her was her father, who seemed unable or unwilling to confront her mother when she commanded him or Patrice into action.

Yet, for someone so controllable, I could have no influence on Patrice. With me, she seemed to be a boulder—unmovable and silent, with immense density. Density not in size but in the volume of air/space displaced with her presence. As I described earlier, Patrice's affect seemed to exist beneath a placid frozen surface, which meant the panic and fear I would see behind her eyes was available only for me to experience, not to talk about. As such, her presence could feel like loud wallpaper, demanding an enormous amount of attention through a passive present-ness that would not subside. She arrives always on time, sits and stares at me, awaiting some magical cure. When week after week she begins by saying, "I'm still vomiting",

I feel her hostility, hopelessness, fear, and challenge. Because she is pregnant, I feel responsible for what is now two bodies sitting with me. Sometimes when I feel too much concern to contain it, I attempt to reach her verbally by wondering aloud about what is going on inside her body. She responds as if she is flicking my concern away. She says she does worry too, and that she really has cut down on vomiting, and that she is now only being sick a small amount after some meals. But to explore this change or her or my worries, would create risky connections between us and between her own awareness and her behaviour. Instead, she needs to shock me to attention and then stare as I squirm with helplessness, experiencing the same tumult I see in her but cannot touch. Her body, her locus of control around which she organizes every moment of her day, all her experiences and meaning-making, now feels completely out of her control. She survives by controlling bodies, so since she cannot control hers, she needs to control mine.

Contextualizing bodies

This paper is centrally about bodies. Bodies become recognizable only as they are connected to a cultural body of meaning-making, and this connection occurs through rituals (Douglas 1966). Ritual gives the individual body a cultural space or capacity for making meaning. The cultural meaning that is made then co-creates individual experience, such that we come into being through rituals. This experience, then, re-inscribes meaning back onto the cultural body. So, as in Butler's (1990) ideas of subversive repetition, each movement we make, each ritual or temporal link[2] we enact, at once locates our bodies within a cultural hierarchy and reproduces that hierarchy. The "trick" of these rituals is that they effectively obscure the links between "individual" intentionalities, cultural control, and the political ideologies supporting them (Bourdieu 1977). So, for instance, going on a diet is seen as an individual choice. Were we

---

[2] I am using temporal linking based on Loewald (1980) and my own previous formulation (Gentile, 2010, in press). Here temporal links are the foundation of development, whereby we learn to make meaning of the present by creating expectation and anticipation based on the unfolding of a future from an accumulation of past experiences. This process is psychological and cultural.

to disassemble the patterns of meaning-making, however, dieting might be identified as a response to a political imperative to control female bodies in order to maintain patriarchal social cohesion. Identifying and exploring the quality and multiple layers of these links enhances our understanding of the connection between the individual and cultural meaning of bodies.

This framework is how I can best discuss the simultaneous and seemingly contradictory meanings of eating disorders as both self-destructive and as a form of resistant survival (Gentile 2007). On the one hand, disordered eating has become a ritualized way of being a woman, which seems to standardize one kind of misogynous cultural body, normalizing the extreme practices required to achieve and maintain it (Orbach 1986; Bordo 1993; Bloom et al. 1994). However, given that the social order relies on the capacity to split off and contain female bodies (see Dimen 1991; Butler 1990; Flax 1990, 1993; Goldner 1991; Bordo 1993; Probyn 1993; Grosz 1994, 1995; Dimen and Goldner 2002), when women take any kind of control over their bodies (whether eating when one is hungry, sleeping when one is tired, deciding when, if, where and with whom one will have sex, selling one's body as physical or sexual labour, or binging and purging) it can also be seen as a form of defiant resistance.

It is this life and annihilation struggle for existence that we ask eating disorder patients to explore. While bodies always speak in relationships, with these patients in particular, bodies become containers, powerful screens for projections, spaces of dissociated interactions. As Petrucelli (2008), Knoblauch (1997, 2000), myself (2007) and others have noted, bodies can become a primary medium for the therapeutic relationship. But using bodies in this way requires grappling directly with political and cultural power, for it is sculpted into our muscles and actions (Sampson 1996). Eating disorders are an excellent example of this complicated multilayered relating.

As others have also noted, eating disorders can be understood as an attempt to resist patriarchal oppression (Orbach 1986; Gutwill 1994; Nasser 1997; Gentile 2007; to name only a few). What has been less discussed is the ever-present racist and ethnocentric nature of this patriarchal oppression. This means the already complicated therapeutic alliance that might be created between two white women's body-minds discussing and enacting the cultural creation and abuse of female bodies in the name of beauty ideals, is rendered even more layered and fraught. Here we also experience the impact of a cultural history where ideals of femininity have been based on exclusion, oppression, and privilege. White, upper-class women were reified as *the* ideal of femininity, which meant that not all women had access to "real" femininity (see Welter 1966; Amott and Matthaei 1996). It is easy to see the continuing impact of these class-based, white supremist ideals as they are still relentlessly exhibited in magazines that feature light-skinned, straight-haired women as the cultural ideal, while presenting non-white women as the "exotic", colonized other, if they present them at all.

Within this complicated mix, it is clear that Patrice's eating disorder is multiply determined. For Patrice, her eating disorder links her individual, South Asian body, to the dominant, white, cultural body by providing a discourse through which she can experience her appetites as appropriately disgusting, as female appetites are in Western culture. It emphasizes the importance of regulating her body as an object of "scaled" measurement. It provides a white majority culture-based organizational frame through which she can enact a "white" female gender through the distrust and control of her non-white body. This has important ramifications. The body, the primary avenue for "knowing" the world (Merleau-Ponty 1962/1996; Grosz 1994, 1995; Dimen 2003; Harris 2005), is distrusted and destroyed as dieting becomes not only normal, but a way of being a woman. But not trusting the body—the site of the development of meaning-making and thus, of knowing the world—leaves Patrice more susceptible to letting other people define her, to tell her what she wants, when to have sex, when to get married. Of course she would have to steer clear of me becoming yet another, in particular white, definer of her world.

Researchers like Striegel-Moore (Striegel-Moore et al. 2002; Striegel-Moore and Smolak 1996; Striegel-Moore et al. 2000) and Thompson (1994, 1996) describe how women of colour may use eating disordered behaviours to cope with the stress of bridging different ethnically marked worlds. Indeed, Patrice described college, an English-speaking school, as the location of her freedom, as opposed to her Hindi speaking home where she obeys her mother and her husband. In this aspect, she is identified with "my" white feminist theory of family as deadening or limiting for women; however, it is important to remember that for Patrice, family is also synonymous with South Asian culture. Thus, she is caught in a horrible tug of war for her allegiance and fidelity. And, if Patrice does use her eating disorder to help her deal with this stress, she is using a behaviour that is identified with white women (despite research to the contrary, see Striegel-Moore and Thompson listed below, and Nasser [1997] and Gentile et al. [2007]), further complicating as well as potentially relieving some of the stress of this conflict. I would say that Patrice's eating disorder also functioned to enable her to inhabit both of these worlds simultaneously. Anzaldúa (1987) described Latinas and Chicanas in the US being located in the liminal spaces of cultural borderlands, bridging languages and divergent cultural gender roles and expectations, remaining between but never within. Patrice's eating disorder may have provided a flesh and blood materiality to a similar hovering status, while she attempts to rid herself of it by ridding herself of her body. It enables her to become a defiant thorn in both her own and the dominant cultural body's side. Through it, she resists the dominant Western cultures and her South Asian culture's traditional female gender roles while also enacting both. So her eating disorder not only resisted me as a therapist but also me as the representative of the white, dominant culture, while at the same time bonding with me as a representative of these contexts.

The maelstrom of bodies in the room

But how do all these layers of bodies and power relate in the room? Patrice is being told what to do by her South Asian husband. Me, her white therapist, runs the Women's Center—a known space of progressive, feminist activism on campus and counselling for relationship violence. We are set up to repeat the dynamics of cross-cultural "helping" relationships that have been critiqued by many feminist and postcolonial theorists (hooks 1984; Narayan 1997; Cheng 2001; Mohanty 2004), where the liberal, educated white woman tells the lower income, woman of colour how best to live her life. We are set up for me to critique her mother's and father's parenting skills like a judgmental ACS (Administration in Children's Services) worker. I can denigrate her husband for being verbally abusive creating another potentially racist/ethnocentric enactment, turning her against him to get her to ally with me, privileging a connection of gender over that of ethnicity, as if they can be separated. Here our differing ethnicities and culturally defined states of privilege lent additional layers of potential meaning to common therapeutic content.

Privilege is invisible to those who have it, so it can be difficult to acknowledge and work with. We have a rubric for analyzing trauma and victimization. Analyzing racial power and privilege, is a relatively new endeavour (Leary 1997; Altman 2003; Moss 2003; Straker 2004; Suchet 2007; Harris 2007). As Bass noted, the privileged must hold both the unconscious racist fantasies that create the features of racism and the larger historical trauma that fuels "unspeakable aggression" (Bass 2003: 31). In other words, I had to analyze my unconscious fantasies (which are commonly experienced and enacted through the body) while holding the "unspeakable" history of aggression, knowing that I represent those aggressors. I must say it is normal for me to discuss power, privilege, trauma, and historical violence during therapeutic encounters with my students, most of whom are ethnic minorities. But given Patrice's general inability to verbalize her experiences, this interaction was difficult. In addition, this more open discussion required a level of dyadic relating that we never reached; said in the knowledge that to have done so might have helped us reach it. So, perhaps her boulder-like demanding physical presence in my office was not just an embodiment of her inability to symbolize her experience verbally, but also a form of a sit-in and an act of self-preservation in the face of potential colonization. So what was being manifest in my body?

My countertransference was decidedly much less feminist in nature than my theorizing. As noted at the beginning of this chapter, I initially feared that Patrice's pregnancy would derail her attempts to change her life and turn her into a statistic. I heaped an unfair responsibility onto her shoulders, which she already felt at home, being one of the first people in her larger extended family to go to college.

Most terrifying for me, however, was watching Patrice surrender so quickly and thoroughly to her pregnancy. She embodied the female body out of control that our culture so fears, as Dimen (2003), Harris (1997) and others have critiqued. Her body, the site of such strong resistance (and complicity), appeared to immediately submit to and disappear within her pregnancy. She gained 60 lbs of weight within the first five months. She was struggling not to gain any more weight, not to vomit, not to eat, to have a healthy baby. I felt completely overwhelmed by her continuing crisis and her inability to talk about what was happening and the reality of needing to keep her and her growing fetus safe. Each session felt like a struggle to find her within her growing layers of protection and aggression.

Searching actively for her was complicated by the fact that as she grew, I found a shameful relief in knowing that I was not growing. This relief was tainted for me by the knowledge that my non-pregnant, seemingly under control body, might be envied by her. As Petrucelli (2008) has noted, because this envy could not be verbalized by Patrice, it just manifested itself in deeper self-hatred and disgust for her self. But there was also an opportunity to display and perhaps flaunt her body's generativity to mine. Along side her spoken feelings of disgust about her pregnancy she described each ultrasound and brought in pictures. As Patrice spun with contradictions—health of the baby/losing weight, anger at her mother and father/complete submission to them, wanting to break up with Anthony/marrying him, feeling disgust at her pregnant body/tentatively enjoying the images of her growing fetus—my experience of relating manifested itself in splitting headaches during her sessions. I, too, was being forced to become a bridge between conflicting expectations. Additionally, I was still furious about her situation. Her pregnancy became, in my mind, a constant reminder of her boyfriend, who then became her husband "simply" because he refused to wear a condom. I colluded with her lack of responsibility, knowing that responsibility in heterosexual relationships is always complicated by patriarchal power (Gentile 2007; Goldner 2004). As I held her (and my) rage, she found her own familiar security in focusing on her weight.

Patrice came more or less regularly until she dropped out of school three months later. I provided her with a referral when we terminated. I was very worried about her because I feared she would not reach out to the referral, but I was also relieved to not have the weekly splitting headache. Patrice returned a year later with a beautiful, animated, and engaging daughter. She was again attending graduate school (so much for my prediction that a baby meant the end of her studying). She had not been able to lose the weight she gained during pregnancy. She still vomited daily but now she also took diuretics. She had stopped breastfeeding after a few weeks so that she could take them without hurting the baby. We had two months of weekly sessions that were occasionally cancelled due to childcare issues (sometimes she just brought the baby along with her).

These sessions were different. She would begin with "You won't believe what the baby did this morning!" or "Guess what Anthony said to me when I asked him to help with the baby?" She still displayed little affect, but the content of her stories, their eagerness to be told, and the occasional lilt in her voice began to express more emotion. With this newly exhibited emotion came a little more space for reflection. As the first two examples demonstrate, this occurred as the baby's body became the body we could relate through. Whether present in the room with us or just an object of discussion, we could admire it and wonder about it. It was a safe body that created a triangulated space making it possible for us to relate as a dyad.

She would speak for most of the session, sharing story after story of how Anthony or her mother had gotten her angry and how she could not fight them. But now instead of automatically dissolving into their desires and commands, she began to describe her passive behaviours designed to drive them crazy. She related with stilted glee how she would set up the playpen directly between Anthony and the television set so that he would have to watch the baby. Although we could explore the different meanings of her intentions when they involved the baby, her eating disorder behaviours were off limits. She did not want to discuss her vomiting or diuretic use. Discussing them would be to connect directly to her body with no baby acting as the buffer. Reflecting on this inability was impossible, too, and immediately ended any space I had felt in the room with her. So we did not talk about her eating. I focused on whatever story she brought in, occasionally checking in to ask about frequency of vomiting or how many diuretics she was taking. While not talking about it, I thought a great deal about it.

Purging as embodiment

Patrice purged but she did not binge. She threw up multiple times per day. After her baby, she began taking diuretics regularly, and lessened the frequency of her vomiting. Using diuretics, as opposed to laxatives or vomiting, is an interesting form of purging. It disrupts not the digestive process, like vomiting and laxatives, but the renal system—a filtering system for the body. It does not evacuate what is eaten, but filters out what is already part of the body. Her vomiting was most likely a way to resist her mother and husband, to get rid of experiences that had already happened. This can function to rid her of her past in order to make the present more tolerable: an embodied form of self-regulation, as I have described elsewhere (Gentile 2007). One could say using diuretics too changes the past (attempting to get rid of the present physical evidence of having been pregnant in the recent past). But here it is more complex.

One of the only times Patrice and I could explore her purging was when she answered my question of why she chose diuretics. She described using them as a way of getting rid of the "heaviness" of her body. Her diuretic abuse may be an attempt to filter out her present physical "heaviness" that is a result of her recently giving birth. But this "heaviness" is most likely not only about the physical weight gain. I described Patrice's presence earlier as being like a boulder with emotional turmoil that I could see as if it was held back under a frozen surface. This heaviness she wishes to get rid of may also be the undigested and unsymbolized turbulence that I experienced in sessions as a heavy weight of responsibility. Her body also has a new centrality in her life as she holds and breastfeeds her baby. She has hated her body, starved it and exercised it to exhaustion trying to live beyond it and now her daughter tethers her to it. Being tied to the site of turmoil is torturous, so it is not surprising that Patrice wants to get rid of all this heaviness.

Patrice spent her pregnancy purging by vomiting and she had a healthy baby. Perhaps she also had to up the anté and begin purging in a way that would create a barrier between herself and her baby, a stronger frozen surface to protect them both. Purging with diuretics provides a reason for Patrice to stop breastfeeding, as she is sure they will hurt the baby. Doing this she regulates the present experience of control and colonization of her body by her baby while she attempts to filter out her "heaviness" from her self to protect her baby from it.

Additionally, given her difficulties with differentiation, breastfeeding might equate to merging. She and her mother were one, why not she and her daughter? She related to me through her baby and she expressed her anger toward her husband by triangulating her daughter; triads are where she was beginning to speak and create a sense of self. Being alone with another, feeding a person through her body, was probably intolerable. A bottle could become the third for them, a physical container filled not with fluids from her tainted body, but from an external source. Through this buffer she could feed and relate to her daughter. Having her create this third herself was important. She needed a relational crowbar to separate her mother from her and her father was not up to this task. Similarly, her husband, although controlling of her, was not actively involved in caring for their daughter—a repetition of her own parenting experience. Introducing the bottle might be an acknowledgement on her part of this need for a third participant in order to regulate contact.

As I noted earlier, I only saw Patrice for two months after the baby was born. We terminated when she said she was too overwhelmed with household responsibilities, parenting, and school to attend our sessions. I again provided a referral, just in case she decided that was a good option. I have many thoughts regarding why it was impossible for her to continue seeing me (we were getting too close; she was beginning to challenge the authority of her mother and husband; she needed to see someone closer to her own cultural background; she really was just overwhelmed with everything she was juggling) because it is never easy to sit with a treatment that is so unresolved. Our relationship contained no particular stellar, defining clinical moment, or an epiphany (I cannot speak for Patrice here). However, it did deepen my capacity to experience and sit with the oftentimes nagging and heavy insistence of bodies to be seen and heard in sessions. Embodied symptoms are complicated, for they function simultaneously as both resistance and complicity, traumatic and subversive repetitions, and the analyst becomes part of the process. Which version of the embodied symptom appears central depends upon our focus. Holding these contradictions simultaneously helps illustrate how eating disordered behaviours are particularly important forms of self-destructive survival that engage the analyst's body-mind as they do the patient's. But focusing on the body and all its expressiveness requires also setting forth a task to consciously engage with political and cultural power, and the resistances and complicities that enable the psychological to come into being in the first place. Indeed, as the embodied, cultural context of relating becomes a focus of analysis, an enlivening, challenging, torturous and necessary way of being with another emerges.

References

Altman, N. (2003). "How white people suffer from racism". *Psychotherapy and Politics International*. 1: 93–106.

Amott, T. and Matthieu, J. (1996). *Race, gender, and work: A multicultural economic history of women in the United States*. Boston: South End Press.

Anzaldúa, G. (1987). *Borderlands/La Frontera: The New Mestiza*. San Francisco: Aunt Lute Books.

Bass, A. (2003). "Historical and unconscious trauma: Racism and psychoanalysis". In: D. Moss (ed.) *Hating in the first person plural: Psychoanalytic essays on racism, homophobia, misogyny, and terror*. New York: Other Press, pp. 29–44.

Bloom, C., Gitter, S., Gutwill, S., Kogel, L. and Zaphiropoulos, L. (eds) (1994). *Eating problems: A feminist psychoanalytic treatment model*. New York, NY Basic Books, pp. 27–39.

Bordo, S. (1993). *Unbearable weight: Feminism, Western culture, and the body*. Berkeley: University of California Press.

Bourdieu, P. (1977). *Outline of a theory of practice*. Cambridge: Cambridge University Press.

Butler, J. (1990). *Gender trouble*. New York: Routledge.

Cheng, A. (2001). *The Melancholy of Race: Psychoanalysis, Assimilation and the Hidden Grief*. Oxford: Oxford University Press.

Collins, P.H. (1990). *Black feminist thought: Knowledge, consciousness, and the politics of empowerment*. London: Routledge.

Dimen, M. (1991). "Deconstructing difference: Gender, splitting, and transitional Space". *Psychoanal. Dial*. 1: 335–352.

Dimen, M. (2003). *Sexuality, Intimacy, Power*. Hillsdale, NJ: The Analytic Press.

Dimen, M. and Goldner, V. (eds) (2002). *Gender in psychoanalytic space*. New York: Other Press.

Douglas, M. (1966). *Purity and danger*. New York: Routledge.

Flax, J. (1990). Thinking *fragments: Psychoanalysis, feminism, and postmodernism in the contemporary West*. Berkeley: University of California Press.

——. (1993). *Disputed subjects: Essays on psychoanalysis, politics, and philosophy*. New York: Routledge.

Gentile, K. (2007). *Creating bodies: Eating disorders as self-destructive resistance*. Hillsdale, NJ: The Analytic Press.

Gentile, K.(2010) (in press). What about the baby?: The new cult of domesticity and media images of pregnancy. *Studies in Gender and Sexuality*. In press.

Gentile, K., Raghavan, C., Rajah, V. and Gates, K. (2007). "It doesn't happen here?: Eating disorders in an ethnically diverse sample of low-income, female and male, urban college students". *Eating Disorders: The Journal of Treatment and Prevention*. 15(5): 405–425.

Goldner, V. (1991). "Toward a critical relational theory of gender". *Psychoanal. Dial.* 1: 249–272.

——. (2003). "Ironic gender/authentic sex". *Studies in Gender and Sexuality*. 4(2): 113–139.

——. (2004). "When love hurts: Treating abusive relationships". *Psychoanalytic Inquiry*. 24(3): 346–372.

Grosz, E. (1994). *Volatile bodies: Toward a corporeal feminism*. Bloomington, IN: Indiana University Press.

——. (1995). *Space, time, and perversion: Essays on the politics of bodies*. New York: Routledge.

Gutwill, S. (1994). "Women's eating problems: Social context and the internalization of culture". In: C. Bloom, A. Gitter, S. Gutwill, L. Kogel and L. Zaphiropoulos (eds) *Eating problems: A feminist psychoanalytic treatment model*. New York, NY: Basic Books, pp. 1–27.

Harris, A. (1997). "Aggression, envy, and ambition: Circulating tensions in women's psychic life". *Gender and Psychoanalysis*. 2: 291–326.

Harris, A. (2005). *Gender as soft assembly*. Hillsdale, NJ: The Analytic Press.

Harris, A. (2007). "The house of difference: Enactment, a play in three scenes". In: M. Suchet, A. Harris and L. Aron (eds) *Relational Psychoanalysis Volume 3: New Voices*. Mahwah, NJ: The Analytic Press.

hooks, B. (1984). *Feminist theory from margin to center*. Boston: South End Press.

Knoblauch, S. (1997). "The play and interplay of passionate experience: Multiple organizations of desire". *Gender and Psychoanalysis*. 1: 323–344.

——. (2000). *The musical edge of therapeutic dialogue*. Hillsdale, NJ: The Analytic Press.

Layton, L. (1998). *Who's that girl? Who's that boy? Clinical practice meets postmodern gender theory*. Hillsdale, NJ: Jason Aronson, Inc.

Leary, K. (1997). "Race, self-disclosure, and 'forbidden talk': Race and ethnicity in contemporary clinical practice". *Psychoanalytic Quarterly*. 66: 163–189.

Leowald, H.W. (1980). *Papers on psychoanalysis*. New Haven, CT: Yale University Press.

Merleau-Ponty, M.M. (1962/1996). *The Phenomenology of Perception* (Trans. C. Smith). London: Routledge & Kegan Paul Ltd.

Mohanty, C.T. (2004). *Feminism without borders: Decolonizing theory, practicing solidarity.* Durham, NC: Duke University Press.

Moss, D. (2003). *Hating in the first person plural: Psychoanalytic essays on racism, homophobia, misogyny, and terror.* New York: Other Press.

Narayan, U. (1997). "Contesting *Cultures:* 'Westernization', Respect For Cultures, and Third-World Feminists". In: L. Nicholson (ed.) *Second wave: A reader in feminist theory.* New York: Routledge, pp. 396–414.

Nasser, M. (1997). *Culture and weight consciousness.* London: Routledge.

Orbach, S. (1986). *Hunger strike: The anorexic's struggle as a metaphor for our age.* New York: W.W. Norton.

Petrucelli, J. (2008). "When a body meets a body: The impact of the therapist's body on eating disordered patients". In: F.S. Anderson (ed.) *Bodies in treatment: The unspoken dimension.* Mahwah, NJ: The Analytic Press, pp. 237–254.

Probyn, E. (1993). *Sexing the self: Gendered positions in cultural studies.* New York: Routledge.

Sampson, E.E. (1996). "Establishing Embodiment in Psychology". *Theory and Psychology.* 6: 601–624.

Striegel-Moore, R.H., Dohm, F.A. and Pike, K.M. (2002). "Abuse, bullying, and discrimination as risk factors for binge eating disorder". *American Journal of Psychiatry.* 159(11): 1,902–1,907.

Striegel-Moore, R.H. and Smolak, L. (1996). "The role of race in the development of eating disorders". In: L. Smolak, M. Levine and R.H. Striegal-Moore (eds). *The developmental psychopathology of eating disorders: Implications for research and prevention.* Mahwah NJ: Gurze.

Straker, G. (2004). "Race for cover: Castrated whiteness, perverse consequences". *Psychoanalytic Dialogues.* 14(4): 405–422.

Striegel-Moore, R.H., Wilfley, D.E., Pike, K.M., Dohm, F.A. and Fairburn, C.G. (2000). "Recurrent binge eating in black American women". *Archives of Family Medicine.* 9: 83–87.

Suchet, M. (2007). "Unraveling whiteness". *Psychoanalytic Dialogues.* 17(6): 867–886.

Thompson, B.W. (1994). *A hunger so wide and so deep: American women speak out on eating problems.* Minneapolis: University of Minnesota Press.

Thompson, B.W. (1996). "Multiracial feminist theorizing about eating problems: Refusing to rank oppressions". *Eating Disorders: The Journal of Treatment & Prevention.* 4(2): 104–114.

Welter, B. (1966). "The cult of True Womanhood: 1820–1860". *American Quarterly.* 18(2): 151–174.

CHAPTER NINETEEN

The incredible shrinking shrink

Janet Tintner, Psy.D.

F ifteen years ago, in my last year of psychoanalytic training, I shed around 50 lbs of weight. The more significant this loss became, the more I wondered if my patients would notice. At the time, I discussed this issue with a supervisor. He encouraged me to consider raising this question with my patients, if appropriate (Blechner 1995; personal communication). He also noted that it would be just as interesting a question were I to gain weight! I don't think I replied. Had I done so, I would have told him, with great certainty, that I would *not* go on that awful trek up the scale again, even though I have a lifetime of doing just that. The question of what a realistic sustainable weight might be did not occur to me.

Over about a ten-year period, I did, of course, regain that weight and then some, at the rate of between five to ten pounds a year. My supervisor's question about potential patient responses nestled in an obscure, but not entirely unconscious, region of my mind. As I got heavier I didn't want to think about my weight. And, my weight gain was so slow it was almost imperceptible. But sometimes, when I had to buy new clothes in larger sizes, for instance, I had to face it. This made me feel awful, so I tried not to think about it. I knew I was getting larger, but most of the time I just couldn't consciously face it.

I was in a state of simultaneously knowing, while also attempting to push this knowledge out of awareness. Were a friend or colleague to ask me how I would feel, or were my patients to verbalize their perceptions, I would have said, "Mortified". Just mortified.

I knew that patients would see my body altering. Over ninety pounds is obvious. Maybe some patients could miss it, but not all or even most of them.

However, there were no overt references to my weight gain amongst my patients. Yet now, I see that my weight gain was a subtext with at least some of them.

As my mind drifts back I see myself unable to relax in my chair opposite a never married man in his late fifties. He comes to see me after a minor stroke and the death of his admired but verbally abusive father. He describes dating legions of women whom he rejects for a variety of minor emotional and physical blemishes. When someone gets close emotionally he becomes critical and even insulting. Around a year into our work he comments derisively on women who "let themselves go". I try to listen objectively. But I also know he's talking about me. As an analyst, I know he needs to find a way to cope with these disturbing feelings of disdain and judgement so they do not disrupt every relationship. One way to do this is to directly discuss how he feels about me. Yet being so vulnerable myself, I want to protect myself from his potentially stinging comments about my size and how much it disturbs him. So I cannot, at this point, facilitate this essential discussion. He leaves shortly thereafter.

Similarly, three middle-aged women, like me, are in the mid-200 lbs range. We discuss their emotions around eating, their attempts at weight loss, from spas to fasts to commercial weight loss programmes. But we never talk about the fact that I too am overweight. These women also leave soon.

While I heard the references to a larger size, I did not invite my patients to elaborate on their feelings. I do not know if an explicit dialogue would have helped, but I believe that my inability to address this issue certainly contributed to the ending of the treatment. My weight was a pertinent factor I chose to ignore. At that time the notion that if I wanted to know if my patients noticed my bodily alteration I would have to directly ask about it, hadn't occurred to me. As I now describe, it took me some time to come to this idea.

Obviously, if I could not acknowledge my size, how could my patients discuss their mixed feelings regarding their own bodies? I did not think this through clearly then, but I did learn enough to change my practice. I realized that, with certain patients, I would have to acknowledge that I was overweight.

So, when, two years later I started seeing a patient who was around the same weight as me, approximately 240 lbs, I soon asked how she felt about my size (Tintner 2007). She said it reassured her because it made her feel I could understand how hard this struggle was. Here the common problem—our weight—became a way of bonding and directly addressing a shameful and stigmatized reality that was so alive in my consulting room. I believe that overweight people feel shame because of the stigmatization in our society. When the social and personal taboos against voicing feelings about a larger body are broken, this may ease this sense of shame.

Finally facing my weight I became interested in bariatric surgery. I gathered information and three years later underwent a lap-band procedure. This procedure is different to the much-popularized and televised Gastric Bypass. It is reversible. It does not involve cutting and repositioning of internal organs. It does not result in a rapid weight loss. I lost about 80 lbs, over nearly two years.

In my clinical work, it was important for me that the band increased my odds of maintaining the weight loss. I could finally hope not to repeat the dreaded humiliating experience of my patients witnessing my struggle before their very eyes. This made it easier—for me. If my odds of staying at a stable size improved, I was more willing to consider inviting patients to verbalize their perceptions.

As I began to lose weight, the question of my patient's reactions again came slowly towards the forefront of my mind. My own work was validated by my reading in the professional literature (for example, Mitchell and DeZwaan 2005) and the popular press (for example, Senior 2005) which described strong responses to weight loss not just for people losing the weight, but also for those around them; especially if the weight loss was dramatic. I knew the period following surgery could be a time of hope, excitement, and even risk-taking. However it could also be disturbing and may lead to disruptions in interpersonal relationships (Tintner 2007). I realized that this was relevant for the therapist/patient relationship. This time I anticipated responses from my patients, and I intended to be open to them.

To my surprise, however, there was no reaction on the part of my patients. "Curiouser" still, as Alice would say, while my patients appeared unfazed, my suite mate's patients noticed and spoke about what they saw. I had been in the same suite with this colleague for sixteen odd years, so I had long been nodding and smiling at, and greeting some of her patients. While my patients said nothing, her long-term patients scrutinized me. It didn't take long before they started to comment. They noticed that as I lost weight I began to experiment with my clothing. Sitting in the waiting room as I emerged from my office they casually but spontaneously scrutinized my appearance. Smiling, encouragingly, they commented on my changing wardrobe. They liked what they had seen the previous week. As I passed by them in the waiting room they asked if I knew that I could now wear more shapely clothing and if I was aware of how becoming it was. Frequently, I was accosted on the way out of the suite with curious and admiring questions. How had I done it? Was I exercising? How did I feel? My colleague commented to me that this was also a topic in individual sessions and in a group she runs (Howard 2005; personal communication). So, my body was a hot topic in my suite, just not in my consulting room.

I began to wonder where that heat was on *my* couch. What was going on? For my long-term patients, noticing I had lost weight meant acknowledging having noticed how heavy I was—and their feelings about that. Socially, was the body, maybe especially obesity, so taboo a subject that it was too inappropriate to voice? Were people afraid of hurting my feelings? Were they afraid of jinxing me? Were they afraid of their own negative feelings? Could I survive their critical feelings about how I looked, or difficult newer feelings emerging in response to the change? Was I warding off responses I might find too disturbing, as I had warded off the hostile comments of the unmarried man I referenced earlier? Was it shallow to wonder about the impact of my appearance?

During this time, observing my patients *not* noticing, I wondered if perhaps I should open the topic up. I was drawn to re-visit Ferenczi, whose volumes had rested on my shelves unread for at least ten years. Even though he wrote eighty years ago I was delighted to find he was wrestling with the very issues that were occupying me.

Speaking specifically about the analyst's physical features, Ferenczi (1928) wrote:

> "Every patient without exception notices the smallest peculiarities in the analyst's behavior, external appearance, or way of speaking, but without previous encouragement not one of them will tell him [sic] about them". (p. 93)

Approaching our patient's critical feelings about us, Ferenczi suggested our technique must be more candid and relentless. He put it like this:

> "In the course of an analysis it is as well to keep one eye constantly open for the unconscious expressions of rejection or disbelief and to bring them remorselessly into the open". (p. 93)

Reading this material validated my inclination to explore my weight loss more actively. Of course my patients noticed! Naturally, it was difficult to talk about! While it was one thing to congratulate or admire in a conventional social interaction, it was altogether another thing to bring it up directly with me, where it would be grist for that perennial analytic mill. If my suite mate's patients had anything negative or conflicted to say, they could say it to her confidentially. For my own patients it was another story altogether. Once we get to it, less socially acceptable feelings may emerge. Saying these feelings aloud directly to me was much more complicated.

Gradually, and/or because I was actively thinking about this issue, I began to receive positive feedback. Mostly observations were limited to the conventional, "You've lost weight". But one patient bursting with enthusiasm said, "Oh! My incredible shrinking shrink!" This was the most effusive response I received. Other responses were more timid yet and still all the feelings expressed were within the bounds of what is socially acceptable.

This was a start, but I knew there was more to say. The less I heard, the more I wondered how to proceed. My training had encouraged me to follow a patient's free associations rather than introduce my own material. Yet I felt that I needed to help my patients overcome their hesitations. I realized also that my failure to question them further suggested that I was unable to hear what they had to say.

If I wanted my patients to speak up I had better indicate that to them in the form of a question (Levenson 1987).

A clinical tale

I turn now to my clinical work which describes the unfolding process of becoming more persistent in my questioning. I focus on one case. This material covers an approximately sixteen-month period following my weight loss. It starts during the period I have just described when I was puzzled by the absence of comment on what my patients saw.

Sasha has been in treatment with me for four years by the time my weight loss is apparent. Sasha does not come for treatment to deal with food and weight. Her focus is on her professional and family life. She is smart and efficient. But it isn't easy to get ahead if you can't ask for yourself. We understand this difficulty in the context of Sasha's overbearing mother. Her mother, an Italian matriach, overtly acquiesces to the men around her overflowing table. But in the kitchen, with her girls, her word is law. Thus Sasha has a lifelong expertise in pleasing. Sasha needs to separate from her mother emotionally by standing up for herself without being engulfing. This is our focus. Issues with eating are secondary. However, size matters to Sasha herself and matters still more to her mother. Her mother's weight just creeps upwards. Sasha oscillates between periods when she gains weight mindlessly and periods during which she monitors every morsel consumed and every calorie burnt. Somewhat successfully, we work towards a regulated mid-point between these extremes. Emotionally, we explore her guilt that, relatively, it is easier for her to control her weight than it is for her mother.

As I lose weight, Sasha glances, maybe smiles. I can only speculate she notices. She is occupied with her own issues. I don't feel I have enough data to justify asking a question about what she observes about me. Tentatively, a few months later, she comments that I look different. I invite her to tell me what she sees. She notes I have lost weight and associates to her mother's struggles. Around that time, her family comes to New York from the Philadelphia suburbs, for their second visit in eight years. Usually Sasha and her family visit them. Watching her mother moving around in New York City comes as shock. At home they go everywhere by car, so Sasha's mother doesn't have to walk.

Coming into our Wednesday evening session after a long weekend visit with her family, Sasha says of her 5' 2", 247 lbs mother:

> "I couldn't believe what terrible shape she was in. She could barely walk one block. We had to plan everything around her and she couldn't do much if it involved walking. I hadn't realized she was so restricted. We went to Times Square to Tkts [Tickets on Sale for Broadway Shows], and we wanted to go to a theatre that was five blocks away and we could see she just couldn't make it. At home I don't see it. But now I'm really scared about what's going to happen to her. She won't go to doctors. But she is so heavy. She ate so much. She couldn't stop stuffing food in her mouth. We had this great meal in Little Italy and when we got back to Brooklyn she wanted us to stop off for coffee and cake. She shovelled down this huge piece of chocolate cake with cream. Then when we got home I wanted to hide the candy we had out, because she didn't stop eating. I couldn't bear to watch her. It was disgusting".
>
> "Could you talk to her about how worried you are?" I ask.
>
> Sasha laughs and says, "You must be kidding! If I said to my mother—'I'm worried about your weight. I'm worried about your health. You need to do something,'—she would be so hurt. And then, she would just get mad at me. She would say it was none of my business. And I would want to say being around you is like being in a fun house with mirrors when everything's upside down and you won't see what your reflection really looks like ... I haven't begun to deal with how sensitive my mother is and how huge a deal this was in my family. And it's really hard to see how disgusting the way she eats is, I would never talk to her about THAT".

Given that I am wondering how my patients see my reflection in their mind's eye's mirror this is a fascinating analogy. More indirect than I would be now, I clumsily ask:

> "What is it like for you to have a relationship with someone when you have to be so sensitive about something that was such a big deal?"
>
> "You mean with my mother?" Sasha answers.
>
> Still tentative, I reply, "Well, as I was listening I wondered what it was like for you when I was so heavy, I wondered if that is a subtext that could also relate to your mother".

In that session, Sasha ignores me, but a few months later, commenting on entrance to my office, she says:

> *"That dress looks good on you. You look skinny". I ask how that made her feel and she says: "It's a weird mix. I feel sad it's still so hard for my mother. Glad you're doing it. Also though I feel that I'm envious of you. I would like to be thinner now. But, I also have this feeling that I don't want to pretend".*

I am confused about the pretending and say so: *"Oh!"*

Sasha says: *"Just now, when you asked how I felt about you, I thought of something my mother did. When we walked down the street and she saw someone really thin she stared. I was embarrassed. Once we were out of earshot, she said: 'Did you see how skinny she was! Those skinny bitches all they think about is the way they look. They can't possibly be happy.' I haven't thought about it in so long. Have I told you about that?"*

> *"No", I reply. "It sounds like the message was, if you were skinny, if you were not like her, you would not be happy".*

Sasha says: *"Yes, I thought that if I was too skinny I would get punished. If I were skinny, my mother would wish for me to be punished".*

> *"Do you remember what it was like for you when I was heavier?" I ask.*

> *"I didn't think about it", she says.*

I find this unlikely, so I persevere:

> *"But looking back, with this history, no feelings? Kind of hard to think there was nothing. Can you stay with it a little as it comes up?"*
>
> *"Well, I remember occasionally worrying if you were OK. I felt protective of you. Not wanting to hurt you. Then when you started losing weight I was afraid of talking about it, afraid of seeing too much. I was afraid you might put the weight back on. Afraid that I thought maybe you were sick. But also I was afraid that if you were on a strict diet, I'd have to get all wrapped up in food again. That I would have to start obsessing and when I do that it never works. It's always best for me when I'm not totally ignoring it, when I'm exercising and just staying in control. But then, when I start weighing myself every day and watching every bite, it's awful".*

Discussion and Conclusion

I have described a broad congruence between my capacity to face changes in my body and Sasha's capacity to face and verbalize her feelings about me and significant others. Sasha herself notes how talking about me leads her to a new examination of her mother's difficulties: "When you asked about how I felt about you, I thought of something my mother did". Similarly, after she starts to observe my weight loss, she starts to understand how much her mother's obesity influenced family life: "I haven't begun to deal with how sensitive my mother is and how huge a deal this was".

However glitches in such interactions often do occur. I had to reconcile my perceptions of myself with those of my patients. If Sasha's view of me diverged markedly from my sense of self, it was difficult to follow up on a line of inquiry. For instance I could have asked Sasha if she thought I was unhappy like those skinny bitches. But, still distinctly curvaceous now, the thought of myself as associated with the skinny girls was too remote from my image of myself to think of that question. Similarly, I did not ask Sasha what illness she thought I might have. Actually, shortly post-surgery I was able to stop taking medications for high blood pressure and mild diabetes because they were no longer needed. Physically I felt so much better that I was shocked by her perception that I might be ill.

I know from my clinical work, discussions with colleagues, and pertinent literature (Petrucelli 2008) that talking about the therapist's body can yield rich clinical material. Yet in certain arenas, I have the urge to pull back, not to go that little bit further that is necessary to elicit disturbing feelings. This illustrates how, even with the best of intentions, it is very hard, as an analyst, to pursue a line of inquiry that touches on issues that are personally painful.

When I take a step back, I observe myself in the throes of a complex process of change over the entire period. Behaviourally, as I lost weight I experimented with exercising and my clothing. I also felt differently. Then I had to integrate these layers of my changing reality to my sense of self. This took and continues to take, time. Professionally, I was also observing my patient's difficulty opening up and thinking about how to help them. My technique shifted accordingly. Personally I felt more open. My questions became clearer. By the end of this time, when a question is avoided, I persist, rather than back off: "Kind of hard to think there wasn't anything".

Correspondingly, during this time, patients underwent a process that can be broadly delineated. In what I view as a first stage, a period of about a year to eighteen months, there was little outward response. During the later stages of this period vague wonderings about whether I had lost weight surfaced. These sometimes turned to conventional congratulations.

The second stage was over the next three to twelve months. Sundry significant sisters, brothers, cousins and friends came out of the eating disorders and substance abuse closets. Ostensibly out of the blue, patients got in touch with a mixture of feelings about these friends and relatives. Maybe it was a way of connecting with me. Or, maybe my patients felt that disturbing feelings were now safer to say. This important material provided significant information about my patients' historical and social lives. However, I was also aware it might have been easier for patients to talk about others than state direct perceptions of me. It may have also been a trial balloon, a test of what or how much I am actually willing to hear.

It is harder for me to distinguish a third stage temporally. This stage is ongoing, individualized, with a larger array of factors coming into play. Sasha's feelings towards me ran the gamut from pleasure at my achievement, to envy that I seemed to be in control as she continued to struggle. She was typical of other patients in her reluctance to voice her feelings. She was also typical of others in her fearfulness of hurting me. To me, these are natural feelings. Unless they are sadistic I think patients may, as Ferenczi (1933) indicates, be as protective of us as they are of their parents.

I think the third stage began as my size stabilized. Visually my body stopped changing. Maybe this helped patients speak their mind. This may be especially true for patients with a history of eating disorders in their family. Sasha has witnessed her mother's yo-yo dieting all her life. She is acutely attuned to how problematic maintenance can be. She understands the absurdity of the easy "lifestyle" changes blithely promoted in the popular media.

All these factors result in deeper openness and insight. Sasha's primary psychological task is to separate from her mother's engulfment, free to embrace and stand up for, her own strength and talent. She finally tells me of her fear that I too will impose my problems on her: "When you started losing weight I was afraid of talking about it, afraid of seeing too much". What, hopefully, is different is that, unlike the women I described earlier, her anxiety about me is out in the open. She does not have to silently and fearfully wonder how I can help her if I myself am struggling. Unlike with her mother, with me she can tell me what she fears, and work it out.

This connection between direct observation of me and an opening up in the therapy has occurred with other patients. Often women find it easier to talk about struggles with their body. Several men tell me that they had chosen me as a therapist when I was heavier, because they assumed sexual feelings would not emerge. They were then confused when other feelings connected to aspects of their issues with intimacy and sexuality began to emerge.

In conclusion, in this paper I describe my patients' difficulties responding to changes in my body size as I gain and lose weight. I trace the interaction between what is known and what is spoken and what is unspoken. The more able I am to be aware of what bothers me about my body, the more I can persist in my questioning. I don't know what patients actually thought during the mindless phase of weight gain because I didn't ask. I speculate they sensed my inability to face myself and they responded accordingly. As I lost weight I was able to ask patients to articulate their perceptions about me. It was still difficult to engage in this process. I was still adjusting psychologically and other factors also came into play. Once I was slimmer, patients may have been more able to allow themselves to acknowledge how heavy I had been. Thus, they also became more conscious of disturbing feelings during that prior stage. They may have felt it was socially unacceptable to voice such feelings. Or, they may have been reluctant to face these aspects of themselves.

Especially in a society obsessed with appearance, obesity is viewed with prejudice and stigma. This is hard for people who are overweight. In principle a psychoanalytic approach goes beyond social truisms and aims to allow for the taboo to be spoken. However, it can be hard for the analyst herself, facing her own issues as well as her own shameful feelings. I wish I had been able to help patients explore their feelings as I gained weight. I couldn't. I would like to think that the course of a treatment is determined by what is happening in our patient's emotional and actual lives. But here, even though patients were able to make significant progress, they only opened up on this issue as I myself changed.

Independent of changes in my body size, I believe that my willingness to ask direct questions was crucial. In order to cross the lines of social and personal norms and taboos patients may need active permission to express the unacceptable. That may require us, as analysts, to expand on our usual associative technique. Rather than make assumptions about the subtext of a patient's communications maybe we need to invite them to tell us directly. Asking a question about how our patient's see us may be viewed as narcissistic and intrusive. However, it also brings the obvious into the open, which may be central to the analytic endeavour (Levenson 1987). In this realm of the forbidden, the unknowable and the unspoken, the function of a question is to open the doors—thereby making what may seem unbearable, actually knowable, bearable and changeable.

A larger body evokes strong feelings in others. Significant weight loss can evoke equally powerful feelings. This is documented in the Bariatric surgery literature, which describes interpersonal and psychosocial responses to weight loss, which can be exhilarating, confusing and even disruptive (Cook Myers 2005; Swan-Kreimer 2005). Obesity may be a particularly potent area of exploration because it is a problem literally worn on the sleeve. In fact, such a body is an arena in which the taboo and the obvious coincide and in which the banal and the significant are concretized in corporeal form. It is a communication that is obvious and ignored at one at the same time. To find out more, even if we may not want to, we have to start asking—and tolerate just how exposed we feel.

References

Blechner. (1995). Personal communication.
Cook Myers, T. (2005). "Psychological Management after Bariatric Surgery". In: J.E. Mitchell and M. de Zwaan (eds) *Bariatric Surgery: A Guide for Mental Health Professionals*. New York: Routledge, pp. 125–144.
Ferenczi, S. (1928/1955). "The Elasticity of Psycho-Analytic Technique". In: B. Mazel (ed.) *Final Contributions to the Problems and Methods of Psycho-Analysis*. New York, pp. 87–101.
Ferenczi, S. (1933). Confusion of Tongues between Adults and the Child. In: B. Mazel (ed.) *Final Contributions to the Problems and Methods of Psycho-Analysis*. New York, pp. 87–101.

Howard. (2005). Personal communication.

Levenson, E.A. (1987). "The Purloined Self". *Journal of the American Academy of Psychoanalysis.* 15: 481–490.

Mitchell, J.E. and de Zwaan, M. (2005). *Bariatric Surgery: A Guide for Mental Health Professionals.* London: Routledge.

Petrucelli, J. (2008). "When a body meets a body: The impact of therapist's body on eating disordered patients". In: F.S. Anderson (ed.) *Bodies in treatment: The unspoken dimension.* Mahwah, NJ: The Analytic Press, pp. 237–254.

Senior, J. (2005). "My life as thin person". *New York Magazine.* Archives www.newyorkmagazine.com/nymetro/health/features/1868/index,May16.

Swan-Kremeier, L.A. (2005). "Psychosocial outcome of bariatric surgery". In: J.E. Mitchell and M. de Zwaan (eds) *Bariatric Surgery: A Guide for Mental Health Professionals.* New York: Routledge, pp. 101–118.

Tintner, J. (2007). "Bypassing Barriers to Change? Bariatric Surgery, Case Material". *Contemporary Psychoanalysis.* 43: 121–134.

PART VII

I KNOW SOMETHING ABOUT YOU: WORKING WITH EXTRA-ANALYTIC KNOWLEDGE IN THE ANALYTIC DYAD IN THE TWENTY-FIRST CENTURY

CHAPTER TWENTY

I know something about you

Jill Bresler, Ph.D.

Psychoanalysts have long struggled with questions about what our patients know, can know, or should know about us, in addition to questions about how we work with what they know. Freud and his colleagues, as well as "analyst's analysts", of necessity have had to move as fluidly as possible between the "real" relationship and the transference relationship (Berman 1995), given the fact that the social milieus in which they practiced often afforded them little ability to maintain personal privacy. Due to the awkwardness of writing about one's patients who are in the field, the professional literature offers little help for understanding the clinical issues that arise in such circumstances.

Although the founders of psychoanalysis and training analysts have had relatively transparent working conditions, analysts have traditionally been taught to strive to be as abstemious and anonymous as possible (Crastnapol 1997). In fact, there was a period of time in analytic history when there were serious discussions about whether or not one should ever drop one's analytic stance, to the point of questioning the advisability of a warm greeting at the beginning of an analytic session (Fox 1984). Expressing one's subjectivity, giving personal opinions, or answering personal questions—each forms of self-disclosure—were strongly frowned upon as they might impinge on a desired state of analytic neutrality. Maintaining such extreme abstinence proved to be impossible for most analysts, and it could not have been popular or even comprehensible to most patients. It's now taken for granted by many that while the analyst's attempt to maintain a sort of free-floating attention and an awareness of bias while attending to the work can be considered to be an attempt at a neutral state of mind, no analyst, no person, presents as a completely neutral individual. Since the anonymity project is doomed, we are led to consider what use may be made of the analyst's unique person.

Over the years, we have come to acknowledge that it may be useful in many instances to share our personal reactions to the patient, that this is, in fact, one of our most important functions. Recently, numerous writers have made major contributions in articulating how the sharing of the analyst's subjectivity can be used to further treatment (Aron 1991; Hoffman 1983; Renik 1995). The use of the analyst's subjectivity in the form of reactions to the patient's material is by and large a sanctioned type of self-disclosure although determining when it will be useful is not simple. Although we are aware that our personal reactions to our patients are inevitable and may be useful, we are still generally counselled to keep factual information about ourselves out of the mix (and are not really prepared for how complicated that may be even for ourselves on a human level, however preferable it may be overall). Given this, somewhat less has been said about how we handle the sharing of more concrete information—not our subjectivities, shall we say, but objective facts about us. Of course certain personal characteristics, such as stage of life, race, and gender, are freely observable, and many other things about us may be surmised by our manner of dress, demeanor, office decor and other valid clues to identity. Some work has been done on the many ways in which potentially unavoidable disclosures of factual information, such as being pregnant (Bassen 1988) or being very ill (Galatzer-Levy 2004), can be managed.

In general, we are still taught to function as though we can and should maintain a high degree of anonymity, to keep the disclosure of personal information to our patients to a very bare minimum. But we are also presented with case material in which the analyst is more revealing and the treatment seems to benefit as a result.

The complicated double message seems to be: "Don't do this because it will compromise the treatment, but if you do—watch out!—the results may be worth it".

Controversy about the effects of disclosing personal information is far from over, with analysts of the same orientation at times making diametrically opposed clinical decisions. Consider the contents of the November/December 2007 issue of *Psychoanalytic Dialogues*. Elise (2007) describes her work with a sexually repressed young woman who thought she saw Elise, who usually appeared in her office dressed in the classic muted therapist outfit, wearing a mini-skirt and hugging a black man on the street. This "chance encounter" becomes the jumping off point for a dramatic and quite productive change in the dynamics of the transference—countertransference. Elise never confirms or disconfirms for her patient whether or not the woman she saw was Elise. She presents this as a technical decision for the betterment of the treatment saying, "I think this is the difficulty to keep in mind regarding these types of potential disclosures on the part of the clinician; concrete answers do not present an equal opportunity for the clinical trajectory" (Elise 2007: 850). This is a clear statement that not knowing fosters a more therapeutic environment. At the same time, Elise questions whether she should be dressing differently in the office—she identifies her work wardrobe as desexualized and wonders about the impact that this may have on her patients. It seems that, for her, indirect disclosure is more comfortable, maybe even therapeutic, perhaps because the analyst preserves the possibility of being non-revealing about the personal meaning of such "disclosure".

In general, the open disclosure of personal information goes so against traditional analytic convention that I suspect it is greatly under-reported, giving us less than optimal conditions under which to study it. In a paper in the same journal, Suchet (2007) describes an experience in which she told an African-American patient that she was born in South Africa and raised as a racist. Suchet and her patient discuss the impact of disclosure, although Suchet is not convinced that they have done the topic justice. Describing in rich detail her sickened internal reactions as she exposes this part of her history to her patient, Suchet (2007: 870–871) writes, "I no longer felt calm. I felt deeply shamed. I felt exposed … . I was losing my footing, spinning into the domain of self-loathing … . I wanted to disown my history". Suchet's description alludes to some of the reasons that analysts prefer not to be known. First, as she describes it, the disclosure is very disorienting, even humiliating. It is upsetting to her, and especially so in the presence of this particular patient. Such strong feelings certainly must wreak havoc on analytic listening. Second, as Renik (1995) has stated, our patients knowing more about us may interfere with their idealized image of the analyst, which may be painful to patient and analyst alike. There are many other reasons to hesitate before disclosing, a topic taken up in more detail elsewhere (Davis 2002).

Incidentally, but germane to this topic, by publishing this article Suchet opens herself up to the possibility that other patients will grapple with this aspect of her history. It is only a matter of time before the articles we write may be available for purchase to a wide reading audience over the Internet. E-commerce has come to psychoanalysis, and reading your analyst's work no longer requires a trip to the library.

In addition, we have been given the same opportunities to learn about our patients in more ways than we might have previously, and we must make decisions about what to do with these possibilities. In rare instances in the past, analysts have had to decide whether or not to read patients' books (Jacobs 1987), but we are now faced with clinical decisions about whether to view their blogs or Facebook pages, read copies of their text-messaging conversations with friends, or listen to music that they have made. Analysts are presented with the possibility of new kinds of abstinence if they choose not to view these materials—the more traditional, but not their only contemporary choice. There are times when learning about a patient through channels other than the patient's report may be useful to the treatment. Although there seems to be some amount of shame and confusion attached to the possibility of "knowing" one's patients via these avenues, more than one analyst I have spoken to has told me that they have Googled a patient or otherwise viewed information about them on the Internet, the easiest way for patient and analyst to engage in extra-analytic learning about one another. In both of the case reports cited above, the analyst made the decision to reveal or not to reveal. At least in that moment, they were in control of the decision to disclose. This is not always the case. The recommendation to keep personal information about yourself out of the room is no longer as easy to follow as it was, say, in the middle years of psychoanalysis. I say the middle years because in its early days, psychoanalysis was conducted amongst a very small group of people who simply knew a lot about each other. It was assumed that the real relationship and the analytic work could co-exist, because it had to. Later on, as analysis became more popular, it remained relatively easy for a very high degree of anonymity to be maintained, unless the patient was in a small town, an analytic candidate at your institute, or was doggedly determined to do research. Now, of course, your political affiliations, the high school you graduated from and the date you graduated, your children's schools, and your publications and affiliations, may all be known in an instant with the miracle of the Internet. And if you think your patients aren't Googling you, think again. Based on what new patients tell me, it is my impression that Googling your prospective therapist is routine practice.

Psychoanalysis is practiced in a world that seems to change faster than ever before, which means that if your career spans the thirty or forty years that you might expect it to, the world will have changed several times over from its beginning to end. Even more than psychoanalytic theory, technology has changed over the last several decades. Changes in technology create changes in how we relate to each other. So much of how we communicate or "know" each other takes place in ways that were once impossible. We e-mail, text, sit in front of computers with cameras and look at each other on screens as we talk. The world seems much noisier and more interactive than it used to be, quite at odds with the quiet, hushed, and enclosed world of psychoanalysis. This is a change that bears reflecting on, as it is more and more difficult to create the kind of quiet, contemplative, closed space that psychoanalysts live in while on their job. Thus a psychoanalytic experience may be in some quite subtle ways even more foreign than it was at its inception.

In keeping with the theme of this anthology, Chapters twenty-one, twenty-two and twenty-three are about alternative pathways to "knowing" each other, focusing specifically on the impact of knowledge that therapist and patient may have about one another that is obtained outside of the treatment room. We've purposely chosen examples in which present-day therapist and patient come to know things about each other via avenues that existed in the past—as, for example, therapist and patient discovering that they happen to know someone in common and when something about one or the other of them is revealed thereby. But one of our examples involves modes of information gathering that simply didn't exist five, ten, or twenty years ago—computer technology—which makes finding out about one another easier, and less controllable, than it has ever been. We have come to have many new sources for knowing things about each other without having to ask questions directly of each other.

We are hoping that these examples will stimulate thought about how we live as analysts in today's world. Some of the things that have come up for us as we've reflected on the experiences we are going to describe include the following: What exactly is the place of anonymity in today's analytic encounter? What do we do about the fact that our patients may know things about us that we would not wish them to know, simply because of technology? What do analyst's analysts, or small town practitioners, have to teach us about how to live more transparently as analysts and the advantages and pitfalls of doing so?

Does non-disclosure create a more "analytic" atmosphere? Are there instances in which it is preferable? Instances when it is not? How do you tell the difference? What does it mean for a patient to be curious about our personal lives? What are the benefits of curiosity? How do you know when curiosity is problematic, or pathological? What should the patient do with his or her curiosity? How about the analyst? What type of connection is established when one person relates to another via the Internet, or when one person follows another's life via Google?

How does the analyst live in a world where he or she is faced with Facebook, My Space, Internet dating, and other new forms of interacting that are increasingly normalized? Does the analyst, who is generally concerned with anonymity, of necessity become a creature who lives outside of his or her culture? We are hopeful that you will find these clinical examples thought-provoking, and that they will provide you with the beginnings of a framework for how to think about this increasingly common phenomenon.

References

Aron, L. (1991). "The patient's experience of the analyst's subjectivity". *Psychoanalytic Dialogues*. 1: 29–51.

Bassen, C.R. (1988). "The impact of the analyst's pregnancy on the course of analysis". *Psychoanalytic Inquiry*. 8: 280–298.

Berman, E. (1995). "On analyzing colleagues". *Contemporary Psychoanalysis*. 31: 521–539.

Crastnapol, M. (1997). "Incognito or not? The patient's subjective experience of the analyst's private life". *Psychoanalytic Dialogues*. 7: 257–280.

Davis, J.T. (2002). "Countertransference temptation an the use of self-disclosure by analysts in training: A discussion for beginners". *Psychoanalytic Psychology*. 19: 435–454.

Elise, D. (2007). "Analytic voyages: Surprises at sea: Replies to commentaries". *Psychoanalytic Dialogues*. 17: 847–857.

Fox, R. (1984). "The principle of abstinence reconsidered". *International Review of Psychoanalysis*. 11: 227–236.

Galatzer-Levy, R.M. (2004). "The death of the analyst: Patients whose previous analys died while they were in treatment". *Journal of the American Psychoanalytic Association*. 52: 999–1,024.

Hoffman, I.Z. (1983). "The patient as interpreter of the analyst's subjectivity". *Contemporary Psychoanalysis*. 19: 389–422.

Jacobs, T.J. (1987). "Notes on the unknowable: Analytic secrets and the transference Neurosis". *Psychoanalytic Inquiry*. 7: 455–509.

Renik, O. (1995). "The ideal of the anonymous analyst and the problem of self-Disclosure". *Psychoanalytic Quarterly*. 64: 466–495.

Suchet, M. (2007). "Unravelling whiteness". *Psychoanalytic Dialogues*. 17: 867–886.

CHAPTER TWENTY ONE

Double exposure …
Sightings of the analyst outside
the consultation room

Barry P. Cohen, Ph.D.

lthough the psychoanalytic inquiry seems predominantly
designed as an exploration of the patient's psyche, personal
history, intrapsychic, and interpersonal dynamics, the analyst, as a participant observer in the process, inevitably presents him
or herself to the scrutiny of the patient. What patients allow themselves to observe and to know about their analysts in the consultation room provides the analyst with an in vivo experience of their
ability to perceive, to tolerate, to attend and to selectively in-attend
aspects of the "other" in the interpersonal situation.

Each analytic dyad represents the interaction between the unique
individuality of the patient and the unique individuality of the analyst. Each analytic session offers a multitude of choice points where
patients and analysts can make overt their observations, hunches,
and reactions regarding what they know or perceive of the other, as
well as what the other seems to know about them.

The notion of maintaining analytic anonymity seems not only
an impossible goal but perhaps an archaic and undesirable one as
well. How do we foster curiosity and help our patients overcome
their selective in-attention, while developing the ego strengths of

observation and critical questioning if we "hide" aspects of our individual selves? But even for many analysts whose theoretical beliefs and practices would have them forego the notion of analytic neutrality and anonymity, the default position of the therapist is often a non-revelatory one in terms of our personal experience, life history and, at times, subjective experience. Do we experience self-revelation as a choice, an intervention, and a departure from the typical analytic stance, or do we consider self-revelation an integral part of the mission of joint discovery and mutual recognition of the analytic dyad? How do we avoid, on the one hand, unnecessarily mystifying our patients by withholding aspects of ourselves without, on the other, imposing aspects of ourselves on them in a manner that is irrelevant, unwanted, or counter-therapeutic?

Surrendering to the inevitability of being known by our patients can feel somewhat liberating in the sense that we no longer need to control the uncontrollable, or prevent the un-preventable. But in fact the responsibility for what to self-disclose, or how to respond to the patient's observations and inquiries regarding our unique individuality, or when to call attention to our unique individuality, involves a continuous process of critical thinking and judgement.

But what about those times when the disclosure is totally out of our control, where the choice is not a deliberate or conscious one, or where in fact there is no choice exercised on our part at all? What about those instances when the patient gains access to information or an experience of us outside of the consulting room? Are these moments to be feared or welcomed? What impact do they have on the analytic process and how do both patients and analysts integrate these extra-analytic experiences into the treatment relationship? What is our counter-transferential experience of being "known" by our patients outside of the boundaries of the consulting room and our roles as analysts and, in a manner of speaking, without our consent? If in the analytic inquiry we encourage our patients to utilize all of their powers of perception to identify the attributes and tendencies of the people who inhabit their interpersonal world, why would we not welcome extra-analytic encounters as an opportunity to further the process? What is it that can make us anxious about being seen, experienced, or known by certain of our patients outside of sessions but not others?

Robert

Robert presented for therapy at the age of sixty-three, a few months after retiring from a job in the public sector. He had experienced a sudden onset of dysphoria, and sought help with his symptoms as well as assistance in finding meaningful post-retirement activity and a social life.

Robert had lived a very limited and socially avoidant life. He considered himself inept at human interaction. He would often say that he felt as if he had "woken up in the middle of the game", and while everyone around him knew the rules, he had no clue. His work had provided him with a structure to his day, and a meaning to his life, but only a veneer of interpersonal relationships. Even though he had worked in the same location for decades, he was close to no one at his job. He had never been married, nor had any significant history of dating; he told his colleagues at work that he was a widower, so that they would not think that he was a social misfit. He had a few long-standing friends outside of work, but he saw them infrequently, and when he did, he was often consumed with anger and contempt for what he invariably experienced as their insulting and mean-spirited behaviour. He felt trapped in these relationships ... unwilling to relinquish them and suffer the resulting loneliness and isolation, but unable to take much pleasure in the companionship that they offered.

He was suspicious of others and his reality testing was tenuous at times. He often provided me with stories of how some "jerk" in the supermarket, the bagel store, or the post office had coughed or sniffed loudly within his earshot, which Robert took as a covert communication that they were insulting him and implicitly saying that they thought he was crazy. At times he would reply with a cough or loud sniff of his own, as a form of retribution. He was certain that others saw him as a monster of some kind and found the frequent reminders of this fact quite painful.

Robert's stories of his family of origin and childhood were few in number and sparse in detail. Whereas he claimed that his age had made it difficult to recall more details, we came to understand that in his family, relatively little was said, feelings were not expressed or explained, and curiosity into the behaviour, motivations and decisions of others was actively discouraged. Robert had developed his own narrative which had filled in many of the blanks. It seemed clear that Robert had to adapt in his family by paying very close attention to subtle and few clues, from which he would extrapolate an entire narrative, and that the subtext of the narrative was to beware of the risks inherent in questioning or probing those around him.

Not surprisingly, my own relationship with Robert was tangled, complicated, and difficult. At his very first session he informed me that he had almost not come at all. He had requested an appointment by leaving his full name on my answering machine. When I called him back, I asked for "Robert". When he came to see me, Robert explained that he felt insulted by my use of his first name and was certain that I was fully aware of the social imperative to address others by their title and last name. He could not conceive of the possibility that asking for him by his first name meant something different to me than it did to him, and this was emblematic of so much of my struggle with Robert. I frequently did not recognize myself in his reflected appraisal of me.

He came to sessions prepared with a mental agenda, a well-rehearsed story about an incident in his life, and a complete explanation about it which he presented as if there was nothing for me to add. What he wanted in return was merely my validation of his cleverness, insight, and the progress that he was making in therapy. He took great umbrage when I responded in any way which did not support what he was saying, which, it so happens, I frequently did. He wanted me to be predictable, unchanging and to fit perfectly into his generic conception of what a therapist should be, which was a classical Freudian blank slate analyst—hardly the image I had of myself.

Robert and I struggled to form a treatment alliance. He experienced our interactions as a continual effort on my part to test him and on his part to avoid humiliation. He could not accept help, an interpretation, or a suggestion without feeling "less than" me, so he would repeatedly reject what I offered. Even my questions were thwarted. Robert would anticipate and pre-empt my inquiry by saying that he understood what was "behind" my questions and commenting on where he thought I was heading without ever answering the question I had actually asked. When I attempted to explore his inner experience, my efforts were often misunderstood and misperceived by him, and as a result, I felt constricted and constrained. When I asked him a question which he did not expect, he would be thrown for a loop, tell me he was not prepared to answer, and accuse me of coming at him "out of left field". If my choice of words was too sophisticated, he complained that I was demonstrating my intellectual superiority over him. If my choice of words was too simple, he accused me of patronizing him and insulting his intelligence.

His responses often left me in a state of personal confusion. Did I mean what I thought I meant or was Robert picking up unconscious motives and enactments that I was unable to acknowledge to myself? I frequently left our sessions feeling badly about myself, wondering if I was more competitive, nasty and sadistic than I had ever imagined myself to be.

Robert did not feel entitled to ask me direct questions. He would comment or make observations about me, filling in the "blanks" with what he assumed was true of all psychologists, or using his own frame of reference to infer my motives, attitudes and values, while anxiously deflecting any attempt I made to fill in the blanks myself. Despite my openness and willingness to explain myself, he claimed that direct inquiry on his part represented an "invasion" of my "privacy". If I expressed interest in any particular reaction he had to me, he would often reply that he was "like that with everyone," denying anything unique or even of particular interest in our own relationship.

While Robert was busy protecting my privacy, I struggled with my desire to be known, or at least to be perceived more accurately by him. At times I would question him about his perceptions, beliefs and assumptions about me, and invite him to ask direct questions regarding areas of mystification. He would often get anxious at these moments, fearing that he would "fail the test" and telling me how uncomfortable he was with any discussion about our own relationship. In his view, I was pushing for greater intimacy and he was fighting to maintain a safe distance. He once told me that he would rather use me as an "ATM machine" than see me as a "bank teller". I sought a more direct interpersonal involvement with Robert, to help him overcome his fears of intimacy and the dread associated with revealing himself to others. I felt pulled to reveal myself directly to him, while at the same time feeling inhibited by the panic he experienced when confronted with a more intimate interaction.

In the third year of our treatment, Robert began to take me in, albeit in his own way, in small bites and with a great deal of anxiety. He began to identify me with one of his nephews. In one session, he described watching this nephew patiently answer his young son's questions, and expressed gratitude that I gave him the chance to question me as well.

Around this time I informed Robert that I would be leaving my part-time job at a local hospital and increasing my hours in private practice. The following is a dialogue from a session in which he had been discussing dreams of being "left behind", which reflected his concern that I would be less attentive to him when I added more patients to my practice.

Robert: *"I was concerned about you. I wondered if your being tired was related to the change you made in your job. I remember the difficulty I had in adjusting to retirement, and I wondered how it was going, if it was taking its toll. I'd have the same concern about anyone I know who's making this kind of change".*

BC: *"Anyone who's making this change?"*

Robert: *"I know, I know. There I go saying I feel the same way about everybody. I was concerned ... curious about you. Well I'm starting to get anxious about this, talking about my feelings toward you. But I have admiration for what you've done, standing on principle and leaving your job. I think of you like my nephew, who's just graduated from school, making it on his own. I would never ask you, it would be an invasion of your privacy, but I think about all of these things ... insurance benefits, the impact on your family."*

And in the next session:

Robert: *"I've been scared since I talked about my feelings about you. It's an understatement to say that I'm not used to talking about these things. I don't even like to acknowledge that I'm in a relationship with you."*

And in a session a few weeks after that:

Robert: *"You know, I'm having more feelings lately and I'm finding them a real intrusion in my life. I'd rather be doing the crossword puzzle. I feel ridiculous talking about my feelings. It's like what they say ... you're peeling the layers off the onion, getting deeper and making me feel things I don't want to feel."*

A few weeks later:

Robert: *"It worries me that I've gotten to be dependent on this, on coming here. I've been talking about my concern about you terminating treatment, and I realize that it could be a problem for me. I mean, I'm used to coming, it's a structured part of my week."*

BC: *"But you're talking about your attachment to me."*

Robert: *"I get nervous even when you ask me to talk about our relationship. It's silly, I know, but I prefer still to refer to it as the situation here. I mean I know that you are caring for me, and seem to show an interest, but I'm still not sure of what is your professional facade and what you feel personally."*

And in the next session:

Robert: *"Recently I've felt more comfortable in here, more willing to express myself. I feel that over the past several weeks I've been interacting more like a real person here, and not like I am dealing with my ATM machine."*

And in the subsequent session:

Robert: *"I prefer to use other people as metaphors. I feel that I can talk more openly when it's not about the person I'm talking to. Well, here goes ... it should come as no surprise that I like you. There I said it, and the world didn't end. I guess that's a small step. Maybe if I live to be 235 years old, I'll reach all of my goals."*

And finally in the very next session:

Robert: *"I had a surreal experience yesterday ... I was flipping through the channels and I saw you and your family on television."*

I immediately realized what he was referring to. My wife and I had a neighbour who produced a show for cable television regarding financial matters. He had offered us several months previously what appeared to be a low risk/possible reward deal. In exchange for interviewing us on camera regarding our financial situation, we would receive the advice and suggestions of experts regarding investments and the management of household finances. What made it seem like a low risk was the obscurity of the program and the fact that it was going to be shown on a Saturday afternoon. My wife and I assumed that the only people we knew who would ever see it would be a select few family and friends we made aware of its existence.

The television crew came into our house, where they filmed us making a snack and playing with our two young children. We answered very specific questions about our incomes, our assets, and our goals for the future and received some fairly standard, and ultimately not at all helpful, financial advice. One of the ironies of the experience was that the cable network decided to put this particular episode of this obscure show on one of their video loops that play in airports and other public venues. In our own personal version of the movie *Groundhog Day*, for months after its initial showing we kept receiving phone calls from some friend or family member saying something to the effect of, "Hey, I was waiting for my flight in the Dallas airport and I saw you on TV!"

My reaction to being revealed in this way to Robert was a mixed one. It was an out of control experience for me, and I felt some momentary panic trying to recall which details of my life would be news to him while attempting to anticipate the myriad of reactions he might have to learning my actual income, seeing my wife, watching me play with my children, viewing images of my home, and hearing about my financial status at what was still an early period in my career. With Robert, nothing was simple. Would he think I was "rubbing" this information—these revelations showing my loving connections to my family—"in his face"? Or would he feel proud and responsible for his percentage of my income? Or perhaps disdainful about my modest income at the time?

In some ways though, I welcomed the fact that he had seen the show. I thought that this might help him see me for who I was and lower his inhibitions about questioning and interacting with me in a direct manner. Since it came about inadvertently, I could avoid my

usual dilemma of calculating the inherent risks and benefits of pushing him to see what could be seen about me, to know what could be
known, and could avoid the feeling (and his frequent accusation)
that I was forcing myself on him.

Robert's reaction to the television show was positive and, in some
ways, entirely characteristic. He felt good about seeing me and my
family, and said that it "completed" the feeling that I was just like his
nephews, that is, part of the family. He stated that the domestic scene
was the same as he had seen countless times with his nephews and
nieces and their kids. I asked him if there was any sense of invading
my privacy, to which he said, "On the contrary ... I felt a little bit like
you were invading mine. After all, *you* were in *my* living room." He
had no other questions about my participation in the show, feeling
that I had answered them when I had initially explained the genesis
of the program.

Robert's viewing of the show seemed like a non-event, which disappointed me. While I recognized that there was something loving
in the way he took me in as a family member, I was left with a very
familiar feeling, that he had not had any new or unique experience
of me at all. Despite an extremely personal and penetrating view of
my life outside of the consulting room, it seemed that nothing at all
had changed for Robert in his sense of me or in our relationship, and
the potential gateway did not facilitate any direct exploration of our
relationship. I was his nephew before he saw the show, and I was
the same nephew after viewing it. I was left feeling like I often did
with Robert ... not completely invisible, but not entirely recognizable either. He had treated the new information as he had processed
information about me in the past, that is, ignoring much of it, and
internalizing the rest as material he had already known about me.

Upon further reflection, I realized that my experience of this
interaction as a "non-event" was related to the way that Robert had
already begun to engage me differently in the recent months. I had
become like a nephew to him because he had begun to trust me and
to experience me as a predominantly caring and benevolent person
in his life. He knew that I not only tolerated, but welcomed his direct
observations of me, even if he rarely chose to pursue those observations beyond their initial cataloguing. Perhaps the details of my personal life revealed in the television show were in-attended by Robert
because they were truly irrelevant to him. What mattered to Robert

was that the interactions he viewed of me with my wife, my children and the camera were congruent enough with his own personal experience of me to corroborate and validate his perceptions, which allowed them to be seamlessly incorporated into our ongoing relationship. This was a significant development for a man who so often felt that he could not trust his perceptions of others, and who so frequently felt betrayed and threatened in his interpersonal relationships.

Robert and I continued to work together for another nine years. He made significant changes in his life, developing a full calendar of ongoing activities with a new network of friends, as well as an affectionate romantic relationship. He continued to be plagued by doubts of his own perceptions, as well as the humiliation and hurt from the perceived slights and insults of others. However, he demonstrated remarkable perseverance in maintaining these relationships, and tolerating their ambiguity and uncertainty.

Robert maintained his intense involvement with me, which at one point entailed commuting an additional twenty-five miles each way to continue our work when I re-located my office. His sense of me as a benevolent and supportive presence in his life never ceased to be confounded by moments of distrust and alarm, and his fear of his own dependency. Over time he began to delicately ask me more direct questions and requested that we call each other by our first names, although he seemed to wince in pain at times when I took him up on the offer. I continued to struggle with the alien aspects of his reflected appraisals of me. He never again referred to his viewing of the television program.

The experience with Robert raised several questions for me. Are these extra-analytic experiences to be feared or welcomed? What is our counter-transferential experience of being "known" by our patients outside of the consulting room, and at times without our "consent", and how would I have experienced a different patient seeing that television program? For a patient who struggles to incorporate the unique individuality of the analyst, can these extra-analytic experiences actually be helpful? Do they matter at all? Are the ways that we are internalized by our patients during a prolonged and intensive treatment so robust that few singular events can truly transform and change them? Or did this extra-analytic experience of me provide Robert with a corroboration of his transferential perceptions necessary to sustain and develop his involvement with me?

CHAPTER TWENTY TWO

Who's afraid of Google?

Caryn Gorden, Psy.D.

"I did something really bad, and you're going to be very upset with me," Alex said tearfully as his session began. Alex, who I have been seeing for nine years, is my most challenging and also one of my favourite patients. I initially met him on the inpatient psychiatric unit of a hospital, where as a nineteen-year-old college freshman he was admitted involuntarily for major depression and suicidality. Extremely curious and intelligent, Alex, who is now a twenty-seven year-old veterinarian student, has a traumatic history of sexual abuse and suffered the loss of his only sibling to suicide when she was nineteen. He has identified as gay since early adolescence.

Even after a fair amount of encouragement Alex remained secretive about the bad thing, though he stated feeling guilty and concerned about how angry he thought I would be. Outwardly I maintained my composure, gently questioning whether the bad something was of a self-injurious nature, given that he had a history of cutting. Inwardly, however, I was filled with a sense of certain dread that Alex had surreptitiously gained access to my office, scrutinizing patient notes and personal papers. I struggled to remain rational and continued to inquire about the matter, but to no avail; Alex remained tightlipped as I felt my face flush and my heart race.

Though my fantasy seems off the wall, the surrounding elements of reality, which I will discuss, paired with the concurrent dynamics regarding disclosure that Alex and I had been consciously and unconsciously playing out, served as a lightening rod for my heightened panic. Following are the factors that facilitated my hyperactive imagination. During office hours my suite relied on a combination lock system that allowed patients to let themselves into the waiting room for their scheduled sessions. At the time of this episode my personal office had no lock nor did my closet where I stored confidential records and private papers. Similarly the preceding day I had noticed that my space heater was on though I had no memory of having used it. It therefore seemed conceivable to me that Alex, knowing that I did not work on Fridays, had let himself into the suite while the other therapists were in session and entered my office. My thoughts regarding Alex's incursion might still seem completely paranoid were it not for the fact that his history abounded with secrets and betrayals, which he generally uncovered through secretive manoeuvres, thereby repeating and re-enacting his familial veil of secrecy and its exposure. Rummaging through his father's desk drawer had yielded detailed police reports and newspaper clippings indicating that his sister's death, whose cause was previously unknown to him, was an undeniable suicide. Similarly he had located his father's will in his office file cabinet and learned that he was leaving everything to his second wife. In fact I had already been subject to Alex's extra-analytic attempts to "know me" as he discovered what he believed was my college yearbook after serendipitously learning that I was a graduate of his university.

Additionally at some earlier point in his treatment, after asking me about my dissertation, he remarked that perhaps I wasn't who I said I was; that most likely I hadn't really written a dissertation, as he was unable to find it. Although it was never articulated I imagined that what he was really interested in were the acknowledgements so that he could determine the identity of my significant others and their relationship to me. Therefore, although a break-in seemed unlikely and irreconcilable with how I generally experienced Alex, it also seemed plausible that given his childhood traumas of abuse, mystification and betrayal, and frequent mistrust in his own perceptions of things, he may at least have considered such a trespassing.

Further attempts to understand my dreaded fantasy recall Racker's (1957) case example of the analyst who upon leaving his office to get his patient change for the thousand pesos he has given him, imagines that his patient will take back the money and claim that the analyst took it with him when he left the office. Racker's vignette illustrates his theory regarding countertransference thoughts: where the analyst's spontaneous ideation or fantasy about the patient is based on what the analyst already knows about the patient. He explains the similarity of the analyst's fantasy and the patient's fantasy as springing from a symbiotic psychological connection between the two unconscious's that allows the analyst to have, without prompting, thoughts that correspond to the psychological constellation in the patient. In line with this thinking it is possible that I deeply intuited Alex's fantasy in part because the issue of trust was a critical and unyielding undertow from the very start of his treatment.

Alex often questioned me about my personal life, while deflecting any attempts I made to explore his fantasies or feelings, continuously insisting that he was merely curious. I understood Alex's questions as attempts to sort out who I was, to assess whether or not he could trust me. He frequently baited me, saying things like, "How do I know who you are? ... I don't even know what your favorite colour is;" or, "How do I know ... maybe when you're not in your office you're dealing drugs!" Alex did not believe that he already knew me or at least certain critical aspects of who I was from being in the room with me all these years. He brushed off as insignificant any assertions I made about having disclosed from time to time my countertransference feelings. I attributed Alex's inability to trust his perceptions of me to his own traumatic history of abuse and introjected insanity, which left him uncertain about the accuracy of his reality and necessitated continued external verification and validation.

I was reluctant, however, to answer most of Alex's questions about my personal life, believing that it could be mostly burdensome rather than therapeutic. As Alex tended to overprotect his parents, I felt that any personal disclosures might inhibit him from discussing feelings and fantasies he imagined would clash with mine, and that it could result in closing off the analytic space. I was cautious too as Aron (1991) suggests about establishing my own subjectivity, fearing that it might deprive him of the opportunity to discover me as a separate subject in his own way, which seemed critical given his deep distrust and inability to rely on his own take of the world and others. Finally I was concerned that Alex would use my personal revelations to withdraw, as it would provide him with reasons to distrust me; that in discovering the inevitable differences between us, he would employ them to explain why I couldn't possibly understand him or the painful issues he contended with.

I appreciate that disclosure—particularly of my vulnerabilities—can potentially help my patients truly believe that in spite of disappointment and frailty they can lead a good life. However, I am also aware that as an analyst, and particularly with patients who are preoccupied with the dynamics of power, I am sometimes uncomfortable exposing my weaknesses and failures, and that perhaps my theoretical standing regarding personal disclosure may at times function as a safe hiding place. I imagine, therefore, that my decision to remain reticent was influenced in part by my awareness of Alex's potential sadism and malignant self-sufficiency. Further, his questions felt more like attempts to recalibrate the asymmetry of power in the consulting room, and less about a genuine desire to know me. In retrospect I understand that Alex suffered enormous shame and rage in what he experienced as the "one-down position". Feeling less powerful hindered his ability to share intimate thoughts and feelings when he felt that I shared none. Though I understood the shame he felt about revealing his pain while mine was left unarticulated, I believed, but perhaps also hid behind, the idea that my doing so may have perpetuated his shame over what he might then interpret as my greater strength and power in accepting and sharing my weaknesses.

I eventually understood that what was at stake for Alex explained why my countertransference disclosures were experienced as insufficient and unsatisfying. I felt Alex's questions as demands—they stimulated a great deal of pressure and internal discomfort. I did not believe that responding to them could be valuable if they emerged, as Bromberg (2006) elaborates, out of a wish to prove my honesty or trustworthiness to counter his mistrust. Further his demands rendered it impossible for my personal disclosures to spontaneously and organically surface in the moment. I felt as though Alex and

I were caught in an inextricable double bind. If I chose to avoid his questions we would be re-enacting his old traumatic history of mystification, where his parents were most often misleading or evasive. Alternatively if I chose to share details regarding my personal life which might not be therapeutic but rather burdensome, I would similarly be re-enacting aspects of his childhood trauma of over-stimulation or seduction; where roles were reversed and boundaries crossed. I believe I shared some of this dilemma with Alex, but that too provided no relief. As a result we got locked in a power struggle, a relational knot which neither of us seemed able to loosen or untie.

My experience with Alex around this period of impasse was best captured by the transference–countertransference position Davies and Frawley (1994) delineate in *Treating the Adult Survivor of Childhood Sexual Abuse* as the sadistic abuser and helpless, impotently enraged victim. Alex and I alternately took turns playing out both sides of this relational constellation. The aspects of abuse and victimization seemed unavoidable between us, due to the asymmetry in our relationship, which Alex felt most acutely through my non-disclosure of personal information. My subsequent discomfort and sense of constraint as a result of his constant and seemingly indiscriminant questions led me to experience him as demanding and manipulative, and myself as victimized. While we remained stuck in this cyclical enactment, our individual disavowed shame got passed back and forth between us like a hot, but secret potato.

Back to the confession scene … as soon as the unnerving (above mentioned) session ended, I searched through my notes and papers to clarify what, if anything, had been tampered with. In addition to concluding that none of my files had been disturbed I subsequently discovered that my suitemate had used my office that morning and had turned on my space heater. As I began to breathe more easily I wondered why I had imagined this intrusion. No doubt it had some significant meaning. It was not something that had ever before crossed my mind with other patients and never before even with Alex. Though Alex's need to know me had been an ongoing theme since the beginning of treatment, it didn't explain why I was now having this fantasy.

As I continued to ponder the possible reasons for my flight of fantasy, things began to shift into focus and I became *more* convinced that

Alex had engaged in an extra-analytic expedition, most likely in the form of an internet search. Naively, I was not yet "afraid of Google"; I suppose I had no reason to be. I had never Googled myself, and was quite certain that there was nothing private that could render my personal life transparent. Indeed I was quite wrong! Following my hunch about Alex's extra-analytic research I gathered up the courage to Google myself. I was astonished and quite upset to discover that my daughters' school had posted an annual contribution that my husband and I had made, which now came up when my name was typed into the search bar. Furthermore, as my husband and I have different surnames, access to the family name provided a whole new cache of information.

Meanwhile Alex remained silent about the really bad thing he claimed to have done. He was, however, agitated and worried about how I would react when he finally confessed, though in classic style he let it slip that it was entirely my fault. He was scheduled then to be out of town for a week and said he would consider telling me prior to leaving. He didn't however tell me then or after he returned. During this period Alex continued to focus on his sexuality, which had been an ongoing subject for several months. He was despondent and convinced that success in his profession necessitated his remaining closeted. He ranted about the judgement he was certain others passed about his being infantile, undeveloped and dysfunctional because he was "queer" and happier alone than as part of a gay couple.

He frequently declared that heterosexuals who married despite the fact that gay people were denied that same right lacked integrity and morality. Any attempts I made to explore what else was at play, or any thoughts I expressed about things not being so black or white, seemed to further enrage him and fill him with hopelessness about my understanding him or his dilemma. Instead a frozen angry silence hovered in the space between us, and any previously shared self-reflectivity we had, collapsed and now seemed irretrievable.

A couple of months elapsed. Our work which had been marked in the past by moments of rupture and repair and even instances of impasse now felt particularly deadlocked. Alex appeared furious; although he insisted that he was merely indifferent and disinterested in our work together. He asserted that it was I who had changed, but could only explain how or what was different in very vague, incomprehensible terms that did not resonant with my understanding or experience. After some time, Alex requested a consultation, stating that he could not work things out directly with me and I gave him the name of a well-respected senior colleague.

Following the consultation, my colleague shared, in addition to some other observations, that Alex had confessed a crime, which he promised he would share with me. Apparently there *had been a break-in* of sorts, and Alex had in fact intruded on my privacy and my personal life. As I had fleetingly surmised, Alex had Googled me, and armed with my husband's family name, had gone on a "phishing expedition". What I hadn't guessed was that he had discovered one of my twin daughter's blogs which made some reference to her being "queer". Alex irrationally chose to believe that I was not privy to this information about my daughter and hence doubly felt that she couldn't share with me the bad thing that he had done. Alex however did not keep his promise to tell me.

After allowing two sessions to go by without mention I raised the matter with him. In addition to being angry at my colleague for revealing his secret, which further justified his continued distrust of the entire analytic community, Alex openly blamed me for his extra-analytic research. He insisted that, had I been willing to be more open and disclosing with him, he would not have needed to furtively search for himself. Similarly, he claimed that disclosing my daughter's sexual status would have been therapeutic, as he would have felt more understood. I didn't fully agree with him as I anticipated, irrespective of my revelations, an inevitable enactment of his experiencing me as a duplicitous and withholding other. Given that I had sort of known for a time about Alex's misdeameanour, save for the particular details, I had already processed some of the raw feelings and therefore was able to respond with greater curiosity and less shock and anger. I did, however, feel like Alex had crossed a line in bringing my family into our enactment, though no doubt he had already experienced their presence in the consulting room— explicitly, as I had stated at one point in an effort to demonstrate my understanding of him, that I had close relationships with other gay people, yet implicitly as I didn't identify who it was. However I was therefore quite curious why Alex persisted in imagining that I was unaware of my daughter's sexual preferences. It seemed as though it made Alex feel simultaneously more powerful and protective towards me, and also facilitated once again his transference to me as the unseeing, uninvolved parent who needed caretaking, and alternately the helpless, impotently enraged victim.

Despite my initial external composure, this event exploded into a kaleidoscope of many different thoughts and feelings. At first what seemed ironic was Alex's professed need to know me so that he could trust me, and how my unwillingness to yield to his intrusions caused him to distrust me as a person and as an analyst. Synchronistically, his intrusion resulted in my greater sense of distrust and vulnerability regarding any personal disclosures, and my further retreat into anonymity. It is noteworthy then that the critical element that Alex claimed he needed to know, which was whether or not he could trust me, ended up not only obscured but also temporarily foreclosed.

In retrospect, given the intersubjectivity of our pairing Alex's violation of my personal space was inevitable. Despite its aggressive nature, it also represented an opportunity for a new and reparative interaction, since my response to him was neither sadistic nor shaming and I clearly was accepting of my daughter's sexuality. Yet it also initiated another cycle of abuse. This time the configuration was that of me, the analyst as victim and Alex, my analysand, as abuser. In this round of "paranoid ping-pong" (Racker 1957: 318) I experienced the aggression and ruthlessness of Alex's intrusion and need to know me, regardless of the unspoken boundaries of privacy and trust that he ultimately traversed. Yet we seemed to have emerged from this rabbit's hole, if only long enough to catch our breaths.

Alex's extra-analytic incursion helped me to see more of the wisdom in taking a risk and sometimes disclosing personal information to a patient. It helped me appreciate Hoffman's ethos (2006) that acts of omission can be just as damaging as acts of commission. Our notions regarding the possibility and achievement of analytic anonymity of our personhood are no longer valid; which of our patients know about us, what they know, how they know and whether and which parts they disclose to us that they know is no longer something we get to choose. Although we still have control over how we respond to these extra-analytic disclosures, whether or not it interferes with or facilitates the treatment depends on many factors, including the nature of the analytic relationship between the analyst and the analysand, and what may be going on in their individual lives at the time. Knowing the same extra-analytic information at different moments in the treatment can yield very different responses in the patient. For what can be comforting at one point can at another time be experienced as malignant and may forestall momentum (Richman, 2006).

Clearly the terrain of relational thinking regarding the judicious disclosure of our own subjectivity and personhood is shifting and being challenged even if it is in ways that we fear leads to greater ambiguity, uncertainty, and complexity. As it appears inevitable that the internet is here to stay (and in fact it is impossible to erase oneself completely and achieve invisibility), our theories, philosophies, and techniques regarding our personal privacy must accommodate the shifting landscape and require further exploration, negotiation, and development.

References

Aron, L. (1991). "The patient's experience of the analyst's subjectivity". *Psychoanalytic Dialogues.* 1: 29–51.

Bromberg, P. (2006). *Awakening the Dreamer.* New York: The Analytic Press.

Davies, J.M. and Frawley, M.G. (1994). *Treating the Adult Survivor of Childhood Sexual Abuse.* New York: Basic Books.

Hoffman, I.Z. (2006). "The myths of free association and the potentials of the analytic relationship". *International Journal of Psychoanalysis.* 87: 1–18.

Racker, H. (1957). "The Meanings and Uses of Countertransference". *The Psychoanalytic Quarterly.* 26: 303–357.

Richman, S. (2006). "When the analyst writes a memoir: Clinical implications of biographic disclosure." *Contemporary Psychoanalysis,* 42: 367-391.

CHAPTER TWENTY THREE

Six degrees of separation ... When real worlds collide in treatment

Susan Klebanoff, Ph.D.

F ive years into treatment with Melina, a Greek-American author in her thirties, a strange coincidence occurred. She was talking in detail about a good friend from Princeton whom she had previously mentioned only briefly. Then she described her friend's father, a prominent academic. Melina was planning to give him a copy of her recently published book, in hopes of getting positive feedback and an offer to write a review. My thoughts flashed briefly, and presciently, on my uncle, himself a Princeton professor. Then Melina said, "Perhaps you've heard of him", mentioning my uncle's best-known book, followed by his name. Oh my god, I remember thinking, that's Uncle Max, which means that Melina is good friends with my first cousin. I nodded my head yes, to indicate that I'd heard of him, but said nothing more about it. The process I went through in the following few days is the focus of this paper.

Initially I felt relieved about my withholding stance with Melina. At least this time I had protected analytic neutrality. The transference could remain pure and uncomplicated by the unnecessary self-disclosure. However, because I am a relational psychoanalyst and believe that the true transformational moments in treatment come about from exactly the kind of opportunity for authentic and spontaneous connection that I had just passed on, I started to wonder why I had chosen that particular second to wrap myself in a more traditional stance. After all, my patient did not even know that she was holding personal information about me. It's not as if she sought it out. What's more, there was nothing terribly revealing about the information she held. I could have let the moment pass silently or mention that we were related (as I had with other relatives and other patients). But this time my acute anxiety allowed me to do neither comfortably, which was the tip off that more was going on here than superficially appeared. When I reviewed Melina's history, and reflected on how certain themes echoed throughout my own life, it became clear that such an enactment was bound to occur.

Melina entered treatment because she felt she was "living a lie". In her first session she explained, "I have two separate lives and need to learn to put them together". She had recently purchased an apartment with her long-time boyfriend with whom she was living. However, she had not told her family about this relationship. She visited home and attended holidays alone, pretending to be single. Aspects of this life seemed almost farcical at times (two phone lines in the apartment, for example, and rules about who could answer which one). But any comedic element was at sharp contrast with Melina's reserved and thoughtful manner, her intelligence evident in her striking green eyes, peering out from under a heavy lid of dark thick bangs. Melina's boyfriend was tired of their charade and wanted to get married, but she was frozen. Her parents would object to an interfaith union (she was Greek Orthodox, her boyfriend was not) and she was terrified that she would either be disowned by her family or that her boyfriend would leave. She could not imagine putting her two worlds together and both of them being able to survive.

As I got to know Melina better, it became clear that there was, in fact, a pattern of secret-keeping in the family designed to protect each other from various truths that they all feared would lead to destruction. Most of these secrets had to do with protecting Melina's older sister, Laura, who had cerebral palsy, from understanding the truth about her limitations. Melina was encouraged to have little social independence from the family to avoid making Laura jealous or upset. Birthdays were *"family only* events", dating was actively discouraged, and no one in the family was allowed to drive, save for

Melina's father, all supposedly to "protect" Laura from feeling left out. Melina's parents did not even attend her high school or college graduations because "What would we do about your sister?" These complicated dynamics, revolving around shame and guilt, powerlessness and social isolation, formed the emotional backdrop of Melina's family experience and helped to generate a life-long pattern of internal and external compartmentalization. Much like the blonde, teenaged daughter she identified with from the popular 1960s television sitcom, *The Munsters*, what was considered "normal" in the outside world was considered strange at home, and what was "normal" at home was often considered strange outside. A serious boyfriend was a "normal" developmental milestone but also a threat to the family's stable dysfunction.

We explored Melina's rational and irrational fears about telling her family of about her boyfriend, as well as the emotional drain of keeping her two lives so separate. I supported her goal of no longer holding her relationship secret. Eventually, she did tell her mother about her boyfriend and there was a frightening several month rift after she did so. In fact, her mother hung up on, her upon hearing the news on the phone. However, reconciliation was achieved in time, Melina's boyfriend met the family, and they went on to get married, though her parents were, as usual, "unable" to attend themselves.

A few years later, I learned that there were other family secrets with even more serious consequences. After much sustained work in therapy to resolve conflicts around motherhood, Melina and her husband decided to have a child. Unfortunately, seven months into her pregnancy, Melina developed a rare and life-threatening syndrome. The only way to reverse this syndrome was by emergency caesarean, following which Melina remained at high risk of having a stroke. For days it was unclear whether Melina or her premature baby would survive. I remember feeling, when visiting the hospital on Melina's request, a weight of responsibility, symbolically standing in for her mother and bridging her two worlds. Her parents had called daily and lovingly but had not travelled east from the middle of the country to visit when she was ill.

Several months later, after she and the baby had recovered, Melina learned some shocking news from a relative she was interviewing for her book of personal essays. She learned that every single woman on her father's side had suffered from this same syndrome.

Most died in childbirth; others chose to avoid the danger by never getting pregnant. By keeping this information a secret, Melina's parents had denied her the ability to make an informed decision, which had almost cost her her life. I wonder if unconsciously Melina's mother's wish for her daughter not to move forward with marriage was, in fact, protective, tied to her fears for Melina, both in reference to developing this syndrome in childbirth, as well as the fear of her giving birth to another damaged baby, like Laura. In retrospect, I also wonder whether Melina's mother's initial response to hearing that her daughter had a serious boyfriend (she had said "I think I'm having a stroke" before she hung up on her) was a dissociated warning to Melina about the danger in her future, should she marry and bear a child.

Somehow, and, I guess inevitably, secret-keeping made its way into our work. While not by nature a therapist who is comfortable keeping secrets, by not "owning" my uncle right away, and simply nodding when I heard his name, I did, in fact, keep a secret for several days. Once I realized that I was unconsciously participating in this malignant family pattern, I understood that this was an opportunity to explore the anxiety and fantasy around secret-keeping, as well as the manifest content of the secrets themselves. I had learned that for Melina secrets—whether kept through ignorance, shame or dissociation—were simply too dangerous not to share.

Many themes emerged as I explored my own anxiety in this enactment. On a concrete level, I was concerned that my relationship to her friend's family would be "outed" anyway and that Melina would be upset that I had withheld this information in an ingenuous manner. While my uncle, my cousin and I do not share the same last name, I am mentioned with my full name in the acknowledgements section of Melina's book with a vague but flattering description as her "guardian angel". Since Melina was planning to give my relatives a copy of her book, I know that if they read the acknowledgements, it would be natural for them to ask Melina how she knew me. There was no way of knowing when or if this may occur, as people may read books months or even years after they initially receive them. Melina was doing well and likely to terminate treatment sometime soon. I did not want to chance her finding out that I had withheld this information when we were no longer in a position to work it through together.

Another theme that came into play in processing this enactment was that of stories and their ownership. Melina's book was a collection of personal essays with many about her extended family and their experience in Greece. Melina's parents could not understand their daughter's interest in these stories or their public appeal and disapproved of her writing about them for commercial purposes. The question, "Whose stories are they?" kept coming up in treatment, and needed to be worked through many times. But exploitation did not seem to be the motivating force behind the book. The stories were written with warmth and deep appreciation for their cultural context. I supported her need to claim these stories as her own, and as a writer, in print.

However, the coincidence with my uncle complicated matters for me. I recognized some wish to claim my uncle as part of *my* family story, and not to share him with Melina. I was concerned that in telling I could be acting out some sibling like rivalry for my uncle's attention. I shared my patient's respect for this brilliant man and certainly would have welcomed the opportunity to receive praise from him on *my* work too. By claiming my uncle, did I competitively want to let Melina know that I had a closer connection than she did to this mutually admired figure? My envy had come up once before in treatment and I wondered if it was rearing its ugly head again, or at least that it may be perceived that way.

The previous August, Melina had given me a copy of her book's galleys to read. I was impressed with the seriousness and sociological scope of her work. But Melina felt I was not sufficiently enthusiastic about her writing and was disappointed in my reaction. When I was honest with myself, I realized that my lack of enthusiasm was probably related to my own envy—which I eventually shared with her—for accomplishing something that I had always wished to do myself.

I was also concerned about another way that my telling could reawaken Melina's feelings of envy. She had described growing up feeling "less than", as an ethnic outsider in a wealthy Jewish suburb in the Midwest. Melina knew that I was Jewish and had spoken of her wishes to have grown up in a sophisticated and intellectual, Jewish home like the one she imagined I had. Hearing I was related to this academic star might provide validation of her fantasy, though, in fact, my home and upbringing were quite different from that of my cousins. I felt I had to be careful not to lend misleading support for her idealization, especially as her fantasy dovetailed so nicely with my own wishes.

Even if my "telling" did not set off Melina's envy, I was concerned that my disclosure might transferentially be experienced like her parents, who were not able to remain with her and praise her accomplishments. She was clearly proud of knowing my uncle personally. If I were seen as "trumping" her by announcing my biological connection, could I also be seen as dismissing her success, implying that she did not belong in such lofty circles (and that I did)?

Lastly, this dilemma stirred personal doubts and insecurities about claiming my own family stories as they pertained to my uncle. I had grown up hearing all the family lore and taking part in a communal pride regarding his accomplishments. However, while I love and respect him, others in the family certainly have closer relationships with him. And my mother, his sister, had herself become a bit of an outsider in her family of origin, moving far away from the intellectual and socialist values she had been raised with. So, I wondered, as her daughter, did I really have the right to claim these roots for myself?

Thus, Melina and I shared a concordant identification in reference to our shared outsider status in specific aspects of our lives, and complementary sources of shame (her physically impaired sister and unsophisticated parents; my bourgeois mother). This identification laid fertile ground for the enactment. We each desired to prove ourselves intellectually through a relationship with the same learned man we both admired. Another therapeutic dyad, or even another uncle, would have likely yielded a different set of concerns or a different enactment entirely.

Despite the multitude of transference and countertransference issues, my own discomfort in the secret-keeping role, along with the life-endangering backdrop of secret-keeping in her family, and my fervent wish to maintain as honest a relationship as possible with my patient, prompted me to reveal my connection to my relatives, and deal with whatever complications were to arise.

The next session I asked Melina if she had had any thoughts about our prior meeting. She said no but quickly realized that I had something to say. When I told her that the prominent academic she mentioned was my uncle, and that her friend was my first cousin, her first reaction was embarrassment. She was worried about any negative comments she had made about her friend. "I'm sorry", she said, "I didn't know". "Of course not", I told her, "there's no way that you could have known",—and I explained, truthfully, that she knew my cousin much better than I did, allowing her to both save face and own her own experience with this young woman. She was also worried that she had sounded like a schoolgirl when talking about my uncle, and expressed that she now felt embarrassed by exposing her wish to "get" something from him. This brought up familiar feelings of guilt about her potentially exploitive nature that we had already worked on in reference to publishing her family's stories. We also spoke about our shared admiration for my uncle. This was an authentic moment of connectedness and mutual recognition that was moving for both of us and also helpful in demystifying the idealized transference. Melina thanked me for telling her and saving her from the humiliation she would have experienced by finding out this information any other way. Our personal worlds had collided but our relationship had survived.

I realize this session may present a fairy tale ending, following my careful and angst ridden unpacking of the therapeutic dilemma involved. But Melina's response was consistent with her tendency to minimize problems, in this case, making it easier for me, much as she didn't want to make trouble for her already burdened mother. The timing of this incident was also relevant. We were approaching the end of treatment and were mutually protective of our wishes to end the work on a positive note. It is not surprising, then, that I dragged my heels in calling Melina to ask for permission to tell this story in print, holding in mind the possibility that other material could emerge years after the incident and our termination. I felt the need to ask for permission for many of the same reasons I chose to self-disclose in the first place.

As a postscript, I should mention that I have seen my relatives numerous times since Melina terminated and that the connection has never come up. I suspect they never read the acknowledgements section and only glanced at the book; much like Melina's parents, who predictably never fully read *her* book. I believe Melina and I were both caught up in the dread of having people see our names and our stories in print in order to mask our even stronger wishes that they would, in fact, cut our names in print and be suitably impressed.

In retrospect, when I think of this therapeutic dilemma in the context of dealing with extra analytic information, what strikes me as most important is not where the information comes from, or even what the information may be, but the meaning that the particular information has to the therapist and to the patient involved, as well as to their shared process. For the most part, I believe that the emotional and intellectual journey we took to unpack that particular therapeutic moment was a worthwhile venture. But I must admit, sometimes I have my doubts. Reality can look so much simpler outside of the psychoanalytic lens.

My husband recently visited with my uncle and commented on the bulging book shelves lining his home. "Have you actually read all these?" he innocently asked. "Of course not", my aunt replied. "People are always sending us books, I don't know why. Sometimes we take a look, but mostly we just put them on the shelf".

PART VIII

OMISSIONS OF JOY

CHAPTER TWENTY FOUR

Instances of joy in psychoanalysis: Some reflections

Joseph Canarelli, L.I.C.S.W.

Reading Ken Corbett's remarkable essay, "More Life" (2006), I was struck by his title, which comes to Corbett from a phrase in Tony Kushner's play, *Angels in America* (1955). Over the following days, I found the phrase evoking impressions of Corbett's essay, thoughts about joy, recent events in my life, memories of the play—a dizzying mix of sources and stories. Through it all, I found myself returning to the words "more life" as if they were demanding something of me. I was feeling my way toward what the phrase might mean, more than grasping it in some easily knowable way.

This talk is being written in the hope of turning some light on one facet of "more life": the experience of joy in and, we hope, as a result of, psychoanalysis and psychotherapy (terms which, for the purpose of this paper, I shall use interchangeably). I'll share some thoughts on joy and, in the heart of these reflections, will tell you something about a period of time during which I worked while holding to myself a precious yet troubling secret: the joy of finding myself newly in love. While relational psychoanalytic literature continues to free analysts to write frankly about our lives and work—and the interplay between them—much of this writing is concerned with grim life experiences (for exemplary instances, see

Gerson [1996]). Sharing my thoughts with you, I hope to provoke our thinking together about the relationship between the therapist's private joys and the therapeutic dyad.

I suspect we've all experienced something like the following: The patient opens the session announcing, "I don't have anything to talk about today. It's been a good week"—a good week apparently running counter to this patient's idea of what constitutes a session's proper subject matter and emotional tenor. Other patients have wondered, crankily, why they should have to pay me to talk about feeling well, as if that were somehow less interesting or crucial than feeling unwell.

As a profession we mirror this attitude; we have to. Being a therapy, we're concerned with ameliorating patients' misery and anguish. We hope to create possibilities for more nuanced understandings of and more engaged, spontaneous ways of relating to oneself and to others—ways we hope will be so surprising and particularized that we cannot know in advance precisely what shapes they will assume. We hope for more life. However, in the necessary process of moving again and again with our patients through their pain and suffering, pain and suffering become central or privileged terms of our practice and discourse.

But what of the margins to these central terms? What about that good week? What about joy? I believe that we take for granted that we sort of know what we mean by a "good week" and "more life"— or at least until recently I have taken it for granted. But more life isn't simple. It is multiple and various, encompassing pains as well as pleasures, labour as well as play. More life includes reinvigorated living with and through the inevitability of sorrow, loss and anguish. A colleague (Silver 2007; personal communication) describes the goal of her work as enabling her patients to authentically face, and with a (relative) lack of defensiveness, whatever they feel about that which life presents them: more life here, then, meaning celebrating and suffering on one's own terms.

More life is also about possibilities for pleasure and playing, good sex and terrific songs, moments of contact and recognition within the analytic pair as well as in the larger world. It could be simply sitting in a cool, quiet solitude; or deeply appreciating one's skills and senses while preparing a meal; or reading at its best, when, to borrow from Winnicott, it's a form of being alone in the presence of another (Winnicott 1958).

Approaching the topic of joy, I realized how little thought I'd given to it, realized, in fact, that I was hard-pressed to say what I meant by it. I felt a little like the satirized figure who says about pornography, "I don't know how to define it, but I know it when I see it!" Panicking about not knowing what I was talking about—a moment of feeling the "oy' in joy—I reached for my dictionaries. The Shorter Oxford English (1993: 1453) defines joy as "vivid pleasure arising from a sense of well-being or satisfaction; exultation; gladness, delight; an instance of this". Webster's (1993: 1222), in typically American fashion, cites "the emotion excited by the acquisition or expectation of good".

As a topic within psychoanalytic discourse, joy most often is implicit in our ideas of what constitutes a good or a better life during and after a good(-enough) treatment. Buechler's paper, "Joy Within the Psychoanalytic Encounter" (2002), is a rare instance of an analyst writing explicitly about joy. In the paper, Buechler shares a number of experiences of well-earned joy between herself and her patients. She differentiates "two fundamental opportunities for joy in the treatment process ... the joy of affirming uniqueness and the joy of transcending it ... Both ... fortify the relationship, allowing it to weather its inevitable challenges" (p. 613). Joyful moments aid the dyad in tolerating the interplay of progress and stalemate, of revitalization and enervation, characteristic of our work. Buechler captures beautifully these two opportunities for joy: the joy of being a part of and the joy of being apart from—but, importantly, "apart from" without alienation.

Thinking of joy, we may more easily call to mind the joys of commonality and contact than those of solitude and a strongly asserted individual bent. As an example of the latter, Buechler offers a telling case vignette. A professionally accomplished patient tells her about a meeting she recently attended. Buechler notices that while the topic of the meeting was one about which her patient has strong feelings, her patient was silent throughout. Her silence becomes the focus of her analyst's attention. Buechler states:

> *Transferential and countertransferential factors, in the broadest sense of both terms, led me to assume the patient's silence at the meeting was born of reticence, inadequate self-worth, truncated ambition, difficulty with assertion. Intuiting my assumptions from my focus, the patient*

*confronts me. Why couldn't her silence at the meeting be, simply, her
brand of participation, just as her forceful confrontation of me in the
session reflects her values about when it is important to speak up?*
(p. 620)

As they examine their conflict, they elaborate upon ways in which
they differ—their "potentially endearing (or maddening) peculiarities. Unlike the joy of finding commonalities ... this is the joy of
knowing someone by appreciating small (and large) differences"
(ibid.). The point I wish to underscore is that as these differences
are elaborated upon, they paradoxically create a point of contact, an
instance of communal difference. Additionally, the patient's experience at the meeting makes beautifully clear that what may appear to
be isolation and withdrawal may actually have nothing to do with
feeling alienated; that, in fact, a rich solitude and singularity are as
much opportunities for joy as are companionship and contact. Being
with oneself when one is being very particularly oneself, can be as
joyful an experience as any other.

I'm reminded of Louis, a psychotherapy patient I saw many years
ago. He was one of the few patients who didn't cancel his session the
day of a very serious hurricane. This didn't surprise me since Louis
was an intense, volatile man who regularly sought out experiences
others find extreme. He walked into the office wet, winded, and
elated. In a rush of words he described his walk across town through
powerful hurricane winds. He'd found it thrilling. I said, "Yeah, the
inside and the outside were the same ..."—meaning: finally your
inner storminess and power is being met and held by a storminess
which isn't yours; you're not alone and you're still you. The joy of
these moments—his in the storm and ours within in the session—
was simultaneously about contact and similarity *and* about separateness and difference. These are instances of joy which suggest that its
two faces may be less sharply differentiated and binarized than I've
been making them out to be.

What about the analyst's joys which occur outside of the office?
What happens to, and because of, these joys as we sit with patients?
I'll approach these questions by turning to the personal situation
which brought me to my topic.

About two years ago I relocated to Seattle after having lived in New
York City for more than thirty years. In the years just before my move,

the atmosphere of the city had begun to feel dense with memories. Looking at storefronts on certain streets, I could count back the names of the businesses previously occupying those spaces. Addresses had become markers of—memorials to—old friends, lovers, therapists, acquaintances, tricks, encounters friendly or antagonistic—and, unavoidably, memorials to past "I's". Some days I felt haunted, the spaces I moved through heavy with ghosts and recollection.

While this same density could have been, and once had been, sustaining and holding, now the air itself felt melancholic and heavy. The ghosts had co-opted too much space, and in their company I became dispirited. Then something surprising occurred: I met someone wonderful and we fell in love—noisily and perplexingly. His emotional commitments were taking him to Seattle and about one year later, after more than a little turmoil, I followed suit.

The period I want to focus on is that period of time after I'd decided to leave New York, but hadn't yet worked out what I was going to tell my patients when, and if, they asked why I was leaving. I was clear that I was comfortable explaining that "New York fatigue" had bred a desire for a simpler, slower way of life. But—another surprise—the idea of also telling them that a relationship was taking me away caused me unease. It apparently still does: I wrote "taking me" as if going hadn't been my choice. The fact of the matter was that giving love as the reason for my move felt somehow embarrassing, even undignified, as if it lacked sufficient weight. As an explanation, love seemed frivolous to me.

Clearly what and whether to tell my patients had to be decided case by case according to their and my own, individual needs and states of mind at any given moment in our process of ending the face-to-face part of our relationships. I'm not advocating thoughtless self-disclosure. Nor do I believe that I owed them a "full explanation" (as if that were ever a realistic possibility). But whether I did or did not tell any of them that I was leaving to pursue a new relationship, my response to the prospect of telling them so remains curious to me. And the fact is that they ended up sitting with a therapist not simply having his own, separate experience but with one who was experiencing himself holding back a joyful yet somehow shameful secret.

One might think about this by considering Slavin and Kriegman's (1998) argument that "conflict in the therapeutic relationship [derives] from the inherently *diverging interests* of analyst and patient" (cited in Aron and Harris 2005: 77; emphasis in original). Think cancellation policies and holiday breaks. I suspect some patients felt their curiosity about my leaving was only partly answered; I'm sure some sensed me holding something back. In the end, I simply had to accept the fact that, revelling in loving and being loved, I didn't want to place that loving in what I imagined would be the line of fire of their anger and envy. I wanted it just for me.

My fellow panellists (at the conference at which this paper was given originally—Chapters twenty five, twenty six and twenty seven), have been thinking about joy and its relationship to shame. My shame and feelings of unease over my patients knowing that I was in love clearly has antecedents in my personal life history. (And I would include internalized homophobia as a possible precursor.) However, I don't want to dismiss them out of hand as "just my problem". What I hope can be useful to us is pondering the sense that joy and its causes are lovely and thrilling, for sure, but that somehow and at some times, they may feel shameful, suspect, and disorienting. We're often ambivalent about them. Consider a mother who is excited *and* feeling guilty as the last of her children leave home, or any of us painfully leaving the familiarity of home, friends, and patients to risk pursuing some exciting new endeavour we cannot be sure will turn out well.

Further, as analysts we may feel, at least in part, that understanding joy is less pressing a need than what might feel like the more necessary and urgent project of understanding human destructiveness, a project which has held our attention for more than a century. In the wake of the twentieth-century's endless bloodletting and despoliation—what Dorothy Dinnerstein (1970; personal communication) called our seeming love affair with death—it can be terribly difficult even to entertain the possibility of hope, let alone joy. Understandably, the idea of happy endings has received a bad rep: more often than not it seems, it leaves us feeling lied to, betrayed. "Opportunities for joy" (Buechler 2002) can appear to be yet another endangered species.

But in a gesture which recapitulates our daily clinical efforts at sustaining hope and creating affiliation and idiosyncrasy, I return now to "more life", which, as I've said, is not necessarily easy or even very attractive. It can be strenuous and destabilizing. At times, however, accepting these very difficulties may point to a way through them. I once realized that to wrestle with the devil you must first embrace him. That, too, can be an opportunity for joy. In "The Way It Is", a poem she wrote during the Vietnam War, Denise Levertov said (1975):

> *Like a mollusk's, my hermitage*
> *is built of my own cells.*
> *Burned faces, stretched horribly,*
>
> *Eyes and mouths forever open,*
> *weight the papers down on my desk.*
> *No day for years I have not thought of them.*
>
> *And more true than ever the familiar image*
> *placing love on a border*
> *where, solitary, it paces, exchanging*
> *across the line a deep attentive gaze*
> *with another solitude pacing there.*
>
> *Yet almost no day, too, with no*
> *happiness, no*
> *exaltation of larks uprising from the heart's*
> *peatbog darkness.*

Levertov's poem illuminates the dialectic of suffering and pleasure involved in joy. Joy emerges from moments and periods in which we move out of the mundane and/or dreadful. In some of these moments, we may find ourselves in a self state which is bordered, discrete and radically alive; in others we feel ourselves to be permeable, fluid, and equally alive—like those jubilant larks emerging from our heart's rich, contradictory darkness.

Joy is felt, too, in moments when "a part of" and "apart from" are not easily distinguishable but, instead, overlap or ebb and flow— joy, then, being created by the tension between the two: like Louis, my former patient, separate within the hurricane while at one with its storminess. Or like an analyst and patient in moments when the border between them is at once a site of joining and demarcation, that border making it possible for each to recognize herself as well as the other as separate instances of common being. The joy of that.

References

Aron, L. and Harris, A. (2005). *Relational Psychoanalysis, Vol. 2: Innovation and Expansion*. Hillsdale, N.J.: The Analytic Press.
Buechler, S. (2002). "Joy in the Analytic Encounter: A Response to Biancoli". *Contemp. Psychoanal.* 38: 613–622.
Corbett, K. (2006). "More Life: Centrality and Marginality in Human Development". *Psychoanal. Dial.* 11: 313–335.
Dinnerstein (1970). Personal communication.
Gerson, B. (1996). *The Therapist as Person*. Hillsdale, N.J.: The Analytic Press.
Kushner, T. (1995). *Angels in America: A Gay Fantasia on National Themes*. New York, N.Y.: Theatre Communications Group.
Levertov, D. (1975). *The Freeing of the Dust*. New York: New Directions Press.
Silver (2007). Personal communication.
Slavin, M.O. and Kriegman, D. (1998). "Why the Analyst Needs to Change: Toward a Theory of Conflict, Negotiation, and Mutual Influence in the Therapeutic Process". In: L. Aron and A. Harris (eds) *Relational Psychoanalysis, Vol. 2: Innovation and Expansion*. Hillsdale, N.J.: The Analytic Press, 2005.
The New Shorter Oxford English Dictionary (1993). Oxford, Eng.: Clarendon Press.
Webster's Third International Dictionary (1993). Springfield, MA: Merriam-Webster Press.
Winnicott, D.W. (1958). "The Capacity to Be Alone". In: *The Maturational Process And the Facilitating Environment*. New York: International Universities Press, 1965.

CHAPTER TWENTY FIVE

The underbelly of joy

Rachel Newcombe, L.I.C.S.W.

T
he waiter had just served us our salad, more precisely, a baby arugula salad tossed with sliced red onion and mushrooms. Larry and I knew right away that the traditional wedge of iceberg lettuce with a big hunk of goopy blue cheese was not our salad of choice. We praised ourselves for ordering sensibly, keeping in mind that a rather large T-bone steak, also to be shared, would be arriving shortly. As for the appetizers, we passed; no mushrooms stuffed with crab or lobster bisque for us. Nope, not even tempted. We knew the healthy way to order. When I think back to that night, Larry and I negotiating the menu and compromising, our steak medium instead of medium rare, I realize how intimate it felt to be making these decisions. There wasn't the low grade bickering that accompanies restaurant dining when a couple has been together for a long time, both people set in their ways, uncompromising and exacting about food preferences. Larry and I are not married but we are most definitely a couple, a psychoanalytic couple.

Everything that happened that night matters; the circumstances leading to eating dinner at Ruth's Chris Steak House are fundamental to my tale of joy and the underbelly of joy, which I realized at a point during this particular evening, was the trauma of loss.

343

I am going to take a small detour before jumping into the night in question and ponder a bit about the culture of psychoanalytic conferences. I don't know about you, but for me, conferences are tricky events. Sometimes psychoanalytic meetings are fabulous, a time for renewal and inspiration while other times they are dispiriting and I feel lonely like I did at the Sandor Ferenczi conference in Baden-Baden, Germany a few years ago. A friend who was also attending that conference said, "For a Ferenczi conference, it certainly felt un-Ferenzian!"

The mystery of a conference is that anything can and will happen depending on the mix of people. In a way, conferences are like blind dates—stirring up feelings of hope and excitement—but in this case what we are hoping for is deeply personal and private. Sometimes what begins as a conscious motive shifts during the course of a conference, other times motives for attending conferences are unconscious, unknown for days or even months afterward, maybe never known. Nevertheless there is one indisputable fact about conferences whether we are presenting a paper or listening to the paper of someone else; always at risk is our identity. Do I dare to be known, flaws and all, or do I hide, unknown to others and even myself?

Judy Vida and Gersh Molad (2008) co-founders of the seminar in the *Autobiographical Dialogue* remind us:

> *Psychoanalysis has had a conflictual relationship with the autobiographical virtually from its inception, beginning with Freud's self-censorship in* The Interpretation of Dreams, *and including his eventual refusal to share with Jung and Ferenczi his complete associations to the dreams they had agreed to analyze mutually on shipboard during the 1909 trip to America. (p. 1)*

Molad (2001: 228) believes there is a regression that occurs when we present at conferences and because of this "as therapists and analysts, we do not tend to risk our identity in the presence of too many other analysts".

When I presented a version of the chapter you are now reading during the APA Division 39, Spring Conference: *Knowing, Not-Knowing and Sort-of Knowing,* I made a conscious decision to risk my identity, whatever this phrase actually means. For me, the greater fear was and continues to be not speaking, which guarantees no chance to be known, not known or even sort-of-known.

The night in question

It is an unseasonably warm autumn evening in Toronto. We are gathered for the annual IFPE (International Forum for Psychoanalytic Education) conference and on this last night Richard Raubolt and his wife Linda invite a small group to their hotel suite for a clandestine cocktail party. While the other conference attendees are milling about at the more traditional post-presidential address party, we are summoned to sip martinis on the seventh floor (aiming for accuracy, it may have been the ninth floor) of the Renaissance Hotel. I'm conflicted about parties; they are a major source of anxiety but I also don't like missing out on a chance for fun. And knowing this about me Larry does not leave any time for waffling, in his "I know what's best" voice he informs me that we are going to this party. Obediently I submit to his directive.

Getting out of the elevator the sound of laughter spills into the hallway and my heart quickens its pace. The door to the suite is ajar and despite anxiety I walk straight in with the confidence I keep on reserve for occasions just like this. There are lots of familiar faces, fellow board members with their spouses and partners. I also see some new faces; people I heard present earlier in the day. Navigating my way through the room of people I glimpse a makeshift bar on a standard hotel desk, curiosity draws me closer. But on this desk there is nothing remotely standard. In place of four water glasses and the customary bottle of overpriced sparkling water there are bottles of gin, vodka, and vermouth. Then I spy cocktail napkins, shiny ice tongs, jars of olives and onions, colourful swizzle sticks and martini glasses. This attention to detail is not wasted on me and I bellow a loud *"yes"* when Linda offers to make me a martini. Caught up in the excitement I add, "Make that a dirty martini".

Looking around the room seeing so many people I enjoy my anxiety begins its descent and quite by surprise I catch myself in the act of having fun. A moment later there's Larry and with just a raise of an eyebrow I register his, "I told you so expression". After about an hour of mingling and many enjoyable conversations Richard announces dinner reservations await us at a nearby steakhouse. In varying degrees of inebriation coats are collected and we make our way down to the lobby. Like children on a fieldtrip we automatically buddy up for our walk to the restaurant. My partner is Billy. He talks about the subject of his latest research, his writing, and what's been going on in his life. Then I do the same.

Finally we reach the restaurant and follow our hostess as she leads us to our table. We begin the game of musical chairs scrambling for the closest seat. In a matter of minutes all the chairs are filled; no one will be left out on this night. I am part of a triad nestled at the head of the table. Directly across from me is Gersh and to my immediate right is Larry; actually Larry and I cheated, making a pact before the evening started that we would sit next to each other no matter what. Sitting to my left is Stuart, someone I don't know well. I've interacted with him briefly at previous conferences and the words we exchange are friendly. We acknowledge each other with the familiarity that comes from years of sharing conference space. When attending conferences I reflexively file mental notes, small details about people I know, but don't really know. It works something like this: Stuart, the analyst from California with the cowboy hat, he usually stands in the back of a room, the person who wrote a book about trauma and the therapist's experience of trauma. Assumptions are neatly boxed and taken home. But on this particular night when I talk to Stuart there will be no need for a box.

Politely our conversation begins. Stuart asks me something about being new to the Northwest and without hesitation I answer. There is something in his voice that conveys a genuine interest as opposed to a question that is a mere pleasantry. I begin to tell Stuart my story, the full story. I tell Stuart I moved from Manhattan, the city where I lived for twenty-five years, the city where I received two different graduate degrees, underwent my psychoanalytic and supervisory training, two analyses, fell in love, married, bought a Classic 7 apartment on Riverside Drive, gave birth to our daughter, and then separated from my husband. I tell Stuart I left everything that was familiar and moved three thousand miles west to a remote island in Puget Sound. I tell him moving to Orcas Island did not come about randomly. Stuart is listening with rapt attention and I continue to talk, answering all his questions. I explain what brought me to the Northwest was romance, a very complicated and wonderful romance, with a woman. I tell him how awful I felt during this tumultuous time of ending my marriage and preparing to leave New York. I tell him it felt as though I were harbouring a secret from my patients. Stuarts nods knowingly. I say, "It doesn't matter that my patients and I worked together until my very last day because I still judge myself harshly for leaving, for abandoning them". Stuart reaches out and touches my hand. I tell him that I feel shame and finally I say, "It was a very traumatic time for me".

I've always resisted using the word "trauma", believing that the word should be used sparingly, limited to events that truly require such a signifier. When people ask me about my move to the Northwest I say that terminating was very difficult, indeed one of the most painful events I have ever lived through, all the while knowing that the words "difficult" and "painful" do not adequately capture my experience. Perhaps the words I use are not important. I am reminded of Ernest Schachtel's (1959) idea that "in the spoken word, language can become evocative of experience even if the most hackneyed words are used, provided that the speaker is in touch with their experiential referent" (p. 190). On this particular evening words are not hackneyed and we are both speaking from our experiential referents. Stuart understands what I am saying; he is bearing witness to my loss, the trauma of many endings—and for the first time in two years I feel less traumatized.

I write this last sentence and quickly switch to www.refdesk.com where I use the online dictionary, checking the definition of trauma, preemptively defending myself should you, my reader, challenge me of its usage, briefly forgetting that the experience of trauma is in the psyche of the beholder. Stuart does not question my use of the word "trauma" nor does he lecture me about terminating with patients. He knows that I have judged myself plenty. In place of judgement, what Stuart offers me is a gift of understanding. He knows my paradox: the newfound joy in my life co-exists with the trauma of many endings. I live with this paradox everyday and it makes me more aware that in our profession of psychoanalysis, the personal is the professional, the two are inextricably bound.

At this point I am going to take another small detour and ask a question: "Why are we unforthcoming when sharing our life stories with each other?" What are we afraid of, being judged? Or as my colleague Joseph Canarelli (2008; personal communication) asked me, "What is it in ourselves that we are fearful is going to be judged?" Is it character, morality, or personality? Here's my hypothesis; none of us want to hear the five words that have the power to sting, "You are not well analyzed". *Ouch*. This statement deserves at least one lengthy paper (or book) defining what it means to be "not well analyzed". Implicit in this statement is that somehow we don't measure up to a universal professional standard.

In the process of moving to the Northwest I had to pack and unpack many boxes and it seems that I lost my checklist telling me how to spot the signs of a well-analyzed analyst. Instead of panicking I decided to engage in unscientific research turning to friends, new and old colleagues and countless journal articles hoping to compose a new list. This was harder than I thought. I like to think of myself as an apt researcher but on this mission I came up empty handed—there was no universal list to be found. However, during my research I enjoyed talking with colleagues and spending quality time with Freud, Ferenczi, Horney, Jung, and Sullivan. In this historically important group of mavericks I read about betrayals, fierce professional competition, an extra-marital affair or two, rumours about sex with patients, and hidden sexual orientations. It seems our forefathers and foremothers had their share of personal drama; their underbellies are well documented in the psychoanalytic history books. Admirably, none of these five stopped working in the face of personal conflicts.

I don't think I stand alone in wondering why we adhere to the myth that well-analyzed analysts have tidy lives that are exempt from unruly disruptive events, good or bad. There is a small glitch with this myth—it's a myth! Unfortunately the myth is perpetuated when we remain silent, when we forget that to be human means that we have an underbelly, that tender region of our being that tells us who we are.

I don't recommend dispensing with privacy or running around indiscriminately sharing the personal details of our lives. Indiscriminate sharing with virtual strangers can often leave the recipient feeling like they just engaged in a one night stand. Rather, my desire is to stimulate thinking about our conscious personal omissions—*how* and *what* we decide to conceal or reveal, not with our patients, but with each other, what I describe as collegial self-disclosure.

Collegial self-disclosure puts our reputation at stake. Yet worrying about professional reputation restricts our ability to share major life events, profound thoughts, joys, and uncertainties. It's a bind. We remain silent and isolated (described best by Frieda Fromm-Reichmann) or we talk and risk being judged. Even though we don't like to admit it, analysts are known to be harsh when critiquing one another. I don't stand apart from this because I, too, have been judgmental of colleagues. Where did we learn to be this way?

I view the problem as originating from the belief that as analysts we hold ourselves to a higher standard. We vigilantly observe each other, whispers turning to rumbles when colleagues reveal anything less than what we perceive as a well-analyzed life. For example, a well-analyzed analyst would never get divorced, have an affair, file for bankruptcy, be the parent of a teenager who is expelled from school, or gain fifty extra pounds in weight. These events happen to the other analyst. Not to us.

Sandra Buechler, an analyst from the William Alanson White Institute, is an essential contemporary voice in the ongoing dialogue about our topic under discussion, the analyst's omissions of joy. Beuchler's (1988) article that first caught my eye opens with the following:

> I would like to treat the profession of psychoanalysis as though it were a culture. We are not born into this community, but choose to enter it. During our initial period of acculturation, we must learn its language, its moral codes, and its behavioral ethics. We adapt to its hardships and find ways of enjoying the rewards it offers. Depending on our natural endowments, personalities, and experiential backgrounds we fashion different roles for ourselves in this culture. (p. 462)

Embracing Buechler's idea that the profession of psychoanalysis is a culture generates hope that personal narratives, underbellies included, can be viewed as a source of psychoanalytic knowledge, theory as lived. Psychoanalysis is not the only profession with thoughts about exposing underbellies. When political columnist Katha Pollitt wrote an essay in *The New Yorker*, about taking driving lessons, web stalking her ex-boyfriend, and her boyfriend's desire for oral sex in the morning, feminists and journalists went wild, they couldn't get their opinions out fast enough. As you can imagine, some journalists were jubilant while others chastised her, asking why a serious journalist would write about such personal matters. Rebecca Traister, a Salon.com writer, responded to Pollitt's essay beginning with the question, "What's wrong with serious women writers exposing their soft underbellies to the world?" Later in this essay she gets to the heart of the matter:

> It's time we grew up and realized that it is possible to exhibit both intellectual strength and personal weakness simultaneously. And that when a woman chooses to lift her cerebral robes and expose herself in surprising or disconcerting ways, she should be judged on the artfulness and grace with which she does so, not on the body that she reveals. (p. 3)

It comes as no surprise that readers' responses to Traister's essay resulted in a flurry of letters to the editor. One reader wrote, "Telling the whole story, warts and all, is a valuable contribution to our understanding of what makes humans work". Sadly, the letter was signed anonymous.

Many years ago a patient gave me a copy of the poem, *The Space Heater* by Sharon Olds. The poem captures an ephemeral moment when a patient observes the analyst contorting his body to unplug a heater in order to make the temperature more comfortable for the patient. Observing the analyst reach for the plug behind the couch reassures the patient of the analyst's humanity, his underbelly, and this is when she knows she can place her trust in him. I recommend this poem as an example of the union of knowing between patient and analyst.

Concluding my tale of joy is more challenging than I imagined. Deciding when to stop and how to close is another instance in which there is self-revealing and uncertainty but psychoanalysis teaches me to embrace and surrender to this uncertainty. There are unexpected moments in life when heaters are unplugged, martinis are mixed and questions are asked. I borrow language from Carole Maso (2000) to describe these times:

> A place where we are for a little while endlessly possible, capable of anything, it seems fluid, changing, ephemeral, renewable, intensely alive, close to death, clairvoyant, fearless, luminous, passionate, strange even to ourselves. (p. 115)

These are the moments of psychoanalysis, of life.

References

Buechler, S. (1988). "Joining the psychoanalytic culture". *Contemporary Psychoanalysis*. 24: 462–469.

Canarelli, J. (2008). Personal communication.

Maso, C. (2000). *Break every rule: Essays on language, longing, and moments of desire*. Washington, D.C.: Counterpoint.

Molad, G.J. (2001). "Mutual training of developmental trajectories: The shaping of dialogue between analysts in conference space". *Int. Forum Psychoanal.* 10: 227–234.

Molad, G.J. and Vida, J. (2008). Syllabus for "The Autobiographical Dialogue Seminar", held February 2008, Sunland, California.

Olds, S. (22 January, 2001). The space heater. *The New Yorker*. p. 68.

Pollitt, K. (22 July, 2002). Learning to drive. *The New Yorker*. p. 36.

Rebecca Traister, R. (September 26, 2007). "The feminist who made me blush". Retrieved 1 March, 2008, from: http://www.salon.com/mwt/feature/2007/09/26/pollitt/index.html

Schachtel, E. (1959). *Metamorphosis*. New York: Basic Books.

CHAPTER TWENTY SIX

The intersubjectivity of joy

Karen Weisbard, Psy.D.

This paper is an attempt to further grapple with the tension between a one-person and two-person psychology that relational psychoanalysis seeks to elaborate (Mitchell 1997; Bromberg 1998; Corbett 2001). This tension has been described as autonomy and influence, as the dialectic between the ability to preserve the self while being many or to be oneself while seeking the therapist's help to be different, and as the interplay of centrality and marginality—having mental freedom along with the wish for containment, conformity, and acceptance. My personal experience of this dialectic has most often been felt as a need to be independent, separate, and unique and my desire to be dependent, connected, and found worthy and lovable by others. My writing plan was to "hole myself away" with my books, articles, and notes yet I sit at my dining room table with my family downstairs watching a movie. I could have left the house but I could not leave. I have to do my work but I want to be near and needed by those whom I love.

Many psychoanalytic theorists have posed that the human condition is characterized by the desire to stand separate and the need to be attached. We must both live without and with others in order to be fully alive. This life-long endeavour is tinged with many affective states and behavioural outcomes. In this paper I am most interested in the states of loss, shame, and joy as they are manifest and experienced in this struggle. Erich Fromm (1947, 1956) proposed a solution to the human condition in his concept of "relatedness"—the synthesis of closeness and uniqueness. He suggested that productivity in the form of responsibility, care, respect and knowledge of the other person would resolve our bind. This is what he meant by love. Margaret Mahler (1972) felt that it was in the rapprochement subphase of the separation–individuation process that "man's eternal struggle against both fusion and isolation" (p. 338) offers its best resolution. Here the child realizes his "smallness" and separateness, and the separateness of others. Thus he must feel his need for them.

Jessica Benjamin (1990), however, offers us the impossibility of resolving the human condition. At just that moment that we stand on our own, we need the other to recognize us standing there; apart from them yet intricately tied to them. She suggests that our psychic make-up is always located somewhere on this tension line. She poses intersubjectivity as a developmental achievement for bearing this tension. Through the mother's acts of independence the child is offered the opportunity to experience her mother as someone with her own mind. In turn the child can experience herself as having a separate consciousness as well as a shared state of being with the other. The child can feel that she and mother, she and others, have a shared humanity in that their minds are designed similarly. This provides for the capacity for mutual recognition. For Mahler, the crisis of rapprochement is in recognizing one's smallness and need for the other, which carries the potential for shame and guilt. For Benjamin, the crisis is also a source of pleasure in the discovery of the other and of the affective connection that such discovery affords.

I would like to suggest that experiences of joy potentiate the development and/or deepening of intersubjectivity and that intersubjectivity can shift and deepen experiences of joy. This mutual influencing contains feelings of loss and shame. Opportunities for joy exist throughout life and yet, for many, joy is an experience they cannot claim. The complex relational conditions of recognition need to exist for joy to be felt and for loss and shame to be bared. Sometimes these conditions are set without our intention and joy arrives unbidden. We can take notice and receive it, enjoying the pleasure it brings. Other times we may take a more active stance and seize the chance. Whether actively sought or simply cherished, joy seems problematic. Joy, as differentiated from pleasure, is more difficult in that it must broker the tension of self and other, either actual others or internal other selves. For example, I cannot enjoy a beautiful day or a good book unless I can temporarily let go of all that presses in around me and feel that I am not *actually* letting go of my responsibilities to myself or to others. For me, one struggle with joy is in allowing myself to feel fully joyful in the face of another's pain. At this moment I am lost in the other (two-person psychology) but have also lost grounding in my own self-experience. One psychologist patient experiences this to the extreme and wonders how she can be happy and grateful for her life when so many of her patients and people in the world are suffering. As a professional, I have felt that my sources of personal joy are superficial and thus for me shameful. I imagine that a serious, intellectual analyst feels joy only in these endeavours and not in the athletic or domestic venues in which I feel them. I have felt anxious and guilty in my joy. I worried what colleagues would think if they knew of my joy. Would it bring me less respect, fewer referrals? Would it evoke envy and would I be able to stand that envy? Often hiding my joy, or the sources of it, felt like the safer route. Most notably for me was how separate I felt in my joy. Sometimes this was a very lonely feeling, other times a private, cherished experience. Like any affective state, joy shifts and undergoes multiple ways of being held. Yet there is something about joy that can feel dangerous, either by the experiencing self or the observing other, whether that other is external or an internalized other.

Joy follows a complex trajectory and affords us the chance to move beyond the struggle of separation or connection, or choosing between self and other. I want to use images of movement to describe the phenomena of "pure joy" and "intersubjective joy". Experiential descriptions of joy often use this terminology—untethered/tethered, floating/grounded, out of my mind/in my body, blurry/clear. While I speak of conditions for joy in recognition, I do not mean to invoke linearity or causality even though there may be contingency. I liken the experiences of pure joy and intersubjective joy to the practicing and rapprochement subphases of Mahler's theory of the separation–individuation process. While developed as a stage theory it can be thought of in the contemporary double helix model in which one moves back and forth, in and out, and around pure joy and intersubjective joy. Joy as evolving and revolving yet connected to a centred place may help it feel less dangerous and more easily graspable. In joyful experiences one becomes acutely aware of oneself and of one's separateness in this wholly individual experience. And at the same time, one is afforded the opportunity to feel connected to the outside world, to humanity, and thereby to others. Images of movement further connote the trajectory of life. What is well-known to relational analysts is that all is not lost if it does not happen in childhood, and that relationships and experiences in adulthood are transformative as well.

Pure joy has much in common with the descriptions of the practicing subphase of the separation–individuation process. It can be characterized as an envelope full of discovery of one's autonomous functions. We feel the world is our oyster. We are on a "joy-ride" in which we are intoxicated by our own faculties, and in being so drunk we are impervious to bumps, pain, and obstacles. We can be oblivious to those around us as we are so absorbed in the elation of our ride. Eventually pure joy shifts, and yet the feeling of danger seems to lie in the uncertainty of it. Will we come out of it? What if we don't? What price in future consequences will we pay for our joyful journey? One patient recalled her younger self doing cartwheels in her secluded backyard without underwear. When her mother observed this, she yelled, "Don't ever do that again!" My patient has wondered since what was the danger? What should she never do again? The opportunity for recognition of an alive, risk-taking, carefree self was missed and instead shame, loss, humiliation, and confusion were felt. Her pure joy shifted away from the possibility of recognition to isolation. This woman has a life-long struggle with depression and expression of her "forbidden" identities.

We can become afraid of the possible addiction to the feeling of pure joy and have seen pure joy become a narcissistic state where one believes he can be an island unto himself. Maybe some people are afraid to feel joy precisely because it can feel so isolative and unmoored. The anchoring we need is in recognition which provides the reassurance that joy, like any self state, will shift. It is being able to feel that this is "one you"—not all of you. While this may be relieving or disappointing from a multi-state perspective, it is certain. Joy shifts to an intersubjective experience when the impossibility of our omnipotence intersects with the recognition of our self and others as intimately and intricately related. This is the centring that we need in order to feel the fullness of joy. And joyful experiences can deepen experiences of intersubjectivity. I would like to next describe how this interplay of joy and intersubjectivity came about in a personal experience of my own.

Two years ago, I began playing competitive team tennis. I thought that to improve my game, I needed to play year round, not just when the weather was nice outside. I did not know anyone on the team when I began. I slowly realized that this group of professional women, who had been together for many years, had ambitions to win a national championship at their high intermediate level of play. As we became the undefeated Seattle team, then the winners of local play-offs, we were on our way to regional champions and ultimately to final round play at Nationals. At that juncture we lost, ending our ride by becoming the second best team in the nation.

As the team progressed so did I. My skills certainly improved but the biggest transformation was in my time and psychic commitment. All I wanted to do was play tennis. I felt valued, wanted, and encouraged by my new found social group. This was in sharp contrast to recent experiences I had been having as co-director of the psychoanalytic training institute in my city. No doubt part of my exhilaration in tennis was fuelled by my sense of escape from that conflictual orbit, not unlike the child of the rapprochement subphase who now has the mobility to leave the mother and experience different orbits more at her own will.

Where clinical work had always been my haven in times of personal trouble—I could forget about myself for a short while—it now became my prison. Empty hours were chances to sneak out and hit a few serves and I relished rather than sweated no new referrals. My family graced me with their patience and support. One day, however, when I left the house dressed in my work clothes my son said, "Bye Mom, have fun, hope you win". At that moment I had a dim warning that I no longer existed as a full person to my child. I had become only a tennis player. My transformation had perhaps gone too far but I could not stop to heed its warning. I was as committed to pure joy as I was to the team goal. My orbit contained thrills of winning, highs of physical improvement, pleasures of camaraderie and cooperation toward a shared goal, and protection from feeling the professional losses in my institute.

As the child who "hatches" out of differentiation into the practicing subphase, the child in the rapprochement crisis awakens too as he realizes that his parents are separate individuals with their own needs and interests. It is in this transitional space that we, both the doers and the observers (or done to's), might be most prone to shame. As I was awakened by my son's comment, I recognized that I had been isolated, absorbed, and indifferent to his needs and pain. While he did not actively shame me, comments from others led me to know that they were envious, scared, and felt abandoned by the unbridled, damn-be-the world aspects of my joy. In my exhilarant state I felt imposed on as if I was being asked to "curb my enthusiasm". Internally, I accused them of rigidity, uptightness, cowardice, and malice, thereby shaming them in my judgement.

Benjamin states that the rapprochement crisis is first experienced as a conflict of wills: you and I don't want the same thing. A space must open up between ourselves and others such that we can move into mutual recognition. It is in that space where we can think and recognize that we are not in a struggle about things. Rather we are different subjects and as different individuals we want different things. I held this thought as a rationalized comfort in what was more accurately neglect of my family and my institute. Sometimes my attitude conveyed indifference to the different needs of others. This was not mutual recognition as I wasn't about to budge in either my attitude or behaviour. Intersubjectivity had yet come into play. I was still absorbed in pure joy.

After almost winning nationals, my joy ride was winding down. I still played in tennis tournaments and on another higher level team—but it wasn't the same. This reached its head when I made it to the finals of a tournament and the match was scheduled for the same time that I was supposed to be taking my son to Little League Day at the Seattle Mariners (baseball for those who might not be so inclined). As my attempts to reschedule the final failed, and as I agonized over which event to miss, I finally, and shamefully, realized that this need not be a difficult choice. I forfeited the final and went to the baseball game. I was grateful for what had transpired within me. I felt rescued from my inclination to deny the effect I was having on those closest to me. For me, this was a crisis of intersubjectivity in which I deepened my sense of what it means to be separate and connected, unique and close. The earlier joy I had felt with my winning team was gone and could not be recaptured on my own. I had to wrestle with my complex individual needs and the complex needs of my son. We had to both exist as subjects. Benjamin (1990) states, "The wish to absolutely assert the self and deny everything outside one's own mental omnipotence must sometimes crash against the implacable reality of the other" (p. 192).

The experience of my initial joy and its evolution remains a powerful place holder in my psyche. The potentiation and penetration of both joy and intersubjectivity highlights the necessity of expanding our world to the outside environment, even beyond relationships, to other things that exist in our life—sports, nature, music, and so on. The interplay of joy and intersubjectivity has the hallmarks of Fromm's productiveness. This dialectic demonstrates the fervor and urgency that so motivated Fromm in that it makes us realize how tragic it is to waste a life in seeking either closeness or uniqueness. This evolution to the outside world can occur through a deepening of intersubjectivity in the therapeutic encounter. For my patient, Eva, our work enabled her to recapture experiences of joy in her own life. She discovered pleasure in the outside world through knowing the inside of other minds, thus ending her terminal experience of isolation, and leading her to greater connection, mutual recognition, and intersubjectivity.

Eva did not have the capacity to stand separate. From the time she first came to see me, when she could not cope with her daughters' adolescent individuation processes, to the second episode of treatment, Eva could not bear to be disconnected from her children who were now in their twenties. She did not experience their efforts to become their own women as just that and even made possible by her own great accomplishments and efforts for them. Instead she felt rejected and hated. She felt her neat, clean, and classy self was revolting to them. She was in fact disgusted, shocked, and abhorrent of much of their behaviours. It did not help that the daughters could be very crude in their efforts to form separate identities. They posted highly sexualized displays of their bodies on My Space and felt enormous rage and contempt toward Eva's husband who was her business partner. He was indeed a very successful conservative businessman as contrasted with Eva's ex-husband and father of her daughters, who was a disheveled, anti-establishment, wildly passionate alcoholic. The daughters also identified with Eva's own gypsy heritage, of which she was both ashamed and proud.

Eva would experience her separateness from her daughters as being out in the middle of the ocean without land in sight and no life jacket or life raft. She would respond to calls from them for a ride, for money, or for food with immediate urgency, setting aside anything else that she might be doing. She did the same for her younger, deeply disturbed sister. She would spend hours on the phone with her or at her home as the sister cried and threatened to kill herself. This relationship while motivated by care and fear was also motivated by guilt and shame at not being as impaired as her sister. Eva had been sexually abused by her older brother and did not understand how her sister, who allegedly was not abused, could hardly function. She often thought her sister must have also been abused but could not remember it. Eva could not give herself credit for confronting her abuse, receiving lots of help for herself and her family, and for establishing strong relationships with others, both in and outside of her family of origin.

Eva felt very much like a failure in her inability to stand separate, and humiliated by her difficulty setting limits with these hurtful and somewhat destructive individuals. Through our work, Eva began to recognize the subjectivity of the other. By understanding and elaborating her subjective experiences, she was able to see that her daughters were expressing many aspects of who they were, some of which were wonderful, which she knew, and some of which were worrisome and concerning. As she began to discern the differences in her own affective states, each experience of their expressed identity was not felt as a catastrophic ending of their relationship. In recognizing her own multiplicity, Eva became more expressive and proud of herself and of her daughters. Whereas before she felt shame that they were not getting married and having babies like the children of her friends, she could now recognize them for their unique selves.

A turning point in the treatment came when Eva's husband arranged for them to go to Tahiti for three weeks. With much angst and fear of being away from her daughters, of being in that ocean with no life jacket, Eva asked me if she should go. With no hesitation I said absolutely yes. My joy at Eva's growth and my desire to see her more self-regarding undoubtedly fuelled my response. And my fervor and intrinsic assurance that she would not be as alone as she feared fuelled Eva's ability to enjoy her holiday. When she returned, Eva told me of her experience at being in a condominium much less accommodating and beautiful than her own home. She said she broke down and didn't know if she could adapt to this less than ideal place, again expressing the need for the outside and inside to match to feel a sense of comfort. After some time, she did however assimilate and find a way to live in that culture and her own. She happily showed me pictures of her dancing with the natives to illustrate how immersed and alive she had become.

We also talked about her trip as a cross-cultural experience that she could use to exist more comfortably with her daughters. She had to cross over from her own comfortable world into their sparser one. They were in a developmentally appropriate place where they were relatively resourceful and content. She did not have to feel badly for them or make their worlds more like her own. She could enjoy her life with less shame and guilt as she no longer saw herself as depriving them. She could claim her world as her own creation and theirs as this too.

After her trip, Eva enrolled in tango dancing, a gift given to her by her daughters many months prior. That she could now attend classes with her husband and not be on call for others 24/7 was further indication of her ability to separate and stand more on her own and still be in the same city as those who needed her. But the joy she experienced in dancing was the added gift that furthered her individuation. One evening after dancing, her sister called in deep distress. Eva began to talk to her, settling in to the idea that her evening would be spent on the phone. Somewhere in the course of the conversation, Eva "woke-up" and thought, "I could spend my time on the phone or I could hang up and go make love to my husband". She told her sister that she needed to go, and joined her husband.

Several months after that evening, Eva told me that she felt ready to end treatment. More able than ever to place herself as a subject Eva no longer felt stranded and at the behest of her anxieties. Being able, perhaps for the first time, to see others as subjects that existed with all their complexities, neither she nor they had to be only need-satisfying objects. They could each live in their own lives, with both the pleasures and pains of being human. The psychic imprint of our work and the joys she came to experience both with me and away from me provided the centring that she needed in order to move out of the protective and claustrophobic relational orbits she had so thoroughly inhabited.

Conclusion

To stand separate is not to stand alone. It is to stand with a foot in the domains of the self and a foot in the domains of the other. While attempting to recognize the subjectivity of the other, we still are subjective selves whom we equally cannot forget. Sometimes we don't just have a foot in each camp. Sometimes we are sunk hip-high in the domains of self and barely have a toe-hold in the domains of the other. This could describe my experience of pure joy in the early phases of my tennis journey. Sometimes the converse can be true, as I believe it was with Eva, where she barely had a place to stand within her own self. We are always calibrating these stances such that intersubjectivity always exists. It doesn't always feel or look that way. We need to modify our positions in order for a deeper, more comfortable, and perhaps more lasting hold to be found.

In this paper I have tried to elaborate how intersubjectivity can potentiate joy and how joy can deepen experiences of intersubjectivity. Loss and shame are experienced at crisis places along the way as we shift between self and self–other states. Experiencing these affects may sober joy but intensify intersubjectivity. Yet one experiences exhilaration at the increased capacity to recognize one's self and others thereby intensifying joy. As psychoanalysts and psychotherapists we are always working on this tension line. Our attention to the lives of others may cause us to neglect ourselves. When we feel that we must tend to ourselves due to dire circumstances we may feel less shameful—we didn't have a choice. But when we desire to tend to ourselves and choose to go away from others toward some other Other, we may feel more prone to loss and shame. Our own awakening to that which we neglected in our own lives deepens the dialectic between intersubjectivity and joy. Sandra Buechler (1997) calls psychoanalysis the "passionate" instead of the "impossible" profession (p. 304). In her writings she encourages each of us to find full psychic life by having access to all of our emotional states, to live fully, and to bring that passion for life into the consulting room. As I have tried to elaborate, this is easier said than done for to tend to self and other brings a host of complex and difficult emotions that requires our attention and struggle.

Attention to joy and the passionate life place us squarely in the face of our intersubjective dilemma and forces us to wrestle with the human condition. The desire to be our own unique person and the desire to love and be loved by others must place subjectivity on the front line. Omissions of joy are omissions for intersubjective growth. The more fully alive we become, the more available we will be to our patients, to ourselves, and to the others in our lives.

References

Benjamin, J. (1990). "Recognition and Destruction: An Outline of Inter-subjectivity". *Psychoanalytic Psychology*. 7: 33–47.

Bromberg, P. (1998). *Standing in the Spaces*. New Jersey: The Analytic Press.

Buechler, S. (1997). "The Right Stuff: The Analyst's Sensitivity to Emotional Nuance". *Contemporary Psychoanalysis*. 33: 295–306.

Corbett, K. (2001). "More Life: Centrality and Marginality in Human Development". *Psychoanalytic Dialogues*. 11: 313–335.

Fromm, E. (1947). *Man for Himself: An Inquiry into the Psychology of Ethics*. New York: Holt and Co.

Fromm, E. (1956). *The Art of Loving*. New York: Harper and Row.

Mahler, M.S. (1972). "On the First Three Phases of the Separation–Individuation Process". *International Journal of Psychoanalysis*. 53: 333–338.

Mitchell, S.A. (1997). *Influence and Autonomy in Psychoanalysis*. New Jersey: The Analytic Press.

CHAPTER TWENTY SEVEN

The healing power of joy

A discussion of Chapters 24, 25 and 26

Sandra Buechler, Ph.D.

> *It has been said there is not much*
> *Freude (German for joy) in Freud's*
> *psychoanalytic psychology.*

> (Emde 1992: 5)

In this discussion I would like to suggest that the emotion of joy is uniquely able to modify the impact of all the negative emotions. Elsewhere (2008: 115) I call joy the "universal antidote". I believe that feeling real joy can help us bear life's most painful moments of loss, fear, anger, regret, anxiety, shame, guilt, and other emotions. But what is joy, and how does it lend us this resiliency?

Heisterkamp (2001) defined joy in contrast to anxiety. "Joy can be considered as a basic form of resonance. Psychodynamically, joy is complementary to the feeling of anxiety. Whereas anxiety reflects psychic distress in connection with problems of structuring, joy is the expression of successful (re)structuring. It is the feeling of self-discovery, of a new beginning, and of self-renewal" (p. 839).

Later, Heisterkamp concludes that, "Whenever we gain new land from the sea of unconsciousness, when we succeed in finding more satisfactory environments for the workings and longings of the id, joy emerges" (pp. 858–859)

What can these three, rich papers tell us about the nature and power of joy? Starting with Rachel Newcombe's paper, in Chapter twenty five, I infer that:

1. Joy is, at least sometimes, about moments of relief from the sadness, loss, and loneliness of the human condition.
2. Revealing oneself heals, perhaps, because it assuages the loneliness, so we have enough strength left over to bear the sadness and loss.
3. The patient in Sharon Olds' poem feels empathy for her struggling doctor. I would suggest that empathy for the analyst is very often a highly significant aspect of therapeutic action. When a patient sees how hard we struggle to reach out, to find the right word or action, it can evoke in the patient the feeling of being profoundly cared about, as well as empathy for our baffled effort. But I believe that part of the meaning of that reaching out is that it is against a backdrop of comparative silence, the white canvas whose contrast helps colour come alive. In an analogy with Sharon Olds' poem, I ask, if it weren't for the analyst's general stillness would the times when he gropes for an outlet (so to speak) be such a gift, and have so much meaning?

Newcombe's paper seems to me to sing of the joy of escape. Escape from social inhibition, the fear of shame, and the inherent loneliness of being the only one who sees things from our personal, unique perspective. And then, there is that special, magical moment when two say "yes" to the party. Or when a patient fumbles for words that might release her analyst's warmth, and the analyst responds. When need is understood and met in an act of pure kindness. Perhaps this harkens back to the first kindnesses extended to us, the earliest hungers capably tended to. Maybe whenever our need is still in an unformulated state and yet someone understands us, meets us, and satisfies us, we feel joy. The joy, perhaps, of the full underbelly.

In response to Weisbard's (Chapter twenty six) and Canarelli's (Chapter twenty four) papers I will touch on two topics—how joy promotes growth and when it points us inward versus outward.

Generally, does joy tend to isolate us, locking us into private experience, or does it promote interpersonal relating?

First of all, it seems to me that joy promotes growth mainly by giving us strength to go on. Moments of joy can lend colour to life. When I look into a child's laughing eyes my heart leaps and I know that this, too, exists. Alongside life's grief, opportunities for joy still beckon. The memory of those eyes can re-frame everything. Yes, there is still loss, pain, and regret. But there is also those eyes, and that bundle of joy.

Does joy mostly point us inward or outward, toward each other? Is it inherently solipsistic or relational? Or, does joy come in different flavours, and some of us have a greater taste for inward joy, while others prefer joys that bring them into relational contact? Or does joy evolve developmentally, so that our joys mature and grow wiser, and, perhaps, more interpersonal over time? Are interpersonal joys further along in a developmental progression? In other words does life experience bring a greater capacity for a more relational joy? Or is joy more simply human than otherwise, Janus faced from the start, looking inward and outward from our earliest through our last days?

A paradox at the heart of joy is that, I think, it can accompany both the finding of one's particular self and the loss of the boundaries of individual identity. Fromm once said: "Joy, then, is what we experience in the process of growing nearer to the goal of becoming ourselves" (Fromm 1976: 106). Surely, as analysts, we know what a joy it can be for someone to more fully recognize her own characteristic ways of being human and living life. But it is also true, as the emotion theorist Cal Izard said, that, "Joy is often accompanied by a sense of harmony and unity with the object of joy, and, to some extent, with the world. Some people have reported that in ecstatic joy they tend to lose individual identity, as in the case of some mystical experiences associated with meditation" (Izard 1977: 271).

So, it seems that joy can accompany our greater awareness of individuality, as well as our temporary escape from it. How can we understand this? I would suggest that it is important, first of all, to distinguish joy from pleasure. Many widely available experiences may bring pleasure, but joy is nearer the soul. In joy I think we are often one step closer than usual to awareness of both our unique particularity and our shared interpersonal humanity. In some moments of joy where, for example, a child takes its first steps, or a patient dares new self-awareness, we know that life itself has been affirmed. These seeming reminders of our common humanity wouldn't mean as much without our investment in this *particular* child or patient; this *particular* instance of life. So, I would say, the deepest joys remind us of both the private, singular and the shared, interpersonal aspects of being human.

Canarelli mentions "more life" and gives us wonderful examples of it. He raises the question of why we would be ashamed of our joy. I ask whether it could be that it is not the joy, itself, that threatens us with shame, but, rather, our total surrender to joy. Canarelli tells us that when he wrote of love "taking him" away it seemed to him as though he had tried to convert his active choice to move for the sake of love into something passive, as though if a force took over he wouldn't feel guilty and ashamed of being frivolous enough to choose his own love and joy over staying with his patients. I am suggesting a somewhat different reading of the situation. Maybe Canarelli's phrase, "taking me away" was exactly right emotionally. Maybe we do surrender to love's powerful force, as we surrender to joy. And maybe, in Manny Ghent's unforgettable language, we confuse joyous surrender with shameful submission. Maybe we are easily shamed by our love and joy and avoid talking about them because we feel it would be admitting that we have been conquered.

But all three of these authors are not afraid to say when love and joy have taken them over. Personally, I can not differentiate the joy I feel in solitary moments from instances of joy with patients or others. My joy listening to Bach or looking at Rembrandt's self-portraits seems like the same lift as the joy I feel when a patient and I come upon a new awareness in a session. Something feels as though it is locking into place with a palpable rightness and my heart cries, "That's it!" As Heisterkamp suggested (above) we have gained new land from the sea of unconsciousness. We understand something a little better. In some small way we encompass more of what it means to be alive. Just as I feel I see more of life when I try on Rembrandt's eyes, and hear more of life when Bach is my prism, Dostoevsky, too, can stretch the limits of my understanding. Re-reading his *Notes from the Underground* I feel the joy of the absolute rightness of the words. They fit. They are the only words that could have been so right.

As sometimes happens in a session they carry understanding a touch further, bringing me, bringing us, more life.

References

Buechler, S. (2008). *Making a Difference in Patients' Lives: Emotional Experience in the Therapeutic Setting*. New York: Routledge.

Emde, R. (1992). "*Positive* emotions for psychoanalytic theory: Surprises from infancy research and new directions". In: T. Shapiro and R. Emde (eds) *Affect: Psychoanalytic Perspectives*. Madison Conn.: International Universities Press.

Fromm, E. (1976). *To Have Or To Be?* New York: Harper & Row.

Heisterkamp, G. (2001). "Is psychoanalysis a cheerless (Freud-less) profession? Toward a psychoanalysis of joy". *The Psychoanalytic Quarterly*. 70: 839–871.

Izard, C. (1977). *Human Emotions*. New York: Plenum Press.

INDEX